GUATEMALA IN REBELLION

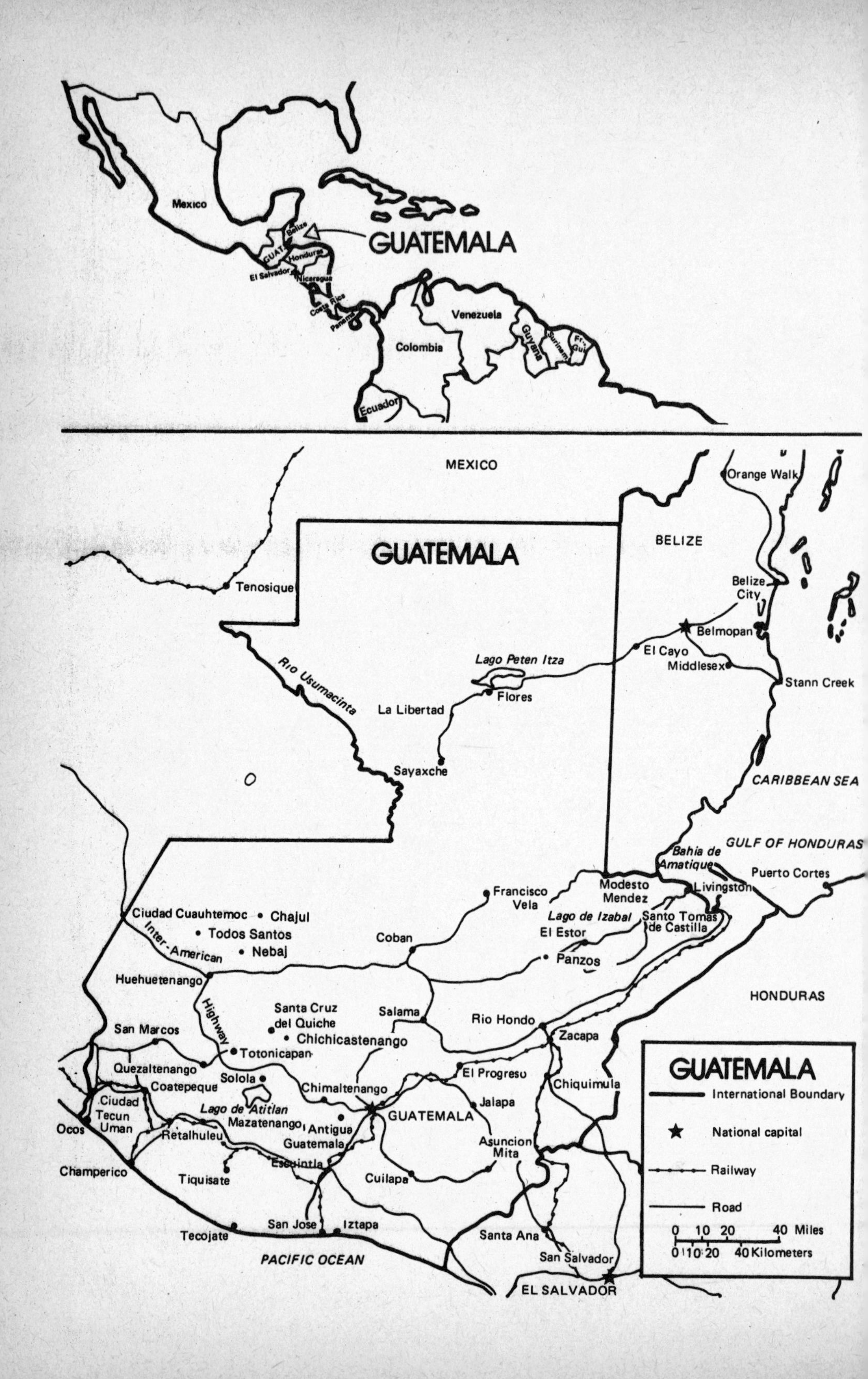

Mexico
GUATEMALA
Belize
GUAT.
Honduras
El Salvador
Nicaragua
Costa Rica
Panama
Venezuela
Guyana
Surinam
Colombia
Ecuador
MEXICO
GUATEMALA
BELIZE
Orange Walk
Tenosique
Belize City
Belmopan
El Cayo
Middlesex
Stann Creek
Lago Peten Itza
Rio Usumacinta
La Libertad
Flores
Sayaxche
CARIBBEAN SEA
GULF OF HONDURAS
Bahia de Amatique
Puerto Cortes
Livingston
Modesto Mendez
Francisco Vela
Lago de Izabal
Santo Tomas de Castilla
El Estor
Panzos
Ciudad Cuauhtemoc
Chajul
Todos Santos
Nebaj
Inter-American
Coban
Huehuetenango
Highway
HONDURAS
Santa Cruz del Quiche
Salama
Rio Hondo
San Marcos
Chichicastenango
Zacapa
Totonicapan
Quezaltenango
Coatepeque
Solola
El Progreso
Chiquimula
Chimaltenango
Ciudad Tecun Uman
Lago de Atitlan
GUATEMALA
Jalapa
Ocos
Retalhuleu
Mazatenango
Antigua Guatemala
Asuncion Mita
Escuintla
Champerico
Tiquisate
Cuilapa
San Jose
Iztapa
Tecojate
Santa Ana
PACIFIC OCEAN
San Salvador
EL SALVADOR
GUATEMALA
International Boundary
National capital
Railway
Road
0 10 20 40 Miles
0 10 20 40 Kilometers

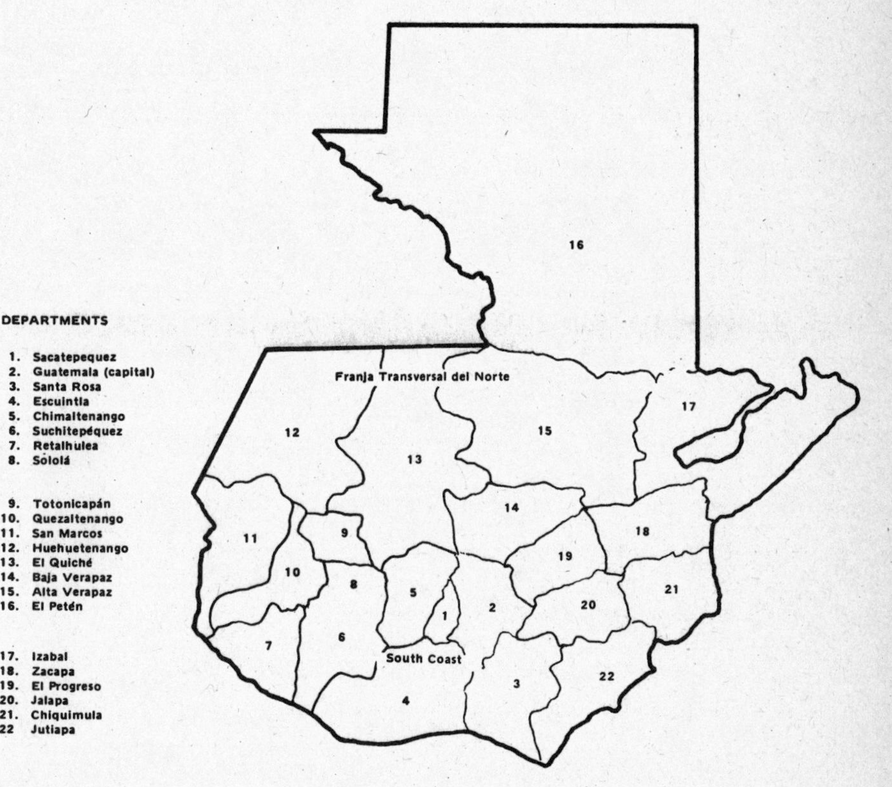
DEPARTMENTS
1. Sacatepequez
2. Guatemala (capital)
3. Santa Rosa
4. Escuintla
5. Chimaltenango
6. Suchitepéquez
7. Retalhulea
8. Sololá
9. Totonicapán
10. Quezaltenango
11. San Marcos
12. Huehuetenango
13. El Quiché
14. Baja Verapaz
15. Alta Verapaz
16. El Petén
17. Izabal
18. Zacapa
19. El Progreso
20. Jalapa
21. Chiquimula
22 Jutiapa
16
Franja Transversal del Norte
17
12
15
13
14
18
11
9
19
10
8
21
5
2
20
1
7
6
South Coast
22
3
4

GUATEMALA in rebellion: UNFINISHED HISTORY

George Maynes, U. S. military attaché, and Indian women in Nebaj, 1982. *Photo credit: Jean-Marie Simon*

Edited by
Jonathan L. Fried,
Marvin E. Gettleman,
Deborah T. Levenson,
and
Nancy Peckenham

GROVE PRESS, INC./NEW YORK

"The Mayas Discover Spain," by A. Recinos, © 1953 by University of Oklahoma Press, reprinted by permission. "The Domination of Indian Women and the Birth of the Ladino," by Severo Martínez Peláez, from *La Patria del Criollo*, reprinted by permission. "Land and Labor After Independence," by Alain Y. Dessaint, reprinted with permission from *América Indígena*, Vol. XXII, No. 4, October-December, 1962. "Debt Labor in the 1940s," by Maud Oakes, from *The Two Crosses of Todos Santos: Survivals of Mayan Religious Ritual*, Bollingen Series 27. Copyright 1951 © 1969 by Princeton University Press. Reprinted by permission. "Colonial Heir: The Indian Community in the 1950s," by Eric Wolf, from *Sons of the Shaking Earth*, copyright © 1959 by Eric Wolf. Reprinted by permission of University of Chicago Press and the author. "A Case History of U.S. Subversion: Guatemala, 1954," by Max Gordon, from *Science & Society*, Summer, 1971, Vol. 35, No. 2. Reprinted by permission. "To Defend Our Way of Life: An Interview with a U.S. Businessman," by Allan Nairn. Reprinted by permission of the author. "The Alliance for Progress: Development Program for the United States," by David Tobis, from *Monthly Review*, January, 1968. Reprinted by permission. "Guatemalan Victims," by Frances Moore Lappé and Nick Allen, © 1982 by the New York Times Company. Reprinted by permission. "Guatemala: Central America's Blue Chip Investment," by Allan Nairn. Reprinted with permission from *Multinational Monitor* magazine, a publication of the Washington, D.C.-based Corporate Accountability Research Group. "Guatemala: Going Bananas," Copyright © 1980 by Roger Burbach and Patricia Flynn. Reprinted by permission of Monthly Review Press. "The Militarization of the Guatemalan State," by Gabriel Aguilera Peralta, from *Polemica*, No. 1, reprinted by permission. "Manuel Colom Argueta's Last Interview," from *Latin American Political Report*, reprinted by permission. Latin American Newsletters publish a series of newsletters on Latin America. Details are available from Latin American Newsletters, Boundary House, 91 Charterhouse Street, London EC1, United Kingdom. "A Guatemalan General's Rise to Power," by Raymond Bonner, © 1982 by The New York Times Company. Reprinted by permission. "Behind Guatemala's Military Power," reprinted by permission of The Institute for Policy Studies. "Guatemala: A Government Program of Political Murder," reprinted with permission of Amnesty International. Copyright © 2/81 Amnesty International Publications. "The Guatemalan Trade Union Movement (1976-1977)." by Miguel Angel Albizúrez, reprinted with permission from *Latin American Perspectives*, Spring & Summer, 1980. "Fight the Fare Increase," reprinted by permission of *Noticias de Guatemala*. "Coke Adds Life?" by Robert Morris, excerpted from *ICCR Brief*, November, 1980. Reprinted by permission. "My Country, Let Us Walk Together," by Otto René Castillo, reprinted by permission of Editorial Universitaria Centroamericana. "The Road to Liberty Passes Through Organization," by J. Antonio Bran, reprnted by permission from *Cuadernos de Marcha*. "Religion and Revolution: A Protestant Voice," reprinted with permission from *Christus*, Nos. 554-555, pp. 50-51, *Centro de Reflexion Teologica*,

Apdo. Postal 19-213, Colonia Mixcoac, 03910 Mexico, D.F. Mexico. Testimony of a Guatemalan indigenous women from El Quiché (February, 1982) in "Search and Destroy in Chupol: Daily Life in Occupied Guatemala" printed by permission of Christine Piotter. "Guatemalan Indians Crowd into Mexico to Escape the Widening War," by Marlise Simons, © *The Washington Post*. Reprinted by permission. "The Foco Experience: The Guerrillas' First Years," by Pablo Monsanto, reprinted by permission of *Punto Final Internacional*. "The People Become Guerrillas," from *Noticias de Guatemala*, reprinted by permission. "Strategic Guatemala: Next Red Plum in the Hemisphere?" by Edward J. Walsh, reprinted with the permission of *National Defense*, Journal of the American Defense Preparedness Association. "Wrong Central American Policy," by Wayne S. Smith, © 1982 by the New York Times Company. Reprinted by permission. "Elections: Symbols of Democracy?" by N. Santana, reprinted by permission of NACLA and the author. "Did History Lie When It Promised Peace and Progress?" by Eduardo Galeano, from *Proceso*, May 15, 1982, reprinted by permission.

First Hardcover Edition published in 1983
10 9 8 7 6 5 4 3 2 1

First Evergreen Edition published in 1983
10 9 8 7 6 5 4 3 2 1

Library of Congress Cataloging in Publication Data
Main entry under title:

Guatemala in rebellion.

Bibliography: p. 325
Includes index.
1. Guatemala—History—1945- . 2. Guatemala—Foreign relations—United States. 3. United States—Foreign relations—Guatemala. 4. Guerrillas—Guatemala. I. Fried, Jonathan L.
F1466.5.G794 1983 972.81 83-1420
ISBN 0-394-53240-6
ISBN 0-394-62455-6 (pbk.)

Manufactured in the United States of America

GROVE PRESS, INC., 196 West Houston Street, New York, N.Y. 10014

About the Editors

Jonathan L. Fried has lived in Guatemala and is a reporter on Central American affairs who frequently contributes to *The Guardian*. Professor of History at the Polytechnic Institute of New York, Marvin E. Gettleman is the editor of *Vietnam: History, Documents and Opinions* and an editor of *El Salvador: Central America in the New Cold War*. Deborah T. Levenson has lived in Guatemala and teaches Latin American history at New York University. Nancy Peckenham is an anthropologist and journalist who, in 1979, conducted research in Guatemala on land settlement programs. Her articles have appeared in *Multinational Monitor*, *Latin American Perspectives*, and *Win* magazine, among others. The editors and members of the National Writers Union.

Contents

INTRODUCTION
by Guillermo Toriello Garrido*

WITH great enthusiasm I have agreed to write these introductory words to what I believe is a major book about my country. I do so not only because this volume constitutes a serious and accurately documented analysis of the dramatic repression and genocide practiced by the military and endured by the Guatemalan people for the past twenty-eight years, but also because it is edited and written by a group of North American scholars. This work will familiarize all readers in the United States with the true image—captured impartially and with objectivity—of a noble people, descendants of the Maya, who after almost five centuries of the most cruel and repressive exploitation, have rebelled against injustice and now struggle to attain their liberty and economic independence.

Despite previous writings by journalists and religious and academic authors, "the case of Guatemala" has been virtually ignored by wide sectors of the North American public, or is known only by distorted views of its tragic reality. Let us see to what we can attribute the distortion, and what examples of it we can cite.

In 1943, with the exception of Costa Rica, Central America was governed by four criminal dictators: Nicaragua by Anastasio Somoza García, murderer of Augusto César Sandino; Honduras by Tiburcio Carias Andino, great repressor of his countrymen; El Salvador by Maximiliano Hernández Martínez, who in 1932 massacred more than thirty-two thousand peasants and opponents of his regime; and Guatemala by Jorge Ubico, champion of the Fugitive Law (which in practice meant that a captured enemy or opponent of the government usually wound up shot in the back, justified by the accusation that he had tried to flee). These four dictators ranked as Generals, the highest military position achievable in Central America.

In the year 1943 the situation that prevailed in Central America was ideal for political and economic domination by the United States: four generals in power, four brutal dictatorships, a "graveyard silence" throughout all the region, but above all an absolute guarantee for North American investments in the "banana republics," as they have disrespectfully been called.

In the first months of the year 1944, after a few unsuccessful attempts, a group of Salvadoran civilians and military men succeeded in overthrowing the govern-

---

*Dr. Toriello was simultaneously Guatemalan Ambassador to the United States, to the Organization of American States, and to the United Nations from 1952 to June 1954, at which time President Jacobo Arbenz Guzmán named him Minister of Foreign Relations. After the 1954 coup Toriello went into exile in Mexico where he wrote a number of books on the history of his country, including *La Batalla de Guatemala* (Mexico City, 1955). He is currently a vice-president of the Guatemalan Committee of Patriotic Unity. This piece was translated by Marianne Dugan, Ernesto Castillo, and the editors.

ment of General Hernández Martínez. However, the repressive apparatus of the dictatorship remained intact and power unfortunately continued to rest in the hands of a most backward and reactionary military. To this very day, the military exercises real power in El Salvador, both against the popular will, implementing fierce repression, and with the decisive support of the present government of the United States.

But the situation was different in Guatemala in 1944. After nearly seventy years of civilian and military dictatorships, our people—through heroic and historic periods of struggle during the months of June and October—forced the ouster of the tyrant Jorge Ubico, who had reigned for fourteen years using the tools of blood and fire. General Ponce Vaides, Ubico's successor, was in turn ousted when his intention to break the promise to hold elections became clear. October 20, 1944 is a most memorable date, for on that day a truly democratic process was begun in Guatemala. A patriotic, popular, and nationalistic process was initiated, led by the Revolutionary Junta made up of Captain Jacobo Arbenz, Mayor Javier Francisco Arana, and the civilian Jorge Toriello Garrido. These men promised to govern for only five months and they kept that promise.

Those five months witnessed the promulgation of a new and advanced Constitution of the Republic. The country held absolutely free elections for president and deputies of the National Congress. For ten years the people and this government struggled to maintain democratic representation. Ideological and party pluralism were in effect. Freedom of religion, press, and association were guaranteed. Civil and political rights, as well as human rights, were exercised.

Other important laws were passed, such as the Social Security Act and the Code of Labor Statutes. By recommendation of the United Nations a moderate agrarian reform law was enacted, affecting only uncultivated land, whether owned by nationals or foreigners. The United Fruit Company, which possessed large uncultivated estates, thus found this law applicable to its holdings.

The overthrow of El Salvador's genocidal General Maximiliano Hernández [in 1944] caused little worry to the U.S. State Department, for the status quo in El Salvador remained unaltered after that event. On the other hand, "the case of Guatemala" put the department into a state of alert. Guatemala sought to construct a totally independent and modern capitalist system, thereby breaking the scheme of traditional domination. This act was absolutely intolerable to the United States. At the strong urging of the State Department, the CIA and the Pentagon were called in to help terminate what was considered a bad example to other countries of the Americas.[1]

Never before in the history of the United States has such an untruthful and slanderous campaign been promoted against a Central American country as was undertaken by the State Department, the CIA, and the Pentagon with regard to

---

1. See Stephen Schlesinger and Stephen Kinzer, *Bitter Fruit: The Untold Story of the American Coup in Guatemala* (Garden City, N.Y.: Doubleday & Co., 1982).—AUTHOR'S NOTE.

Guatemala from 1944 to 1954. They made Guatemala appear as if it were a "beachhead of international communism," "a threat to the oil wells of Texas" and "a danger to the Panama Canal"; but above all "a threat and a danger to the solidarity of the hemisphere." The most serious result of this deceitful campaign was that it succeeded in confusing and misinforming the North American people. This tactic went to such extremes that some people actually believed—in addition to all the other dangers and threats mentioned—that Guatemala was a great power intent upon destroying the United States. Therefore, it had to be obliterated.

Now, after more than twenty-eight years, fresh light has been shed upon this shameful campaign of lies, a campaign waged not only to uphold the interests of the United Fruit Company, but also to maintain the system of economic and political domination the United States sought to exert in the Central American region.

In June 1954, an unjustifiable intervention and armed aggression by the United States culminated in a coup by Guatemalan military officers, bribed by and acting in collusion with the U.S. embassy, that overthrew the constitutionally elected president, Jacobo Arbenz. Since then, the U.S. State Department has helped to install and maintain nine military governments in our country. Let us take a look at the bloody and senseless results obtained for the Guatemalan people during these nine administrations.

Over ninety thousand persons have been assassinated in Guatemala from June 1954 to the present date. This does not include those who have merely disappeared. In its last two years alone, the Lucas García government buried fourteen thousand of its countrymen; among these were ninety-seven professors from the University of San Carlos in Guatemala City, more than five hundred students, forty-seven journalists, fifteen Catholic priests and two Protestant ministers, one hundred ninety Catholic lay workers, hundreds of teachers, intellectuals, workers, and trade union leaders and thousands of Indian and ladino campesinos.

On the other hand, this barbarism against our people has resulted in very favorable economic and political gains for the United States. In 1944, there existed in Guatemala only three powerful North American monopolies: the United Fruit Company, International Railways of Central America, and the Electric Bond and Share Company. Together these three companies formed a supranational government controlling our ports and lighthouses, railroad transportation, electric power, and international telephone and telegraph lines. They were protected by the dictatorships until the overthrow of Ubico.

Currently, and as a result of the support lent by the United States to the last nine military dictatorships, there are seventy-seven U.S. transnational companies that have taken control of our economy. They possess our natural resources and riches in areas such as mining and hydrocarbon industries, and agriculture. They also have gained control of thirty-seven formerly independent Guatemalan companies. At the same time the armed forces have also come under substantial U.S. control. Besides political support, Washington supplies arms and has financed and trained more than 2,300 Guatemalan officers in counterinsurgency, including torture techniques and other "dirty war" tactics employed in the unjust war against Vietnam.

These facts are ignored by the noble people of the United States. North Americans have been led to believe that the Guatemalan struggle against their military executioners is a communist movement, simply a part of the confrontation between East and West. Or they are tricked into believing assurances that the Soviet Union and Cuba are the originators of the rebellion not only in Guatemala but in El Salvador. Naturally the United States hides the truth about the genocide committed by the military against our people; the hunger, the malnutrition, the disease, the unemployment, the repression and the system of violence and terror institutionalized by the state.

The administration of ex-president Jimmy Carter imposed sanctions against the military government of General Romeo Lucas García for continuous violation of human rights in Guatemala. Now, after the military coup of March 23, 1982, we watch with tremendous anxiety the dramatic effort being made by President Reagan before the United States Congress, urging it to lift the military arms and economic embargo against Guatemala.

In appears that the communications of President Reagan to the Congress are based upon reports received from the U.S. embassy in Guatemala, and the account of Stephen Bosworth, Deputy Assistant Secretary of State for Inter-American Affairs—who recently visited Guatemala—describing the new government of General Efraín Ríos Montt as having ended the genocide, human rights violations, and repression.

Such reports not only deny the truth but directly contradict testimony given in Washington by two Congressional envoys, Representatives Stephen Solarz and Tom Harkin, who after visits to Guatemala both affirmed: "The massacres of civilians in that Central American country continue, although the government has halted the violence in the capital city." Solarz said, "I am much less inclined to resume military support after this trip," and Harkin added, "There appears to be a resumption of the war against the Indians of the rural areas." [2]

The truth of the matter is that after General Lucas García was replaced, his successor, General Ríos Montt, was advised to reduce the number of political crimes in the capital while intensifying the ferocious repression against unarmed campesinos in the countryside, where the guerrilla groups operate. This involved application of "dirty war" techniques applied by the United States in Vietnam—indiscriminate murder of men, women, even pregnant women, the elderly, and children; establishment of "strategic hamlets" (virtual concentration camps for the rural population); a "scorched earth" policy—the razing of villages, killing of livestock, the burning of crops and forests. Through horrifying crimes of mutilation, castration, beheading, crucifixion, and burning people alive, the army hoped

2. *Excelsior* [Mexico City], May 23, 1982.—AUTHOR'S NOTE.

to undermine the mutual trust between campesinos and guerrilla organizations, which have attempted to defend rural areas from the army's repression.

Finally, to complement this strategy of counterinsurgency. the mass media and newspapers have been used to falsely accuse the guerrillas of having been responsible for the atrocities. The army, its paramilitary groups, and state security forces have taken to dressing like guerrillas and campesinos in order to sow confusion and to create the false image of an internal struggle among the campesinos themselves.

Supporting a government that carries out these practices, the U.S. State Department evidently aims to uphold a repressive regime in Guatemala, support the campaign of rural extermination, and supply economic aid so that the enrichment of the military and its accomplices can continue.

But I harbor the hope that the great people of the United States—as inheritors of the high ethical values of their forebears—will, with the same vehemence with which they opposed the Vietnam war, now resist the Reagan Administration's plans to continue aid to the murderers of the Guatemalan people and to the perpetuators of genocide in El Salvador, and will thwart plans to destabilize and oust the popular government of Nicaragua, a government that is a victim of slander and lies similar to those used against my country, Guatemala, from 1944 to 1954.

The complicity and support given by a succession of United States governments to the executioners of our people have drenched our road to liberation in innocent blood; but in the end, we will win. . . .

CUERNAVACA, MEXICO
June 22, 1982

PREFACE

THE four editors undertook the project of compiling this volume with a sense of urgency. In the past, some U.S. tourists visiting Guatemala came back with only the experience of the pseudoreality constructed for them;[1] now even casual visitors cannot help but notice evidence of serious social problems and violent conflict. Long a country wracked by internal struggle and subject to foreign intervention, Guatemala has today reached a crisis in which the destiny of the country is being decided on the political-military battleground of guerrilla and antiguerrilla warfare. Through the readings in this book we hope to make available to a wide audience a varied body of historical and contemporary materials on the background of this crisis, its main elements, and the human hardship it engenders.

A recent study has pointed out the inadequate and misleading images of the Central American countries propagated in school textbooks: a "bridge" between North and South America, and the home of childlike, disputatious populations presumably in need of outside tutelage.[2] Such simplistic notions are dangerous. They function as empty vessels into which almost any content can be poured by official policymakers seeking to shape popular conceptions to accord with dubious policy initiatives. The textbook image has not, by and large, been offset by the mass media. The conspicuous lack of current and background information on Guatemala is at least partially due to the constant harassment of foreign and domestic journalists in that country.[3]

U.S. citizens need to know more about Guatemala, in part because of the

---

1. For an examination of the pseudoreality presented to tourists, see Daniel J. Boorstin, *The Image: A Guide to Pseudo-events* (New York: Atheneum, 1968), Chapter 3.

2. *Interracial Books for Children* [Council on Interracial Books, New York] XIII, Nos. 1-2 (1982).

3. Julia Preston, "Killing Off the News in Guatemala," *Columbia Journalism Review*, January-February 1982.

fateful direct U.S. intervention nearly thirty years ago (See Part I, Chapter II "U.S. Intervention 1954"); and more immediately, because of the fresh interventions that may be in the making by Washington policymakers. All too often U.S. foreign policy decisions are made without full public scrutiny. Only an informed, alert, and active citizenry can prevent the implementation of policies that have in the past had such disastrous consequences for our neighbors to the south. The parameters of intervention—military aid, economic loans, the encouragement of certain social programs, and the dispatch of U.S. advisors and troops—need not be taken as given in Washington's decision making. There is another alternative: not to intervene at all.

The title we have chosen for this volume, *Guatemala in Rebellion: Unfinished History,* merits a brief explanation. Guatemala's history, like that of the rest of Latin America, has been radically interrupted and reshaped by non-Guatemalan forces. The first of these interruptions was the Spanish Conquest, which established a lasting pattern of political and economic domination by foreign and local elites linked to expanding world markets, and of discrimination against Guatemala's non-European native population. The United States overtly interfered in Guatemala's affairs in 1954—when the CIA engineered a coup that ended a modest indigenous attempt to change the country's patterns of dependency and underdevelopment—interference that has continued with the support given the Guatemalan military to rule the country with an iron fist.

Guatemalans have never accepted their situation passively. Guatemala's history since the Conquest has been one of scattered, isolated, but constant rebellion against the social legacy of intervention. Today's national rebellion seeks to set the foundations of a more just society. Only if the Guatemalan people can shape their own destiny will their history of rebellion against an imposed system be finished, and a new historical era, undoubtedly with its own social problems, begin.

In addition to imparting reliable data on Guatemala, the preparation of this book has been prompted by another closely related aim: to provide a framework and a context for thinking about such countries as Guatemala. The reality of present-day Guatemala demands a conceptual framework that includes such categories as colonialism, underdevelopment, and imperialism. Guatemalan society rests on an agro-export economy dominated by foreign capital and subject to the fluctuations of volatile international markets and exchange rates. Some of the readings in this book make attempts to convey these aspects of Guatemalan political economy. Others focus on the political and economic role of the United States in shaping Guatemala's destiny and upholding the privileged military-oligarchy that has attempted to administer the country since 1954. There is also considerable data in these pages on the impact—often lethal—of aspects of the Guatemalan government's social and economic policy on various sectors of the population, as well as the devastating effects of its present-day counterinsurgency.

A theme found throughout the book is the indelible legacy of the Spanish

Conquest and the oppression of native populations, the misnamed Indians.[4] Guatemala is one of two Latin American countries (the other is Bolivia) where, according to most definitions, the majority of the population are Indians, ethnic groups which maintain a distinct cultural life and identity. The poverty of the Maya-descended campesinos [5] is probably the most important reason for the existence of insurgency today in Guatemala, but the cultural-based grievances and solidarity of the Indian ethnic groups certainly is a significant factor. The oppression of workers in the cities and the disaffection of intellectuals (most now in exile) are also essential root causes of rebellion (see Part Three, Chapter I). Together, these opposition forces created the guerrilla struggle which, with ferocious effort, the military and the oligarchy are trying to crush.

Major portions of this book are given over to analyses of the history and components of the resistance struggles. It is a complex story, and the documents and reports here do not constitute the last word, but the materials available suggest that the attempt to fit the fierce contest now being waged in Guatemala into a pattern derived from U.S.-U.S.S.R. Cold War rivalry is either tragically mistaken or a rationale for schemes of intervention. The tendency of Washington policymakers to see the Kremlin's hand in every social upheaval is well known and has been particularly apparent in Central America and the Caribbean, long a sphere of special and political interests of the U.S.[6]

The editors of this book themselves give little credence to the notion that Central American insurgencies are part of some vast international communist plot. Of course nations, even those that call themselves socialist or communist, will often seek influence or advantage in areas beset by internal unrest, but to

---

4. Of course the name "Indian" is a historical misnomer, mistakenly conferred on the Caribbean natives by Christopher Columbus, who had no conception of the fact that he had in his voyage westward from Spain encountered a "new" continent. Believing he had encountered the outlying islands of the East Indies he called the local population he encountered "Indios," Indians. But we use the word "Indian" throughout this book, in part because we lack a clearer one and in part because of the following argument put forward by Indian activist Rigoberta Menchú:

"None of the names given to us—"Indian," "indígena," "naturals" are ours. We know the Spaniards gave us the name Indian because they didn't know where they were; but many of us have realized that at this point the word Indian captures our history and our identity. There is real history in the word Indian and we do not want to separate ourselves from our history so we call ourselves Indians although we Indians have not yet had the chance to sit down in a huge meeting and decide what name best describes us." (Interview with the Editors, June 1982.)

5. Throughout this book we use the word "campesinos" to refer to rural subsistence agriculturalists as well as farm workers. For further discussion of the rural sociology of Guatemala, see Part Three, Chapter II.

6. For an account of the functioning of U.S. anticommunism in a nearby country, see Marvin E. Gettleman, Patrick Lacefield, Louis Menashe, David Mermelstein and Ronald Radosh, eds., *El Salvador: Central America in the New Cold War* (New York: Grove Press, 1981), *passim.* For a more general account, see Michael Parenti, *The Anti-Communist Impulse* (New York: Random House, 1969).

reduce these conflicts to elements in "Moscow's program of aggression in Latin America"[7] is to distort reality beyond legitimate bounds. Yet the view that turbulence in Central America is the direct result of outside communist interference is well represented in the readings of this book. Such a view has become the near-sacred ideology of U.S. government and corporate leaders and their spokespersons, and since Washington wields so much power in the region, any student of Central American politics should be well acquainted with the intricacies of Washington's ideology.

Many of the readings in this book are published here for the first time. Others are drawn from generally inaccessible books, periodicals, and occasional publications. Many items appear nowhere else in English, or are presented here in fresh translation. Official U.S. spokespersons share the pages of this anthology with Guatemalan labor leaders and campesino insurgents, contemporary journalists and historians, sixteenth-century Spanish conquistadores, and their clerical critics. From these many viewpoints readers will be challenged to form their own opinions and convictions; the book then will have served its editors' purpose.

We must explain our inability to describe the precise provenance of several of the contemporary documents included here. This has been necessary to protect the identities of persons who have more than ample reason to fear reprisals from governmental authorities. But we are only too happy to acknowledge the help and support of many people who encouraged this project. We begin with Lisa Rosset of Grove Press, whom we thank for her heartfelt enthusiasm.

We would also like to thank all the people who translated pieces for this book: Jan Perlin, José Braconi, Lisa Vives, Marianne Dugan, Ernesto Castillo, Madeleine Ruehl, Edmond F. Robinson, Jr., David Rodgers, Gabriel Escobar, Javier Bajaña, Raimundo Mora, David Kalke and Dina Briones.

For their invaluable support and criticism we thank Noel Thomas of EPICA (Washington, D.C.), Marcie Mersky and Jean Walsh of the National Network in Solidarity with the People of Guatemala, and Ellen Shrecker.

We also thank Pamela Yates and Tom Sigel, Robert Trudeau of Providence (R.I.) College, David Kalke of the New York Circus, Susanne Jonas of the Institute for the Study of Labor and Economic Crisis (San Francisco), Mark Fried, Robert Morris of the Interfaith Center for Corporate Responsibility, William A. Orme, Phillip Berryman of the American Friends Service Committee, Shelton H. Davis of the Anthropology Resource Center, Milton Jamail, Javier Bajaña, Reggie Norton of the Washington Office on Latin America, Jean-Marie Simon, Anna, César, Dina Bursztyn, Martin Lucas, Steven Schlesinger, A.P., Michael Parenti, Todd Anton, Nicolás Sánchez-Albornoz, Warren Dean, and Rozenn Frère, as well as Norma Chinchilla of the University of California at Irvine, Louis Menashe of the Polytechnic Institute of New York, the staff of the North American

---

7. A characteristic comment from a former U.S. ambassador to Guatemala, John E. Peurifoy, drawn from Reading 11.

Congress on Latin America, the Guatemala News and Information Bureau (Berkeley), Carlos Gallardo Flores of the Guatemalan Social Democratic Party and the Guatemalan Committee of Patriotic Unity (CGUP), Luis Cardoza y Aragón, Guillermo Toriello Garrido and Frank LaRue of CGUP; and special thanks to Rigoberta Menchú of CGUP for her tireless inspiration.

Although the above-mentioned people helped us greatly in the preparation of this book, the responsibility for the choice and presentation of materials was ours collectively. Writing and editing books is supposedly a solitary, individual process; we have learned much about collective work from our efforts to produce this comprehensive, informed anthology on Guatemala. It may very well be that these collective labors deepened our understanding of how people join together in common enterprise, as the Guatemalan people are doing to contend with their suffering. We hope to convey in these pages a sense of this collective effort, from which someday a new Guatemala of justice and peace will emerge.

NEW YORK CITY
July 1982

PART ONE

ROOTS OF REVOLUTION: FROM CONQUEST TO COUP (1524–1954).

Guatemala City shantytown. The tires and debris on top of the houses keep the sheet metal and cardboard roofs from blowing away. *Photo credit: Susan Meiselas*

EDITORS' INTRODUCTION

THE new world the Spaniards discovered in 1524 was thousands of years old. The peoples in the territory of Guatemala, such as the Cakchiquel, the Pokoman, the Ixil, the Mam, the Tzutujil, the Quiché, the Pipil and the Kekchí—known to us today by their languages—were part of the Mayan civilization, which had existed at least since the third century B.C. One of the world's great civilizations, the Mayas produced important works of art in sculpture, ceramics, and architecture. They also created a system of arithmetic, invented the concept of zero, and created a system of astronomy that enabled them to plot the movements of the stars and planets with greater accuracy than anyone else in the world at that time.[1] Mayan social structure was hierarchical and complex: peasants, artisans, and merchants supported priests and warriors in grand style. These societies were neither egalitarian nor ideal, but the material well-being of the Mayas, peasant or priest, was higher before 1524 than at any time since.[2] Cultivators and worshippers of nature, the Mayas supported a population at least as large as Guatemala's current one without the starvation and malnutrition now all too common.[3]

For the Spaniards who conquered, this new world was a frontier in which to fulfill dreams of power, wealth, and position. The Spanish conception of power and position, unlike the Mayan, meant the private accumulation of wealth

1. J. Eric Thompson, *The Rise and Fall of Maya Civilization*, 2nd ed. (Norman, Okla.: University of Oklahoma Press, 1977); Victor W. Von Hagen, *The World of the Maya* (New York: New American Library, 1960).

2. Moises Behar, "Food Nuitrition of the Maya before the Conquest and at the Present Time," in *Biomedical Challenges Presented by the American Indians* (Washington, D.C.: Pan American Health Organization, September, 1968), p. 116.

3. Eric Wolf, *Sons of the Shaking Earth* (Chicago: University of Chicago Press, 1959), p. 31 on population figures.

through the use of land and labor to produce goods to sell abroad. The consolidation of Spanish dominion meant that the territory's economy ceased to be based on the social and economic needs of its population; it became Eurocentric.[4] The present pattern of today's export-oriented agricultural economy has remained essentially unchanged since it began in the sixteenth century. An economy dependent on the fluctuations of the world market, producing cacao and indigo for New Spain (Mexico) and Europe during the colonial period, today Guatemala produces coffee, cotton, sugar, cardamom, beef, and bananas for a primarily North American market.

Modern Guatemala is a society which came into being as a result of the Conquest not only in the economic sense but in social terms as well. The Spaniards and their Guatemalan-born offspring, the creoles, formed the elite of a societal pyramid. Their interbreeding with Indian women created a "half-breed" group, the *ladinos,* who formed an intermediary layer of urban workers, as well as tenant farmers, sharecroppers, and wandering laborers working on Spanish-owned plantations (see Reading 3). The newly baptized "Indians,"[5] the uniform name the Spaniards gave the different indigenous groups, formed the vast base of this pyramid. The Indians were taken from their traditional villages and urban centers and resettled in new villages. Here the Spaniards both leveled them socially, by taking power away from the Mayan elites, and attempted to Christianize them. Although some acted as intermediaries for the Spanish officials and priests, most Indians were relegated to be part-time forced rural laborers on Spanish plantations and part-time peasants, tilling their cornfields for subsistence (see Readings 4 and 5). Coerced by law and violence in the colonial period, an increasing number of Indians are today compelled by hunger to migrate for seasonal work. They leave their highland *minifundios,* lands insufficient to satisfy minimum needs, to work for a subsistence wage on *latifundios,* the large plantations. Excluded from political involvement, Indians have been the backbone of economic life since the Conquest. This exploitation and exclusion has been rationalized by western supremacist and orthodox Christian doctrines, which perceive Indians as childish, backward, and lazy. With the advent of tourism, segments of the ladino upper and middle classes started to see them as "exotic" as well.

Today's population is characterized as fifty to sixty percent Indian and forty to fifty percent ladino, depending on the census takers' definition of ethnicity. But to say it is a country sharply divided between Indians and ladinos would be misleading. In the first place, percentages do not reflect the complexities of successive interbreeding or the subtle cultural ways Indians have affected ladinos, and vice versa. Secondly, "Indian" and "ladino" are not class terms; and the interplay between class and ethnicity has been complex throughout Guatemalan history. Although a small Indian middle class now exists, the power elite and middle classes have traditionally been non-Indian, at first creole and later ladino.

---

4. Murdo J. MacLeod, *Spanish Central America* (Berkeley: University of California Press, 1973).
5. See our earlier discussion (preface) of how the term Indian will be used in this book.

The overwhelming majority of Indians and ladinos, however, have always been poor rural or urban workers, and subsistence agriculturists, although Indians have consistently been treated worse and have suffered special oppression. What poor ladinos have shared with rich ones has been a more Hispanic culture, the Spanish language, and, generally living apart from Indians, spacial proximity. They have also shared a sense of social superiority over the Indians whom they have long held in disdain.

In the early nineteenth century the upper- and middle-class creoles led the movement for independence against Spain in order to liberate themselves from Spain's colonial regulations on Indian lands, burdensome taxes, and trade restrictions which shut off portions of the European market. They blamed Guatemala's extreme poverty and lack of internal development on the Indians' "lack of civilization." They sought European immigrants to "whiten" the population and foreign investment to promote capitalist modernization. Never succeeding in attracting large numbers of immigrants, their visions of capitalist development saw some realization when European demand and prosperity stimulated a coffee boom in the late 1870s.[6] Liberal Party president Justo Rufino Barrios, 1871–1885, promoted important agrarian legislation abolishing Indian village rights to community property holdings in order to free lands for primarily foreign-owned coffee cultivation (see Reading 17). In addition, national legislation both legitimized debt peonage and simply commanded Indians, newly impoverished by these land losses, to work on plantations. Barrios sent a circular to regional officials in 1876 stating: "that the Indian villages in your jurisdiction be forced to give the number of hands to the farmers that the latter ask for. . . ."[7] In the twentieth century, dictator Jorge Ubico instituted Vagrancy Laws obliging the landless and small holders to work or suffer penalties.

By the 1930s Guatemala's agro-export economy was closely linked to the United States and a new boom product, bananas. The Boston-based United Fruit Company was the country's largest employer, landowner, and exporter, as well as the owner of its one railroad and only Caribbean port.[8] United Fruit's economic role was symptomatic of the U.S. social and cultural domination of the country. Guatemalans peered at U.S. goods in store windows, saw U.S. movies, read U.S. comics if they could read, and received world and continental news through U.S. agencies. Guatemala became an apparently mortified society where neither labor

---

6. For an analysis of the historical impact of foreign capital and markets on Guatemala, see Suzanne Jonas, "Guatemala: Land of Eternal Struggle," in R. Chilcote, J. Edelstein, *Latin America: Struggle with Dependency and Beyond* (New York: John Wiley and Sons, 1974), pp. 93–214.

7. Chester Lloyd Jones, *Guatemala Past and Present* (Minneapolis: University of Minnesota Press, 1940), p. 150.

8. On UFCO's role see Thomas McCann, *An American Company: The Tragedy of the United Fruit* (New York: Brown, 1976); Stephen Schlesinger and Stephen Kinzer, *Bitter Fruit: The Untold Story of the American Coup in Guatemala* (Garden City, NY: Doubleday & Co., 1982), Chapter 5.

unions, political parties, nor an independent press were permitted. Even the word "worker" was banned for its inflammatory connotations; "Jesus the Worker" became "Jesus the Employed." Indians, the majority of the people, were barred from the capital's main streets.[9]

Then came 1944 and the "October Revolution" of that year. An alliance of middle-class intellectuals, professionals, and young military men brought to power a reform government which attempted to break with the past. Inspired by Mexico's reformist president, Lázaro Cárdenas, and by the worldwide antifascist and antidictatorial spirit of the World War II years, the Guatemalan reform governments of Juan José Arévalo (1945–1950) and Jacobo Arbenz Guzmán (1950–1954) began a new era. They promoted a labor code, social security, public schools, a land reform based on the purchase of uncultivated lands, industrial development, and intellectual freedom. An attempt was also made to curb the power of the United Fruit Company.

Guatemala's sole interlude in four hundred thirty years in which violence and coercion ceased to be the norm was sabotaged in 1954 by a U.S.-planned, -directed, and executed coup which sent Arbenz into exile. (See Reading 10). In the words of Mexican writer Carlos Fuentes, who along with many Latin Americans watched in shock as the United States intervened, hopes for friendly relations with the U.S. "were now buried inside an iceberg that not even the warm waters of the Caribbean could melt. . . . It was an important year, 1954, because political development in Guatemala was not merely interrupted by violent foreign intervention; it has been continually perverted and poisoned to this very day. . . ."[10]

The material in the next two chapters describes a historical cycle, from the Spanish Conquest to a kind of U.S. conquest in 1954. Seen in this context, present-day Guatemala stands in the shade of its history.

---

9. Luis Cardoza y Aragón, *La Revolución Guatemalteca* (Montevideo: Ediciones Pueblos Unidos, 1956), pp. 75–76.

10. Carlos Fuentes, "Three Dates of Change in Latin America," in Marvin E. Gettleman, Patrick Lacefield, Louis Menashe, David Mermelstein, and Ronald Radosh, eds., *El Salvador, Central America in the Cold War* (New York: Grove Press, 1981), pp. 382–383.

Chapter I:

The Colonial Legacy: A Long Present Past, 1524–1944.

Editor's Introduction

I joined the struggle because of my revolutionary convictions: that is because we ourselves have suffered in the flesh all that inheritance from the invasion of 1524.

—Emeterio Toj, Indian leader of the Committee of Campesino Unity, 1982

GUATEMALA is a country where people have a strong sense that history shapes their present lives. The past is visually evident in the Spanish colonial architecture and Mayan ruins, and it is also politically alive. In the 1980s many people speak of their problems in terms of hundreds of years. Partisan about the present and the future, they are also partisan about the past. Many Guatemalans do not accept, for example, the finality and hegemony implied in the term "Spanish Conquest" and instead call that event an "invasion" as Emeterio Toj does above. Perhaps Guatemalans are particularly historically minded beause, like so many of the old buildings, shaky but standing in this land of earthquakes, social control has never been firmly established or decidedly broken.

Guatemala's history of continual conflict is reflected in the way the past is perceived. The memory of the Spanish Conquest preserved in rural folklore is not a Hispanic memory, but an Indian one. Tecún Umán, the Quiché Indian leader defeated by Conquistador Pedro de Alvarado (see Reading 1) in 1524, has been an Indian hero since that time; so much so that the Guatemalan state has attempted to dilute his meaning as a symbol of resistance by making him a national hero, an official canonization which many Indians reject (see Rigoberta Menchú, Reading 32).

The Indian history of the Conquest is portrayed each year in the mountains when the traditional "Dance of the Conquest" is performed. In this dance the Conquest is reenacted by Indians who wear smiling masks to represent the Mayas and grimacing ones to represent the conquistadores. Year after year this play communicates an element of resistance to an event which took place hundreds of years ago. As Tecún Umán and Alvarado fight, a chorus chants:

> Mighty volcano, fertile mountain, why art thou humiliated by the weapons of the foreigners? Throw forth the flames that burn thine entrails and consume thine oppressors with fire. Long live King Quiché and death to the Spaniards! [1]

Francisco Javier García, the only Indian village director of the "Dance of the Conquest" to have a manuscript about it published, writes:

> The Conquest reminds pure-blooded Indians of the time when Spanish troops, not braver, but better armed, had no other mission than to destroy. For as long as we can remember, the play of the Conquest of the Quiché kingdom has been performed as a tribute to the resistance offered by our ancestors to the invaders.[2]

In this manner Indians spurn an official history which glorifies their conquerers.

It is an indication of Guatemala's continuous lack of social stability that Indians have resisted the process of acculturation. Archbishop Cortés y Larraz's report to the Spanish Crown in 1769 (see Reading 5) describes Indians' profound hostility toward Spanish priests and officials 245 years after the Spaniards had established their rule. What was true in 1769 was still true in the 1930s and continues to be so today: Guatemala's governments have never been able to command the loyalty of the majority.

This chapter presents a long time period, 1524–1944, from the perspective of people of the time as well as Guatemalan and non-Guatemalan scholars. These readings give a sense of the violent, dramatic, and unresolved qualities of Guatemalan history, suggesting today's revolutionary movements are its prophecy.

---

1. Barbara Bode, *The Dance of the Conquest* (New Orleans, Louisiana State University Press, 1961).

2. Francisco Javier Garcia, *El Baile de la Conquista* (Quezaltenango, Guatemala, 1934) quoted in Bode, above, p. 232.

1. *The Spaniards Discover Guatemala* *

BY PEDRO DE ALVARADO

WHEN *the Spanish Conquistador Pedro de Alvarado and his soldiers advanced down the Pacific Coast from Mexico in 1524, the indigenous kingdoms of Guatemala had already received ominous news from Mexico of these bearded warring strangers. As Alvarado describes in this excerpt from a letter to Hernán Cortés, most of the Guatemalan kingdoms, under the leadership of the Quiché and their captain, Tecún Umán, immediately challenged Alvarado's invading army. Initially defeated in battle, the Quiché invited Alvarado to their capital, Utatlán, to negotiate or perhaps, as Alvarado thought, to entrap him. Alvarado burned the city and its chiefs in the name of Christianity and the Spanish Crown.*

SIR: FROM SONCONUSCO I wrote to Your Grace all that had happened to me as far as that place and even something of what was expected to happen further on. And after having sent my messengers to this country, informing them of how I was to come to conquer and pacify the provinces that might not be willing to place themselves under the dominion of His Majesty, I asked of them as his vassals (for as such they had offered themselves to Your Grace) the favour of assistance and passage through their country: that by so doing, they would act as good and loyal vassals of His Majesty and that they would be greatly favoured and supported in all justice by me and the Spaniards in my company; and if not, I threatened to make war on them as traitors rising in rebellion against the service of our lord the Emperor and that as such they would be treated, and that in addition to this, would make slaves of all those who should be taken alive in the war. And having done all this and despatched the messengers, who were men of their own people, I reviewed all my men, both foot and horse. And the next day, on the morning of Saturday, I set out in search of their land, and after marching for three days through uninhabited forest, we pitched our camp and the scouts whom I had sent out captured three spies from a town in their country named Zapotitlán. I asked them what they came for and they told me that they were collecting honey, but it was notorious that they were spies, as it later on appeared. Notwithstanding all this, as I wished to treat them reasonably before compelling them, I gave them another command and requirement [1] as before, and sent them

---

* Letter from Pedro de Alvarado to Hernán Cortés April, 1524, from John Eoghan Kelly, *Pedro de Alvarado, Conquistador* (Princeton, N.J.: Princeton University Press, 1932), pp. 135–139.

1. To satisfy objections by the Dominicans to the conquistadores' treatment of Indians, the Spanish Crown drew up a document called the Requirement, which the Spaniards read to the Indians before making war on them. This curious statement asked the Indians to acknowledge the supremacy of the

to the chiefs of the said town. To none of my requests did I receive any answer. . .

At the end of six days that I had been here, one Thursday at noon, a great multitude of people appeared on many sides and, according to what I learned from them, twelve thousand were from this city and surrounding towns and the others they said could not be counted. From the moment I saw them, I put my men in order, and went out to give them battle with ninety horsemen, in the middle of a plain three leagues long. I left men in the camp to guard it and, at a gunshot from the camp and no more, we commenced to crush them and scatter them in all directions and followed them in pursuit for two leagues and a half until all of them were routed and nobody left in front of us. Later we returned against them, and our friends and the infantry made the greatest destruction in the world, at a river. They surrounded a bare mountain where they had taken refuge, and pursued them to the top, and took all that had gone up there. That day we killed and imprisoned many people, many of whom were captains and chiefs and people of importance.

And when the chiefs of this town found that their people were defeated, they took counsel with all the land and called many other provinces to them, and gave tribute to their enemies and induced them to join them, so that all might come together and kill us. And they agreed to send and tell us that they had wished to be friends, and that again they gave obedience to our lord the Emperor, so that I should enter the city of Utatlán, where they afterwards brought me, thinking that they would lodge me there, and that when thus encamped, they would set fire to the town some night and burn us all in it, without the possibility of resistance. And in truth their evil plan would have come to pass but that God our Lord did not see good that these infidels should be victorious over us, for this city is very very strong, and there are only two ways of entering it; one of over thirty steep stone steps and the other by a causeway made by hand, much of which was already cut away, so that that night they might finish cutting it, and no horse could then have escaped into the country. As the city is very closely built and the streets very narrow, we could not have stood it in any way without either suffocating or else falling headlong from the rocks when fleeing from the fire. And as we rode up and I could see how large the stronghold was, and that within it we could not avail ourselves of the horses because the streets were so narrow and walled in, I determined at once to clear out of it on to the plain, although the chiefs of the town asked me not to do so, and invited me to seat myself and eat before I departed, so as to gain time to carry out their plans. But I knew the danger in which we were, and at once sent some men ahead of me to take possession of the causeway and bridge, so that I could get out on to the plain, and the causeway was already in such a condition that one could hardly get over it on horseback, and outside the city were many warriors, and as they saw me pass out on to the

---

Pope and the Crown over their lands or suffer war and enslavement. Alvarado wrote of the Indians' reply to this demand to serve the Pope and the Spanish King, "They sent me word they did not know either of them."

plain, they retreated, but not so much that I did not receive much harm from them. But I concealed it all so that I might capture the chiefs who were taking to flight and by the cunning with which I approached them, and through presents which I gave them, the better to carry out my plan, I took them captive and held them prisoners in my camp. But, nevertheless, their people did not cease fighting against me in the neighborhood and killed and wounded many Indians who had gone out to gather grass. And one Spaniard who was gathering grass, a gunshot from camp, was slain by a stone rolled down the hill. This land is very full of gullies; there are gullies two hundred estados in depth, and, on account of them, one cannot carry on war and punish these people as they deserve.

And seeing that by fire and sword I might bring these people to the service of His Majesty, I determined to burn the chiefs who, at the time that I wanted to burn them, told me, as it will appear in their confessions, that they were the ones who had ordered the war against me and were the ones also who made it. They told me about the way they were to do so, to burn me in the city, and that with this thought (in their minds) they had brought me there, and that they had ordered their vassals not to come and give obedience to our lord the Emperor, nor help us, nor do anything else that was right. And as I knew them to have such a bad disposition towards the service of His Majesty, and to insure the good and peace of this land, I burnt them, and sent to burn the town and to destroy it, for it is a very strong and dangerous place, that more resembles a robbers' stronghold than a city. . . .

And as far as touches the war, I have nothing more at present to relate, but that all the prisoners of war were branded and made slaves, of whom I gave His Majesty's fifth part to the treasurer, Baltasar de Mendoza, which he sold by public auction, so that the payment to His Majesty should be secure.

I would wish Your Grace to know that the country is healthy and the climate temperate, and well populated, with many strong towns, and that this city is well built and wonderfully strong, and has much corn land and many people subject to it, the which, with all the subject towns and neighbourhoods, I have placed under the yoke and in the service of the royal crown of His Majesty.

2. *The Mayas Discover Spain* *

—From The Annals of the Cakchiquel

For many, the Spanish Conquest of the Americas evokes images of success, glory, and the discovery of a new world. But these notions are in European terms, and only to Europeans was this territory new.

---

* From A. Recinos, *The Annals of the Cakchiquel,* tr. D. Goetz and S. G. Morley, (Norman, Okla.: University of Oklahoma Press, 1953), pp. 119-30, 143.

For the millions who had lived in the Americas for centuries, the Conquest was a traumatic invasion which destroyed their civilization, suppressed their culture, and imposed startling new values in a new historical era. One of the few native documents to survive Spanish rule, The Annals of the Cakchiquel, *from which the following reading is taken, presents the Conquest from an Indian perspective.*

The Cakchiquel, the only Indian group to briefly ally with the Spaniards hoping to win aid against their own enemies, were subsequently shocked by the Spaniards' brutality. After the fall of Quiché, the Cakchiquel joined other kingdoms and launched a general uprising. Rebellions forced the Spaniards to spend twenty years pacifying the native population which they then enslaved. By the mid-sixteenth century, another form of destruction superseded the destruction and disruption of life brought by war, when disastrous epidemics of European origin destroyed at least one-third of the population. It has been estimated that the population of Mesoamerica fell from fourteen million to two million between 1524 and the early 1600s due to disease, the overwork of slavery, starvation, and war which accompanied Spain's claim to a world belonging to other people.

In the previous reading conquistador Pedro de Alvarado describes his entrance into Guatemala, the defeat of the Quiché, and the enslavement of Indians as he saw these events. In the following reading the entrance of Tunatiuh Avilantaro, the Cakchiquel name for Alvarado, the alliance of the Cakchiquel with the Spaniards, the Quiché defeat, the Spanish arrival at the Cakchiquel capital of Yximché, Spanish enslavement, the Cakchiquel rebellion, and the European epidemic are depicted through the eyes of the conquered Cakchiquel.

DURING THIS YEAR the Spaniards arrived. Forty-nine years ago the Spaniards came to Xepit and Xetulul.

On the day 1 Ganel [February 20, 1524] the Quichés were destroyed by the Spaniards. Their chief, he who was called Tunatiuh Avilantaro,[1] conquered all the people. Their faces were not known before that time. Until a short time ago the wood and the stone were worshiped.

Having arrived at Xelahub, they defeated the Quichés; all the Quiché who had gone out to meet the Spaniards were exterminated. Then the Quichés were destroyed before Xelahub.[2]

Then [the Spaniards] went forth to the city of Gumarcaah, where they were received by the kings, the Ahpop and the Ahpop Qamahay, and the Quichés paid them tribute. Soon the kings were tortured by Tunatiuh.

On the day 4 Qat [March 7, 1524] the kings Ahpop and Ahpop Qamahay were burned by Tunatiuh. The heart of Tunatiuh was without compassion for the people during the war.

Soon a messenger from Tunatiuh came before the [Cakchiquel] kings to ask

1. Pedro de Alvarado.—EDS.

2. The present-day Quezaltenango or "place of the quetzalli"—the long green feathers of the quetzal bird worn by the Quiché chiefs who died fighting the Spaniards.—EDS.

them to send him soldiers: "Let the warriors of the Ahpozotzil and the Ahpoxahil come to kill the Quichés," the messenger said to the kings. The order of Tunatiuh was instantly obeyed, and two thousand soldiers marched to the slaughter of the Quichés.

Only men of the city went; the other warriors did not go down to present themselves before the kings. The soldiers went three times only to collect tribute from the Quichés. We also went to collect it for Tunatiuh, oh, my sons!

How they came to Yximché[3]

On the day 1 Hunahpú [April 12, 1524] the Spaniards came to the city of Yximché; their chief was called Tunatiuh. The kings Belehé Qat and Cahí Ymox went at once to meet Tunatiuh. The heart of Tunatiuh was well disposed toward the kings when he came to the city. There had been no fight and Tunatiuh was pleased when he arrived at Yximché. In this manner the Castilians arrived of yore, oh, my sons! In truth they inspired fear when they arrived. Their faces were strange. The lords took them for gods. We ourselves, your father, went to see them when they came into Yximché.

Tunatiuh slept in the house of Tzupam. On the following day the chief appeared, frightening the warriors, and went toward the residence where the kings were. "Why do you make war upon me when I can make it upon you?" he said. And the kings answered: "It is not so, because in that way many men would die. You have seen the remains there in the ravines." And then he entered the house of the chief Chicbal.

Then Tunatiuh asked the kings what enemies they had. The kings answered: "Our enemies are two, oh, Lord: the Zutuhils and [those of] Panatacat. Thus the kings said to him. Only five days later Tunatiuh left the city. The Zutuhils were conquered then by the Spaniards. On the day 7 Camey [April 18, 1524] the Zutuhils were destroyed by Tunatiuh.

Twenty-five days after his arrival in the city, Tunatiuh departed for Cuzcatán, destroying Atacat on the way. On the day 2 Queh [May 9] the Spaniards killed those of Atacat. All the warriors and their Mexicans went with Tunatiuh to the conquest.

On the day 10 Hunahpú [July 21, 1524] he returned from Cuzcatán; it was two months after he left for Cuzcatán when he arrived at the city. Tunatiuh then asked for one of the daughters of the king and the lords gave her to Tunatiuh.

The demand for money

Then Tunatiuh asked the kings for money. He wished them to give him piles of metal, their vessels and crowns. And as they did not bring them to him immediately, Tunatiuh became angry with the kings and said to them: "Why have you

3. The present day Iximché, then the capital ot the Cakchiquel.—EDS.

not brought me the metal? If you do not bring with you all of the money of the tribes, I will burn you and I will hang you," he said to the lords.

Next Tunatiuh ordered them to pay twelve hundred pesos of gold. The kings tried to have the amount reduced and they began to weep, but Tunatiuh did not consent, and he said to them: "Get the metal and bring it within five days. Woe to you if you do not bring it! I know my heart!" Thus he said to the lords.

They had already delivered half of the money to Tunatiuh when a man, an agent of the devil, appeared and said to the kings: "I am the lightning. I will kill the Spaniards; by the fire they shall perish. When I strike the drum, depart [everyone] from the city, let the lords go to the other side of the river. This I will do on the day 7 Ahmak [August 26, 1524]." Thus that demon spoke to the lords. And indeed the lords believed that they should obey the orders of that man. Half of the money had already been delivered when we escaped.

Then we fled from the city

On the day 7 Ahmak we accomplished our flight. Then we abandoned the city of Yximché because of the agent of the devil. Afterwards the kings departed. "Tunatiuh will surely die at once," they said. "Now there is no war in the heart of Tunatiuh, now he is satisfied with the metal that has been given him."

Thus it was that, because of the wicked man, we abandoned our city on the day 7 Ahmak, oh, my sons!

But Tunatiuh knew what the kings had done. Ten days after we fled from the city, Tunatiuh began to make war upon us. On the day 4 Camey [September 5, 1524] they began to make us suffer. We scattered ourselves under the trees, under the vines, oh, my sons! All our tribes joined in the fight against Tunatiuh. The Spaniards began to leave at once, they went out of the city, leaving it deserted.

Then the Cakchiquels began hostilities against the Spaniards. They dug holes and pits for the horses and scattered sharp stakes so that they should be killed. At the same time the people made war on them. Many Spaniards perished and the horses died in the traps for horses. The Quichés and the Zutuhils died also; in this manner all the people were destroyed by the Cakchiquels. Only thus did the Spaniards give them a breathing spell, and thus also all the tribes made a truce with them [the Spaniards] . . .

During the tenth year [of the second cycle] the war with the Spaniards continued. The Spaniards had moved to Xepau. From there, during the tenth year, they made war on us and killed many brave men.

Then Tunatiuh left Xepau and began hostilities against us because the people did not humble themselves before him. Six months had passed of the second year of our flight from the city, or [from the time] when we abandoned it and departed, when Tunatiuh came to it in passing and burned it. On the day 4 Camey [February 7, 1526] he burned the city; at the end of the sixth month of the second year of the war he accomplished it and departed again. . . .

During the course of this year our hearts had some rest. So also did the kings

Cahí Ymox and Belehé Qat. We did not submit to the Spaniards, and we were living in Holom Balam,[4] oh, my sons!

One year and one month had passed since Tunatiuh razed [the city], when the Spaniards came to Chij Xot. . . .

During this year, while we were busy with the war against the Spaniards, they abandoned Chij Xot and went to live at Bulbuxyá.

During that year the war continued. And none of the people paid the tribute.

The beginning of the tribute

Fifteen months after [the Spaniards] appeared in Chij Xot the tribute to the Capitán [Alvarado] was started by Chintá Queh. Here in Tzololá, on the day 6 Tzíi [January 12, 1528] the tribute began. . . .

During this year [1530] heavy tribute was imposed. Gold was contributed to Tunatiuh; four hundred men and four hundred women were delivered to him to be sent to wash gold. All the people extracted the gold. Four hundred men and four hundred women were contributed to work in Pangán on the construction of the city, by order of Tunatiuh. All this, all, we ourselves saw, oh, my sons! . . .

During the two months of the third year which had passed since the lords presented themselves, the king Belehé Qat died; he died on the day 7 Queh [September 24, 1532] while he was washing gold. Immediately after the death of the king, Tunatiuh came here to choose a successor to the king. Then the lord Don Jorge was installed in the government by order of Tunatiuh alone. There was no election by the people to name him. Afterwards Tunatiuh talked to the lords and his orders were obeyed by the chiefs, for in truth they feared Tunatiuh.

Seventeen months after the death of Belehé Qat, the lords had to recognize as king Don Jorge, the father of Don Juan Juárez. . . .

During this year the king Cahí Ymox, Ahpozotzil, went away and went to live in the city. The desire to go away came to the king because the tribute was imposed on the lords as well as on everyone else, and therefore the king had to pay it. . . .

During the course of this year Tunatiuh departed for Castile, making new conquests on the way. Then the people of Tzutzumpan and those of Choloma were destroyed. Tunatiuh went to destroy and to conquer many towns. . . .

[The Annals of the Cakchiquel continue, describing the hanging of many native chiefs, Alvarado's death in 1541, the start of the Cakchiquel's religious instruction under the Dominicans, the grouping of the Cakchiquel into new villages which began in 1547, a volcanic eruption in 1552, a locust attack in 1554 and the epidemic in 1559.—EDS.]

Little by little it arrived here. In truth a fearful death fell on our heads by the will of our powerful God. Many families [succumbed] to the plague. Now the

4. "Head of a tiger," a high mountain near Iximché.—EDS.

people were overcome by intense cold and fever, blood came out of their noses, then came a cough growing worse and worse, the neck was twisted, and small and large sores broke out on them. The disease attacked everyone here. On the day of Circumcision [January 1, 1560], a Monday, while I was writing, I was attacked by the epidemic.

3. *The Domination of Indian Women and the Birth of the Ladino* *

BY SEVERO MARTINEZ PELAEZ

WITH the Conquest came the subjugation of Indian women. At first joined by few Spanish women, the Spaniards sexually abused Indian women. For the Indian woman this sexual exploitation was a humiliating experience based on the Spaniard's economic and social power over her. Even as the number of Spanish women in Guatemala grew, interbreeding between Spaniard and Indian was common. But marriage was not; the Spaniard reserved this institution for the Spanish woman, and it served to provide legal heirs and thus preserve the economic and social status of the Spanish elite and their Guatemalan-born children, the creoles.

Interbreeding did not produce a people who, half-Indian and half-Spanish, could join the ranks of either the Spaniards or the Indians. Instead it created a third group of people, called ladinos, who were considered socially neither Indian nor Spanish. Exempt from the regulations imposed on Indians and without the power of being creole or Spanish, the ladinos came to be, in both the colonial and modern periods, colonos, [1] *sharecroppers, tenant farmers, subsistence agriculturists, wage workers, urban artisans, and eventually its small middle classes. Today the term ladino refers to any non-Indian as well as to culturally assimilated Indians.*

The following is from Guatemalan historian Severo Martínez Peláez's interpretative study of the colonial period, La Patria del Criollo, *which, except for the following excerpt, has unfortunately never been translated into English. This excerpt describes the character of sexual relations between Spaniards and Indians and the genesis of the ladino population. As is the case with many Guatemalan intellectuals, Martínez Peláez can no longer live in Guatemala.*

---

* From Severo Martínez Peláez, *La Patria del Criollo* (San José, Costa Rica: Editorial Universitaria Centroamericana, 5th ed. 1979), pp. 355–360. Translated by David Rodgers.

1. The term *colono* refers to a resident worker on a large plantation who is ceded a small plot of land as part payment for laboring on the plantation.

THE INTERBREEDING OF the Spaniard or the creole with the Indian woman at the time of the Conquest as well as later tends to be falsified by being presented as a biological phenomenon, and even more superficially as an isolated sexual incident.

It would be lengthy and out of place here to explain that human acts, in so far as they are human, are always socially conditioned. But it is easy for anyone to understand the following truth: man cannot carry out any relationship—of whatever nature—that is not conditioned by the value he confers on it and upon those whom it involves; and that the measure or manner of evaluation is necessarily given to him by the type of society in which the relationship is formed and the position he occupies in it.

Thus the Spaniard—or if preferred, the creole—carried out very different acts when he lay down with a Spanish woman and when he lay down with an Indian one. On the biological plane the two phenomena may be very similar, but to us that is of no importance, because we are not trying to understand fecundity, but rather its social conditioners and its historical consequences when it takes place between persons belonging to two different social classes in a given society. The Spaniard had taken the Spanish woman, or had to take her, to the Church, and there, in a ceremony to which the assembled attributed transcendental meaning, he committed himself to live with her in everlasting union, to protect and educate his children, and to make them, and eventually her too, heirs to his goods. These children received certain material goods as well as a certain capacity to conserve and expand them. They entered a group their parents and other families belonged to which also had something to conserve, inherit, and expand. They entered to form part of the dominant class. That destiny had been assigned to them long before their birth in the minds of their fathers, programming their procreation, which had nothing to do with a "blind act."

Nor was the Indian woman simply fertilized by the Spaniard or the creole. Whether she was raped, deceived, bribed, seduced, persuaded, in any case, some situation existed which must be stated. The fundamental condition of the interbreeding of the Spaniard with the Indian woman was, after all, the superiority of the Hispanic over the native—a theme that should be well understood and which we have discussed; not only the pretention of superiority, but effective superiority in terms of economic and social advantage. . . . Economic domination, the lasting essence of the Conquest and the lasting cause of the subordination of the conquered, continued to operate within interbreeding, making it, as we have said, a peculiar aspect of oppression. The Indian woman was not the wife of the Spaniard or the creole who incidently or regularly possessed her. She was to the utmost his Indian concubine (his *barragana* in the judicial lexicon of the era), what in that context meant his extramarital servant, supplying the commodity sex. No law, no moral code obligated the colonial gentleman to his Indian concubine, nor to the children he procreated with her. We have already seen elsewhere—"inheritance of blood, inheritance of power"—how the protection of wealth within a small European nucleus of heirs of the conquest demanded that the nucleus remain closed and its racial character protected; a racial character to which was attributed from the beginning a false significance as a source of distinction in every sense. And the proof that the real preoccupation was of a strictly economic origin lies in the fact that opinion was not bothered by concubine relations and spurious children—common happenings in colonial life—as long as the man's conduct left it clearly understood that these were escapades that did not threaten the structure nor the patrimony of his legitimate family. The colonial aristocracy, the creole class, opened under the pressure of Spanish immigrants; it also opened to expel from its bosom ruined Spaniards; but it remained closed to the people of mixed blood and to the Indians during the respectable lapse of three centuries.

Let us understand then, that the initial interbreeding was an act realized in the context of and as a consequence of the societal inferiority and disadvantage of a woman from the dominated class facing a man from the dominant class. It was the result of a biological union based on profound human disunion and inequality; of fornication as an act of veiled domination or, in many cases, simple and open outrage.

The children of these unions, the original half-breeds, were what they were—workers without patrimony, tossed out in search of middle-level occupations or completely unskilled ones—as a consequence of their parents belonging to two antagonistic classes; and neither could give them a place without bringing harm to their class or themselves. All of this was the result, in the final analysis, of the existence of two classes at odds, and of the limited possibilities of behavior established by the domination of one over the other.

The secondary interbreeding, the multiplication of the half-breeds combining among themselves and with various other groups—including, of course, the Spaniards and creoles themselves—was not nor could be anything else but the prolongation and a compilation of what resulted from the initial interbreeding. The multiplication of beings who were born outside the wealthy dominant group and outside the servile Indian group, was a proliferating of individuals in search of middle-level and inferior vacant positions and occupations. Individuals without inherited property, or authority, or servants, had to make themselves useful in order to be remunerated and in order to survive. Thus, the success and the vicissitudes of that search depended, naturally, on the demand for workers in that society and of the occupational areas in which they were needed. The need for free workers acted as a mold into which the human stream of half-breeds was poured.

4. Seventeenth-Century Colonialism: "A Cheap and Lazy Way of Living" *

BY THOMAS GAGE

INITIALLY the right to the labor and tribute of entire Indian villages was given in trusteeship or encomienda *to individual Spanish conquistadores. By the late sixteenth century the tremendous depopulation of the Indians following the Conquest and under slavery had resulted in a serious attempt by the Spanish Crown to control and ration its dwindling supply of Indian labor. The Crown abolished slavery and replaced it with a system called* repartimiento. *Under the* repartimiento *system the colonial administration compelled each Indian village to pay tribute and supply a share, or* reparto, *of laborers each week in exchange for a nominal wage. By the late sixteenth century the Church had also entered as a force: in the 1540s and '50s the Dominicans led the removal of Indians from their traditional homes. They congregated them in newly built villages near Spanish settlements and supervision. From these villages came the* repartimiento *labor upon which colonial society rested. Thomas Gage, a Dominican friar from England who worked in the Kingdom of Guatemala in the 1630s and '40s, gave the following account of the* repartimiento *system in his book,* The New Survey of the West Indies, *published in England in 1648.*

THE MISERABLE CONDITION of the Indians of that country is such that though the Kings of Spain have never yielded to what some would have, that they should be slaves, yet their lives are as full of bitterness as is the life of a slave. For which I have known myself some of them that have come home from toiling with Spaniards, after many blows, some wounds, and little or no wages, who have sullenly and stubbornly lain down upon their beds, resolving to die rather than to live any longer a life so slavish, and have refused to take either meat or drink or anything else comfortable and nourishing, which their wives have offered unto them, that so by pining and starving they might consume themselves. Some I have by good persuasions encouraged to life rather than to a voluntary and wilful death; others there have been that would not be persuaded, but in that wilful way have died.

The Spaniards that live about that country (especially the farmers of the Valley of Mixco, Pinola, Petapa, Amatitlan, and those of the Sacatepequez) allege that all their trading and farming is for the good of the commonwealth, and therefore whereas there are not Spaniards enough for so ample and large a country to do all

* From Thomas Gage, *The New Survey of the West Indies, 1648* (New York: Robert M. McBride & Company, 1929), pp. 230–234.

their work, and all are not able to buy slaves and blackamoors, they stand in need of the Indians' help to serve them for their pay and hire; whereupon it hath been considered that a partition of Indian labourers be made every Monday, or Sunday in the afternoon to the Spaniards, according to the farms they occupy, or according to their several employments, calling, and trading with mules, or any other way. So that for such and such a district there is named an officer, who is called *juez repartidor*, who according to a list made of every farm, house, and person, is to give so many Indians by the week. And here is a door opened to the President of Guatemala, and to the judges, to provide well for their menial servants, whom they commonly appoint for this office, which is thus performed by them. They name the town and place of their meeting upon Sunday or Monday, to the which themselves and the Spaniards of that district do resort. The Indians of the several towns are to have in a readiness so many labourers as the Court of Guatemala hath appointed to be weekly taken out of such a town, who are conducted by an Indian officer to the town of general meeting; and when they come thither with their tools, their spades, shovels, bills, or axes, with their provision of victuals for a week (which are commonly some dry cakes of maize, puddings of *frijoles*, or French beans, and a little chilli or biting long pepper, or a bit of cold meat for the first day or two) and with beds on their backs (which is only a coarse woollen mantle to wrap about them when they lie on the bare ground) then are they shut up in the town-house, some with blows, some with spurnings, some with boxes on the ear, if presently they go not in.

Now all being gathered together, and the house filled with them, the *juez repartidor*, or officer, calls by the order of the list such and such a Spaniard, and also calls out of the house so many Indians as by the Court are commanded to be given him (some are allowed three, some four, some ten, some fifteen, some twenty, according to their employments) and delivereth unto the Spaniard his Indians, and so to all the rest, till they be all served; who when they receive their Indians, take from them a tool, or their mantles, to secure them that they run not away; and for every Indian delivered unto them, they give unto the *juez repartidor*, or officer, half a real, which is threepence an Indian for his fees, which mounteth yearly to him to a great deal of money; for some officers make a partition or distribution of four hundred, some of two hundred, some of three hundred Indians every week, and carrieth home with him so many half hundred reals for one, or half a day's work. If complaint be made by any Spaniard that such and such an Indian did run away from him, and served him not the week past, the Indian must be brought, and surely tied to a post by his hands in the market-place, and there be whipped upon his bare back. But if the poor Indian complain that the Spaniards cozened and cheated him of his shovel, axe, bill, mantle, or wages, no justice shall be executed against the cheating Spaniard, neither shall the Indian be righted, though it is true the order runs equally in favour of both Indian and Spaniard. Thus are the poor Indians sold for threepence apiece for a whole week's slavery, not permitted to go home at nights unto their wives, though their work lie not above a mile from the town where they live; nay some are carried ten or twelve miles from their home, who must not return till Saturday night late, and must that week do whatsoever their master pleaseth to command them. The wages appointed them will scarce find them meat and drink, for they are not allowed a real a day, which is but sixpence, and with that they are to find themselves, but for six days' work and diet they are to have five reals, which is half a crown. This same order is observed in the city of Guatemala, and towns of Spaniards, where to every family that wants the service of an Indian or Indians, though it be but to fetch water and wood on their backs, or to go on errands, is allowed the like service from the nearest Indian towns.

It would grieve a Christian's heart to see how by some cruel Spaniards in that week's service those poor wretches are wronged and abused; some visiting their wives at home, whilst their poor husbands are digging and delving; others whipping them for their slow working; others wounding them with their swords, or breaking their heads for some reasonable and well grounded answer in their own behalf; others stealing from them their tools; others cheating them of half, others of all their wages; alleging that their service cost them half a real, and yet their work not well performed. I knew some who made a common practice of this, when their wheat was sown, and they had little to do for the Indians; yet they would have home as many as were due unto their farm, and on Monday and Tuesday would make them cut and bring them on their backs as much wood as they needed all that week, and then on Wednesday at noon (knowing the great desire of the Indians to go home to their wives, for which they would give anything) would say unto them: 'What will you give me now, if I let you go home to do your own work?' Whereunto the Indians would joyfully reply and answer, some that they would give a real, others two reals, which they would take and send them home, and so would have much work done, wood to serve their house a week, and money as much as would buy them meat, and *cacao* for chocolate two weeks together; and thus from the poor Indians do those unconscionable Spaniards practice a cheap and lazy way of living. Others will sell them away for that week unto a neighbour that hath present need of work, demanding reals apiece for every Indian, which he that buyeth them will be sure to defray out of their wages. So likewise are they in a slavish bondage and readiness for all passengers and travellers, who in any town may demand unto the next town as many Indians do go with his mules, or to carry on their backs a heavy burden as he shall need, who at the journey's end will pick some quarrel with them, and so send them back with blows and stripes without any pay at all.

5. Eighteenth-Century Colonialism: "The Indians Have an Aversion to Anything Spanish" *

BY ARCHBISHOP PEDRO CORTES Y LARRAZ, 1769

COLONIAL Guatemala evolved into what appeared to be two societies: Catholic Spaniards and creoles living in towns and owning private plantations of cacao, indigo, sugar, and other export crops; Indians residing in rural villages and growing corn on their community-owned fields for subsistence. But although distinct spacially and culturally, those two societies formed a single one. The Spanish towns and plantations, or haciendas, depended on the Indian villages' tribute of foodstuffs and goods to supply the distant Crown and the local officials and priests. The villages also provided, as Thomas Gage describes in the previous reading, the repartimiento *labor which tilled the Spaniards' plantations, built their towns, cleaned their streets and homes, spun their cloth, and hauled their goods. The Spaniards and the Indians developed in relation to, and in the context of, one another.*

It was this relationship which so shocked Archbishop Cortés y Larraz in 1769. A Spaniard sympathetic to Spaniards, the Archbishop was sent to Guatemala by King Charles the Third of Spain, to investigate the condition of the population in the overseas diocese. The exigencies of repartimiento, *the violence priests and officials routinely used against Indians, and the Indian antipathy toward anything Spanish dismayed him. As the following excepts from the Archbishop's report to the King describe, although the Indians had rights to some land during this period, the* repartimiento *left them little time to work it. A system of forced labor,* repartimiento *appears to have rested on violence and not on the structural need of the Indians to work for the Spaniards. This resulted in a society of continuous bitter conflict between Spaniard and Indian. The Archbishop's portrayal suggests a territory occupied by foreigners, rather than settled by them, for 250 years.*

FOR TILLING THE HACIENDAS, the Indians are divided into groups. The hacienda owners demand these groups of Indians for planting and for weeding, whenever their labor is necessary for agricultural production, which is the same time the Indians need to be working on their own land; yet the Indians are taken to distant haciendas, so the result is that the Indian land is not cultivated and

---

* From Pedro Cortés y Larraz, *Descripción Geográfico—Moral de la Diócesis de Goathemala* (Guatemala: Biblioteca "Goathemala" de la Sociedad de Geografia e Historia de Guatemala, 1958). Excerpts translated by Deborah Levenson.

produces nothing. This partitioning of Indians for labor service is done with great violence, without respect for the Indian's own need to work his land, or for his own health, or life, so much so that in Chichicastenango several of these wretched souls, fearing they would perish, brought me money in exchange for their labor service, leaving it on the table so that I would give it to the hacienda owners because they could not go to work. They were sick and left me with the sorrow of not being able to console them. . . .

Three towns have been complaining of their Spanish administrator, who forces them to send food supplies to the port without paying them: for two years the Indians' corn, beans and hens have been taken away violently, so they have experienced two years of calamitous starvation because of which many have died and many have fled the villages. Many have also died spinning cotton which the Spanish administrator makes the Indian women do all year long so they cannot do anything for their families. . . .

The truth is, that at whoever's command, these wretched Indians are tied to the whipping post, men, women, young and old; they are whipped with excessive cruelty, sometimes without any reason at all, and almost always for things which they would not be whipped for if they were not Indians. . . . Of this cruelty I cannot produce greater evidence except to say that frequently enough I hear screams and cries from my room or inn even though the beatings are taking place at a great distance. . . .

The Indians have an aversion and absolute hate for anything Spanish as is generally the case in all of America. They do not like anything Spanish, neither religion, the doctrine or customs. . . . On holy days, the priests and civil servants spend hours pulling the Indians out of their huts and the woods. . . . They start to ring the bells for mass very early and with pauses the bells ring for two hours; the priests go out to look for the people; then the civil officials go out. Some hide, others flee. After some are rounded up and brought to mass, in some places the civil officials guard the church doors, in others they lock them, otherwise the Indians would leave. . . . If these wretched people did not attend mass because they were inactive or lazy, or because they were playing or enjoying themselves, it would be one thing; but it is another to not attend because of a positive repugnance which is so strong that they hide in the woods and hide their children. . . .

The priest in one particular parish reprimands their excesses with prudence, and helps them generously with what they need . . . but with all this they do not give up being Indians. One afternoon, I took a walk and I met an old Indian who spoke Castillian, and had a troop of children, his grandchildren; I stopped to speak with him and asked him to give me one of the children to raise and educate, indicating I would provide every comfort; he responded frankly, saying under no circumstances would he give me a child. Because he responded so forcefully, I pursued the conversation, asking him: "Why do you walk barefoot?" He responded, "Because I am an Indian." I told him Indians were Spaniards like us. He replied he was not a Spaniard, but an Indian. Pursuing the subject, I asked him if he did not want to be a Spaniard. He answered: "No," and since I pressed him repeatedly, he insisted forcefully that he did not want to be a Spaniard. In this incident, one can see clearly the ideas these wretched people have about Spaniards.

6. *Indian Rebellions: 1524-1944*

COMPILED BY THE EDITORS

THE idea that Indians were "grateful to serve" their Spanish conquerors, as a third-grade textbook distributed in the 1960s by the U.S. Agency for International Development (AID) states,[1] is an undocumented stereotype. Perhaps the propagation of the myth of the docile and passive Indian is an attempt to convince Indians that that is what they should be, because that is what they have always been. History refutes the notion of a fatalistic Indian population: the persistence of Indian uprisings since 1524 demonstrates the existence of a significant number of angry and active Indians in every generation.

1524: Quiché captain Tecún Umán and his soldiers were defeated in battle by the Spaniards outside Quezaltenango; later that year, the Cakchiquels began a rebellion against the Spaniards which lasted until 1529.
1530: Uprising among the Chortí.
1556: Uprisings in Verapaz province.
1633: A series of Chol rebellions in Verapaz.
1708: Rebellion in Chiapas, at that time a part of Guatemala.
1748: Mam revolt in Ixtahuacán.
1760: Uprising in Santa Lucía de Utatlán.
1764: Cakchiquel rebellion in Tecpán.
1770: Insurrections in Cobán and Rabinal.
1803: Uprising in Cobán.
1811: Indians invade lands claimed by the Church in Santa Cruz del Quiché.
1813: Revolts in San Martín Cuchumatanes, Momostenango, and Ixtahuacán.
1818: Quiché communities unite in rebellion against tribute payments.
1820: Anastasio Tzul and Lucas Aguilar led a major Quiché uprising in Totonicapán. Tzul proclaimed himself King, abolished tribute, and wrote a new constitution before Spanish troops recaptured the area. In the same year Indians also rose up in Chiquimula and Sacapulas.
1837: Indians in San Juan Ostuncalco rebel against forced labor.
1838: Uprisings in Jumay and Ixtahuacán.
1846: Uprisings in Verapaz, Sololá, Ixtahuacán, Chichicastenango and Cotzal.
1849: Rebellion in Momostenango.

---

1. Quoted in *Guatemala* (New York: NACLA, 1974), p. 30.

1864: Melchoir Yat led a Kekchí rebellion in Alta Verapaz against plantation labor system.
1876: Guerrilla warfare in Totonicapán against the Barrios government.
1885: Indian rebellion in Alta Verapaz.
1898: K'anjobal revolt in San Juan Ixcoy against wage labor and the loss of communal lands.
1905: Another Quiché revolt in Totonicapán.
1906: Rebellion near San Juan Chamelco in Alta Verapaz.
1944: A major Cakchiquel rebellion in Patzicía to protest the loss of lands.

7. *Land and Labor after Independence* *

BY ALAIN Y. DESSAINT

Last day of despotism, first day of the same. —Folk saying

FOLLOWING *independence from Spain in 1821, life for the majority did not substantially improve. Foreign investment in coffee production increased demands for land and labor. As in the colonial period, the state played the role of labor supplier, overseeing a system of forced labor, as scholar Alain Y. Dessaint describes in the following reading.*

New laws were passed aimed at expropriating Indian lands; in 1884 alone, over one hundred thousand acres of Indian land passed into private hands. Indians protested to President Lisandro Barillas the loss of their lands in the 1890s:

> You have ordered us to leave our lands so that coffee can be grown. You have done us an injustice. . . . You ask us to leave the land where our grandfathers and fathers were born. . . . Is it because we do not know how to grow coffee? You know very well we know how. . . . Are we not the ones who sow the coffee on the fincas,[1] wash it, harvest it? . . . But we do not want to grow coffee on our lands. We want them only for our corn, our animals, our wood. And we want these lands where our grandfathers and fathers worked. Why should we leave them? [2]

The similarity to sentiments expressed today is notable. Then and now, loss of land threatens an entire way of village life, and the defense of land is a defense of

* From Alain Y. Dessaint, "Effects of the hacienda and plantation systems on Guatemala's Indians,' *América Indígena* (Mexico City, 22 Oct. 1962), pp. 300–349.

1. Large farms or plantations—EDS.

2. Vera Kelsey, Lilly Obsborne, *Four Keys to Guatemala* (New York: Funk & Wagnalls Co., 1939), pp. 58–59.

that life. Villagers from Baja Verapaz protested their planned relocation to make way for a hydroelectric plant in 1979: "In none of those new places can we live, without palms to make our mats, or firewood, or pasture for our animals. Our wish is to stay living where our Mayan ancestors left us and where, through many years of work, we have built our culture, our villages, our crops, and our lives." [3]

GUATEMALA'S ECONOMY SAW a turnover as rapid as any other ever recorded: whereas in 1860 coffee exports were almost nil, by 1873 over 150,000 quintals [1 quintal = 100 pounds] were exported. Coffee could be grown over a large part of Guatemala, and its price was relatively stable, so that it quickly attracted growers. It began to be produced on a large scale, affecting a large proportion of Guatemala's inhabitants, and dominating its economic life to this day. "Without coffee the whole picture of Guatemala's economy would be different. The amenities that wealth and commerce provide could not exist without it, yet coffee in Guatemala, like cotton in the United States, is beset by a plague of economic ills."

Justo Rufino Barrios and his "Liberal" regime helped the trend in every way. In 1877 Barrios abolished communal ownership of land. "The Liberals at times ruthlessly drove them [Indians] from their holdings, thus making them more dependent on such employment as planters and others might offer." Barrios further divided Indian laborers into three classes: *colonos* who contracted to live and work on haciendas; *jornaleros habilitados* who, in return for money advances, promised to work out such debts; and *jornaleros no habilitados* who promised to work for a time without receiving advances. The *jefe político* of each department handled requests for *mandamientos* [mandatory labor], each Indian serving anywhere from a week to a month each year. The actual engaging of laborers was done by the employer *(finquero, ranchero)* or his agent *(habilitadores, obligadores)* or the ladino agent's Indian agent *(caporales)*. Gradually the *mandamiento* system was superseded in importance by debt-bondage, which was formally recognized in 1894.

Thus, supplying labor to cultivators of commercial crops was still considered a major concern of the government. When Indians began claiming exemption from forced labor by filling small local offices *(ministrales)*, the government abolished the offices; thereby adding some 15,000 men to the labor supply. When too many Indians began to take work outside of Guatemala and then stay there, the government demanded a deposit for each Indian from the recruiting agents.

The powerful new *finqueros* of coffee preferred a strong man in office who could preserve peace, supply the Indian labor they needed and prevent destruction of their property during civil uprisings. Revolutions, when they did occur, never meant real changes permeating the entire social structure, but only a

---

3. *La Pura Verdad* (Quezaltenango, April, 1979).

change of the present office holders for another group of professional office holders.[4]

In 1934 the system of debt bondage was abolished, but a set of "Vagrancy Laws" took its place. These laws forced Indians to work 150 days a year if they cultivated less than one and five-sixteenths *manzanas* of land, 100 days a year if they cultivated more.

Under this kind of government support, foreign investors had early been attracted into Guatemalan coffee production. Germans, especially, found the business profitable, and as early as 1913 produced well over one-third of Guatemala's coffee. Germans, often residing in Berlin or Hamburg, continued to be important coffee producers in Guatemala until World War II, when a large part of their properties was expropriated by the government.

Coffee fincas continued to grow in size and importance. By 1880—barely two decades after its introduction as a cash crop—coffee accounted for over 90 percent of Guatemala's exports. Since that time, coffee has each year (except in 1940) accounted for at least half of the country's exports. As a result, Guatemala became victim to the demand, supply, and price of this one crop in the world market. "Forces were set in motion to bring about important changes in the indigenous economy of the Highlands—a process of change which has been continuous to our day. . . ."

During the October to January harvest of coffee (and before coffee, the harvest of cochineal, indigo, etc.) the fincas need many extra laborers. In her survey, (Elizabeth) Hoyt found that about four-sevenths of all laborers were temporary seasonal workers. This recruitment of harvest help is the means by which the fincas have extended their influence over virtually every Indian community in Guatemala. The *jornaleros* or *temporadistas,* as these seasonal workers are called, are recruited by finca agents who usually live in their town and therefore know who is likely to need extra money each year. The *jornaleros* may go to the fincas either individually or in groups *(cuadrilleros),* in either case being advanced a certain sum to cover the expenses of the trip. . . .

[Anthropologist Ruth] Bunzel reports many illegal tricks used by the local authorities in Chichicastenango to assure the town of prosperity.

> It used to be customary during times of labor shortage, to imprison large numbers of Indians for small offences, especially for drunkenness, and to impose heavy fines. *Obligadores* from some plantation would pay the fine, with a bonus for the Alcalde [town mayor], and the Indian was turned over to the plantation to work off the debt.[5]

4. Leo A. Suslow, *Aspects of Social Reform in Guatemala, 1944-1949* (Hamilton, N. Y.: Colgate University Area Studies, 1949), p. 9.

5. Ruth Bunzel, *Chichicastenango, A Guatemalan Village.* (Locust Valley, N.Y.: Publications of the American Ethnological Society XXII, 1952), p. 173.

The *obligadores* were liberally supplied with cash by their *finqueros*, and hired Indian *capitanes* to make contracts: lending money and buying drinks with the stipulation that it would be repaid by work on the fincas; the *obligadores* and *capitanes* would then keep their eyes on all the Indians they had under contract, and collect a bonus for each when delivered to the finca. "When partway drunk, an Indian will sell his soul for more liquor: upon this the finca system is based." Between October and January

> . . . every few days the bell in Chichicastenango is tolled to commemorate the passing of some citizen who has died "in the finca." The bodies are not brought back. . . . So effectual are the familiar devices of colonial exploitation, alcoholism, easy credit, debt indenture, and liability for debts to the third generation, that once caught in the system, escape is difficult.[6]

. . . The loss of communal lands, which we have seen was at least partly a means to insure a labor supply for fincas, has led to the monopoly of land by a few. Formerly there had been no necessity to work for others since anyone could obtain communal land from the Alcalde according to his needs, today there is a great disparity in land wealth. Some coffee growers have extensive landholdings in the Highlands for the sole purpose of obtaining labor from the Indian tenants. The ladino wishes only to own land, while the Indian wishes to work it and identify himself with it.

> The love of the land, of each man for his own piece of ground, is one of the deepest emotions which he feels; it is at the root of family life and social structure; it is the basis alike of strongest attachments and bitterest enmities.[7]

The accumulation of land, the overcrowding of the Highlands, and soil erosion continue, and the alienated must turn to the fincas.

[For reasons of space we have eliminated most of the footnotes to Alain Y. Dessaint's extensively researched article in this short excerpt. Some of the sources he drew upon are Ruth Bunzel and Leo Suslow, cited above; Elizabeth E. Hoyt, "The Indian Laborer on Guatemala Coffee Fincas" (*Inter-American Economic Affairs*, volume 9 no. 1, 33–46, 1955); Chester Jones, *Guatemala, Past and Present* (Minneapolis, Minn.: University of Minnesota Press, 1940)—EDS.]

---

6. Bunzel, pp. 10–11.
7. Bunzel, p. 9.

8. *Debt Labor in the 1940s* *

BY MAUD OAKES

WHILE in the colonial period Indians were forced by law to work on other people's plantations, in the twentieth century they have been forced by poverty and, until 1945, by law as well. Until the late 1940s, people often did not work directly for wages. Instead villagers borrowed money in times of need or crisis from a local labor contractor. They signed contracts requiring them to pay off small debts working for months on distant plantations where they lived in miserable housing and ate the poorest quality corn.

The following reading is from Maud Oakes's well-known study The Two Crosses of Todos Santos, *a book full of details about life and times in the 1940s in a mountain village. In order to study religious customs and Mayan tradition, Oakes spent two years in the Mam village of Todos Santos Cuchumatán. In her appendix she records what her Mam-speaking neighbors told her about how indebtedness compelled them to work and how local state officials enforced this system of debt labor.*

PATRONA, THE WIFE of my neighbor Domingo, came to see me. Her eyes were swollen from crying. In very incoherent Spanish she told me that Domingo had signed a contract for himself and his son, Andrés, with Señor López, who owned the *tienda* [1] in the village, to work on a coffee *finca* [2] beyond Quezaltenango. She went on to say that she expected her baby in a month and a half, and how could she look after three children, get wood, and plant corn if neither Domingo nor Andrés was there to help her?

Domingo then entered the house and told me the whole story. The year before, he and Andrés were both sick for two months, so sick that they nearly died. In consequence he was not able to plant his corn. When he was better he could not work for he still had no strength. He had only a little corn. He therefore signed a contract with Señor López for money. He was to receive sixteen dollars and for this he and Andrés, aged fourteen, would both have to work sixty-four days picking coffee on the *finca.* They would have to walk there and back, which would take four to five days each way. At the *finca* they would be given huts, too poor to keep out the mosquitoes, and unground corn; nothing else. If they got sick they would get no medical care; and all this for less than one dollar a week apiece.

"If you will pay my debt to Señor López," Domingo continued, "I will work

---

* From Maud Oakes, *The Two Crosses of Todos Santos* (Princeton: Princeton University Press, 1969), pp. 241–242, by permission.

1. store—EDS.

2. plantation—EDS.

faithfully for you; have no fear of it. I will carry cargo for you from Huehuetenango; I will be your *mozo* [3] on your trips." This is how Domingo became my *mozo*, my man Friday. When I went to Señor López to pay Domingo's debt, he said that he thought I was very foolish, Domingo was no good and would never pay off the debt to me. Needless to say, Señor López proved to be wrong.

But to give another experience. One week or so after Domingo became my *mozo*, a young woman with a baby a year and a half old came to see me because she was a friend of my maidservant Simona and had heard from her that I was a kind person. She was sick with malaria. Her baby was very ill with a temperature of 104°. She had just returned from working two months on a *finca*. In fact she had run away from it before her time was up because the baby was ill and because she did not feel well herself. I examined the baby and gave it some medicine, and then gave the mother some food. Before she could finish eating the police came and with them the agent with whom she had signed the contract, to lock her up in the *juzgado*.[4] The agent demanded her arrest and insisted that she be shipped back in a few days to the *finca* to finish her contract. It made not the slightest difference to him that both mother and child were very ill or that it would be freezing cold in the jail.

I went later to see the Alcalde, but he was out so I saw the *secretario* [5] instead. He told me that the woman owed five dollars and fifty cents which she had not yet worked out at the *finca* and one dollar and twenty-five cents for the bus from Quezaltenango to Huehuetenango. He would give her eight days to pay the agent, otherwise he would ship her back. I told the *secretario* that I would be responsible for her debt. She was then let out of the jail. I found out then that she owned no blanket, that all she possessed were the clothes on her back.

9. *Colonial Heritage: The Indian Community in the 1950s* *

BY ERIC WOLF

MOST of the numerous studies of Guatemalan Indians have been written by North American and European anthropologists. Arcadio Ruiz Franco, ex-director of Guatemala's National Indigenist Institute, writes, "What a painful contradiction of our nationalism that it has been foreigners who have come to

3. servant—EDS.
4. local jail—EDS.
5. local official—EDS.
* From Eric Wolf, *Sons of the Shaking Earth* (Chicago: University of Chicago Press, 1959), p. 211-232, by permission of the University of Chicago Press, and the author.

teach us the value of indigenous culture." [1] *It is also a mark of national shame toward Indian culture that Guatemalan funding for anthropological research has not been readily available.*

This anti-Indian atmosphere has made studies of Indian life problematic in yet another sense. Indian activist Rigoberta Menchú thinks her culture has survived because it has been hidden from non-Indians. She says, "Our grandparents guard secrets and pass them on to their grandchildren who have the responsibility to pass them on, so there exists an expression completely enclosed in the Indian. We have guarded secrets, we have kept our identity because we have kept it secret." [2]

Despite this enclosed quality, one can put together some pieces and get a sense of Indian life. Traditionally defined by their use of one of twenty-two languages and one of two hundred and eighty costumes, Guatemalan Indians are also distinguished by a culture which is dynamic and original, combining pre-Colombian, Hispanic, peasant, and local elements. Although this culture has not always in itself challenged the structural relations between Indians and non-Indians, it has countered a sense of social inferiority by stressing the centrality and worth of Indians. In a society which negatively defines them, their own culture positively defines them.[3]

The following reading is from U.S. anthropologist Eric Wolf's classic study of Mexico and Guatemala, Sons of the Shaking Earth, *written in the 1950s. It makes thoughtful suggestions about the economic and social life Indians have constructed within the limits of their historical circumstances. Since the 1950s the situation in many Indian communities has changed. Although the religious and social institutions Wolf discusses are intact, some villagers can no longer afford to, or choose not to, participate in them. Others have joined Catholic organizations and Protestant sects.*

THE SPANISH COLONIST ultimately had access to an apparatus of power managed by others like himself. But the Conquest had deprived the Indian of access to state power. Knowingly, the conquerors had destroyed the connection between the Indian present and the pre-Hispanic past. In dismantling the Mexica state,[4] they had removed also the cortex of the Middle American political organism and severed the nerves which bound communities and regions to the larger economic and political centers. The Indian state was not rebuilt. Royal decree carefully circumscribed the position of the Indian commoners. They were enjoined from wearing Spanish dress and forced to don "Indian" costume, a combination of Spanish and Indian articles of clothing. Indian commoners could not own or use horses and saddles and were prohibited from bearing arms. They had

1. Arcadio Ruiz Franco "La contradicción y La problemática indígena," *America Indigena,* XXXII (April-June, 1972).
2. Interview with the editors, June 1982.
3. Kay B. Warren, *The Symbolism of Subordination, Indian Identity in a Guatemalan Town* (Austin: University of Texas Press, 1978).
4. Also known as the Aztec state.—EDS.

to pay tribute, but, because they paid tribute, they were endowed with economic personality and therefore with judicial personality. They could present their cases in special "Indian" courts and were defined as "free vassals" of the king. They were exempt from military service and from such taxes as the tithe and the sales tax, imposed on Spaniards and others. But legal rights were not accompanied by common political representation. Where Indian officials had once exercised power on the national and regional level, Spanish officials now held sway. The Indian political apparatus had been smashed by the Conquest; and the conquerors were not ill-advised enough to countenance its reconstruction.

With the assumption of power by the Spaniards, the Indian ruling class lost its functions. Some of the chiefs moved to town, adopted Spanish dress and manners, learned to speak Spanish, and became commercial entrepreneurs employing European technology and working land with Indian tributaries and Negro slaves.[5] Spanish law abetted this process by equating them socially with the nobility of Spain and economically with the Spanish *encomenderos.* Since the new law took inadequate account of the pre-Hispanic division between nobility of office and nobility of lineage, granting to all nobles the privileges of hereditary descent, many Indian nobles even added to the pre-Hispanic perquisites of their rank and gained title to lands which had previously belonged either to a community or to a non-hereditary office. Also, the Indian noble who was treated like a Spanish *encomendero* received rights to tribute and personal services and, like other *encomenderos,* began to invest in the process of building capital through capitalist enterprise. Frequently, intermarriage with the conquerors still further dissipated their Indian identity, until they lost touch with the Indian commoners who in the midst of death and upheaval were building a new Indian life in the countryside.

Nobles who remained in the villages, on the other hand, were reduced by loss of wealth and standing to the position of their Indian fellow citizens. Because his person was still suffused with the magic of past power, a former priest or local chieftain here and there assumed a post in a local community, but he soon lost the ability to command tribute or labor-power to which his ancestors had been accustomed. The new Indian communities were communities of the poor, too overburdened to sustain a class that had lost its function.

With the disappearance of the Indian political elite, there also vanished the specialists who had depended on elite demands: the priest, the chroniclers, the scribes, the artisans, the long-distance traders of pre-Hispanic society. Spanish entrepreneurs replaced the *pochteca;*[6] Spanish artisans took the place of Indian feather-workers and jade-carvers; Spanish priests displaced the Indian religious specialists. Soon there was no longer anyone who knew how to make feather cloaks and decorations, how to find and carve jade, how to recall the deeds of

5. Today Guatemala has a small black population, descendants of the slaves brought to Guatemala as well as of runaway slaves from other parts of the Caribbean who set up their own communities on Guatemala's tiny Caribbean Coast.—EDS.

6. Mexican Indian merchants—EDS.

gods and ancestors in days gone by. For a brief period the Indians strove valiantly to learn the new arts of the Mediterranean, and men like Bernardino de Sahagún (1499-1590) and the scholars of the short-lived college of Santiago de Tlatelolco (1536-1606) labored to maintain and enrich the intellectual patterns of Indian culture. But the return to ruralism of the seventeenth century put an end to these hopes and endeavors.

Under the new dispensation, the Indian was to be a peasant, the Indian community a community of peasants. Stripped of their elite and urban components, the Indians were relegated to the countryside. Thus the Indians suffered not only exploitation and biological collapse but also deculturation—cultural loss—and in the course of such ill use lost also the feeling of belonging to a social order which made such poor use of its human resources. They became strangers in it, divided from its purposes and agents by an abyss of distrust. The new society could command their labor, but it could not command their loyalty. Nor has this gulf healed in the course of time. The trauma of the Conquest remains an open wound upon the body of Middle American [7] society to this day.

The strategic unit of the new Indian life was to be not the individual but the Indian community. This the crown protected and furthered, as a double check upon the colonists—ever eager to subjugate the Indians to their exclusive control—as well as upon the Indians themselves, whose individual freedom it wished to curb. To this end, it underwrote the legal separateness and identity of each Indian commune.

Each commune was to be a self-contained economic unit, holding a guaranteed 6.5 square miles of agricultural land, land which its members could sell only after special review by the viceroy. In every commune the duly constituted Indian authorities would collect the tribute and levy the labor services for which the members of the commune were to be jointly responsible (not until the eighteenth century was tribute payment individualized). A portion of this tribute would go into the royal coffers, but part of it would be set aside in a "community chest" *(caja de comunidad)* to finance community projects. Communal officials were to administer the law through the instrumentality of their traditional custom, wherever that custom did not conflict with the demands of church and state. The officers of the crown retained the privilege of judging major crimes and legal cases involving more than one community; but the Indian authorities received sufficient power to guarantee peace and order in the new communes. The autonomy which the crown denied to the Indian sector of society as a whole, it willingly granted to the local social unit.

This model for reconstruction did not envisage a return of the pre-Hispanic community. Yet so well did it meet the needs of the Indian peasant that he could take it up and make it his own. Poised precariously on the abyss of disintegration, the commune proved remarkably resilient. It has undergone great changes since

7. Middle America includes Mexico and Central America.—EDS.

the time when it was first constituted in a shattered countryside three centuries ago, but its essential features are still visible in the Indian communities today, especially in the southern and southeastern highlands. Thus it is still possible to speak of this community in the present tense, to regard the present-day Indian community as a direct descendant of the reconstructed community of the seventeenth century.

The core of this kind of community is its political and religious system. In this system, the burden of religious worship is rotated among the households of the community. Each year, a different group of men undertakes to carry out the tasks of religious office; each year a different group of men makes itself responsible for the purchase and ritual disposal of food, liquor, candles, incense, fireworks, and for all other attendant expenditures. A tour of religious duty may leave a man impoverished for several years, yet in the eyes of his fellow citizens he has added greatly to his prestige. This spurs men to renewed labor toward the day when they will be able to underwrite another set of ceremonies; and a man will sponsor several such ceremonials in the course of his life. Each tour of sponsorship will add to the esteem in which he is held by his fellow men, until—old and poor—he reaches the pinnacle of prestige and commands the respect of the entire community. The essential element in repeated sponsorship is therefore time: the older a man is, the greater the likelihood that he has repeatedly acted as religious sponsor. Thus old age itself becomes a source of prestige for Indians: an old man is one who has labored in the interests of the community for many years and whose repeated religious activity has brought him ever closer to the state of grace and secular wisdom.

Since all men have an equal opportunity to enlist in carrying the burdens of the gods, and thus to gain prestige, the religious system allows all households to be ranked along a scale of religious participation, prestige, and age. At one end of the scale, the Indians will place the young household which has but recently come into existence and whose head is just beginning to play his part in keeping the balance between community and universe. At the other end, he will place the households of the very old, whose moral ascendancy over the community is very great, owing to their years of faithful service and ritual expenditure.

Certainly this religious pattern has Spanish prototypes in the Iberian *cofradía* or religious sodality, a voluntary association of men for religious purposes. But it is also pre-Hispanic in origin. "There were some," says the Spanish friar Toribio de Benavente of the days before the Conquest, "who labored two or three years and acquired as much as possible for the purpose of honoring the demon with a feast. On such a feast they not only spent all that they possessed but even went into debt, so that they would have to do service a year and sometimes two years in order to get out of debt." In the reconstructed Indian community of the post-Conquest period, this religious pattern was charged with additional functions. It became the chief mechanism through which people gained prestige, as well as the balance wheel of communal economics. Each year, religious participation wipes out considerable sums of goods and money; each year part of the surplus of the community is consumed in offerings or exploded in fireworks to please the saints. The system takes from those who have, in order to make all men have-nots. By liquidating the surpluses, it makes all men rich in sacred experience but poor in earthly goods. Since it levels differences of wealth, it also inhibits the growth of class distinctions based on wealth. Like the thermostat activated by an increase in heat to shut off the furnace, expenditure in religious worship returns the distribution of wealth to a state of balance, wiping out any accumulation of wealth that might upset the existing equilibrium. In engineering parlance, it acts as a feedback, returning a system that is beginning to oscillate to its original course.[8]

The religious complex also has aesthetic functions. The *fiesta*, with its procession, burning incense, fireworks, crowds, color, is not merely a mechanism of prestige and of economic justice. It is also "a work of art," the creation of a magic moment in mythological time, in which men and women transcend the realities of everyday life in their entry and procession through the magical space of the vaulted, incense-filled church, let their souls soar on the temporary trajectory of a rocket, or wash away the pains of life in holy-day drunkenness. For the Indians, time is not linear, as it is for the citizens of the industrialized North Atlantic world, where each moment points toward a future of new effort, new experience, and new goals. The Indian scheme of life moves in an endless round, in which everyday labor issues into the magic moment of religious ritual, only to have the ritual dissolve again into the everyday labor that began the cycle. The Indian community has now forgotten its pre-Hispanic past; its past and its future have merged in a timeless rhythm of alternating mundane and holy days.

The social, economic, aesthetic, and ritual mechanisms of the religious complex do not stand alone. They are part and parcel of a larger system which makes political and religious behavior mutually interdependent. For participation in the religious system qualifies a man also for political office. In Indian eyes, a man who has won prestige for himself by bearing the burden of the community in its relations with the gods is expected and—more than expected—required to assume political office. Thus men who have laid down their burdens as religious sponsors will be asked next to serve as community officials. Qualified for office by past religious participation, they are the ones who transact the business of the community: allocating land settling boundary disputes, investigating thefts, confirming marriages, disarming disturbers of the peace, dealing with the emissaries of outside power. A man cannot seek political office for its own sake, nor can he bend political power to his individual end. Power is bestowed by the community, and reallocated at intervals to a new group of officeholders. It is the office that governs men, not its occupant. In this democracy of the poor, there is no way to monopo-

8. Some observers have also seen in this religious complex a mechanism for a ladino elite to extract surplus from the Indian community because most of what is consumed in the fiestas, such as fireworks, candles, and liquor, is bought from ladino entrepreneurs. See Paul Diener, "The Tears of St. Anthony: Ritual and Revolution in Eastern Guatemala," *Latin American Perspectives* (Riverside, Calif., Summer 1978. V. 5) pp. 92–111.—EDS.

lize power. It is divorced from persons and distributed, through election, among all in turn.

The Indian cannot control men; he only wishes to come to terms with them. This process of mutual adjustment has become a group concern. The group counts more than the individual; it limits individual autonomy and initiative. It is suspicious of conflict, tireless in the advocacy of "adjustment." People raised in cultures that thrive on the conflicts of individual with individual would find it difficult to fit into such a community; yet the community can be understood in terms of its context, a larger social order in which men continually fight for power and are ever willing to pay for its fruits the price of their own corruption. In this setting, the Indian community shows great consistency in refusing to play a game that will always seek its first victims among its members. For navigation in troubled water its politico-religious system is a steering mechanism of great resilience.

As the Indian community leveled differences of class, so it obliterated other internal divisions intervening between its jurisdiction and the households that composed. it. The diligent ethnologist may still find, among the Otomí-speakers on the fringes of the valley of Mexico, hamlets based on common descent in the male line and enforced marriage outside the community; or patrilineal kinship units sharing a common name, a common saint, and a measure of social solidarity among the Tzeltal-Tzotzil-speakers of Chiapas, though there too they have lost their former exogamy and the common residence which they possessed in the past. But these examples remain the fascinating exceptions to the general rule that, among Middle American Indians as a whole, common territoriality in one community and common participation in communal life have long since robbed such units of any separatist jurisdiction they may at one time have exercised. This holds also for the divisions called *barrios* or sections, which some have traced back to the pre-Hispanic *calpulli* and which in many cases go back to joint settlement in one community—voluntary or enforced—of groups of different origins, in both pre-Hispanic and post-Hispanic times. In most cases these units have simply been transformed into religious sodalities, each concerned with the support of its special saint and socially amorphous in any context other than the religious, although mutual name-calling, backbiting, or slander of one another's reputation may serve to drain off some of the minor irritations of daily life.

It is the household, then, that makes the basic decisions within both the politico-religious and the economic field, the household being usually composed of husband, wife, and children. Such unions are customarily formed through monogamous marriages; polygyny, the marriage of one male to more than one female, occurs but rarely. An unmarried man or woman is not regarded as an adult member of the community and cannot take up his responsibilities in communal life. A person who has lost a marriage partner through divorce or death must remarry before the community will again ratify the social standing he enjoyed before the breakup or end of his marriage. Nor is it marriage alone that bestows full rights of citizenship. A couple must have children to validate their claim to complete adult status; a sterile marriage quickly falls prey to conflict and divorce. Marriage therefore, and a marriage blessed with children, is the common goal of the Indian men and women.

Economically, a marriage is a union of two technological specialists: a male specialist skilled in field labor and house-building, a female specialist skilled in tending the kitchen garden, caring for the small livestock, making pots and clothing, raising children, preparing the daily meal. The functions of the division of labor and of reproduction take precedence in people's minds over marriage as an outlet for sexual impulses. Marriages are often arranged by the parents of the prospective couple, through the services of a go-between. The Indian man seeks a woman to bear his children and to keep up his home: there is little romantic love. Ideally, people conform to strict standards of marital fidelity. In practice, however, there is considerable latitude for sexual adventure outside marriage, and philandering does not usually endanger the bonds of the union. Nor do Indians engage in sexual conquest as a validation of their masculinity; sexual conquest does not add luster to the reputation of the individual. Exploitation of one sex by the other encounters little sympathy, just as political or economic exploitation of one man by another is not countenanced within the boundaries of the community.

Throughout their marriage, the partners retain a rough equality, though, ideally, wives are held subordinate to husbands. Women own the movable goods which they bring with them into the marriage. If a woman owns land, her husband may farm it for her, but the proceeds from the sale of produce raised on such a field is her own, as are the proceeds from the sales of her handicraft products. If she owns livestock, she retains her rights of ownership. In case of divorce, the family herd is divided equally between the divorcing partners. When one of the partners dies, his property is divided equally among the children; the surviving partner retains his share. Women do not occupy political or religious office, but they help their husbands in making the relevant decisions and in carrying out the attendant obligations. Within the home, the woman has a great deal to say, in strongly marked contrast to her non-Indian sister.

Just as the questions of participation in religio-political life are raised and settled within the household, so the day-to-day economic decisions are also made on the household level. It is the household that plants its fields to crops, that sells its maize or chili, that buys the needed kerosene or pottery. It is the men and women of these unit households who handle the money derived from these sales and act as individual economic agents. This apparent contradiction between the behavior of the Indian as a member of his community on the religio-political plane and his behavior as an economic agent has so impressed some observers that they have lost sight of the communal involvements of the Indian and treated him in terms of capitalist economic theory. Indeed, Sol Tax has spoken of the Indians as "penny capitalists," presumably in contrast to more affluent "nickel" or "dime" or "millionaire" capitalists, thus drawing attention at once to his comparative poverty and characterizing his participation in the wider economy as an individual agent, and a capitalist to boot. Certainly the Indian is poor, and no Middle

American Indian community ever existed on a desert island; it always formed part and parcel of a larger society. Its economic agents, the members of its households, are subject to a wider economy and to its laws. For instance, the value of the money they use and the prices of the commodities they buy and sell are often influenced, if not directly determined, by national conditions. The recent inflation, to name but one case, has affected Indians and non-Indians alike.

But the Indian is not merely quantitatively different in his economic involvements from other members of society. He differs qualitatively from the poor non-Indian Mexican or Guatemalan because he is culturally different from them. Superficially, he may resemble the individual economic agent of classical economics, unrestrictedly exchanging goods in a capitalist market. But he is not a capitalist, nor free of restrictions. His economic goal is not capital accumulation but subsistence and participation in the religio-political system of his community. He handles money; but he does not use money to build capital. It is for him merely one way of reckoning equivalences, of appraising the value of goods in exchange. The Indian works first so that he may eat. When he feels that he has accomplished this goal, he labors to build a surplus so that he can sponsor a ceremony and gain prestige in the eyes of his fellow Indians. In the course of his sponsorship, he redistributes or destroys his surplus by providing displays of fireworks or dressing the saint's image in a new cloak. Clearly, the quality of his involvement in the national economy differs from that of the commercial farmer, industrial worker, or entrepreneur.

Moreover, this pattern of consumption operates within cultural limitations laid down and maintained by his community. When we see the solitary Indian bent over his patch of maize, we seem to see a lone economic agent engaged in isolated production. But this man is enmeshed in a complicated web of traditional rights to land maintained by his community. Spanish rule granted each community sovereign jurisdiction over a well-defined amount of land. With the passage of time, general communal rights over land have become attenuated, usually in favor of a mixed system of ownership, where the richer bottom lands along the valley floors are now owned by individual members of the community, while the community retains communal rights over hilly land and forests. Yet the community still retains jurisdictional rights over land everywhere, rights which remove land from the category of free commodities. The most important of these rights states that members of the community may not sell land to outsiders. This is usually reinforced by a stringent rule of endogamy, which prohibits members of the community from marrying outsiders and thus endangering the man-land balance. Frequently this taboo is strengthened by other sanctions: the right allowing existing members of the community to glean or the right to graze their livestock on any land within the community after the harvest. Such rights frequently imply sanctions in their turn. A man cannot put a fence around his piece of land or grow crops that mature at variance with the crops of his neighbors. Both land and crops are thus subject to negative limitations, even though the actual process of production is intrusted to the several separate households.

Such limitations also apply to the craft products made in a given community.

We may see a woman shaping a pot or a man weaving a hat, and taking pot or hat to market. Again, we apparently see an individual agent engaged in autonomous economic activity. We must however realize that the producer is not "free" to choose the object he wishes to produce and market. What looks like individual craft specialization is but an aspect of a pattern of specialization by communities. There is a general tendency for each community to engage in one or several crafts that are not shared by other communities in its vicinity. Thus, in the Tarascan-speaking area,[9] for instance, Cocucho makes pottery, Tanaco weaves with century-plant fibers, Paracho manufactures wooden objects and cotton cloth, Nahuatzen weaves woolens, Uruapan paints gourds, and Santa Clara del Cobre produces items of beaten copper.

The Indian market is a place where the members of the different communities meet to exchange their products. Such a market brings together a very large and varied supply of articles, larger and more varied than could be sold by any permanent storekeeper in the market town, and does so at prices low enough to match the low income of the Indians. Thus, while the individual producer enters a market that is highly heterogeneous in the variety of goods offered, his particular individual contribution is homogeneous with that of other members of his community. In the characteristic Indian marketing pattern, where the sellers of similar types of objects are arranged together in carefully drawn-up rows, what looks to the casual observer like a mere grouping of individuals is actually a grouping of communities.

We must conclude, therefore, that the Indian's economic involvements are different from those of other participants in the national economy. The individual Indian household is indeed *in* the economy, but not *of* it. For added to the household's general purposes of self-maintenance are the community's purposes aiming at maintaining the Indian social group intact in its possession of land and membership, despite the corrosive influences that continually surround it. A peasantry needs land, and the Indian community defends its land against outsiders through the twin weapons of endogamy and the prohibition of sale to nonmembers. A peasantry faces the risks of class differentiation. As soon as one man accumulates wealth and is allowed to keep and reinvest it, he threatens, in the straitened circumstances of Indian life, to take from others the instruments of their own livelihood. More seriously, wealth breeds power, and power—unless adequately checked—corrupts, stacking the political cards in favor of some men to the detriment of others. Thus the Indian community strives to abolish wealth and to redistribute power. It even frowns on any display of wealth, any individual assertion of independence that may upset the balance of egalitarian poverty. Its social ideal is the social conformist, not the innovator, the controlled individual, not the seeker after untrammeled power. It places its faith in an equality of risk-taking.

It is doubtful whether the Indian community could have achieved these ends

9. Tarascans lived in western central Mexico, around the present-day state of Michoacán.—EDS.

by itself alone. Certainly, without the world beyond its confines, it could not have solved its population problem. Each new generation born to it threatens to upset again and again the balance between mouths to feed and land available to feed them. It can solve this problem only by continually exporting population. To stay in the running, it must continually sacrifice some of its sons and daughters to the outside world, thus ever feeding the forces which it attempts to resist. Increasing its own security by exporting people, it at the same time endangers the security of the larger society. Neither Indian peasant nor colonist entrepreneur, the emigrants fall into no ordered category, occupy no defined place in the social order. They become the Ishmaels of Middle America, its marginal men. Cast out into the shadows, with no stake in the existing order, they are forced to seek their own vindication, their place in the sun. If this is impossible within the social framework, then it must needs be against it. Thus the Indian community perpetually creates a body of potential antagonists, ready to invade it and benefit by its destruction.

Without the outside world, moreover, the Indian can never close the ever opening gap between his production and his needs. Robbed of land and water by the Conquest and subsequent encroachment, the Indian community can rarely be self-sufficient. It must not only export people; it must also export craft produce and labor. Each Indian who goes off to work seasonally in other men's fields strengthens his community; each hat, fire fan, or reed mat sold beyond the limits of the community adds to its capacity to resist encroachment. Each Indian who, in the past, enlisted on a hacienda as a *peón baldillo* thus benefited his community. Paradoxically, he also benefited the hacienda that used his labor. Assured of seasonal laborers who would do its bidding at the critical periods in the process of production, the haciendas welcomed the presence of Indian communities on their fringes. For such a community constituted a convenient reservoir of laborers where men maintained their labor power until needed, at no additional cost to the entrepreneur. Suddenly we find, therefore, that the institution of the conquerors and the institution of the conquered were linked phenomena. Each was a self-limiting system, powered by antagonism to the other; and yet their coexistence produced a perpetual if hostile symbiosis, in which one was wedded to the other in a series of interlocking functions.

If colonists and Indians achieved symbiosis, they did not achieve synthesis. While the great landowners secured virtual political and economic autonomy behind the walls of their great estates, they remained ideologically tied to Spain and, through Spain, to Europe. If the Conquest deculturated the conquered, it also affected the conquerors. First it narrowed the range of patterns carried by the newcomers, only to render them doubly provincial in the enforced readaptation to the ruralism of the seventeenth century. If the Conquest ended, once and for all, the isolation of America from the cultural development of the Old World, the ensuing decline of Spain left the new colonies on the margins of the new and larger world into which they had so suddenly been introduced. Here they suffered the fate of any marginal area isolated from its center of cultural productivity.

At the same time, the Conquest cut the lines of communication with the pre-Hispanic past: the conquerors could not take over the culture of the conquered. But neither could they develop a cultural configuration of their own. Communication with Europe remained formalistic and empty. The intellectual and artistic currency of the Old World was sought more for the sake of provincial display than for the sake of a new vital synthesis. Thus, for example, what is astonishing about the colonial architecture of New Spain is not the degree of indigenous influence in its construction but the virtual absence of it. Churches and palaces were built along European lines, even though greater wealth might render them more ornate or though an occasional decorative symbol might betray the hand of an Indian craftsman as yet untutored in the canons of Occidental art. Similarly, New Spain borrowed from Europe the models of sophisticated thought, first the intellectual formulas of the Counter-Reformation, later those of an Enlightenment tempered with Thomism, still later—in rapid succession—the phraseology of Jacobinism, English Liberalism, Comtean Positivism, only to see the European catchwords produce a sterile harvest in the Middle American soil. Thus the society of the post Conquest period suffered not only from the deepening cleavage between Indian and non-Indian. It also clogged the wellsprings of autonomous cultural creativity. Product of the meeting of two cultural traditions, it should have been the richer for their encounter. But design and circumstance both reduced the capacity of each component to quicken and stimulate the other into new cultural growth, and to be quickened in turn by stimuli from outside. Instead of organic synthesis, the meeting of Indian and Spaniard resulted in a social unity that remained culturally mechanical.

Chapter II:

Reform and U.S. Intervention, 1944–1954

Editors' Introduction

Guatemala has regressed more than a century. . . . Between the Guatemala of 1944 to 1954, with Presidents Juan José Arévalo and Jacobo Arbenz, and the Guatemala from the time it was "liberated" by mercenaries up to this day, there is no possible means of comparison. [*Today's*] *conditions are not even colonial. . . . We are a fiefdom of monopolies and pro-slavery oligarchies.*

—Luis Cardoza y Aragón, 1961 [1]

DESPITE attempts by the Reagan administration to apply traditional Cold War doctrines to the conflicts in Central America, growing segments of North American opinion are now rejecting the notion that an "international communist conspiracy" lies behind every manifestation of popular discontent. Today Nicaragua, Grenada, and Cuba are at the core of Washington's anticommunist scenario evoking the alleged Soviet threat to the security of the hemisphere. In 1954 it was Guatemala. A more detailed look at the 1944–54 period of reforms and the 1954 U.S. intervention that put an end to them is essential for understanding both the contemporary history of Guatemala and U.S.–Latin America relations in general.

The changes undertaken in Guatemalan society in the 1944–54 period, and described in Reading 10, represented a break with Guatemala's past (see Part

1. Luis Cardoza y Aragón, "Guatemala," *Cuadernos Americanos* [Mexico City], año XX, vol. 119 (Nov.-Dec. 1961). For more information about Cardoza y Aragón, one of Guatemala's foremost intellectuals, see Part Two, Chapter I, Editors' Introduction.

One, Chapter I). The democratic reforms of the Arévalo presidency (1945–51) were followed by far-reaching economic reforms under Arbenz (1951–54), including an agrarian reform. In Arbenz's own words in 1951, his aims were

> . . . first, to convert [Guatemala] from a dependent nation with a semi-feudal economy to an economically independent country; second, to transform our nation from a backward nation . . . to a modern capitalist country; and third, to accomplish this transformation in a manner that brings the greatest possible elevation of the living standard of the great masses of people.[2]

Far from spearheading a communist revolution aimed at bringing Guatemala into the Soviet bloc, the democratically elected governments of the period were attempting to involve Guatemala even further in the modern capitalist world of the twentieth century; not merely as a producer of raw materials and foodstuffs for the developed industrial nations, but as an independent capitalist nation, with modern industry and a population economically able to consume the products that industry produces. A "revolution" led by the ladino urban middle class, it nevertheless gave those at the bottom of the social pyramid, the workers and campesinos, a voice in the affairs of the nation and their lives. As essayist Cardoza y Aragón observed, the period was revolutionary only in contrast with the past. The revolutionary element was

> simply, its democratic spirit . . . the fact that in the face of the arbitrariness of many decades and the inertia imposed by panic, the country moved forward and the constitution was fulfilled to an ostensibly greater degree. What was revolutionary was the presence of liberty, the exercise of sovereignty and the struggle for economic emancipation.[3]

The relative importance of ideological, geopolitical, and economic determinants in the U.S. decision to intervene in 1954 has been and will continue to be debated by contemporary political observers and historians.[4] One historical fact is, by now, crystal clear: the U.S. government, using covert methods and Guatemalan mercenaries, did intervene, ending what Cardoza y Aragón dubbed "ten

---

2. Quoted in Jaime Díaz Rozzotto, *El Carácter de la Revolución Guatemalteca* (Mexico City: Ediciones Revista "Horizonte" Costa Amic, 1958), and cited in *Guatemala* (New York: NACLA, 1974, 1981), p. 48.

3. Luis Cardoza y Aragón, *La Revolución Guatemalteca* (Montevideo: Ediciones Pueblos Unidos, 1956), p. 74.

4. One of these analysts, and one of the most prolific writers on U.S. anticommunist doctrine, was Juan José Arévalo himself. Although he was an overt opponent of communism, he wrote a series of bitter denunciations of U.S. anticommunist policies, including *The Fable of the Shark and the Sardines: The Strangling of Latin America* (Buenos Aires, 1956) and *Anti-Kommunism in Latin America* (Buenos Aires, 1959), both of which have been translated into English (New York: Lyle Stuart, 1961 and 1963, respectively).

years of springtime in the land of eternal dictatorship." [5] As ex-Minister of Foreign Relations Guillermo Toriello has pointed out (see Introduction), and the subsequent chapters of this book will demonstrate, the consequences of U.S. intervention for the Guatemalan people have been nothing short of tragic.

The overthrow of Guatemala's decade of reform, in addition, cast a long shadow into the future of all Latin America, and U.S.–Latin America relations. The 1954 coup marked an end to Franklin Delano Roosevelt's "Good Neighbor Policy" (see Part Five, Editors' Introduction). Subsequently the United States embarked on a series of direct interventions in the name of hemispheric defense against communism. Just as Nicaragua and Honduras were used as springboards for U.S. intervention against Guatemala, in 1961 Guatemalan territory was used by the U.S. to train mercenaries for the abortive Bay of Pigs invasion of Cuba. In 1963, convinced he was "soft on communism," the United States supported a coup against liberal President Juan Bosch in the Dominican Republic; and in 1965, the U.S. invaded the Dominican Republic with more than twenty-three thousand marines when a revolt by a constitutionalist wing of the army and a spontaneous popular rebellion led to the fall of the military government. The Popular Unity government of Salvador Allende in Chile was the target of a CIA-planned and -financed campaign that led to the bloody coup of 1973 that installed the Pinochet regime. Today, Nicaragua's young revolution appears to be the object of new covert CIA action, once again using Honduras as the main staging ground,[6] and Soviet and Cuban interference are invoked to justify massive U.S. aid to El Salvador's government in its war with popularly backed insurgents.

A similar war now also rages in Guatemala, and the Reagan administration prepares to renew substantial aid to the current military government. Guatemalans and Latin Americans have drawn many lessons from their experiences of U.S. aggression since 1954; as did some U.S. citizens from the U.S. experience in Vietnam. The Vietnam War, the Bay of Pigs invasion and current events in Central America all point to the same conclusion: successful U.S. intervention against governments and revolutions with strong popular backing may be more difficult to accomplish than it once was.

---

5. Guatemala is often called the "Land of Eternal Spring" for the cool climate of its mountain areas.

6. See "U.S. Approves Covert Plan in Nicaragua," *Washington Post*, Mar. 10, 1982; and "U.S. Said to Plan Covert Actions in Latin Region," *New York Times*, Mar. 14, 1982.

10. A Case History of U.S. Subversion: Guatemala, 1954 *

BY MAX GORDON

THERE is an irony implicit in the title of this essay, its original title. The term "subversion" is widely used by the right in present-day Guatemala to describe what the left is supposedly doing. Max Gordon, a long-time political analyst, uses the term "subversion" in its neutral dictionary definition: "tending to or seeking to overthrow an established government." As such, this term applies exactly to the U.S. government's successful overthrow of the legally established, popularly elected Guatemalan government in 1954. Since the publication of Gordon's article over a decade ago, a small library of books and monographs on the CIA–United Fruit Company coup have appeared, the most recent ones making use of fresh documentary sources opened up by the amended Freedom of Information Act of 1974.[1] *While these new studies yield much new detail on Washington's role in the overthrow of Arbenz, they do not substantially alter the main outlines of the story as Gordon unraveled it in 1971. He has, however, added to this article a postscript written especially for this volume.*

IN THE IMMEDIATE aftermath of the September 1970, Chilean elections which gave a plurality to Salvador Allende, the result was widely referred to as the hemisphere's first case of a Marxist winning a popular presidential election.[2] The communications media compared or contrasted the event with recent radical or revolutionary developments in other Latin American countries, but there was a curious absence of reference to one such development which in some ways is most

* From *Science & Society: An Independent Journal of Marxism* [New York], XXXV (Summer, 1971), by permission.

1. Among these new studies are Thomas McCann, *An American Company: The Tragedy of United Fruit* (New York: Crown, 1976); Blanche Cook, *The Declassified Eisenhower: A Divided Legacy of Peace and Political Warfare* (Garden City, N.Y.: Doubleday & Co., 1981), Chaps. VI, VII; Stephen E. Ambrose, *Ike's Spies: Eisenhower and the Espionage Establishment* (Garden City, N.Y.: Doubleday & Co., 1981), esp. pp. 224–34; Stephen Schlesinger and Stephen Kinzer, *Bitter Fruit: The Untold Story of the American Coup in Guatemala* (Garden City, N.Y.: Doubleday & Co., 1982); Richard H. Immerman, *The CIA in Guatemala: The Foreign Policy of Intervention* (Austin: University of Texas Press, 1982).

2. Writing in the early 1970s, Gordon could not of course describe a parallel even more compelling between Guatemala and Chile: the destabilization of the Allende regime by the U.S. government in alliance with right-wing groups in Chile, and the ouster and assassination of Allende in 1973. For an analysis of the events in Chile, see James Petras and Morris Morley, *The United States and Chile: Imperialism and the Overthrow of the Allende Government* (New York: Monthly Review Press, 1975).—EDS.

relevant to the Chilean phenomenon. The Arbenz government of Guatemala was popularly elected in 1950, with the support of a small, fledgling communist party, and was overthrown in 1954 in a counter-revolution, planned and executed from Washington amid allegations that it was a Marxist regime dominated by communists.

For a few weeks in mid-1954, world attention was focused on this event, but memory of it has long since dimmed. As a result Washington's role has not been clearly defined in the light of later evidence, at least in this country, and the long-range political, economic, and social consequences have escaped assessment. Yet the conspiratorial and covert nature of Washington's subverting intervention, and the dynamics of interrelated political and economic developments within Guatemala during the regimes of Arbenz and his democratic predecessor Arévalo, cannot properly be overlooked in any effort to evaluate or predict the course of events in Chile or other Latin American nations experiencing varying political upheavals such as Peru and Bolivia.

There are, of course, large differences of time, scale, national structure, and political configuration between Arbenz's Guatemala and lands currently experiencing revolution in Latin America. But despite these differences Fidel Castro, who prepared for his Cuban struggle in a Mexico City teeming with refugees from the Arbenz regime, was doubtless profoundly influenced by the Guatemalan experience in shaping his attitude toward the United States and in evolving his concept of an effective national revolutionary structure in a country within Washington's proclaimed domain. It is, then, worth resurrecting the details of that experience.

I. The U.S. Role

In May 1954, Secretary of State John Foster Dulles complained at a cabinet meeting that while world opinion could be marshaled against external aggression, "it is quite another matter to fight against internal changes in one country." The United States had to act alone in "taking a position against a communist faction within a foreign country." Most countries, Dulles said, "do not share our view that communist control of any government anywhere is in itself a danger and a threat."[3]

The nation's power was at the moment directed particularly against "communist factions" in two small, underdeveloped countries. One was Vietnam, then in the process of establishing its political independence from France, following military liberation under communist leadership. The other was Guatemala, where a communist-supported bourgeois regime was attempting to break through the institutions of an oligarchic peonage-ridden agrarian society—in which U.S. firms wielded considerable economic power—and to establish a modern national society within a bourgeois democratic framework. Guatemala's population was a tenth of

3. Sherman Adams, *First Hand Report* (New York, Harper & Row, 1961), p. 124.

Vietnam's, and Washington's "fight against internal changes" was brief and successful. The circumstances of its success affected not only future Guatemalan development; it exerted its subtle influence on the pattern of Latin American development generally.

For some years after Arbenz departed from the scene, U.S. Latin Americanists either dismissed Washington's intervention as simply one of lending its good offices or professed lack of knowledge of its extent. In the past decade, however, any doubt concerning the primacy of Washington's role in organizing and executing the coup which deposed Arbenz has been resolved by the testimony of leading participants. Whiting Willauer, United States Ambassador to Honduras in 1954, told a Senate subcommittee in mid-1961 that because of his experience in fighting communism in the Far East, he had been selected for the Honduran post as part of a CIA-devised plan to overthrow the Guatemalan government. His specific task, he testified, was to assist an anticommunist invasion force being assembled in Honduras. He described himself as part of "a team" whose "principal man" was John E. Peurifoy, Ambassador to Guatemala. Other members were the ambassadors to Nicaragua and Costa Rica, as well as "a number of CIA operatives," who were "helping to equip and train the anticommunist revolutionary forces." Willauer further testified that he had had to keep a reluctant Honduran government "in line so they would allow this revolutionary activity to continue based on Honduras." Following the success of his mission, he said, CIA Director Allen Dulles informed him that "the revolution could not have succeeded but for what I did." [4]

The thrust of Willauer's testimony received general confirmation in a 1963 memoir by Miguel Ydígoras Fuentes, president of Guatemala from 1958 to 1963 and Arbenz's chief conservative opponent in the 1950 presidential election. Ydígoras wrote that in 1953 Walter Turnbull, a retired United Fruit Company official, introduced him to two CIA agents who offered "to lend their assistance" to overthrow Arbenz. But Ydígoras found "unacceptable" the terms of this assistance, which included "favoring" the United Fruit Company and its subsidiary, the International Railways of Central America; destruction of the railway workers union; establishment of "a strong-arm government, in the style of Ubico [former dictator]"; and repayment of expenses incurred in the overthrow. Later Ydígoras was informed by Colonel Castillo Armas, another conservative foe of the regime, that he had consented to an offer of aid from official U.S. agencies, as well as from Honduras, Nicaragua, and Santo Domingo, in heading a movement to overthrow Arbenz. Ydígoras agreed to assist Castillo in return for a pledge of free elections following the overthrow.[5]

In his memoir, *Mandate for Change,* Eisenhower also substantially confirmed

---

4. Internal Security Subcommittee, U.S. Senate Committee on the Judiciary, 87th Congress, 1st session, *Hearings on Communism in the Caribbean,* part 13, July 27, 1961. Testimony of Whiting Willauer.

5. Miguel Ydígoras Fuentes, *My War with Communism* (Englewood Cliffs, N.J.: Prentice-Hall, Inc., 1963), pp. 49–50.

this definition of Washington's initiating role. Soon after Peurifoy became ambassador in October of 1953, the then President concluded, on the basis of Peurifoy's reports, that the United States had to act quickly to counteract communist influence in Guatemala. The first step was "to marshal and crystallize Latin American public opinion" at the Tenth Conference of the Organization of American States at Caracas in March of 1954.[6]

Eisenhower then described his efforts to quarantine arms shipments to Guatemala, U.S. airlifting of arms to Honduras and Nicaragua, the invasion of Guatemala by Castillo's rebel forces from Honduran training bases, and his decision to replace with modern planes the old fighter-bombers flown by U.S. pilots, which Castillo's forces had lost in bombing expeditions against Guatemala City. As part of the CIA-devised plan Peurifoy, on the strength of his anticommunist performance in Greece, had been selected as ambassador to Guatemala. An exploration of why Washington took on that role, and with what long-range effect, requires at least a cursory examination of the character of the 1944–54 revolutionary regime in Guatemala, the nature of United States interests there, the actual course of events leading to the coup, and the aftermath.

II. The 1944–54 Revolution

A democratic revolution in 1944 overthrew the oppressive 13-year dictatorship of General Jorge Ubico and opened the way for drastic changes in Guatemala's social and economic life during the presidencies of Juan José Arévalo and Colonel Jacobo Arbenz Guzmán. The country possesses the geographic prerequisites for an abundant, diversified agriculture. Yet the mass of the population lives in poverty. According to the 1950 census, about 70 percent of those economically active in the 2,500,000 population were engaged in agriculture. Under the Ubico dictatorship, the peasantry—whether landless or small plot owners—worked for five to 20 centavos a day (a centavo is equivalent to a U.S. cent). Indians, a majority of the population, were compelled by vagrancy laws to work up to 150 days a year on coffee plantations for five centavos daily, as well as three weeks on public roads without pay. Malnutrition was widespread and Indian life expectancy was less than 40 years, as against 50 years for the ladino. Illiteracy, 70 percent overall, was reported to be 90 to 99 percent in largely Indian communities.

The land-ownership pattern was, and is, the familiar one in Latin America. Two percent of landowners possessed 72 percent of the land, and 90 percent owned or operated 15 percent of the land. Farms with 1,115 acres or more, 0.3 percent of all farms, contained more than half of all farmland in the nation. Before the 1952 agrarian reform, 80 percent of cultivable land in the large plantations surrounding the overpopulated villages in the central highlands was unused, whereas some three-quarters of farmers owned no land at all or had only small

6. *Mandate for Change* (Garden City, N.Y.: Doubleday & Co., 1963), pp. 422–26.

plots. The result was not only peasant poverty, but enormous underutilization of labor and land resources, a narrow domestic market, the need to import foodstuffs which could be produced domestically, and an economy almost wholly dependent on the U.S. coffee and banana markets.

Three U.S. corporations—United Fruit, International Railways of Central America, and Electric Bond and Share—received substantial concessions under the dictatorship, which gave them considerable power over the nation's economy. United Fruit and the IRCA totally monopolized the nation's rail and port facilities, while an Electric Bond and Share subsidiary provided more than 80 percent of the nation's electricity. The absence of any government control over the operations of these corporations resulted in inordinately high transport costs for all shipping except that of United Fruit produce, and in their control over all cargo moving in and out of Guatemala. Transport inadequacy, high rates, discriminatory service, and preferred tax and other privileges gained under contracts negotiated with the Ubico regime were criticized by the International Bank of Reconstruction and Development, which made a detailed study of the Guatemalan economy at the Arévalo government's request. The IBRD declared that inadequate transport facilities and monopoly rates, in particular, were probably the greatest single barrier to Guatemalan industrial development and cultural integration, and it suggested that the resistant U.S. companies accept contract modifications, as demanded by the Arévalo government, to permit greater government control of rates and construction of new port facilities.

The contracts granted, among other things, substantial exemption from future tax and labor laws. This was estimated to have saved the three United States corporations, in one year, just about half of what they would have paid under the nation's tax laws, or an annual loss to the government of some 2,000,000 quetzales (a quetzal is equivalent to a U.S. dollar). Their economic power gave the three corporations substantial political power which led the IBRD to suggest that foreign companies should "refrain from any political activity and should accept perhaps less reservedly than they have in the past, the need to adapt their legal status and their policies to changed conditions." [7]

In addition, unrestricted transfer of foreign corporate dividends to the United States—added to the transfer abroad of savings by Guatemalan landowners—resulted in a substantial drain of funds needed for growth. In the late forties, payments to foreign residents on income from foreign investments averaged $4,-600,000 annually, a sum made possible by the contractual exemption of the three U.S.-owned companies from the profits tax paid by indigenous business firms. The foreign corporations opened new areas of Guatemala to economic exploitation, built its only railroad, gave it electricity and extended social welfare programs to their employees not enjoyed by other workers. But in return they

---

7. International Bank for Reconstruction and Development, *The Economic Development of Guatemala: Summary of a Report of a Mission* (Washington, D.C., 1951), p. 81.

monopolized vital economic areas, reduced farmers to dependent status, distorted the economy, stultified its further growth, and gave important political backing to its most conservative elements in maintaining a reactionary, oppressive, poverty-ridden society. For these services United Fruit Company investors received, according to an estimate in 1936, an annual return of 17¾ percent in the years 1899 to 1935.[8]

A combination of World War II rhetoric about world freedom, the example of the social achievements of neighboring Mexico's Cardenas regime, a war-created inflation, and an evolving nationalism sensitive to the country's backwardness led to the overthrow of the Ubico dictatorship by a coalition which included elements of the lower middle classes, students, intellectuals, urban workers, peons, and an important section of the mestizo military leadership influenced by nationalist currents. A teacher living in exile, Juan José Arévalo, was overwhelmingly elected president in December of 1944 and a new constitution, adopted early in 1945, marked the initiation of radical, political, social, and economic changes.

The constitution provided extensive guarantees of individual liberties and "social guarantees" with respect to labor, public employment, family, and culture. Large plantations were deemed illegal and the government given the power to expropriate with indemnification; natural resources were declared public property. Labor provisions included the eight-hour day, minimum wages, regulation of child and female labor, severance pay, paid vacations, a social security system, the right to organize and strike, and labor tribunals for settlement of disputes. Politically, the constitution emphasized legislative supremacy, freedom of political parties, secret ballot, an apolitical military force, municipal autonomy, and an electoral system with the compulsory secret ballot for literate males, optional public voting for illiterate males, and optional secret voting for literate, but not for illiterate females.[9]

Almost immediately after assuming office, Arévalo acted to implement several provisions of the constitution. New schools were constructed; a social security system, initially to protect against accidents and illness, was established; an elaborate labor code gave urban and rural labor the right to organize and strike, protected workers from unjust dismissal and accorded them severance pay for loss of jobs without cause, set up labor arbitration courts and required that labor hired by foreign corporations be 90 percent Guatemalan. An Institute for the Development of Production (INFOP) was established, as was an Indian Institute designed to integrate the Indian into the national society while preserving his culture. Health and sanitation programs were developed and a Department of

---

8. Charles D. Kepner, *The Social Aspects of the Banana Industry* (Columbia University Studies in History, Economics and Public Law, No. 414, 1936), pp. 22–23, 208.

9. Kalman H. Silvert, *Guatemala, A Study in Government* (Middle America Research Institute, Tulane University Publ. No. 21, New Orleans, 1954) and Nathaniel Whetten, *Guatemala, The Land and the People* (New Haven: Yale University Press, 1961) provide detailed descriptions of the 1945 Constitution.

Physical Education established. The Social Security Institute launched an ambitious 20-year program to build 67 hospitals throughout the country.[10]

Introduction of the institutional framework for a modern bourgeois democratic "welfare state" did not, of course, result in promptly establishing such a state. The process was necessarily plagued by sharp resistance of the still-powerful landowning aristocracy and foreign corporations, particularly to features which threatened their cheap rural labor supply; conflicts among the various groups comprising the governing coalition, and within these groups, for personal power; and the inevitable problems generally arising out of efforts to reform a stagnant, stratified, largely isolated and tradition-bound illiterate rural society. But progress was striking. Government expenditures for education rose, in real terms, some 155 percent from 1944 to 1950. Expenditures for "extraordinary" social purposes (chiefly school and hospital construction) tripled in 1945 and doubled again by 1950. Overall, real government expenditures doubled in the decade between 1939 and 1949, with about 60 percent of the increase due to the expansion of public activities into new areas which included the new ministries of Public Health and Social Assistance, and Economy and Labor. An expert group of U.S. economists concluded in a 1950 study that the pattern of government spending had resulted in a "moderate" redistribution of income in favor of Indian peasants and low-income urban families. Better schools, more hospitals and similar social improvements, the economists reported, strengthened the entire economy by increasing labor productivity. Summing up the Arévalo Administration's economic record, the U.S. economists wrote that it had laid the institutional foundation for its announced policy of supporting the development of new industries, fostering improvements in agricultural production, providing social capital for continued growth, planning more economic utilization of the country's resources, and granting social security to the nation's workers.[11]

The Arévalo regime did not, however, attempt to reform the antiquated land tenure system, thereby leaving unfulfilled the deepest desire of the Indian—obtaining his own land. And it did not basically revise a tax structure which hardly

---

10. Useful accounts of the genesis, accomplishments, and problems of the Arévalo and Arbenz governments, include Silvert; Whetten; Frederick B. Pike, "Guatemala, the United States and Communism in the Americas," *Review of Politics*, Vol. 17 (April, 1955); Franklin D. Parker, *The Central American Republics* (New York: Greenwood Press, 1964); Mario Rodriguez, *Central America* (Englewood Cliffs, N.J.: Prentice-Hall, Inc., 1965). For the above, see also Richard A. LaBarge, *Impact of the United Fruit Company on the Economic Development of Guatemala, 1946-56* (Middle America Research Institute, Tulane University Publ. 29, New Orleans, 1960), p. 48; UN Economic and Social Council, Economic Commission for Latin America (ECLA), *Policies Affecting Foreign Investment in Guatemala*, March 29, 1950, p. 6; Notes of the Month, "The Social Revolution in Guatemala," *World Today*, Vol. 10 (July, 1954), 280–81; *Hispanic-American Report* (H.A.R.), Feb., 1949, p. 10. H.A.R. contained, until its demise in the mid-60s, informative monthly reports on each Latin American country.

11. John H. Adler, E. R. Schlesinger, and F. C. Olson, *Public Finance and Economic Development in Guatemala* (Palo Alto, Calif., Stanford University Press, 1952), pp. 20, 142.

touched the relatively swollen incomes of the wealthy, nor did it revise the privileged contracts of U.S. corporations. The IBRD study of 1950–51 estimated that a reform tax measure which Congress failed to pass, and essential readjustments of contracts with foreign firms, could have brought the government some $4,000,000 additional for economic expansion annually.

Restructuring the land tenure system became the preoccupation of President Arbenz, elected in December of 1950. Arbenz was determined to transform Guatemala into a modern capitalist state, to free it economically from dependence on world coffee prices and to wrest control of the economy from the U.S. corporations dominating it. He launched four major projects to these ends: a highway to the Atlantic Coast to undercut the transport monopoly of the International Railways of Central America; an Atlantic port to compete with the one controlled by the Railway and the United Fruit Company; a national hydroelectric plant to lessen dependence on the Electric Bond and Share subsidiary; and an agrarian reform program which would greatly increase land and labor utilization and hence expand agricultural production, particularly of domestically consumed foodstuffs. To finance the program, the administration increased export and import taxes, as well as taxes on luxuries and alcoholic beverages, and sought congressional enactment of income and capital gains taxes.

The agrarian reform measure, designed both to maintain a broad political coalition behind Arbenz and to leave production undisturbed, permitted expropriation only of uncultivated land on farms of more than 223 acres. Legal expropriations consisted mainly of idle lands taken from 1,059 properties with an average size of 4300 acres. Compensation took the form of bonds with a maximum maturity of 25 years at 3 percent annual interest, the amount based on declared value for tax purposes as of May, 1952. Government land, mostly taken from German coffee growers during the war, was allocated either to individual peasants or to cooperatives. Plots allocated varied from 8½ to 12 acres of cultivated land, and from 26 to 43 acres of tillable, uncultivated land. Annual rentals were set at 5 percent of the value of produce for expropriated private lands and 3 percent for government land. Credit facilities to aid peasants in receiving and developing land were established through a National Agrarian Bank.

Land reform records were destroyed after Arbenz was overthrown, and estimates of its extent vary. A 1965 report of an agency of the Organization of American States estimated that about 100,000 peasants actually received land in the 18 months that the law was in operation. About 1,500,000 acres were distributed for which the government paid $8,345,545 in indemnities. Credit to land reform beneficiaries and other small farmers amounted to nearly $12,000,000. Among the lands expropriated were 1700 acres owned by President Arbenz and 1200 acres owned by Foreign Minister Guillermo Toriello.[12]

---

12. The report of the Inter-American Agricultural Committee (CIDA) of the O.A.S. appears as an appendix in Eduardo Galeano, *Guatemala: Occupied Country* (New York, Monthly Review Press, 1967, pp. 123–32. [For Toriello's own reflections on the coup of 1954 and its background, see his Introduction to this volume.—EDS.]

The most striking feature of the Arévalo-Arbenz period was the organization and activity of the working class and peasantry, resulting in the development of new and powerful groups—political parties, peasants' associations, agrarian committees for land allotment, labor unions, women's organizations. By 1954, half of the 600,000 workers and peasants were organized, 100,000 in trade unions and 200,000 in peasants' unions. One consequence was a series of bitter strikes throughout the period, directed chiefly at the largest and most resented employers, the U.S. corporations. A second consequence was intense strife on the countryside as landowners resisted expropriation, a process aggravated by militant peasant groups not overly concerned with the niceties of a law which they understood to entitle them to land ownership. A third consequence was at least the beginning of breakdown of the isolation of the Indian communities. The privileged and relatively unhampered activities of the three dominant U.S. corporations were checked, the absolute social control of the upper classes was broken, the aristocratic social structure shaken, and the process of evolving a single national culture out of a pattern of local cultures begun. This did not occur, of course, without agonizing strife within the country and hostile pressures from without, culminating in the dismantling of the Arbenz government.

III. Opposition and Counter-Revolution

A land-owning class so long politically dominant, and dependent on government repression for a labor supply at wages of 5 to 20 cents a day, was not about to accept even the mild reforms of the Arévalo regime without a struggle. From the outset, plots to overthrow his government compelled Arévalo repeatedly to restrict, for limited periods, personal freedoms guaranteed by the Constitution. During the six years of his term, some 25 to 35 uprisings either occurred or were uncovered in the planning stage. Inevitably, too, conflict developed within the coalition backing Arévalo between middle-class elements who feared the revolution would go too far, and more radical elements concerned chiefly with ending the poverty and low status of worker and peasant. Sections of the military which had initially supported the revolution began to develop hostility to it partly because of fear of losing their traditionally dominant role and partly because of their connections with middle-class groups desiring to limit the revolution.[13]

Important strikes against United Fruit and the IRCA occurred in 1946, 1948–49 and 1950–52. In the 1948–49 struggle, the government was heavily involved on the side of the workers. Before it was settled, the pillars of Boston politics in the U.S. Congress assailed the Guatemalan Government in behalf of the United Fruit Company. The Company not only has its offices in Boston, but is closely linked with Boston's First National Bank and the Old Colony Trust Company, two venerable, prestigious institutions which "consolidated their interest" in 1929.

---

13. Silvert, *Guatemala*, pp. 11, 16; Whetten, "Land Reform in a Modern World," *Rural Sociology*, Vol. 19 (Dec., 1954), 332–33.

The First National is the Boston Registrar Bank for United Fruit, and the Old Colony Trust is its Transfer Agent. In February of 1949 Republican Senator Henry Cabot Lodge charged on the Senate floor that the Guatemalan labor code had been devised to discriminate against United Fruit, and the Company faced a "serious economic breakdown" because of communist-influenced activity. A week later, Democratic Majority Leader John McCormack accused "a minority of reckless agitators" of trying to penalize United Fruit for "being American." Republican Congressman Christian Herter, also of Boston, followed by threatening to introduce legislation cutting off funds from countries discriminating against U.S. firms.[14]

Within a year the United States, in the grip of an anticommunist cold war hysteria, was witnessing a journalistic drive to establish Guatemala as a "red menace" in Central America, though the first communist convention in late 1949, registered a membership numbering less than 40.[15] While the prestige of the mostly youthful communists was high as a result of their leadership in building the unions, their political influence on a government level was generally slight. In the U.S. stress was laid on the alleged communist leanings of many of Arévalo's associates and on the "party line nature" of some of his New Deal-like reform policies. While insisting that he would not suppress the communists because he wanted to maintain a democratic government, Arévalo finally succumbed to pressures from Washington and formally banned communist organization. In one of his last acts he confiscated an issue of the communist publication *Octubre*, which had recently made its appearance.[16]

Arbenz likewise experienced continual tension, particularly as a result of conflict with U.S. corporations. He was harassed, too, by developing militant right-wing organizations and the initiation of repeated demonstrations demanding the ouster of alleged communists from his government—a movement which coincided with, and may have been stimulated by, enactment of the agrarian reform law.[17] The Republican accession to power in Washington in January of 1953 held more drastic consequences for his regime. The new Secretary of State, the nation's leading champion of "containment," was uninhibited by considerations of sovereignty in pursuing a vigorous anticommunist course in the name of national security. Moreover, as the editor of the journal *Inter-American Economic Affairs* charged in a detailed review in the fall of 1953, the Eisenhower Administration

---

14. *Congressional Record*, 81st Congress, First Session, Vol. 95, Part 1, Feb. 14, 1949, pp. 1172–73; Part 2, Feb. 21 and 24, pp. 1464 and 1496. The relations between United Fruit and the two Boston banks, and between the banks themselves, are described in *Moody's Manual of Investment* (p. 313 in the 1954 edition) and *Moody's Industrials* (p. 1852 in the 1954 edition).

15. Ronald Schneider, *Communism in Guatemala, 1944–1954* (New York, 1958), pp. 21, 55, 71, 75; Silvert, *Guatemala*, pp. 58–59.

16. *H.A.R.*, March, 1950, April and December, 1951; Schneider (above) Chap. 4 *passim;* William Krehm, "A Victory for the West in Guatemala?" *International Journal*, Vol. 9, 1954, 297.

17. *H.A.R.*, December, 1951; March and April, 1952.

quickly subordinated "Good Neighbor" considerations to the overt, immediate pressures of U.S. banking and business interests.[18]

For Guatemala, these tendencies in Washington were reinforced by a foreign policy staff, several of whose key members were or had been personally in the legal, financial, or political orbit of the United Fruit Company. Secretary of State Dulles's law firm had represented the company in negotiations with pre-1944 dictatorial Guatemalan regimes and had served as legal counsel for IRCA. John M. Cabot, Assistant Secretary of State for Latin American Affairs, was the brother of Thomas D. Cabot, a director of the First National Bank of Boston. Robert Cutler, presidential assistant for national security affairs and Eisenhower's liaison with the National Security Council, was president of Old Colony Trust prior to his Washington appointment. The board chairman of Old Colony Trust was also board chairman of United Fruit. In 1956, after the destruction of the Arbenz government, Cutler returned to Old Colony Trust as board chairman. Secretary of Commerce Sinclair Weeks was a director of the First National Bank of Boston both before and after his service in the cabinet. Robert D. Hill, who as Ambassador to Costa Rica participated in the plan to subvert the Arbenz government, was assistant vice-president of W. R. Grace and Company before his appointment in late 1953. The Grace Company was active in Guatemalan commerce and also had its difficulties with the revolutionary regimes. Hill later became a director of United Fruit.[19]

Eisenhower's assumption of the presidency coincided with the initiation of Guatemalan land reform, which included the expropriation of some 240,000 acres of the United Fruit Company's Pacific Coast holdings. Another 173,000 acres on the Atlantic Coast were expropriated a year later, leaving the company with 162,000 acres on both coasts. The company had no more than 50,000 acres under actual cultivation, or about 9 percent of its pre-reform holdings of some 565,000 acres.

Based on the company's own declared valuation for tax purposes the government offered $600,000 as compensation for the expropriations. The company insisted that the expropriated Pacific Coast land alone was worth over $15,000,000 and obtained State Department intervention on behalf of its claim. Guatemalan officials noted that aside from the requirement of equal application to foreign and native landowners of the law providing for compensation based on declared valuation, Pacific coastal land at Tiquisate—the company's most important—had been given to the company for construction of a port which was never built, and

18. Simon G. Hanson, "The End of the Good Neighbor Policy," *Inter-American Economic Affairs*, Vol. 7 (Autumn, 1953), 3–49.

19. For Dulles's law firm connection, *I. F. Stone's Weekly*, June 28, 1954; for officers of First National of Boston and Old Colony Trust, *Moody's Manual of Investments* and *Polk's Bank Directory*, appropriate years; for officers of United Fruit, *Moody's Industrials*, appropriate years; for Robert D. Hill, *Who's Who in America*, Vol. 33, p. 919. Hill's role in the CIA plan was described by Willauer (see note 4).

Atlantic coastal land had been acquired by various manipulative techniques, often over the protests of municipalities.[20]

In March of 1953, less than two months after Eisenhower's inauguration, Spruille Braden, an ex-assistant secretary of state for Latin America, in a widely publicized address at Dartmouth College, heralded the Eisenhower Administration's drive to oust Arbenz by attacking U.S. policy toward Guatemala as "namby-pamby" and projecting an ideological position which the Administration soon adopted. Since communism was "blatantly international and not an internal affair," Braden declared, its suppression "even by force" would not constitute intervention. Braden was later described by the British *New Statesman and Nation* as public relations director of the United Fruit Company when he made the speech, a connection not publicly noted at the time. He admitted to this writer that he was then "consultant" for the company. In a follow-up statement, Braden specifically attacked the new "so-called agrarian law" and its application to United Fruit.[21]

The Guatemalan government was then increasing its pressure on the U.S. corporations for contract revision, and the resulting friction was aggravated by the contagious character of the process. In Costa Rica, liberal presidential candidate Jose Figueres was demanding that the rate of United Fruit Company profits paid to the government be increased from 15 to 50 percent. And in Honduras and Panama the company's workers were striking, while the governments also pressed for contract renegotiation. As the *New Statesman and Nation* later observed, these developments led the U.S. State Department to conclude that United Fruit interests in all Central America were threatened by the Arbenz government's policies. Company interests in Central America included 3,000,000 acres of land, 2,000 miles of railway, and 100 steamships.

Late in January, 1954, the Guatemalan government charged a "gentleman's agreement" between Colonel Castillo Armas and General Ydígoras Fuentes to overthrow Arbenz by organizing an invasion from Honduras and Nicaragua. It presented documentary evidence which implicated the United States as financier of the movement. It claimed that a former U.S. Army Colonel, Carl Studer, had gone to work for United Fruit and was in charge of training an invasion force. Arms had already been smuggled into Guatemala via the IRCA, it said, to equip a subversive fifth column in the Tiquisate area of the United Fruit Company. *The New York Times*, commenting that the documentary evidence "possibly was obtained through a falling out" of Castillo Armas and Ydígoras, obviously accepted the charges as true. In his memoirs, Ydígoras later confirmed their accu-

20. Anna Louise Strong, "Guatemala, A First Hand Report," *Monthly Review*, March, 1954, 560–61.

21. *The New York Times*, March 13 and 26, 1953; *New Statesman and Nation*, June 26, 1954, 821; author's telephone interview with Braden, April 25, 1969.

22. *Bulletin of the Guatemalan Information Bureau*, Guatemala City, February 1, 1954; *The New York Times*, January 30, 1954; Ydígoras, *My War with Communism*, 50–51.

racy, complaining that his "gentleman's agreement" with Castillo had fallen into Arbenz's hands "by some act of treachery." Washington, typically, dismissed the charges by stating that a denial would give the story a dignity it did not deserve, and that it was in line with "the usual propaganda charges against the United States." [22]

In March of 1954, Dulles came to the 10th Inter-American Conference at Caracas determined to "marshal and crystallize" Latin American opinion behind the move to destroy the Arbenz regime. Guatemala's foreign minister, Guillermo Toriello, fought back by charging Washington with seeking a return to "big stick" and "dollar" diplomacy, using anticommunism to disguise its opposition to popular progress. He argued that Latin America required liberation from the United States in order to deal with the "real problem" of human misery, poverty, and social backwardness. Dulles's resolution, which called for action against communism without prior consultation, received unconditional support only from Nicaragua, the Dominican Republic, El Salvador, Peru, and Venezuela—all under dictatorships. He was compelled to accept amendments requiring prior consultation and asserting that each American state had the right to choose freely its own form of government and economic system, the latter proviso inserted in an effort to block application of the resolution to Guatemala. The resolution, as amended, was passed but Argentina, Mexico, and Guatemala—embracing one-third of Latin America's population—refused to support it, the former two abstaining.

The reaction among many Latin Americans was that dollar diplomacy had returned to the Americas. One delegate reportedly maintained that Toriello had "said many things some of the rest of us would like to say if we dared." The Uruguayan spokesman declared bitterly, "We contributed our approval without enthusiasm, without optimism, without joy, and without feeling that we were contributing to the adoption of a constructive measure." The Mexican journal *Humanismo* reported that as one result of the conference, Toriello was "the most popular name recalled by the people of America. . . . He interprets the music we like to hear and he attacks the things we disapprove. . . . He saved his country and covered himself with glory." [23]

A month after Caracas, the State Department formally demanded $15,854,849 compensation for United Fruit Company properties expropriated on the Pacific Coast alone. Guatemala denied Washington's right to intervene, charging violation of its sovereignty.[24]

In May the State Department, learning that a shipment of Czech arms had reached Guatemala, charged large-scale Soviet military intervention and claimed Honduras and Nicaragua faced invasion from Guatemala. The idea that, in the circumstances, Guatemala would thus furnish the United States with a legal basis for open intervention was fantastic, but the claim gave Washington the excuse

---

23. Quotations are from J. Lloyd Mecham, *The United States and Inter-American Security* (Austin, Texas, University of Texas Press, 1961), pp. 441–45. See also Mario Rodriguez, *Central America*, p. 155.

24. *Moody's Industrials*, 1954, p. 1849.

for supplying Nicaragua and Honduras with arms for use in the intended invasion plan. In fact Guatemala had tried vainly for years to buy arms from the U.S., from other western hemisphere countries and from Western Europe, but Washington had quietly instituted a boycott. The Guatemalan government complained that this boycott was so effective that it could not even get pistols for its police force or "low-caliber" ammunition for the Hunting and Fishing Club of Guatemala. Meanwhile the U.S. was furnishing arms to neighbors who made no secret of their intent to overthrow the government by violence. Guatemala also emphasized its legitimate right to trade freely with any nation in the world; it was "not a United States colony" and it rejected "the pretense of that government to control the legitimate acts of sovereign countries." [25]

Even among Guatemalan anticommunists, Arbenz's insistence on the right to buy arms gained some support. The view was shared, as well, by other nations in the western hemisphere and western Europe. Two days before Guatemala was invaded, Washington publicly requested the "maritime nations of the free world" to embargo arms to Guatemala and to permit searches of friendly ships on the high seas. All European governments approached rejected the request, as a curtailment of the traditional right of freedom of the seas.[26] In Britain, according to a June 19 *Times* dispatch, the attitude was that the Atlantic was not Dulles's "private preserve." Moreover, Europeans were not persuaded that the Guatemalan regime was communist. And if it was, this was its right.

Within Guatemala, middle-class supporters of the regime were frightened by Washington's virulent hostility and the consequent diplomatic isolation being forced upon the country. The growing internal and foreign opposition, in turn, led Arbenz to lean increasingly upon the zeal and energy of the communists in behalf of his program. Prominent in the organization of labor and peasants, they helped to stimulate mass popular backing and enthusiasm for land reform, which had become for him the line of division between friends and enemies, they provided technical and political advice, and they supplied essential background information on the major issues confronting him. Moreover, his general attitude—shared by European and most other democratic rulers outside of the United States—was that any legal curbing of communists was undemocratic. In his annual message to Congress in the spring of 1954, he defended the right of communists to function legally and declared that any attempt to isolate them would be suicidal for the revolutionary government.[27]

Constant talk of armed rebellion among the regime's foes suggested that they knew they could not defeat the regime politically though they operated freely, a

---

25. Guatemalan Embassy, *Statement of the Government of Guatemala*, Washington, D.C., May 21, 1954.

26. *H.A.R.*, June and July, 1954: Arthur P. Whitaker, "Guatemala, the O.A.S. and the U.S.," *Foreign Policy Association Bulletin*. September 1, 1954, p. 6.

27. Schneider, *Communism in Guatemala*, pp. 190–93; Pike, *Guatemala, the U.S., and Communism*, pp. 244–46.

judgment confirmed by the U.S. State Department itself in a report prepared before Arbenz's overthrow but published after it. The report declared that Arbenz's party held the political initiative "while the opposition has for the past 18 months become sterile and ineffectual." Seeking to blunt Washington's hostility, Arbenz offered to negotiate differences between his regime and United Fruit, and to sign a nonaggression pact with Honduras. He also asked for a face-to-face meeting with Eisenhower. The proposals were rejected; Washington was not interested in compromise with a regime whose destruction it was preparing.[28]

On June 18 Castillo Armas invaded Guatemala from Honduras with a few hundred men. The invaders captured a few towns and were driven back from some. The main military action involved frequent bombings of Guatemala City and other key points from U.S. planes flown by U.S. pilots hired by the CIA and based in Nicaragua. They had virtually no air opposition since the chief of the small Guatemalan air force had deserted in the company of the ex-deputy chief of the U.S. air force mission in Guatemala, under circumstances indicating that the U.S. officer may have been a CIA agent in the country since 1952.[29]

Workers' and peasants' paramilitary groups were organized in various parts of the country, but the military refused to permit them arms even though Arbenz ordered it. On June 27, representatives of the army corps demanded Arbenz's resignation. Apparently unnerved by his isolation from the army and unwilling to face a large-scale civil war, he capitulated. Communists made vain, intensive efforts to persuade him to organize civilian resistance, but with his resignation they and other leading government backers became demoralized and fled to foreign embassies.[30]

Arbenz's replacement by the chief of the armed forces, Colonel Enrique Diaz, was arranged through Ambassador Peurifoy. When Diaz pledged to continue the struggle against Castillo, Peurifoy secured his resignation at gunpoint, and after some complex negotiations, in which the U.S. envoy acted as arbiter between Castillo and army officers in Guatemala City, Castillo emerged as president.[31]

A Communist Party post-mortem analysis in 1955 charged that Peurifoy had ordered the army leaders to demand Arbenz's resignation and that he had threatened destruction of the capital by U.S. superfortresses based on Panama if Arbenz refused to resign. The C.P. statement claimed nonetheless that Arbenz's resignation was unexpected and unnecessary, and that it had created paralysis and

28. U.S. Department of State, *Intervention of International Communism in Guatemala.* Publ. No. 5556 (Washington, D.C., 1954), p. 40. For Arbenz offer, see *H.A.R.*, June, 1954.

29. *The New York Times,* June 8, 1954. See also David Wise and T. B. Ross, *The Invisible Government* (N.Y., Random House, 1964), p. 177n.

30. Schneider, *Communism in Guatemala,* pp. 310–13; Political Commission of the Central Committee of the Guatemalan Workers' Party, *North American Intervention in Guatemala and the Overthrow of the Democratic Regime, 1955* (mimeograph translation).

31. Wise and Ross, *Invisible Government*, p. 179; *H.A.R.*, July and August, 1954; Philip B. Taylor, "The Guatemalan Affair: A Critique of U.S. Foreign Policy," *American Political Science Review,* Vol. 50 (September, 1956), 797.

confusion among the masses. It attributed the resignation to Arbenz's essentially bourgeois outlook and to the fact that the bourgeois parties, comprising the main elements of the government coalition, feared the consequences of an armed struggle of workers and peasants. The Party confessed that it had not known how to "mobilize the masses" independently in order to "pass over to the offensive." This, it declared, was due to its uncritical acceptance of the leadership of the bourgeoisie in the 1944–54 revolution and its failure to recognize the need for an independent, and united, policy of worker and peasant organizations.[32] Whatever the causes, capitulation of the communist top command along with Arbenz and his government left no one to provide the necessary leadership for popular resistance to Washington's takeover.

In a 1956 account of the overthrow Arévalo's ambassador to Moscow, Luis Cardoza y Aragón, cited an interview with Arbenz in the Havana periodical *Bohemia* in which Arbenz insisted that Peurifoy had pressured army officers to demand his resignation. He said he had decided to turn over power to Colonel Diaz, his Army Chief of Staff and a political intimate, on condition that Diaz continue to fight the invasion from Honduras and preserve the gains of the revolution. He admitted that Peurifoy's dismissal of Diaz within hours indicated that his resignation had been a grave error. Cardoza suggested that Diaz was dismissed from office by the U.S. ambassador because he refused to arrest and execute, on Peurifoy's demand, a number of people whom Peurifoy had listed as communists.[33]

Washington's subversion of the Guatemalan government caused shock in Latin America and Europe. In the UN General Assembly in October, the Ecuadorean and Uruguayan delegates delivered angry protests. The national legislatures of Argentina and Uruguay condemned the "aggression against Guatemala" and the rightist Chilean Chamber of Deputies invited all Latin American legislatures to express jointly their repudiation of Washington's "armed intervention." Non-leftist political elements normally friendly to Washington joined in the criticism voiced by students, intellectuals, and labor leaders in Brazil, Cuba, Ecuador, Costa Rica, Colombia, Argentina, and Mexico; violent anti-U.S. demonstrations took place in Chile and elsewhere; and in Honduras the affair led to defeat of the reactionary regime in the 1954 elections. British Labor Party Chief Clement Atlee declared in Parliament that the intervention was "a plain act of aggression" and that the principles of the UN had been subordinated to hatred of communism. There was widespread doubt that the Arbenz government was communist-dominated, and suspicion that the "communist smear" was used by Washington as a pretext for aiding the United Fruit Company.[34]

32. Guatemalan Workers' Party, above.

33. Luis Cardoza y Aragón, *La Revolución Guatemalteca* (Montevideo, 1956), pp. 204–211.

34. Latin American reactions are reported in *H.A.R.*, November, 1954; Rodriguez, *Central America*,

IV. Guatemala after Arbenz

Following Castillo's ascension to power, the 1945 Constitution was suspended and he was granted power to rule by decree. Ubico's secret police chief was restored to his former post, as were several other officials of the Ubico regime. A National Committee for Defense against Communism was established, with unlimited powers of arrest. Warrants were dispensed with, and *habeas corpus* rights cancelled. Press and speech freedoms, operative under the Arévalo and Arbenz regimes, were eliminated, and all criticism of the government outlawed as part of the program of "combating communism." A penal code provision against insulting the president or his administration was enforced, causing strong resentment even from the pro-government press.[35]

Many were executed and thousands jailed. Since much of the persecution occurred in the rural areas, it went unreported. The regime effectively liquidated trade union and peasant leaders throughout the country. In Tiquisate, a principal United Fruit site, 17 union leaders were reportedly shot. The Confederation of Latin American Workers charged that 45 leaders of a United Fruit Company strike, settled just before the Castillo uprising, had been executed, as were other local union and peasant leaders. The anthropologist John Gillin, studying an Indian village, learned that nine village leaders were summarily executed by Castillo's army, including five young literate Indians. Many others fled into exile or hiding. A study of another Indian village revealed that 100 supporters of agrarian reform were arrested and others chased into the hills. The chief young radical leaders were sent to Guatemala City for trial; their fate was not indicated.[36]

From the viewpoint of Guatemala's economic and social development, the most harmful measures were the repeal of the Agrarian Reform Law of 1952, the reversal of land reform already achieved, and the virtual destruction of the trade union and peasant movements. Castillo dissolved the trade unions for a 90-day period to permit their reorganization free of communist influence. They never reorganized, in part because of government and employer resistance and in part because there were no replacements for the union leaders eliminated. In the strongly anticommunist *American Federationist* of September, 1954, Serafimo Romualdi, Inter-American Representative of the AFL-CIO, charged the major Guatemalan concerns with deliberately dismissing not only "communist ele-

---

p. 35; Mecham, *U.S. and Inter-American Security*, pp. 451–52. Atlee statement is cited by Taylor, "The Guatemalan Affair," pp. 804–5. Suspicion of "Communist smear" and reactions are reported in *New Statesman and Nation*, June 26, 1954, 817–19.

35. John Gillen and Kalman Silvert, "Ambiguities in Guatemala," *Foreign Affairs*, April, 1956, 480; Whetten, *Guatemala*, p. 338; *H.A.R.*, August through November, 1954; Rodriguez, *Central America*, p. 28.

36. Kalman E. Silvert, *The Conflict Society* (New Orleans: Hauser Press, 1961), p. 119; Gillen and Silvert, *Foreign Affairs* (above), 477; Reuben E. Reina, *The Law of the Saints: A Pokomam Pueblo and Its Community Culture* (Indianapolis: Bobbs-Merrill, 1966), p. 93.

ments" but all active unionists. Romualdi declared it to be "generally accepted that the decree dissolving the banana and railway unions was issued at the insistent request" of United Fruit and the IRCA.[37]

A 1962 report by the U.S. Bureau of Labor Statistics declared that the labor movement had declined to 16,000 members from "over 100,000" during the Arbenz administration. Capable trade union leaders were lacking, the report said, and protection of labor's right to organize "is absent," despite Guatemala's labor code and formal adherence to the International Labor Organization. The BLS report also charged that Guatemalan Labor Code provisions for minimum wages and overtime pay were not being enforced. Under cover of fighting communism Guatemalan business, foreign and domestic, managed to get rid of the labor movement which, as the BLS report said, had "become a significant factor on the national scene" under Arévalo and Arbenz. They also got rid of much of the pre-1954 social legislation. Emasculation of the unions was accompanied by a decline in real wages.[38]

In agriculture, abrogation of the Agrarian Reform Law led to a return to former owners of almost all land distributed under the law, including the expropriated United Fruit Company land. The 1965 report of the Inter-American Agricultural Development Committee (CIDA) of the Organization of American States put the matter succinctly: "All the gains achieved under the Arbenz agrarian reform program were virtually nullified." Peasant organization was outlawed, peasants active in these organizations or in the reform program were blacklisted, and in 1957 wage reductions were decreed for farm workers on about 75 percent of the large plantations. New agrarian laws were passed in 1956 and 1962, but by 1967 only some 22,000 families had received a total of 400,000 to 500,000 acres, as against the 100,000 peasants who had received 1,500,000 acres in less than two years under Arbenz. The new laws provided for colonization of undeveloped land, with no change in land tenure, and at least some of the "colonizers" were military men who received the land through influence and rented it out. Farm credit under Arbenz had totaled $12,000,000; in the five years from 1962 to 1967, it totaled $300,000. A definitive 1960 study of Guatemala by a U.S. scholar characterized the post-1954 attempts at land reform as a "costly failure." Solon Barraclough, UN specialist on Latin American agrarian problems, observed in 1968 that the process of developing large-scale plantations at the expense of subsistence farmers continues in Guatemala, that semi-feudal share-labor agreements still exist widely, and that ex-government officials and labor organizers are still jailed for advocating land reform and higher farm wages.

In 1955–1960, the U.S. contributed more than $110,000,000 in direct assistance to Guatemala, in addition to various other types of aid. The $36,000,000 given in 1956–57 was a fourth of the amount received by India, with more than 100 times

37. Romualdi charge is cited in U.S. Bureau of Labor Statistics, *Labor Law and Practices in Guatemala*, Report No. 223 (Washington, D.C., December, 1962), p. 11.

38. BLS report, above, pp. 10, 11, 17–20, 30.

the population. In return for this assistance, Washington ensured the survival of regimes subservient to it and gained freedom from labor and government harassment for U.S. firms, as well as liberal concessions to other U.S. corporations interested in doing business in Guatemala. While large-scale American aid and high coffee prices permitted a substantial development of the economy for a few years after Castillo Armas took power, the improvement did not endure. Economic statistics for Guatemala are unreliable and contradictory, and the state of the economy is dependent upon world coffee and banana prices. Within these limitations, however, it is worth noting that according to some government figures the *per capita* national product rose 3.6 percent a year from 1946 to 1953, and slightly more than 2 percent a year from 1955 to 1966. Agricultural production from 1955 to 1965 reportedly rose by little more than half the rate of population increase, and food production recovered to the 1953 level only in 1966.[39]

The inequality in income distribution has become more pronounced. Alberto Fuentes Mohr, leading Guatemalan economist who served successively as finance and foreign minister in the recently replaced Montenegro government, reported in 1968 the annual *per capita* income of subsistence farmers and agricultural laborers—about two-thirds of the population—was $87 in 1950 and $83 in 1968 (with prices about 6 percent higher). For the wealthiest 7 percent of the population *per capita* income rose about 30 percent during this period. There is a continual job crisis in the country with the total labor force increasing at a rate of 80,000 and industry creating only some 1,500 new jobs annually. Summing up the effects of Arbenz's overthrow, Fuentes Mohr observed in 1968 that "for the great majority of the Guatemalan population the maintenance of a defective land tenure system and the outlawing of labor and peasant organizations meant that their incomes were kept at subsistence or very low levels." [40]

Post-Arbenz politics have been dominated by reactionary military strongmen who have effectively prevented the emergence of significant trade union and peasant movements. Briefly, Castillo Armas was assassinated in 1957. An election staged by a military junta for a successor was so fraudulent that public clamor compelled a new one and General Ydígoras Fuentes was elected. Recurrent dis-

---

39. CIDA report, 1965, in Galeano, *Guatemala: Occupied*, pp. 117, 132; Alberto Fuentes Mohr, "Guatemala," in Claudio Veliz (editor), *Latin America and the Caribbean, A Handbook* (New York: Praeger, 1968), 201–02; Whetten, *Guatemala*, pp. 166–173; Solon Barraclough, "The Agrarian Problem," in Veliz (ed.), *Handbook*, above, pp. 491—92. Economic data, including indices used to adjust for price changes, were taken from several sources, including Economic Commission for Latin America, *Policies Affecting Foreign Investments in Latin America*, 1950, p. 5; International Development Bank, *Institutional Reforms and Social Development Trends in Latin America*, 1963, p. 179; UN Statistical Office, *Per Capita National Product of Fifty-Five Countries*, 1952–54, Statistical Papers, Series E., No. 4.; *UN Statistical Yearbook*, 1968; International Monetary Fund, *International Financial Statistics*, 1968; UN Food and Agriculture Organization, *Production Yearbook*, 1967, p. 29; Richard LaBarge, *Impact of United Fruit*, p. 48.

40. Fuentes Mohr in *Latin America, A Handbook*, pp. 201–203; IDB, *Social Progress Trust Fund, 8th Annual Report* (Washington, D.C., 1968), 180–81.

closures of corruption, rising unrest among workers and peasants because of his economic austerity measures, and even rightist opposition to his efforts at mild reform, kept Ydígoras's regime in continual state of crisis. His cooperation with the CIA in permitting the use of Guatemalan territory as a staging ground for the Bay of Pigs adventure stimulated such widespread hostility that he was compelled to declare martial law.[41]

Late in 1962, from his exile in Mexico, ex-president Arévalo announced his presidential candidacy in 1963. The enthusiastic popular response again led to martial law. *New York Times* correspondent Tad Szulc reported that according to the general view, Arévalo "had the support of Guatemala's peasants, workers and youth—as well as some middle-class groups—and that he could easily win a free election." [42] Defense Minister and strongman Colonel Enrique Peralta Azurdia foreclosed on this by taking over as dictator and cancelling the 1963 elections. Three years after the event, the *Miami Herald* of Dec. 24, 1966, described a meeting alleged to have taken place in President Kennedy's office where, on the insistence of Ambassador to Guatemala John O. Bell, the decision was taken to cancel the elections in order to prevent Arévalo's return to the presidency.[43] Peralta had no trouble receiving recognition from Washington though he exiled and imprisoned not only leftists but members of the center, while keeping the country in a state of siege.

In presidential elections in 1966, from which leftist parties and candidates were barred, the nominee of the "liberal" Revolutionary Party—Julio Méndez Montenegro—unexpectedly won a plurality. The Party was acceptable to Peralta since it had supported his 1963 coup. Lack of a majority threw the election into Congress, controlled by the Revolutionary Party, but Méndez was permitted to take office only after assuring Peralta that the military would retain its independence and its command positions. Local governors, as well as regional commandants, are appointed by the central government and are overwhelmingly military men.[44]

Army and right-wing terrorist organizations retained a free hand in wiping out guerrilla groups which had developed out of an army officers' revolt in 1960 and had gained considerable influence in several rural areas. By the end of 1967 the army and right-wing terrorist organizations, through a campaign of rural slaughter, appeared to have largely inactivated the guerrillas on the countryside. Under cover of antiguerrilla activity, noncommunist leftists were sought out by the terrorists and eliminated. Estimates of these killed between mid-1966 and early

41. Rodriguez, *Central America*, pp. 30–32. The political character and developments of the early post-Arbenz regime are described by Rodriguez, Whetten *(Guatemala)*, Parker, and monthly reports of H.A.R. throughout the period.

42. March 31, 1963.

43. The report is confirmed in essence in Jerome Levinson and Juan de Onis, *The Alliance that Lost Its Way* (New York: Quadrangle Books, 1972), pp. 84–85.

44. J. W. Sloan, "The 1966 Presidential Elections in Guatemala," *Inter-American Economic Affairs*, Vol. 22 Autumn, 1968.

1968—intellectuals, students, workers, peasants who sought to organize or protest against what they considered the ills of Guatemalan society—have ranged from 2,800 to 9,000. Salaries, weapons, uniforms, arms, and vehicles of these anti-guerrilla groups, it has been charged, were supplied by the U.S. and the Alliance for Progress.[45] As a result of the apparently effective drive against them in rural areas, Guatemala's guerrillas appear to have shifted their activity to Guatemala City and to have resorted increasingly to individual terror as a weapon.

In national elections in the spring of 1970, Colonel Carlos Arana Osorio, candidate of the extreme right-wing National Liberation Movement—founded by Castillo Armas—won the presidency. Colonel Arana's credentials for national leadership were earned as commander of the Zacapa Garrison which conducted a war against rural guerrillas and their suspected sympathizers among peasants and students, with such brutality that President Mendez was compelled to dismiss him and send him off to Nicaragua as ambassador. As Colonel Arana assumed office on July 1, the outlook for Guatemala was one of continued political instability, reciprocal terror, and the incapacity of a reactionary regime—backed by the landowning elite and protected by U.S. power—to resolve the profound economic, social, and political problems of that unhappy country.

By its intervention in Guatemala, Washington destroyed the thoroughgoing bourgeois democratic reforms of the Arévalo and Arbenz regimes which both radicals and liberals—U.S. and Latin American—have long maintained are essential to Latin American social and economic progress, and to which the Alliance for Progress has presumably been dedicated. It is clear, from the historic record, that the United Fruit Company was influential in the U.S. operation. Yet it would be greatly oversimplifying to ascribe Washington's course solely to protection of the company's interests. The cold war and its domestic reflection, McCarthyism, were then at their most intense period and were a major factor in the determination of that course. The relationship would appear to have been reciprocal. Whereas the cold war and anticommunist hysteria provided the public cover for government action in behalf of the company, United Fruit personnel facilitated the CIA's cold war task of subverting the Arbenz government.

As consequence of the abortion of Guatemalan social development attendant upon Arbenz's overthrow, the country has suffered intensified poverty, social chaos, and a rule marked by terror and repression. This has given rise to a guerrilla movement which in its desperation has resorted to kidnapping and killing of U.S. diplomatic personnel, including the first U.S. ambassador ever to be assassinated. Analyzing the murder of Ambassador John Gordon Mein and two earlier killings of U.S. military personnel in Guatemala, a *New York Times* dispatch from

45. "Guatemala, the Ferocious Cure," *London Economist*, January 6, 1968, 22; Norman Gall, "The Legacy of Che Guevara," *Commentary*, December, 1967, 31–34. See also the Statement of Father Thomas Melville, suspended Maryknoll priest, in *The National Catholic Reporter*, January 31, 1968, reprinted in Galeano, *Guatemala: Occupied*, pp. 149–59. The figure of 9,000 killed was cited recently by a Mexican church official (*Siempre*, Mexico City, January 13, 1971, p. 33).

Guatemala City (September 8, 1968) linked the guerrilla attacks on U.S. officials directly to Washington's contribution to the overthrow of Arbenz, who, it declared, was still a hero to leftists and university youth. The failure of "mediocre rightist military regimes" after Arbenz to alleviate Guatemala's grave economic and social problems, the dispatch said, was productive of "the most deadly forms of extremism." Ironically it was a U.S. president, John F. Kennedy, who warned an Alliance for Progress meeting in 1962 that "those who make peaceful revolution impossible will make violent revolution inevitable."

Postscript

In the dozen years since the above article was written, a wealth of documentary materials and personal memoirs dealing with the U.S. subversion of the Arbenz regime has become available. These include State Department archives, a memoir by a United Fruit Company public relations officer, accounts by CIA officials involved, etc. These materials add many details, fleshing out the tragic story, but they do not challenge any aspect of the above account; they confirm all of it. [See p. 45 note for a listing of this material—EDS.]

The State Department records do permit a sharper definition of the lawless nature of the Eisenhower administration's brutal destruction of the Arbenz government, the incredible lengths to which top echelons—including the President—went to accomplish this destruction, the uninhibited lying and deception used to cover up what administration leaders knew to be outside the law. Most Americans cannot believe their government capable of such blatantly outlaw practices and outrageous mendacity, hence the process continues—if perhaps in somewhat less blatant form. In the summer of 1982, the Reagan Administration is clearly duplicating in Nicaragua, El Salvador, and Guatemala various aspects of the Eisenhower-Dulles performance of 1954.

The plan for bringing down Arbenz, drawn up in mid-1953 by a special CIA-State Department Guatemala Group, included training a "liberation" force of mercenaries and dissident Guatemalans at a United Fruit plantation in Honduras; developing a massive media campaign for spreading fear, intimidation and disinformation designed to frighten Guatemala's military leadership into deserting Arbenz and to stimulate capital flight; and crippling the economy through economic sanctions and other destabilizing measures. An invasion from Honduras by the "liberation" force, following intense disinformation and destabilization activities, was calculated to result in popular uprisings and military disaffection. Bombing by planes furnished by the U.S., piloted by CIA-hired mercenaries (mainly ex–U.S. military pilots), and flown from Honduras and Nicaragua under CIA direction, was to accompany the invasion.

In practice the invasion, commanded by Castillo Armas, was simply a front for U.S. propaganda claims that the Guatemalan struggle was a case of domestic insurrection.[46] Yet, there was no insurrection, no significant military defections and no widespread erosion of popular support for Arbenz. The decisive factor was the bombing. The small Guatemalan air force, crippled by inability to break through the U.S. arms embargo (in force since 1948, when social measures affecting United Fruit's privileged position were enacted), was unable to defend against the air offensive. Several villages were leveled and the capital city strafed several times. When antiaircraft artillery brought down a few planes, a meeting of Eisenhower, the Dulles brothers, and other State Department personnel decided to send additional planes, in the face of Assistant Secretary of State Henry Holland's warning that this could expose the illegal U.S. intervention.[47]

Confronted with the threat of continued and expanded bombing of his defenseless country and blocked by his military from distributing arms to local militia forces, Arbenz capitulated to increasing pressures from his military officers that he quit. When his designated successor, army chief Enrique Diaz, refused to arrest and execute Arbenz supporters named by U.S. Ambassador Peurifoy, the Ambassador forced his resignation and imposed his own choice as president of the presumably independent country—Castillo Armas, who had been selected almost a year earlier by the CIA-State Department Group to take over after Arbenz's elimination. The choice was made with the approval of the United Fruit Company.[48]

Perhaps because the McCarthy craze was then at its peak, the U.S. press was marshaled in behalf of the anti-Arbenz campaign to an extraordinary degree. Initially United Fruit undertook the marshaling. In January 1953, Thomas McCann was assigned to a public relations post "related to the expropriation of our lands in Guatemala." His department "had only one task: to get out the word that a Communist beachhead had been established in our hemisphere." By early 1954 the United Fruit campaign, masterminded by Edward L. Bernays, the noted "father of public relations," had created "an atmosphere of deep suspicion and fear" concerning the Guatemalan government.[49]

The State Department and CIA were equally busy in marshaling the press for the camouflaged version of events in Guatemala. Harrison Salisbury, in his "uncompromising look at *The New York Times*" (*Without Fear or Favor*, Times Books, 1980), describes the extraordinary lengths to which the Dulles brothers went to control the news. *Times* correspondent Sidney Gruson was then covering

---

46. Schlesinger and Kinzer, *Bitter Fruit*, pp. 108–17; Cook, *Declassified Eisenhower*, pp. 229, 232, 239, 244–46, 270–71.

47. Schlesinger and Kinzer, *Bitter Fruit*, pp. 22, 104, 111. The story of the actual coup from the "invasion" of Castillo Armas's force of less than two hundred men until Ambassador Peurifoy managed to make him president of Guatemala, is told in Cook, *Declassified Eisenhower*, pp. 279–86; Schlesinger and Kinzer, pp. 192–97, 205–14.

48. Schlesinger and Kinzer, *Bitter Fruit*, pp. 120–22.

49. Thomas McCann, *An American Company*, pp. 41, 44–45; Schlesinger and Kinzer, *Bitter Fruit*, p. 90.

Guatemala. Salisbury observes that as a competent journalist, Gruson knew too much and was too capable of uncovering facts for the Dulles brothers to want him on the scene. Thus, when Gruson left Guatemala temporarily on personal business, the Dulles brothers pressured *Times* publisher Arthur Sulzberger into preventing his return while the coup was launched. They "did not hesitate to employ slanderous and duplicitous means to persuade Sulzberger, . . ." Salisbury declares. The means included vague hints about Gruson's possible associations.[50]

Why the incredible U.S. preoccupation with the Arbenz government? State Department documents reveal an early Eisenhower Administration concern with the "attack" on United Fruit, its rail subsidiary in Guatemala, the U.S.-owned Electric Light and Power Company, as well as with Guatemala's decision to explore for oil exclusively with domestic capital. But other economic and political motives also were present. By 1953 Europe had recovered economically from the war's devastation and, as the Arbenz government maintained, was beginning to compete aggressively in Latin America. The United States feared Guatemala's example of economic independence in the face of this challenge to its virtual monopoly and was thus trying to intimidate the other hemispheric nations.[51]

State Department documents also betray concern for U.S., access to vital raw materials found in Latin America, and a fear that "ultranationalism" presumably fanned by communists would disrupt that access. In 1952 a presidential commission on strategic raw materials—the "Paley Commission"—had located Southeast Asia and Latin America as rich sources of these materials. The Eisenhower Administration had revealed marked sensitivity about Southeast Asia as a source, contributing to its determination to divide Vietnam in two. In 1953 it had subverted Iran's democracy because of oil. And while Guatemala itself was not an important source, Washington feared the impact of its independence on its neighbors.[52]

Politically, Eisenhower's election campaign had pledged a roll-back of communism and the GOP's McCarthyite wing was clamoring for action in that direction. It could not be attempted in Eastern Europe and Guatemala provided a cheap appearance of the pledge's fulfillment. It did not really matter that in fact Guatemala was not communist.[53]

In the essay that won Jeane Kirkpatrick her job as Reagan's ambassador to the UN, she argued that traditional societies are ruled autocratically and often brutally, that there are extremes of wealth and poverty, that the poor are very poor and the rich have no concern for the poor. But these societies will remain undisturbed unless the Russians or Cubans inspire revolution. Hence the United States must oppose any disturbance of the *status quo*.[54]

---

50. Salisbury, *Without Fear or Favor*, pp. 480–82.
51. Cook, *Declassified Eisenhower*, pp. 231, 238, 275–76.
52. *Ibid*, p. 257
53. Schlesinger and Kinzer, *Bitter Fruit*, p. 101.
54. Jeane Kirkpatrick, "Dictatorship and Double-Standards," *Commentary*, Nov. 1979, pp. 34–45.

Guatemala demonstrated the absurdity, indeed sheer hypocrisy, of the Kirkpatrick thesis. No one in her right mind could charge that the 1944 revolution was imposed by Russia—the inspiration came from Roosevelt and the New Deal, and from Cárdenas in Mexico—nor was there any sign of Soviet inspiration in 1954. Castro's Cuba, of course, was not around. And the dreadful poverty currently suffered by Guatemala's peasantry is not a consequence of the *status quo* of traditional society but of its reimposition by the United States in 1954. Kirkpatrick's explicit advocacy of U.S. support for authoritarian rulers who seek to maintain the extremes of wealth and poverty, and to keep the poor very poor, was anticipated by the U.S. in Guatemala. The Reagan Administration of which she is a part is still at it in Guatemala, as elsewhere in Latin America.

—July 1982

11. Whose Intervention in Guatemala, Whose Conspiracy? *

By John E. Peurifoy

READERS *should not take too literally Peurifoy's disclaimer in this speech to a Congressional committee that, as U.S. ambassador to Guatemala, he limited himself to the chaste role of mere "diplomatic observer." According to formerly classified data he was up to his ears in the conspiracy to overthrow the allegedly "communist-controlled" government of Jacobo Arbenz Guzmán, sending a fateful telegram to Secretary of State John Foster Dulles that, according to Stephen Schlesinger and Stephen Kinzer, "rang the death knell on Arbenz's presidency."* [1] *A former elevator operator in the U.S. Senate, Peurifoy rapidly climbed the career ladder in the foreign service, becoming ambassador to Greece during the overthrow of the left and the reintroduction of a monarchy, and serving as ambassador to Thailand after his stint in Guatemala. During the U.S.-backed air attacks on Guatemala City in June 1954, Peurifoy reportedly "cut a dashing figure":*

> Dressed in natty clothes, with a confident smile and a free-wheeling command style, he charmed the press corps. He dropped tidbits of information, confided

* Peurifoy's testimony on October 8, 1954, before the subcommittee on Latin America of the U.S. House of Representatives Select Committee on Communist Aggression, reprinted in U.S. Department of State *Bulletin*, November 8, 1954.

1. Schlesinger and Kinzer, *Bitter Fruit: The Untold Story of the American Coup in Guatemala* (Garden City, N.Y.: Doubleday & Co., 1982), p. 138.

private thoughts to correspondents and drank with reporters at the American Club downtown in the midst of the aerial bombardment. All were struck by his courage; none realized that he knew precisely when the raids were coming and where the bombs or bullets were expected to hit.[2]

The air attacks were the final factor that impelled Arbenz to resign. Once the Guatemalan president who so offended U.S. officials and the United Fruit Company, had been overthrown, the ambassador's wife, Betty Jane Peurifoy, dashed off a bit of doggerel verse to commemorate the event:

Sing a song of quetzals,[3] pockets full of peace!
The junta's in the Palace, they've taken out a lease.
The commies are in hiding, just across the street;
To the embassy of Mexico they beat a quick retreat.
And pistol-packing Peurifoy looks mighty optimistic
For the land of Guatemala is no longer Communistic! [4]

Complete with references to alleged Communist Party control of national institutions, government terror against "anti-communist citizens," party members' trips to the Soviet Union for "training and instruction," instigation of unrest in neighboring countries, an arms shipment from a Soviet bloc country, and the specter of a Soviet beachhead close to U.S. shores threatening "our vital interests and security," Peurifoy's testimony could be easily compared to recent U.S. charges against Nicaragua [5] and the State Department's White Paper on "communist interference" in El Salvador.[6]

. . . BEFORE BEGINNING MY testimony, I would like to take this opportunity to explode a popular and flattering myth regarding the part that I personally played in the revolution led by Colonel Castillo. My role in Guatemala prior to the revolution was strictly that of a diplomatic observer: to inform my Government regarding events there and, when requested to do so, to advise the responsible officials in the Department of State on policy matters concerning Guatemala. The first and only active role that I played in the events last June was to lend my good offices to assist in negotiating the truce between the forces of Colonel Castillo and the military junta that was established in Guatemala after President Arbenz resigned. And even this role, Mr. Chairman, was undertaken only at the

2. Schlesinger and Kinzer, *Bitter Fruit*, p. 186.

3. The quetzal is not only the national bird and symbol of Guatemala, it is the name of Guatemala's currency, which is, significantly, pegged to the dollar.

4. *Time* Magazine, July 26, 1954.

5. See George Black and Judy Butler, "Target Nicaragua," NACLA Report on the Americas (New York) XVI no. 1 Jan-Feb, 1982, p. 6.

6. See Gettleman et al., *El Salvador: Central America in the New Cold War*, readings 35–37.

request of the junta. The revolution that overthrew the Arbenz government was engineered and instigated by those people in Guatemala who rebelled against the policies and ruthless oppression of the Communist-controlled government.

It is my understanding, Mr. Chairman, that the purpose of your hearings is to determine:

1. Whether or not the government of President Arbenz was controlled and dominated by Communists.

2. Whether or not the Communists who dominated Guatemala were in turn directed from the Kremlin.

3. Whether or not the Communists from Guatemala actively intervened in the internal affairs of neighboring Latin American Republics.

4. Whether or not this Communist conspiracy which centered in Guatemala represented a menace to the security of the United States.

My answer to all four of those questions is an unequivocal "yes."

The Arbenz government, beyond any question, was controlled and dominated by Communists. Those Communists were directed from Moscow. The Guatemalan Government and the Communist leaders of that country did continuously and actively intervene in the internal affairs of neighboring countries in an effort to create disorder and overthrow established governments. And the Communist conspiracy in Guatemala did represent a very real and very serious menace to the security of the United States.

And with your permission, Mr. Chairman, I would like to add a fifth point; that menace still continues in Latin America. The Red conspiracy in Latin America has not been completely crushed. The loss of Guatemala represents a serious setback to the Kremlin, not a final defeat. As President Castillo pointed out in a statement before your committee, the democratic forces have merely won the first battle in a long war.

Of course it is true that the seriousness of the threat to our security has been greatly diminished since Colonel Castillo's successful revolution. Nevertheless, as long as this conspiracy is active—and I fear that will be for many years to come—the menace will continue to be a very real one in this hemisphere.

That is the reason why I think your committee is rendering a very substantial service to the American people in holding these hearings. Your committee is alerting the public to the danger to us represented by Moscow's program of aggression in Latin America. As you know, Mr. Chairman, it is exceedingly difficult for our Government to formulate effective policies to combat a situation as serious as this one without the support of a well-informed public. . . .

Communist Control of Arbenz Government

I believe that an incident which occurred shortly before I became Ambassador to Guatemala illustrates conclusively the fact that the government was under the complete domination of the Communists. One of the principal programs of the Communist Party in Guatemala was the agrarian reform, which they used as a weapon to gain political control over the farmworkers and the landless peasants. I understand that an officer of the Department of State may testify before your committee at a later date and will be prepared to give you a more detailed discussion of the agrarian reform law. For the purpose of my testimony, it is sufficient to state that under the agrarian reform law President Arbenz was the final arbiter of any and all disputes concerning the expropriation of land and its redistribution among the peasants. Owners of expropriated land were denied the right of appeals to the courts. Nevertheless, one Guatemalan landowner did appeal. And on February 6, 1953, the Supreme Court of Guatemala rocked the government and particularly the Communist Party by announcing, as a result of a 4-1 vote, that it would hear the landowner's appeal.

The decision was immediately and angrily denounced by the Communists, who charged that it was in violation of that section of the law denying the right of such appeal. Carlos Manuel Pellecer, Victor Manuel Gutiérrez, José Manuel Fortuny, and other Communist leaders demanded that the court be impeached. The next day a resolution was submitted to the Congress by a Communist deputy, was immediately passed, and the entire court was impeached. New judges were quickly appointed, including the one who had voted against granting the hearings, the decision was hastily reconsidered by the new court, and the owner was denied the right of appeal.[8]

Mr. Chairman, I submit to this committee that, when the Communist Party can demand and get the dismissal of a Supreme Court of a country, then the Communist Party, for all practical purposes, controls the government of that country.

This, however, is only one illustration of the degree of control that the Communists exercised over the government of Guatemala during the regimes of Juan José Arévalo and Jacobo Arbenz.

The facts of Communist penetration of the Guatemala Government and of the political, economic, and social life of the nation are well known to your committee. It is hardly necessary for me to recall the salient features—that of the 56 members of the Guatemalan Congress 51 were members of the "national front" supporting Arbenz and dominated by its Communist members; that principal Government agencies in agriculture, social security, propaganda and public information, education, and labor were in the direct hands of the Communist Party; that the labor organization of the country was entirely dominated by Communist-controlled unions affiliated with the Communist Western Hemisphere labor arm, the CTAL, and with the worldwide Soviet labor instrument, the WFTU. In addition, the press, radio, and public forum were increasingly warped

8. For a balanced view of the Guatemalan Agrarian Reform Program of 1952 and its implementation (coming to conclusions at sharp variance with Peurifoy's), see Reading 10; Schlesinger and Kinzer, *Bitter Fruit*, pp. 54–56; and a 1965 report by the Inter-American Agricultural Development Committee of the Organization of American States, reproduced in Eduardo Galeano, *Guatemala: Occupied Country* (New York: Monthly Review Press, 1967), pp. 123–132.—EDS.

into tools of Communist propaganda and relentlessly being closed to anti-Communistic patriotic Guatemalans. The Guatemalan delegates to international organizations such as the United Nations, the Organization of American States, and the numerous regional and functional agencies of international cooperation which have been set up to aid the worldwide cause of peace were mere spokesmen for Soviet aggression and deception.

Part of Kremlin Strategy

This Communist penetration in Guatemala was the most striking example of the Kremlin's strategy in Latin America. Busy with power expansion into Europe and Asia, the Red rulers of Russia have long pushed their conspiracy in Latin America as a diversionary tactic which, while showing no immediate gain of territory under their domination, would at least weaken and harass our defenses. By creating a beachhead within our own zone of vital security, from which sabotage and subversion could be achieved against us and our neighbors, the Kremlin aimed at promoting anarchy within the Western Hemisphere; they aimed at demoralizing this hemisphere by breaking its unity against Communist aggression and throwing the inter-American system into a state of confusion and dispute. They sought to divert Latin American attention from their depredations and crimes in Europe and Asia by pushing forward Spanish-speaking front men who, in native accents, accused the United States of the aggressions and crimes which the Soviet itself was actually performing.

The Communists in Guatemala were working for these Soviet aims under consistent and disciplined Soviet control. This control was exercised directly through the Communist Party itself. Seven of the 11 members of the Party's political committee are known to have visited the Soviet Union, 6 of them having made trips in the past 2 years. José Manuel Fortuny, the Party's Secretary General, took his most recent trip to Moscow from November 5, 1953, to January 12, 1954. The Party's leaders in labor unions, agrarian unions, and teacher unions all visited the Soviet Union in recent times, at least within the past 2 years, as did also leaders of Communist-front organizations such as the youth organization, the women's organization, and the university students' front.

The effectiveness of the training and instruction given to the Guatemalan Communists while in the Soviet Union was immediately manifest in the close integration of the Communist institutions in Guatemala with Soviet policy. No case of Soviet direction was more clear than what occurred after the return of Fortuny last January. A press and propaganda campaign, stirring alarm over resistance of anti-Communists to the Arbenz regime, was immediately cranked up in the endeavor to prepare public opinion for the blow to fall. Then, at the end of January 1954, the dramatic announcement was made of the uncovering of a subversive "plot," with the sinister note of foreign intervention, linking the United States by innuendo as "the country of the North" from which direction and aid were allegedly being furnished the "plotters."

This set the stage for wholesale arrests of anti-Communist citizens and for subsequent imprisonment, torture, and even murder. Many who were later released, beaten and broken, were pushed across the frontiers into Mexico and Honduras by the vicious truncheon-wielding police. These victims of Communist suppression comprised outstanding leaders in the free labor movement, the decent citizenry who did not bow down to a Communist state ruled by Arbenz. Your committee is well aware that these tactics of brutal suppression and terrorization of the opposition are characteristically the last blow of communism in a country outside of the Soviet Union before complete seizure of power. . . .

Threat to Guatemala's Neighbors

The threat of Soviet communism, which is dedicated to expansion, conquest, and ultimate world revolution, was therefore not directed against Guatemala alone but to its peaceful and vulnerable neighbors. The Guatemalan people were the first nation in the hemisphere to suffer Communist control, but others were marked for conquest. The Guatemalan Government, as a tool of Soviet policy, aimed at disruption of the peace of the area by cynically maintaining a sustained campaign to undermine their governments.

Your committee has already heard testimony to the effect that the principal Communists of Central America had received refuge, aid, and comfort in Guatemala. Many of them had even been rewarded with government jobs. These foreign agents of communism were thus able to use Guatemala as a base for their operations against their home countries. They were assisted in their subversive activities by scores of Guatemalan Communists and many Spanish Communists who were given visas to Guatemala during the early years of President Arevalo's regime. The increasing flow of propaganda material and trained agitators from Guatemala into the neighboring countries of El Salvador, Honduras, and Nicaragua became so overt that each of these governments, at various times, found it necessary to close their borders to Guatemalan travelers and to invoke rigid restrictions on all travel. . . .

One of the most blatant examples of intervention by Guatemalan Communists in the affairs of neighboring republics was the strike which paralyzed Honduras for 8 weeks last spring. The success of their efforts came to startled public attention on May 1, 1954, when a general strike broke out in the northern area of the country and continued for a period of 8 weeks. There had been no previous labor disturbances in Honduras, no negotiations for contracts pending, and no rejections of workers' petitions. The duration of the strike would have been impossible without substantial help from abroad.

There is ample evidence that the strike was planned, instigated, and directed from Guatemala and was undoubtedly intended to unseat the Honduran Government. Help to the strikers was channeled through Guatemala and consisted not only of guidance and instructions but surely of the material aid publicly promised by the Communist-dominated Guatemalan National Federation of Labor, for a minimum calculation of the cost of the strike, involving as many as 44,000 workers over a period up to 8 weeks, would indicate it to be not less than three-quarters of a million dollars. No such sums of money were ever collected among the strikers in Honduras and could only have come from a foreign power. The Honduran Government, which had seized a Guatemalan military plane which flew into the northern area of the country without authorization a month before the strike, found reason to expel three Guatemalan honorary consuls who had been appointed to small towns in the strike zone only a few months before. The damage to the economy of Honduras was very considerable and was clearly a part of the Communist plan to disrupt Central America.

Arms Shipment in May 1954

The jars and jolts to Guatemala's neighbors in Central America through strikes, political agitation, and subversion were evidences of the growing Communist threat, but it was during the critical period of the spring of 1954 that the Soviet made its big stab to solidify its strength in Guatemala. This was the shipment of arms on the S.S. *Alfhem*, which came into Puerto Barrios on May 15, 1954. The cargo manifest was fraudulent, listing as glassware and laboratory equipment some 2,000 tons of modern arms for the Arbenz government, packed in more than 15,000 cases. The cargo, which was of Czech origin, had left the Communist port of Stettin, Poland, about 3 weeks before and pursued a zigzag course across the Atlantic, giving false destinations three times en route.

The Guatemalan armed forces were not without arms, and their numbers were already at least equal and probably superior to the total armed forces of the three immediate neighbors, El Salvador, Honduras, and Nicaragua. The Soviet primarily intended to drive a wedge into the middle of this continent. The four Central American Governments, Honduras, El Salvador, Nicaragua, and Costa Rica, all communicated to the Department of State their request for joint measures against the introduction of further armed force into the area. Our Government was moving rapidly to present this threat to all members of the Organization of American States, for action by the inter-American system, when the movement by Col. Castillo Armas in late June 1954 overthrew the Communist government which had acquired the arms.[9]

How thoroughly the Arbenz government was following the dictates of the

9. In a fascinating account of the "secret voyage of the *Alfhem*," the historians Schlesinger and Kinzer mention that the United States had imposed an embargo on arms shipments to Guatemala as early as 1948 (apparently in response to a Guatemalan law passed at the time threatening the power of foreign corporations in the country). The arms shipment to Guatemala included worthless antitank guns (no Central American government had tanks) and artillery built to move on modern highways, which did not exist in Guatemala. Many of the small arms were unworkable. (*Bitter Fruit*, Chap. 10, esp. p. 152.) In any case, Castillo Armas did not return the material when he took power, despite its Communist manufacture.—EDS.

Soviet Union was clearly shown during this crisis in the incident of the nonaggression pacts. At a moment when the alarm of Guatemala's neighbors was highest over the *Alfhem* shipment, the Guatemalan Foreign Minister ostentatiously sent cables to the Governments of Honduras and El Salvador, protesting friendship and offering to sign treaties of nonaggression with them. The very term used, "nonaggression pact," was a giveaway of the inspiration whence this maneuver came. It is a Soviet term, unfamiliar to Central American diplomacy and almost unheard of in the relations of our hemisphere, which has a long and honored history of peaceful settlement of disputes by the machinery set up in our inter-American system. The nonaggression pact idea has repeatedly been used as a tactic of deception. Indeed, if we could write an accurate dictionary definition of the term "nonaggression pact," it would be "(a) Agreement between Stalin and Hitler on August 23, 1939, just before outbreak of World War II which paved way for Nazi attack and was later used to conceal preparation for war between Russia and Germany; (b) Any similar agreement, apparently for peaceful purposes but concealing intent to make war." Guatemala's smaller neighbors were not deceived and rejected the invitation, reminding the Guatemalan Government that no need for such a pact exists between peace-loving neighbors. Indeed, Honduras invited Guatemala to show its peaceful purposes by ceasing to support the strike in northern Honduras.

The Guatemalan Communists also planned high-level infiltration of all Central America, but in this adventure their plans were too ambitious and failed. . . .

Threat to U.S. Security

I need hardly refer to the menace of this Soviet attempt to win Central America as aimed at our own vital interests and security; this is self-evident, for geography alone supplies the reason. Central America lies almost at our southern borders, no more than 3 hours' flying time by modern warplanes from the Gulf ports and even nearer to our greatest strategic installation anywhere in the world, the Panama Canal. If any part of this area should fall under Soviet power, it would shake the foundations of our defenses. The Soviets know that. They were willing to pay a very high price in funds, manpower, organization, propaganda, and subversive skills to gain a base in Guatemala. And we know that the hard-headed, practical men of the Kremlin dedicate their best efforts on objectives which strike closest to the United States. For if we should weaken and succumb, the road would lie open to their domination of the whole world.

Thus, the struggle of the Guatemalan people to throw off the Communist control was as much a struggle for the safety of Guatemala's neighbors, and ourselves, as it was to regain their own liberties.

In conclusion, Mr. Chairman, let me state that the menace of communism in Guatemala was courageously fought by the Guatemalan people themselves, always against the superior odds which a police state has over the decent, patriotic citizen. Communist power was broken by the Guatemalans alone, and their deeds of heroic sacrifice deserve and will always receive the admiration and applause of our own people. They fought the battle which is the common battle of all free nations against Communist oppression, and they won the victory themselves.

President Eisenhower and Secretary Dulles have both publicly pledged our support to the new Government of Col. Castillo Armas [10] and our aid to the Guatemalan people. It is my earnest hope and confidence that all feasible means to extend this aid will be promptly developed, so that Guatemala may resume its place as a prosperous and progressive member in the family of free nations.

12. *The Kremlin Out to Destroy the Inter-American System* *

BY JOHN FOSTER DULLES

FORMER *President Eisenhower's Secretary of State John Foster Dulles expresses here the semiofficial North American view of communism in conflict with the American way of life. In the words of historian Stephen Ambrose, Dulles was a*

> devout Christian, highly successful corporate lawyer, something of a prig, and absolutely certain of his own and his nation's goodness. . . . All the world wanted to be like the United States of America; the common people everywhere looked to America for leadership; Communism was unmitigated evil imposed by a conspiracy on helpless people; . . . there could be no permanent reconciliation with Communism because "this an irreconcilable conflict." [1]

These ideological principles played a major role in guiding Dulles's policies toward Guatemala in 1953–54, but another factor was the Secretary's close links to the U.S. business firm most directly affected by government policies in Guatemala, the United Fruit Company (see Reading 10). Recent studies strongly sug-

---

10. Castillo Armas was assassinated in 1957, possibly by gangsters employed by the Dominican dictator, Rafael Trujillo. Peurifoy died in a car crash in Thailand, his next diplomatic assignment, in 1955. Arbenz lived in exile until his death in 1971. (Schlesinger and Kinzer, *Bitter Fruit*, Chap. 15.)—EDS.

* Excerpts from the text of a radio and TV address, in U.S. Department of State, *American Foreign Policy, 1950–1955, Basic Documents* (Washington, D.C.: U.S. Government Printing Office, 1957), Vol. I, pp. 1311–1315.

1. Stephen E. Ambrose, *Rise to Globalism: American Foreign Policy, 1938–1980*, Rev. ed. (Baltimore: Penguin Books, 1980), pp. 188–189.

gest the determinative role of United Fruit in engineering the overthrow of the Arbenz government in 1954,[2] a point Dulles was at great pains to discount at the time.

TONIGHT I SHOULD like to talk with you about Guatemala. It is the scene of dramatic events. They expose the evil purpose of the Kremlin to destroy the inter-American system, and they test the ability of the American States to maintain the peaceful integrity of this hemisphere.

For several years international communism has been probing here and there for nesting places in the Americas. It finally chose Guatemala as a spot which it could turn into an official base from which to breed subversion which would extend to other American Republics.

This intrusion of Soviet despotism was, of course, a direct challenge to our Monroe Doctrine, the first and most fundamental of our foreign policies. . . .

In Guatemala, international communism had an initial success. It began 10 years ago, when a revolution occurred in Guatemala. The revolution was not without justification. But the Communists seized on it, not as an opportunity for real reforms, but as a chance to gain political power.

Communist agitators devoted themselves to infiltrating the public and private organizations of Guatemala. They sent recruits to Russia and other Communist countries for revolutionary training and indoctrination in such institutions as the Lenin School at Moscow. Operating in the guise of "reformers" they organized the workers and peasants under Communist leadership. Having gained control of what they call "mass organizations," they moved on to take over the official press and radio of the Guatemalan Government. They dominated the social security organization and ran the agrarian reform program. Through the technique of the "popular front" they dictated to the Congress and the President.

The judiciary made one valiant attempt to protect its integrity and independence. But the Communists, using their control of the legislative body, caused the Supreme Court to be dissolved when it refused to give approval to a Communist-contrived law. [Jacobo Guzmán] Arbenz, who until this week was President of Guatemala, was openly manipulated by the leaders of communism. . . .

If world communism captures any American State, however small, a new and perilous front is established which will increase the danger to the entire free world and require even greater sacrifices from the American people.

This situation in Guatemala had become so dangerous that the American States could not ignore it. At Caracas last March the American States held their Tenth Inter-American Conference. They then adopted a momentous statement. They declared that "the domination or control of the political institutions of any American State by the international Communist movement . . . would constitute

2. See the listing of these books, many of them making use of formerly secret documents, p. 45, note 1.

a threat to the sovereignty and political independence of the American States, endangering the peace of America."

There was only one American State that voted against this declaration. That State was Guatemala.

This Caracas declaration precipitated a dramatic chain of events.[3] From their European base the Communist leaders moved rapidly to build up the military power of their agents in Guatemala. In May a large shipment of arms moved from behind the Iron Curtain into Guatemala. The shipment was sought to be secreted by false manifests and false clearances. Its ostensible destination was changed three times while en route. . . .

In the face of these events and in accordance with the spirit of the Caracas declaration, the nations of this hemisphere laid further plans to grapple with the danger. The Arbenz government responded with an effort to disrupt the inter-American system. Because it enjoyed the full support of Soviet Russia, which is on the Security Council, it tried to bring the matter before the Security Council. It did so without first referring the matter to the American regional organization as is called for both by the United Nations Charter itself and by the treaty creating the American organization.

The Foreign Minister of Guatemala openly connived in this matter with the Foreign Minister of the Soviet Union. . . . The Security Council at first voted overwhelmingly to refer the Guatemala matter to the Organization of American States. The vote was 10 to 1. But that one negative vote was a Soviet veto.

Then the Guatemalan Government, with Soviet backing, redoubled its efforts to supplant the American States system by Security Council jurisdiction. However, last Friday, the United Nations Security Council decided not to take up the Guatemalan matter but to leave it in the first instance to the American States themselves. . . .

Throughout the period I have outlined, the Guatemalan Government and Communist agents throughout the world have persistently attempted to obscure the real issue—that of Communist imperialism—by claiming that the United States is only interested in protecting American business. We regret that there have been disputes between the Guatemalan Government and the United Fruit Company. We have urged repeatedly that these disputes be submitted for settlement to an international tribunal or to international arbitration. That is the way to dispose of problems of this sort. But this issue is relatively unimportant. All who know the temper of the U.S. people and Government must realize that our overriding concern is that which, with others, we recorded at Caracas, namely, the

---

3. Dulles himself introduced the resolution in Caracas, the purpose of which was "to condemn Guatemala without actually mentioning its name, as well as put in place the juridical authority with which to defend Operation Success, code name for the CIA-arranged coup against the Arbenz government in the face of anticipated protests." Stephen Schlesinger and Stephen Kinzer, *Bitter Fruit: The Untold Story of the American Coup in Guatemala* (Garden City, N.Y.: Doubleday & Co., 1982), p. 143.—EDS.

endangering by international communism of the peace and security of this hemisphere.

The people of Guatemala have now been heard from. Despite the armaments piled up by the Arbenz government, it was unable to enlist the spiritual cooperation of the people.

Led by Colonel Castillo Armas, patriots arose in Guatemala to challenge the Communist leadership—and to change it. Thus, the situation is being cured by the Guatemalans themselves.

Last Sunday, President Arbenz of Guatemala resigned and seeks asylum. Others are following his example. . . .

The events of recent months and days add a new and glorious chapter to the already great tradition of the American States. . . .

In conclusion, let me assure the people of Guatemala. As peace and freedom are restored to that sister Republic, the Government of the United States will continue to support the just aspirations of the Guatemalan people. A prosperous and progressive Guatemala is vital to a healthy hemisphere. The United States pledges itself not merely to political opposition to communism but to help to alleviate conditions in Guatemala and elsewhere which might afford communism an opportunity to spread its tentacles throughout the hemisphere. Thus we shall seek in positive ways to make our Americas an example which will inspire men everywhere.[4]

---

4. One of the persons "inspired" by the events in Guatemala, although not in the sense implied by Dulles, was an Argentinian physician, Ernesto [Che] Guevara, who was living in Guatemala at the time, and who later joined Fidel Castro's guerrilla war against the U.S.-backed Cuban dictator, Batista. "It was Guatemala," wrote Guevara's first wife, "which finally convinced him of the necessity for armed struggle. . . ." (Quoted in Schlesinger and Kinzer, *Bitter Fruit*, p. 184).—EDS.

Part Two:

THE COUNTER-REVOLUTION TAKES HOLD

Advertisement on road near Guatemala City. *Photo credit: Susan Meiselas*

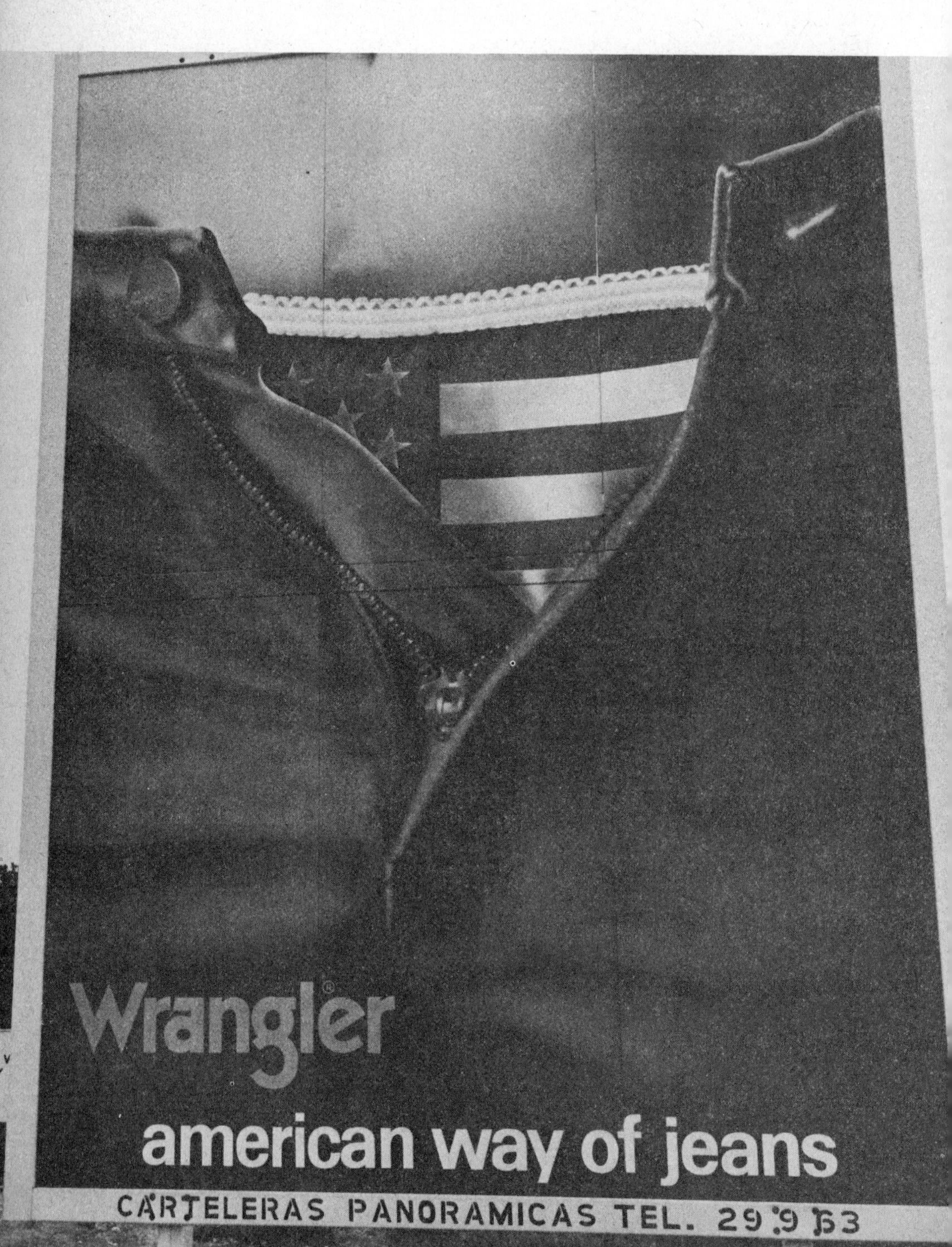

EDITORS' INTRODUCTION

TO members of Guatemala's conservative military hierarchy and their compatriots in the economic sphere, the 1944–54 experiment in democracy was but an aberration, and the coup a victory over dangerous radicals. After the coup against Arbenz they began putting the pieces back together again, guided and encouraged by the United States. A counterrevolutionary model of government was created, based on the exclusion of the democratic elements that had held power briefly in the early 1950s. While conflicts among the groups that remained and could compete for power certainly gave the new cycle of governments its own distinct expression, the design of the model bears the stamp of U.S. government strategists from the State Department, the Agency for International Development, and the Military Assistance Advisory Group. The elements of that model, also introduced elsewhere in Latin America in the 1960s, are an economy dependent on imports from the United States; a government tightly controlled by the military; a security apparatus inspired by U.S. counterinsurgency specialists; and over this, the rhetoric, but emphatically not the practice, of democracy.[1]

After World War II, U.S. businesses were exploring cheap, profitable methods of production, and Guatemala, after 1954, offered a secure investment opportunity. U.S. companies opened factories in Guatemala, forming partnerships with the few Guatemalan business and military figures already engaged in commerce or

1. Many writers have discussed this model imposed by the United States in Latin America in the 1960s. See North American Congress on Latin America, *Guatemala* (New York: NACLA, 1974); Gary MacEoin, *Revolution Next Door* (New York: Holt, Rinehart and Winston, 1971). The details of a U.S. police training program in Brazil and Uruguay in the 1960s are vividly portrayed in A. J. Langguth, *Hidden Terrors* (New York: Pantheon Books, 1978).

agricultural production.[2] The Central American Common Market (CACM), created under U.S. guidance, aimed at supplying an expanded outlet for goods produced locally with U.S. capital. By the mid-1960s, Guatemala was the major producer of goods within the CACM, as well as the Central American country with the most U.S.-financed industries. Foreign aid, as David Tobis shows, was channeled into building an infrastructure to support these industries (see Reading 14).

The Alliance for Progress, President Kennedy's attempt to head off another Cuban revolution in Latin America by developing "peaceful change," [3] was a three-pronged approach to development: social, economic, and military. As Ronald Steel points out, the Alliance for Progress failed to make social reforms because "Washington's fear of communism was even greater than its desire for reforms. . . . Within four years after the Alianza was launched at Punte del Este, civilian governments were toppled in no less than seven countries: the Dominican Republic (twice), Guatemala, Ecuador, Bolivia, Argentina, Peru, and Brazil." [4]

Many of the Alliance for Progress development projects increased social stratification in small villages and shifted production from satisfying basic local needs to satisfying the needs of the world market. Dependency on foreign goods, such as fertilizer, encouraged indebtedness to U.S. lending agencies (for similar types of problems in a post-Alliance development project, see Reading 15). Mounting loans, repaid with interest, siphoned profits from the receiving countries' gross national products. The effects of the Alliance for Progress in Guatemala were not unlike those in Colombia where the Director of Agriculture commented, "What we actually did was to mortgage the country in order to save a ruling class that was headed for disaster." [5]

Under the Alliance for Progress, U.S. government officials also came into Guatemala with their plan to use Guatemala as a component of their foreign policy initiative in the Caribbean and Central America. The Central Intelligence Agency (CIA) surfaced in Guatemala again in 1960 where Cuban exiles and mercenaries were trained at the farm of large landholder Roberto Alejos Arzú for the Bay of Pigs invasion against Cuba.[6] By 1965 legal experts were advising Guatemalan officials on how to draw up a new constitution, based on the U.S. model. Foreign policy experts in President Johnson's State Department attempted to establish the facade of democracy in Guatemala and applied heavy pressure on

---

2. For an excellent analysis of the economic development of this period, see Suzanne Jonas, "Guatemala: Land of Eternal Struggle," in Ronald H. Chilcote, and Joel C. Edelstein, eds., *Latin America: The Struggle with Dependency and Beyond* (New York: John Wiley & Sons, 1974) pp. 169–215.

3. See Richard J. Walton, *Cold War and Counterrevolution: The Foreign Policy of John F. Kennedy* (New York: Viking Press, 1972).

4. Ronald Steel, *Pax Americana* (New York: Viking Press, 1968), p. 218.

5. Gary MacEoin, *Revolution Next Door*, p. 90.

6. See David Wise and Thomas B. Ross, *The Invisible Government* (New York: Bantam, 1964), pp. 22–52.

the military to accept civilian candidate Julio César Méndez Montenegro as president in the 1966 elections.[7]

The military was reluctant to share power with people outside its private circles. Professionalized by U.S. counterinsurgency experts in the 1960s,[8] the military was empowered to suppress the emerging revolutionary organizations, some of which had sprung out of an aborted coup attempt by young army officers in 1960. Under government sanction bands of civilian vigilantes and death squads roamed streets and countryside, killing suspected subversives (see Reading 24). Rather than responding positively to the popular dissastisfaction which fed the guerrilla movement of the 1960s, the military alienated increasingly larger segments of the general population. As unrest spread, the military government instituted a complex network of control based on the intimidation and assassination of opponents. A cycle of repression emerged: the military, in pursuit of its own goals, touched off more unrest.

By 1970 the military had dispensed with civilian figureheads within the Guatemalan government and its leaders began to expand into the commercial sector, often in competition with independent business interests within the country (see Reading 18). During the presidency of General Carlos Arana Osorio (1970–74), the military began to buy up private companies and to establish its own independent economic base, such as the Bank of the Army. The military's increasing incursion into the economy reached unprecedented heights under the government of General Romeo Lucas García (1978–82). Personally, and through his cousins, members of the García Granados family, Lucas amassed a fortune. He acquired, probably illegally, thousands of acres in the Northern Transversal region and promoted the construction of a road passing his estate that was underwritten by public debts to international lending agencies (see Reading 18). By the end of his term credit was monopolized by the public sector to pay for projects whose inflated budgets included enormous profits for public administrators. Lack of credit for private enterprise and the corruption of Lucas and those closely related to him provoked opposition among generals and party leaders who plotted the successful overthrow of Lucas and his successor, General Angel Aníbal Guevara, in March 1982 (see Reading 22).

The United States continued to support and arm this "model" government through much of the 1970s, ignoring the gross manipulation of power by Guatemala's leaders. In 1977 human rights issues, raised by Jimmy Carter, resulted in a freeze on arms sales to Guatemala. When Reagan won the presidency the outlook for renewed relations between the two countries improved. Quickly dissociating himself from Carter's human rights initiative, Reagan reintroduced the strategies

---

7. See Stephen Kinzer and Stephen Schlesinger, *Bitter Fruit: The Untold Story of the American Coup in Guatemala* (Garden City, N.Y.: Doubleday & Co., 1982), Chapter 15.

8. It has been estimated that twenty-eight U.S. soldiers had been killed in Guatemala as of January, 1967. See John Gerassi, "Violence, Revolution and Structural Change in Latin America," in Irving Horowitz et al., eds. *Latin American Radicalism* (New York: Random House, 1969), p. 491.

and rhetoric of the 1950s, the ideology of an era which created the present Guatemalan government. With the installation of General Ríos Montt in the presidency in March 1982, the U.S. State Department argues that Guatemala has broken with its infamous past and pushes for renewed aid to the Guatemalan government, a model counterrevolutionary government.

Chapter I:

A Fertile Investment Opportunity

Editors' Introduction

I spent 33 years and 4 months in active service as a member of our country's most agile military force—the Marine Corps. I served in all commissioned ranks from a second lieutenant to Major-General. And during that period I spent most of my time being a high-class muscle man for Big Business, for Wall Street and for the bankers. In short, I was a racketeer for Capitalism. . . .

Thus I helped make Mexico . . . safe for American oil interests in 1914. I helped make Haiti and Cuba a decent place for the National City Bank boys to collect revenues in. . . . I helped purify Nicaragua for the international banking house of Brown Brothers in 1909–12. I brought light to the Dominican Republic for American sugar interests in 1916. I helped make Honduras "right" for American fruit companies in 1903. In China in 1927 I helped see to it that Standard Oil went its way unmolested.

During those years, I had, as the boys in the back room would say, a swell racket. I was rewarded with honors, medals, promotion. Looking back on it, I feel I might have given Al Capone a few hints. The best he could do was to operate his racket in three city districts. We . . . operated on three continents.

—U.S. Major General Smedley D. Butler, *Common Sense,* 1935

HAD Major Smedley Butler remained in service he might easily have stopped off in Guatemala when the CIA intervened to protect the interests of the United Fruit Company in 1954. Since that time Guatemala has attracted more U.S. corporations than any other Central American country. In the late 1950s, the

1960s, and 70s, U.S. investment expanded from agriculture to manufacturing textiles and chemicals, food processing, mining, oil, and tourism.

A recent brochure describes Guatemala's investment advantages:

> Just two and a half hours from New Orleans, in the heart of Central America, a new American frontier has been opened. Both aggressive multinational corporations and lone entrepreneurs have discerned the path of progress into the future and discovered that it leads to Guatemala. In the vernacular of the early frontiersman, the country is "busting wide open." There are excellent reasons why Guatemala is the most highly-favored site for new investment right now—political and economic stability, resources, modern support facilities.[1]

The reality behind this "vernacular of the early frontiersman" is that Guatemala became a "most highly-favored site" because it yields high profits: wages have been kept low, unions are continually attacked, and materials are relatively cheap. What has been good for U.S. investors has been disastrous for Guatemalans. After years of U.S. investment, this "new American frontier" has a per capita income of $800 a year, with a few earning far more and many earning far less, and an unemployment rate of 20 percent with an additional 50 percent underemployed. Life expectancy is 53.2 years, 82 percent of the children under 5 years of age suffer malnutrition and 20 out of 100 die before they are 4 years old.[2] The Nutrition Institute of Central America and Panama has predicted massive starvation in the countryside; in the cities hundreds of thousands live in tiny shacks without portable water, electricity, or sewage. Not only are most people poor, but they have been getting poorer and poorer since the 1960s. The United Nations has established that a person needs a minimum of 2,236 calories daily; in Guatemala, 42 percent of the population consumed less than 2,236 calories in 1965, 70 percent in 1975 and 80 percent in 1980.

Despite the fact that the statistical data reveal a deeply flawed economy, the government in Guatemala City issues optimistic and hopeful plans and projections. For example, its 1980 *Social Action Plan* projects an efficient, humane policy package under which a whole range of housing, nutritional, and medical needs of the impoverished groups in Guatemala would be adequately met. But as the director of Social Planning admitted after publication of the plan, the government lacked the resources to carry out even a small portion of the proposed programs.[3] It would be more accurate, however, to say that the government and

---

1. National Export Promotion Centre of Guatemala (Guatexpro), *Make the Right Investment: Get to Know Guatemala* [Guatexpro, Guatemala City, 1979] p. i.

2. Consejo Nacional de Planificación Económica PASO: 1980 Plan de Acción Social (Guatemala, 1980), pp. 16–19.

3. Interview conducted by Nancy Peckenham with Edgardo Castañeda, Guatemala City, August 1980. Considered a liberal within the Lucas administration, Castañeda was assassinated several months later.

military leaders diverted these resources to finance their own personal projects and schemes (see Reading 16).

The subject of this chapter is the impact of U.S. aid and investment on the Guatemalan economy since 1954. The readings include an interview with U.S. businessman and long-time Guatemalan resident Fred Sherwood, who voices a strong pro-private enterprise and anticommunist perspective. Several other articles analyze U.S. capital as a conservative force which has intensified inequality and poverty (see Readings 14, 15, 16, 17).

13. *To Defend Our Way of Life: An Interview with a U.S. Businessman* *

BY ALLAN NAIRN

FRED Sherwood is one of hundreds of U.S. businessmen who operate in Guatemala. As an ex-president of the American Chamber of Commerce in Guatemala, Sherwood is considered a leading spokesperson for the North American business community and has been frequently interviewed by journalists, appearing on a CBS Report *in March 1982. In 1954 he flew with the CIA-backed air force supporting Castillo Armas and since then his investments in Guatemala expanded with the nationwide development of a policy encouraging foreign corporations to set up business in the country. The complicity of U.S. businessmen with the Guatemalan government's program of intimidation of labor leaders is firmly tied into their mutual defense of the economic status quo. A North American colleague of Sherwood explains why change threatens business: "[A businessman] would expect at least 30, 35 percent at* least, *return on equity." How does one respond to a bothersome labor leader? "Shoot him or eliminate him. Assassinate him. Murder him. Whichever word is most applicable."*[1] *In the following interview Sherwood elaborates on his approach to doing business in Guatemala.*

Sherwood: I've been down here for thirty-five years. First I was with intelligence with the Air Force here. I'm a commie hater. I don't want any part of communism. And that's what we have here. Don't get it mixed up with labor. Labor we handle. But the commies don't want to settle

* Excerpts from Nairn's interview with Fred Sherwood (Guatemala City, September 1980), by permission.

1. From Nairn's interview with another businessman who requested anonymity.

anything. And I just had it in our own factory and I'm not talking about theory or anything else. I've got 350 [workers] and I saw the commies try to take it over. I'm not talking about labor. We had no labor problems. They came in and, organizing from the outside, they hit us like a ton of bricks. . . . It was done to other factories, [like] this Coca-Cola plant. [See Reading 29—EDS.] It's commies! They talk about labor leaders, labor leaders. Sure they were labor leaders but they were commie labor leaders. Just like in my place. They came in and they fell on us and, honest to God, we were all on our knees. They came in on a Sunday. They got about fourteen of our workers. And they had it all organized. They met on Sunday. Sunday late, Sunday night.

Q: They called the workers together?

Sherwood: Well, just fourteen of them. And the workers were not to blame. They're just poor dumb guys that they got together [and] convinced. And they said, "We're going to make a demand of seven dollars a day." That is the point of the commies. They make economic demands which they *know* cannot be met. And then when it's refused they say, "Well, they won't give you this." They know themselves they can't be met. . . . It seems like their goal is to disrupt the economy by any means they can. In April, right in the middle of the sugar crop they put up roadblocks and they burned cane trucks and they put up blockages in front of the sugar mills, and that sort of thing. And it wasn't so much to demand, it was just to disrupt. The president is a very strong man and extremely anticommunist and he immediately called all the sugar cane in, put a minimum wage down. They were paid by the ton. They were very happy with it. The workers were not unhappy. The commies came in and made them unhappy. . . .

Q: The State Department says that the government hasn't been doing enough to deal with the death squads. Do you think that's reasonable?

Sherwood: Hell no. Why should we do anything about the death squads? They're bumping off the commies, our enemies. I'd give them more power. Hell, I'd give them some cartridges if I could, and everyone else would, too. They're bumping off our enemies, which are also the enemies of the United States. Why should we criticize them?

Q: Do all the U.S. businessmen feel the same way?

Sherwood: Of course, they do. After all, they're trying to do business. The commies are trying to stop them from doing business. That's all in the world the commies want to do. They want to stop the economic growth. Because, you know, the commies are very well organized. But they can't do anything unless [people are unhappy]. Somebody with a full stomach and a job is not gonna risk his life in a revolt.

You've *got to* get hungry and you've got to get to the point where you're not afraid to die. You'd rather die than go on living. Then you're going to have a revolution. And in order to do that they've got to break the economy. And that's exactly their goal. Why the hell should we criticize the death squad or whatever you want to call it? Christ, I'm all for it.

Q: I get the feeling that . . .

Sherwood: It's a hell of a violence going around. No one approves of violence. I don't. I'm not for it. But if it's a question of them or me, I'd rather it be them. . . . We grew up on the basis of private enterprise. Private ownership of capital. Yet our Ambassador, on instructions from Carter, went down [to El Salvador], "Goddamnit, you divide up that farm. Your farm, boy, now you got too big a farm." . . . It's nothing secret. Redistribution of property, nationalized. He pushed for the nationalization of the bank. Now how the hell would you feel if all foreign banks were nationalized? . . . Here they've given up all this land. But these peasants, they don't know how to run something. Really, I'm not downbeating them, but they don't. They're dumb, damn savages. And when you give them fifty acres, well, they don't know how to do it. And no one around there is going to show them. . . . How the hell, what do you think would happen if we went down to the King Ranch in Texas and said, "Goddamnit, we're going to divide up your farm and give it to your cowboys?" And that's exactly what we did in Salvador. . . .

Q: What was Laugerud [President from 1974–78] like?

Sherwood: You know, I sat with him for six hours in Miami over a bar in a private home. This was about—well, damn near a year before they elected him. He had just decided to run. . . . And he told me, he said, you know, "Arana got all the credit, but I'm the guy who pulled the trigger."

Q: On what?

Sherwood: On these guerrillas we had here. This was in the late sixties. And that was when this guy Montenegro was president. Although he was very anticommunist, he was just approaching it in a very, say, a Carter manner, you know, legally and all that. . . . But, you know, they had a guy who defected from the guerrillas. It was very funny. And they called him the man with the green hood. Now, I met him one time and he scared the hell out of me. (Laughs)

Q: He was wearing a green hood?

Sherwood: He was down the highway. They had a blockade. They did this every once in a while. And this guy, of course, knew every one of these guerrillas. And he had this green hood. All you saw were two eyes and a mouth. The grin, you see. And they stopped me and said, "Get out of the car." And I got out and this guy comes over and (laughs) he said the other guys, when they get them, they shoot 'em right there.

Q: Right there in the . . .

Sherwood: They kill them. And I tell you, it cured them. . . . Most writers and congressmen, when they come down they're looking at the situation with the eyes of an American, you know. They used to come down and say, "Oh, the poor Indian." But shit, I wonder how many of them ever been down in the ghetto in New York, or in Washington, to see how the people live down there? They think poverty only exists outside the United States. They forget that the United States has had two hundred years to develop into the country we are. To develop a democracy. These countries aren't ready for democracy. They can't handle that. Believe me, I used to be just like the rest of Americans. I think democracy is really good and everybody should have a vote and all that. But when you think that 60 percent of the people here can't read, they're not interested, and they don't want to know anything about democracy.

What is really good and effective here is to have a real good, strong president who says, "Goddamnit, do this." And there's really nothing wrong with it. . . . Take Somoza. I knew Somoza and his father very well, and, Christ, Nicaragua prospered all the time they were in power. You can say anything you want about him—I don't approve of him but, nevertheless, Nicaragua prospered. He was a son-of-a-bitch but he'd do anything the United States asked him. I'll never forget the old man one time, his father, we were sitting having a drink and he said, "You know, it doesn't mean a goddamn whether I like the United States or if I hate them." And he says, "You tell me tomorrow, 'Tacho, kill all the communists.' And I'd go out and kill them." (Laughs) He was a mighty practical man.

14. The Alliance for Progress: Development Program for the United States *

BY DAVID TOBIS

THE following piece, written in 1967, reviews several years of Alliance for Progress development: the U.S. Agency for International Development proj-

* Reprinted from *Monthly Review* [New York], January 1968, by permission.

ects it funded, its relation with the Central American Common Market, and U.S. private investment as well as the Alliance's contribution to the militarization of the Guatemalan state. The author, David Tobis, was a major contributor to Guatemala, *a landmark study published in 1974 by the North American Congress on Latin America.*

AT ONE TIME Guatemala was called a "Banana Republic." The United Fruit Company owned the only railroad, the only public telegraph system, Puerto Barrios (the only Atlantic sea port), and 460,000 acres of arable land in the country. But today the situation is very different. The railroad and port have been sold to another United States company, the telegraph system is now owned nationally, and most of the Fruit Company's land has been sold. Criticism can no longer be leveled against one "imperialistic" foreign company.

Today there are many foreign investors in Guatemala. Conditions in the country have been made favorable for these investors. There are no transfer restrictions of any kind on foreign-owned assets, dividends, and interest. There is no fixed amount of profit which must be re-invested in industry. The industrial laws of 1952, which gave preferential treatment to domestic capital over foreign capital, were repealed in 1959. Today new foreign industries are exempt for ten years from payment of duties on imports of construction materials, factory machinery and equipment, raw materials, and automotive vehicles for industrial use. These industries receive exemption from payment of taxes for five years and a 50 percent reduction of taxes for the following five years.

The United Fruit Company no longer controls all the foreign investment in Guatemala. But 92 percent of the $117 million of foreign investment still comes from the United States; and three United States companies, IRCA (International Railroad of Central America), Empresa Eléctrica, and United Fruit Company (UFC) own 43 percent of the total.

In addition to what United States companies already have invested in Guatemala, International Nickel is beginning a mining project in the eastern part of the country. In a few years the investment will be $60 to $80 million. This will be the largest single investment in Guatemala. The nickel, however, will not be processed in the country and therefore will not lead to earnings for Guatemala but only for the North American company.

One of the basic problems of United States manufacturing investment in Guatemala is that it has gone exclusively into the production of consumer goods, luxury items, and only to the assembly of durable goods. This type of investment does not lead to the industrialization of the country but merely provides the means for distributing North American products.

To perpetuate the favorable position the United States has as the principal foreign investor in Guatemala, an elaborate system of loans, called "aid," has been developed. The United States Agency for International Development (USAID) loans money to Guatemala for industrial development. The requirements for receiving loans are few. The industries which are eligible are: (1) those which are not in competition with products from United States companies, and (2) those which will increase the sales of products imported from the United States. In addition, if a Guatemalan industry can be developed which will stop the import of a foreign product, other than from the United States, that industry can receive a loan.

Besides making loans to Guatemalan industries, the United States foreign "aid" program also makes loans to United States companies to invest in underdeveloped countries. As reported by USAID, Washington "will finance up to 50 percent of the cost of pre-investment surveys undertaken by United States investors." The government also provides as part of foreign aid a program of investment guarantees for United States companies abroad. The aggregate of such loans is well over $2 billion.

The trade relations of Guatemala with the United States have also been detrimental to the development of the country. In 1964 Guatemala imported $38 million more than it exported, and $36 million of this unfavorable balance was with the United States. It is interesting to note that from 1947 to the present there have only been three years when Guatemala has had a favorable balance of trade—from 1952 to 1954, the years when Jacobo Arbenz was the President of Guatemala. It was, of course, the reformist Arbenz government which was overthrown in 1954 by the joint effort of the CIA and the United Fruit Company.

In an attempt to diversify the international markets with which Guatemala trades, the Central American Common Market (CACM) has been developed and is now being promoted by the United States aid program. The basic problem with the CACM is that the five Central American countries essentially produce the same commodities—raw materials and agricultural products. The goods which are traded between the Central American countries in the Common Market are primarily machinery, industrial items, and processed foods. It is on these items that tariffs have been eliminated in the Common Market. United States corporations are the main producers of these items in the five Central American countries. Furthermore, any producer who can provide 50 percent or more of the trade for any industry will have free-trade privileges. This allows large United States firms to have near monopoly rights and makes it more difficult for new or small industries to enter the Market. Today, 48 percent of all the trade in the Central American Common Market is from United States companies.

The Deputy Chief of the United States Embassy in Guatemala was asked if he felt that the CACM was a greater benefit to the United States than to the Central American countries. He replied: "The Central American Common Market is in the self-interest of the United States but fortunately our selfish interests coincide with those of the Central American countries."

The United States government claims that it is attempting to help Guatemala and other Latin American countries to "develop." To this end it has organized what is called in Spanish the *Alianza para el Progreso*. In English this can be translated, the "Alliance *for* Progress" or the "Alliance *Stops* Progress." Unfortunately it is not only the name of this program that has a double meaning.

Last year, through the Alliance, the United States provided $220 million for development loans in Latin America—a truly impressive figure. Most of this "aid," however, does not lead to the development of Latin America. In a booklet distributed by USAID it is reported that "about 85 percent of the United States bilateral aid is 'tied' . . . so that the money would be spent on United States goods and services." Such "aid" only leads to increased markets for United States-produced goods and makes it more difficult for Latin American producers to compete in their own countries.

An example of how this "aid" works is seen in the road-building project sponsored by USAID in Guatemala. USAID and the Export-Import Bank are each providing about $6 million for the Río Hondo Road Project. This road will connect Puerto Barrios (the major Atlantic port, owned by IRCA) with Honduras. The $12 million principal plus roughly $5 million in interest has to be paid back to the United States in dollars, which puts a heavy burden on Guatemala's balance of payments. The machinery for the construction must all be bought in the United States. The engineers, the contractors, and the supervisors are all from United States companies. Three United States firms—Nelloteer, Poteshnick, and Harrison—are paving and constructing the road. Brown & Root Overseas, Inc., are the supervisors of the construction. When the road was begun in 1961 under an Ex-Im Bank loan, the United States company Thompson-Cornwall, Inc., had the original contract. It is interesting that Thompson-Cornwall is the same company that constructed the United States airbase at Retalhuleu. This was the base from which United States planes left Guatemala for the Bay of Pigs invasion in that same year.

What the United States government essentially has done through the Export-Import Bank and USAID is to use taxpayers' money to subsidize the exports of large United States companies. By the Export-Import Bank's own figures, the Bank is currently "financing 10 percent of all United States exports."

The United States government claims that the road which is being built to connect Puerto Barrios with Honduras will aid Guatemala and Central America in two ways. First, the project will create jobs in the *Oriente* portion of the country where the *guerrilleros* are concentrated and "will show the *campesinos* in that area that we are doing something to help them." But the money which will be spent to pay Guatemalan salaries is only a small percent of the total loan.

Second, the United States claims that the road will increase Common Market trade between the Central American countries. But Puerto Barrios is primarily used as the port of entry for United States products which are to be sold in the Central American countries. The other Central American countries have little use for the Atlantic port in Guatemala. The road will therefore be of greatest benefit to the United States companies that export to Central America.

Another way in which United States foreign "aid" helps Central American countries is seen in a project sponsored by ROCAP (United States Regional

Office for Central America and Panama).[1] An important ROCAP official related this story:

> The project was to build highway CA-12 in Nicaragua. It is an unimportant road except for the fact that it leads to one of Somoza's *fincas*. ROCAP officials were opposed to the project because they felt that it would not help the development of the Central American Common Market. They changed their minds, however, when representatives from the CIA told them that the road was part of Somoza's payment for allowing United States pilots who flew in the Bay of Pigs to leave from Nicaragua.

Because of projects like this and because of the CIA involvement in the 1954 overthrow of Arbenz to protect the interests of the United Fruit Company, the CIA has become known as the Corporation for Investment Abroad.

A recent USAID project is also of interest. The United States lent $200,000 to Guatemala to purchase 54 Ford cars to be used by the police in fighting *guerrilleros.* In addition 300 bullet proof vests were given by USAID to the Guatemalan police. When the cars arrived, they were publicly blessed in the Central Plaza by the Archbishop.[2] USAID tried to avoid publicity about its participation in this project, since the United States government does not want to be openly connected with any counter-insurgency operations. But all the Guatemalan papers carried articles about the loan, and USAID's role is widely known.

In addition to the economic assistance which the United States lends Guatemala, the United States also provides equipment and money for military development. This aid, however, is not as generous as one would think. Most military "assistance" is in the sale of equipment. The Chief of the United States Military Mission in Guatemala, Colonel John Webber, reported that 7 percent of the entire Guatemalan budget each year is used to buy United States military equipment, some of which is new but most of which is used, out of date, and useless to the United States. This 7 percent comes to well over $12 million a year. The United States then, through its "aid" program, sends technicians to train the Guatemalans to use the equipment they have bought. But total military aid and grants to Guatemala for the last fifteen years ($9,100,000) is less than the amount of money which Guatemala spends each year to buy our surplus equipment.

The reason for this military program was summarized by Colonel Webber: "There is hardly any business of this sort with third nations. These other countries would like to get their foot in the door and make some of these sales, but they can't. There's a lot of money involved."

The sale of United States military equipment is going on throughout the world. About $2 billion of United States military equipment is sold abroad annually. This military build-up not only increases the possibility of international

1. ROCAP is similar to USAID but is for the entire Central American region.
2. Archbishop Casariego expounds on religion in Guatemala in Reading 36.—EDS.

wars but also leads to internal repression within the receiving countries. And finally, the money which, for example, Guatemala spent last year for United States military equipment could have been used to decrease the 75 percent illiteracy rate, or to lower the 10 percent infant mortality rate, or to raise the average per capita yearly wage of $200.

If the United States were truly interested in developing Central and South American countries, it would pay equitable prices for the mineral and agricultural products of Latin America. In the past ten years there has been a 10 percent *increase* in the import price of United States products. In the same time period there has been a 25 percent *drop* in the export price of Latin American products.

If the development of Latin America were the sincere desire of the United States, it would listen to the requests of the Latin American countries and eliminate "tied" loans, substituting instead tariff preferences for Latin American exports.

But this is not in the interest of United States corporations. They need consumers. If Latin America develops her own industries, their markets will be restricted. If the prices of Latin American raw materials are increased, the United States industries which are dependent on these commodities will be hurt.

Peter Valky, the Deputy Chief of the United States Mission in Guatemala, stated that "The United States basically has a foreign policy based on self-interest." If this be the case, do not call "tied" loans aid; do not call "the sale of military equipment" assistance; do not talk about the Alliance *for* Progress. Do not call it the United States Agency for International Development; rather call it the Agency for International Development of the United States.

[For reasons of space we have eliminated most of the footnotes in this piece. Students interested in studying this topic in greater depth may consult the following sources referred to by David Tobis: The United Fruit Company, *La Empresa Estadounidense en el Extranjero*, 1958; Banco de Guatemala, *Investing in Guatemala*, 1966 and *Sector Externo: estadisticas*, 1966; U.S. Agency for International Development (USAID), *La Empresa Privada y la Alianza para el Progreso, Foreign Aid Through Private Investment*, and *Chart of American Assistance to Guatemala;* David Wise and Thomas Ross, *The Invisible Government*, (New York: Bantam, 1964); John Gerassi, *The Great Fear in Latin America* (New York: Macmillan, 1963); The Chase Manhattan Bank, *World Business*, July 1966; *New York Times*, July 21, 1967.—EDS.]

15. *Guatemalan Victims* *

BY FRANCES MOORE LAPPÉ AND NICK ALLEN

FRANCES Moore Lappé, author of Food First: Beyond the Myth of Scarcity, *and* Diet for a Small Planet, *is a co-founder of the Institute for Food and Development Policy. Together with Nick Allen, a researcher at the Institute, she gives us a look at how a contemporary development project, similar to those proposed under the Caribbean Basin Initiative, functions in a small community.*

THE ECONOMICS OF Central America, designed to serve the rich, have failed to meet the needs of the poor majorities. This is the core of the crisis there. Will President Reagan's proposed new economic aid program help transform these unjust, inefficient economies? Or will it exacerbate the crisis, strengthening the economic and political structures that have kept Central Americans poor and hungry for so long?

In evaluating the possible impact of the proposed aid, we studied a Guatemalan agribusiness project that is the type of United States Government-subsidized "free-enterprise" venture that the Administration is promoting in its Caribbean Basin plan. (The plan would offer tariff and tax incentives for corporate investment in "nontraditional" agriculture, such as cucumbers, pineapples, tomatoes, and cut flowers.)

In 1975, Alcosa, a Guatemalan subsidiary of Hanover Brands, based in the United States, began contracting with peasants to grow cauliflower and broccoli, which were processed and shipped frozen to North American supermarkets. Alcosa is partly financed by the Latin American Agribusiness Development Corporation, a consortium of big banks and agribusiness firms supported by the Agency for International Development.

An A.I.D. study, "The Social Impact of Agribusiness," provides evidence of the damage caused by a United States-supported agribusiness project inserted into a repressive, oligarchical society such as Guatemala's, El Salvador's or Haiti's.

Alcosa, the study says, recruited poor highland farmers, who gave up their corn, bean and cabbage patches to specialize in cauliflower. While at first their income increased, by 1980 many farmers were suffering substantial losses. They were able to survive only by going heavily into debt to Alcosa for hybrid seeds and insecticides and to itinerant merchants for other goods. While Alcosa loans were interest-free, "Alcosa paid itself first, even if that meant . . . 3 months of no-income farming."

When Alcosa stopped buying vegetables in one village, the farmers protested

* Reprinted from *The New York Times,* May 28, 1982, by permission.

that "there was nothing to eat." The study went on: "Their children had been forced to quit school and leave home to seek work as farm labor or domestic servants."

Alcosa often chose as its managers Ladinos, a privileged ethnic minority in the highlands, thus "reinforcing the existing inequality," the study asserted.

Why didn't the peasants fight more vigorously to protect their interests? The study tells us that they knew that "informal leaders of peasant groups were being gunned down daily in other parts of the country."

Defenders of such projects would point to the increased incomes of some farmers and the relatively good wages and working conditions at the Alcosa packing plant. But projects like Alcosa do not get to the heart of the problem: the political and economic powerlessness of poor majorities. Moreover, such projects further infect the roots of the social crisis by strengthening the position of local elites and foreign interests.

In one village out of 17, the Alcosa project did succeed both for the company and the farmers. What made the difference was a strong peasant cooperative that had enough clout to negotiate a better contract with the company. Since the co-op had its own agronomists, farmers did not have to rely on Alcosa's advice. The agronomists said: Use smaller doses of cheaper insecticides and intersperse corn with cauliflower. Thus, the farmers did not have to give up their staple food crop. The A.I.D. report said: "The cooperative exists to serve the needs of its members, not the requirements of a Guatemala corporation [Alcosa] or its corporate owners in the United States."

In the last two years, Guatemalan security forces' repression of this type of peasant initiative has accelerated, resulting in the destruction of peasant co-ops and other self-help efforts and the assassination of hundreds of their participants. Two peasant organizers we met in 1978 have disappeared; one was forced underground, the other killed, for the "crime" of teaching neighbors better farming techniques.

While many United States citizens rightly oppose military aid to such repressive governments, they find economic aid acceptable. When will we learn that, rather than a different kind of aid, what is needed is a different kind of recipient? As long as recipients of our aid, in Central America and elsewhere, are governments protecting economic and political structures that deny power to most citizens, that aid—military or economic—will not only fail to end the problems of hunger and poverty but rather will aggravate inequalities at their core.

16. Guatemala: Central America's Blue Chip Investment *

BY ALLAN NAIRN

"WE are trying to ensure your investments and we would like all the organizations and the businessmen that are able to invest in Guatemala. . . . We guarantee your investments. The government has said so. The president has said so. The judges have said so. Those in charge of the security of the country have said so. I want all North Americans to come and invest in Guatemala." So said General Benedicto Lucas García, former Army Chief of Staff, November 1981.

In this piece Allan Nairn, a free-lance writer and researcher, provides a glimpse into the complex network of mutual support among American businessmen in Guatemala, their political backers in the United States, and leaders of Guatemala's business, political, and military communities.[1]

IN THE EYES of a Guatemalan labor leader who recently went underground after an army death squad came calling at his home, 1981 will be grim. "This will be the year of poverty and hunger for Guatemala," he says.

A Bank of America executive, who recently increased his Guatemalan lending capital as a show of confidence in the country's future, has another view. "The economy is very, very strong at this point," says Keith Parker. "This year should be excellent. If we as a bank were looking to lend money to a government, if we looked at it strictly on the numbers, Guatemala would be A-1, before any other Latin country."

These men are looking at the two faces of Central America's largest economy (1980 GDP in excess of $7 billion). After decades of U.S. intervention and domination, Guatemala has emerged as a classic case of dependent development. The economy is doing well by conventional business standards. There is a diversified and cosmopolitan oligarchy, a thriving multinational sector with more than 200 U.S. firms, and—for the majority of the population—some of the most abject poverty in the Western hemisphere.

The 1954 coup (instigated by United Fruit Company and implemented by the CIA), which overthrew the elected reformist government of Jacobo Arbenz, cast the die for the next 27 years of Guatemalan politics and economic development.

* Reprinted from *Multinational Monitor* [Washington, D.C.], May 1981, by permission.

1. Nairn's interview with a U.S. businessman in Guatemala offers a more intimate look at these relationships. See Reading 13.—EDS.

The structural underpinnings of today's Guatemala—inequitable land distribution, reliance on export agriculture, extensive penetration by multinational capital, and repressive, military-oligarchic government—were locked in place and insulated from democratic challenge by the post-Arbenz regimes.

According to the most recent Guatemalan census, two percent of the population owns 65 percent of the land. On the large estates, 60 percent of the land lies fallow. Roughly two-thirds of the population earns its living by working on the land as permanent or temporary farm labor on the large estates or as owners of "subsistence" plots of 2.5 acres or less. In recent years, many such plots have been expropriated by large growers and military officers. Each year more than 500,000 peasants unable to find work in the highlands migrate in search of seasonal work on coastal plantations. Guatemala's population is 7 million.

Guatemalan farmland is primarily devoted to export cash crops, led by coffee, which accounts for 36 percent of export income, as well as cotton, sugar cane, cardamom, beef and bananas. Guatemala has recently joined Brazil as Latin America's only exporters of natural rubber, a commodity whose market is expected to grow as oil prices drive up the cost of synthetic rubber.

The agro-export base is supplemented by an industrial sector which grew at 9 percent per year through the late 70s and now employs 20 percent of the Guatemalan workforce. Industry is dominated by low technology, low-wage producers of consumer goods for the working and middle classes of Guatemala and Central America. There are, however, not enough jobs to absorb the agricultural labor surplus, resulting in an estimated unemployment rate of 20 percent coupled with 50 percent underemployment.

As an open economy whose external trade equals half of its Gross Domestic Product, Guatemala is tied to swings in the world market. Thirty percent of its trade is with the United States. In 1979 and '80 the U.S. recession hit Guatemala hard, pulling down GDP growth rates, which had been running around a vigorous 5 percent, and pushing inflation, which had been running at a rate *lower* than that of the U.S. and far lower than most Latin countries, above 15 percent.

Guatemalan exports also suffered when the country's second largest trading partner, the nations of the tariff-protected Central American Common Market, imported fewer goods due to the revolutions in Nicaragua and El Salvador. Guatemala has always enjoyed a large balance of trade surplus in its dealings with its less industrially developed Central American neighbors.

Tourism, which in good years has been the country's third largest source of foreign exchange, dropped precipitously in 1980 and '81 due to international publicity about the government's political repression, which claims the lives of 30 to 40 peasants, workers, clerics, and politicians each day.

But despite these external shocks, multinational bankers and executives agree that Guatemala is still a sound and profitable place to invest. The main export commodities are expected to draw good prices in the coming year, the economy's reaction to the recession was much milder than that of many Third World countries, foreign exchange reserves are strong, and both the public and private sectors enjoy one of the lowest external debt ratios in Latin America. Oliver Sause, executive director of the American Chamber of Commerce in Guatemala, claims that "Guatemala has so many resources going for it that it is possible that it could ride out a major political onslaught."

Any onslaught against the Guatemalan oligarchy would also be an attack on some of the world's most powerful multinationals. For unlike El Salvador, where the United States' direct economic interests are minor, Guatemala represents a $400 million U.S. export market and has direct investments to the value of at least $300 million—a figure which is sure to grow as oil development picks up.

The multinational presence in Guatemala has diversified considerably since the days when United Fruit ran the country like a corporate fiefdom. Perhaps the most powerful firm in Guatemala today is Bank of America, which is surpassed only by the government as a source of agricultural capital. Due to government restrictions on local banks, Bank of America is also the only institution in the country permitted to make loans in excess of $5 million, giving it the inside track on all major projects. As the principal founder of the Latin American Agribusiness Development Corp. (LAAD), Bank of America also helps direct the country's main source of venture capital for "non-traditional" export enterprises.

In addition, the bank is a potent behind-the-scenes political force. It is the only corporate member of the Amigos del País, a right wing Guatemalan business group which lobbies for U.S. weapons sales to Guatemala and pays the public relations firm of Michael Deaver, President Reagan's closest personal adviser, a $13,000/month retainer. Bank of America has many of the country's most powerful landowners, industrialists and military men among its clients, including the nation's president, General Fernando Romeo Lucas García, to whom the bank extended a personal loan to purchase his 7,000-acre cattle estate in the oil-rich Northern Transversal Strip.

The largest industrial enterprise in Guatemala is the EXMIBAL nickel mine owned by International Nickel of Canada (80 percent) and Hanna Mining of Cleveland (20 percent). When plans for the mine were announced in the late 60s, massive public protest led to the establishment of a public commission of inquiry. Two of the three commissioners were assassinated; one of them, a paraplegic congressman, was machine-gunned in the back as he left the Congress in a wheel chair. The mine was approved, on terms favorable to EXMIBAL, and a mining code, drafted by EXMIBAL executives, was enacted to regulate its operations. This January the mine was shut down for a year due to low nickel prices and the high cost of oil used in the smelting process. At its peak, the mine brought in roughly as much foreign exchange as the entire tourism industry.

With the exception of Goodyear, which owns rubber plantations and a tire factory, and Del Monte,[2] which owns old United Fruit banana estates employing

---

2. For an overview of Del Monte's operation in Guatemala see Reading 17.

more than 10,000 workers, most of the multinationals in Guatemala are U.S. manufacturing plants which produce for the Central American market and employ 100–250 workers. These firms include Riviana Foods, Weyerhaeuser, Philip Morris, Colgate-Palmolive, U.S. Steel, Richardson-Merrell, Warner-Lambert and American Standard.

The Guatemalan government is known for its eagerness to cooperate with foreign investors, and the community of U.S. and Guatemalan businessmen is perhaps the most tightly integrated economically, socially and politically in all of Latin America. Joint ventures, intermarriages and political collaboration through the American Chamber of Commerce (which has dozens of Guatemalan members) and the Amigos del País (which has many U.S. members) are the rule for local and foreign members of Guatemala's ruling elite. Unlike the situation in many dependent economies, Guatemalan and U.S. investors have avoided fundamental clashes of interest. The government does not regulate the financial operations of multinationals, and helps them suppress labor agitation. The multinationals honor the turf of local monopolies held by old Guatemalan families (e.g., the Novellas control cement, the Castillos beer and glass), are generous with local stock participation, and defend the Guatemalan military regime in the U.S. political arena.

While the oligarchy and the multinationals have prospered together, the population that does their work has been literally fighting for survival. Even Sause of the American Chamber of Commerce admits that "Guatemala has in the past been guilty of the crimes of repressing the peasants, failure to provide social development for the poor, failure to provide opportunity." Sause contends this is changing, but virtually every available indicator of peasant and worker living standards suggests that while changes have indeed taken place since President Lucas García assumed office in 1978, they have overwhelmingly been for the worse.

Urban workers, generally thought of as the most "privileged" popular sector, have been subjected to an unprecedented campaign of government terror aimed at destroying unions which press demands for improved wages and working conditions. One-hundred and ten labor leaders were assassinated in 1980—roughly two per week. The rate has increased in 1981. Guatemalan and multinational manufacturers responding to the recession by seeking to cut wage costs, have been laying off their work force *en masse,* then rehiring temporary workers who will again be laid off in a few months. In this way, companies such as Alimentos Kern, a Riviana Foods subsidiary and a notorious practitioner of the layoff gambit, keep their workers at the lowest salary grades, preventing them from moving up the pay scale provided by the national labor code, and discouraging union organization. Unlike more capital-intensive investments in countries such as Puerto Rico, manufacturing multinationals in Guatemala are concentrated in low wage, labor-intensive industries. They depend on the country's depressed wage structure—where daily industrial wages range from $2.50 to $4.50—for their profitability.

Since the mid-1960s wages have failed to keep pace with inflation. This is a serious problem for a workforce that was living near subsistence to begin with. It is a critical one for the rural campesinos, many of whom have simultaneously been confronted with loss of their homes and jobs through eviction from large estates and unclaimed land; exploitation by "contratistas" who hire groups of temporary female coffee pickers and often pay them less than half the minimum wage; occasional deduction of wages by large growers such as millionaire Robert Alejos of the El Salto sugar cane plantations; and systematic spraying of toxic pesticides on fields filled with workers.

In 1964 the Nutrition Institute of Central American and Panama (INCAP) estimated that subsistence food, clothing, shelter and transportation needs for a family of five would require a "vital minimum wage" of $7.00 per day. By 1979 the vital minimum had risen to $9.10 per day. Yet according to the National Workers Confederation (CNT)—an umbrella organization for Guatemalan unions—the average daily wage covered only 33 percent of this subsistence requirement. The 1981 average wage is not enough to cover the *1964* vital minimum.

Given such a wage structure, full time child labor, often beginning at age seven or eight, is near universal in rural Guatemala. Families are often split when fathers or mothers leave home for months at a time to look for work. Guatemalan infant mortality, according to the government's preliminary census last November, has surpassed that of Haiti; 56 percent of children die before the age of five.

Starvation wages are nothing new for Guatemalan peasants. What has made 1981 particularly trying has been the inflation of the prices of basic foodstuffs and rural transportation. Corn, sugar, and liver have doubled in price; in some areas, black beans have tripled. Because of the headlong development of export cash crops, cultivation of subsistence food has been neglected. Guatemala has had to *import* much of the corn and beans which, in meager proportions, keep its rural population alive.

A crisis of rural misery would pose little threat to the Guatemalan economic system which has precipitated and survived many such crises before. But with the revolutions in Nicaragua and El Salvador and the slowly growing strength of the Guatemalan guerrilla movement, which has sunk deep roots among the Indian population, the ruling elite will have to respond. The options are to ameliorate the crisis or to repress those who seek to give it political content. The first solution would require redistribution of income, restructuring of the economic system, or a massive infusion of outside capital—none of which are in prospect. The Guatemalan oligarchy, supported by multinational corporations, has instead chosen the strategy of repression, to be carried out by the military-dominated government.

There are, to be sure, sources of friction between the government and the business elites. Multinational executives seeking contracts for government public works projects are complaining about skyrocketing bribery rates and cavalier treatment which is out of keeping with the nation's traditional subservience to U.S.

capital. Corruption which extends beyond routine pillage of the public treasury has aroused the ire of numerous businessmen; last year's coffee harvest was hurt when government officials stole funds earmarked for a coffee-fungus prevention program.

The economic prognosis for Guatemala, like everything else in that country, varies by class. For the masses of agricultural and urban workers, the self-perpetuating, post-1954 regime of army officers, ruling on behalf of local barons and multinational executives, offers no economic hope and considerable physical peril. For the corporate economy, the key factors in the economic future are world commodity prices, and the degree to which the Reagan administration succeeds in restoring business-as-usual to the Central American Common Market. The essential requirement is that the army's strategy of repression continues to prevent foreign and even Guatemalan capital from fleeing the country.

Guatemalan businessmen express a fervent desire to stay and fight for the privileges of their class. American firms, while calling the families of some U.S. executives back to the States, have stopped short of disinvestment. Some, such as Bank of America, have *increased* their Guatemalan exposure, especially since the Reagan victory. The American Chamber of Commerce continues to enthusiastically back the Lucas regime in lobbying on Capitol Hill and through cash contributions to the Guatemalan government's extensive international public relations campaign.

In its moment of impending political conflagration, the full spectrum of Guatemala's dependent economy stands strikingly on display. Peasants starve in the hills and priests are cut down in the streets, but Guatemala remains a "good place to do business."

17. *Guatemala: Going Bananas* *

BY ROGER BURBACH AND PATRICIA FLYNN

ALTHOUGH the term "banana republic" has never accurately described Central American economics, U.S. banana companies have a long history in the region (see Reading 10). The labor practices established by the United Fruit Company, and continued by Del Monte, provide an example of how a foreign corporation creates a stratified labor force while using its influence to avoid costly government regulations. Roger Burbach and Patricia Flynn, former staff mem-

* From *Agribusiness in the Americas* (New York: Monthly Review Press, 1980), Chapter 11, pp. 207–214, by permission.

bers of the North American Congress on Latin America, are currently members of the Center for the Study of the Americas (CENSA), in San Francisco.

TALKING TO A reporter from *Forbes* magazine recently, Del Monte's chairman, Alfred Eames, mused, banana trees "are like money trees. I wish we had more of them." Unlikely as it may seem, eight short years ago Del Monte did not own a single banana tree. But today, the corporation owns or controls an estimated 38,000 acres of banana plantations in Costa Rica, Guatemala, and the Philippines. It is one of the three U.S.-based multinationals that dominate the world banana economy: Del Monte, Castle & Cooke, and United Brands together account for 70 percent of the world's $2.5 billion banana trade. Because of this dominance, the companies also exercise considerable influence on the economic life of the banana-producing countries, many of which depend on banana exports as a principal source of foreign exchange.

The kingpin of Del Monte's banana empire is its plantation in Guatemala, which was purchased from the old and infamous United Fruit Company in 1972. When Del Monte took over from United Fruit, it stepped into the shoes of a company that had long been the symbol of U.S. imperialism in Central America, particularly in Guatemala. As Guatemala's largest landowner and major foreign investor, United Fruit had dominated the country's economy, exploiting its natural resources and workers and consistently opposing organized labor, and it was the leading force in pushing for the CIA-engineered overthrow of the progressive government of Jacobo Arbenz in 1954.

By the time Del Monte entered the picture, United Fruit had lowered its political and economic profile in Guatemala and the rest of Central America as part of a sophisticated strategy to rationalize its operations and undercut nationalistic resentments. But beneath this facade, Del Monte continues the old tradition of the United Fruit Company in Guatemala. It still operates as though it were above the law; it is allied with the most reactionary elements within the Guatemalan bourgeoisie; it manipulates its workers to avoid labor unrest; and along with the other banana companies, it has tried to torpedo efforts by Central American governments to gain greater control over their natural resources. Like the United Fruit Company, Del Monte reinforces economic underdevelopment and political reaction in Guatemala, and acts as a formidable obstacle to change.

The Guatemala plantations that Del Monte took over from United Fruit in 1972 are the most productive in Central America, assuring Del Monte's position as a major force in the world banana trade. For United Fruit the acquisition meant the future erosion of its dominance, unchallenged before the 1960s when it controlled 75 percent of the world trade.

Ironically, the original impetus for Del Monte's entry into the banana business in 1968 came from the United Fruit Company itself. In an apparent bid to take over the food processing company, United Fruit purchased a large chunk of Del Monte's stock. To thwart the takeover attempt Del Monte went out and bought a banana company—the one line of business United Fruit was legally blocked from acquiring. A 1958 antitrust ruling had found United Fruit guilty of monopolizing the banana trade, and in fact the company was under court orders to sell off about 10 percent of its banana operations. With the purchase of the Miami-based West Indies Fruit Company and its Costa Rican subsidiary, the Banana Development Corporation (known as BANDECO), Del Monte was able to make its first inroads into the U.S. banana market.

The banana business proved highly profitable and Del Monte began looking for ways to expand its Central American holdings. Again, United Fruit provided the opportunity. The final deadline for United Fruit's required divestiture was approaching, and the company still had no buyers when Del Monte approached United Brands (which had purchased United Fruit in 1970) with a purchase offer for its Guatemala plantations. By the end of 1970 the two companies agreed that Del Monte would purchase United Fruit's holdings in Guatemala for about $10 million, provided the Guatemalan government agreed.

For Del Monte, Guatemala was the ideal place for expansion. Not only would the plantations there double the company's banana production, but just as important, fifteen years of U.S.-sponsored counterrevolution since 1954 had made the country safe for U.S. investors, providing the kind of "stable" political climate Del Monte demands wherever it operates. However, Del Monte had one formidable obstacle to overcome—a provision of the Guatemalan constitution that prohibits the sale of border lands (as United Fruit's lands were defined) to foreign interests. To complicate matters further, several purchase offers were put forward to Guatemalan nationals, including two entrepreneurs who had even lined up bank loans. But in the best tradition of U.S. multinationals overseas, Del Monte did not let ethics or legal technicalities stand in its way.

Despite personal lobbying visits by Del Monte executives to then president Carlos Arana and several cabinet officers, in late 1971 the government denied permission for the purchase. Not to be deterred, company officials simply dipped deep enough into corporate coffers to change the Guatemalan government's decision. Following the advice of then ambassador to Guatemala, Nathaniel Davis, to retain a local "consultant," in the summer of 1972 Del Monte hired Domingo Moreira, a Cuban-born Guatemalan entrepreneur. Moreira agreed to help swing the deal in return for a $.5 million "consultant's fee." He soon proved his political clout. Even before the Guatemalan government officially reversed its position, Del Monte received the go-ahead from the government to conclude the deal with United Brands. One month later, in September 1972, Arana formally issued a decree approving the sale.

Del Monte, of course, claimed that there was no bribe involved, since the corporation did not make any direct payment to a government official. But the truth of the matter is that Del Monte was carefully covering its tracks. The $.5 million fee was paid through several of the company's Panamanian shipping subsidiaries and charged to general and administrative expenses. Thus, Del Monte managed to stay within the formal limits of the law by satisfying Securities and Exchange requirements that accurate records be kept, and no secret slush funds be used to channel funds abroad. Del Monte also went to great lengths to conceal the transaction with Moreira. No company record was ever made of his name, and Del Monte has promised never to reveal his identity.

In spite of Moreira's disclaimers that no bribery was involved, in Guatemala the universally accepted assumption is that Moreira handed over a good-sized chunk of his "fee" to then President Arana. Some sources in the Guatemalan bourgeoisie even claim to have personal knowledge of the transaction.

But more important than the question of the impropriety of the payment is what the Moreira connection reveals about Del Monte's ties with the most reactionary and corrupt elements of the Guatemalan bourgeoisie. Moreira is a fast-dealing entrepreneur whose holdings have expanded greatly since he came to Guatemala from Cuba. He is a well-known backer of conservative political forces in Guatemala and has close ties with a group of rightwing business executives who promote their political and personal gain through Mafia-like tactics. In Nicaragua he had business links with former dictator Anastasio Somoza.

Plantation Enclave

The United Fruit plantations Del Monte took over lie in the hot tropical lowlands of northeastern Guatemala, not far from the Atlantic coast ports which face the markets of Europe and the United States. The most notable change at the plantation since Del Monte's takeover are the new signs on company buildings. They now read BANDEGUA, for Banana Development Corporation of Guatemala, the subsidiary that runs Del Monte's operations there. Recognizing that the plantation system developed over the years by United Fruit serves its interests well, Del Monte has made few basic changes. In fact, several of the workers interviewed by NACLA[1] wondered whether the company had really changed ownership.

For the $20.5 million Del Monte finally paid to United Brands in 1972, the company acquired 55,000 acres of prime agricultural land, plus an agro-industrial complex that stretches from plantation to port. It also inherited a position of privilege and influence that had long characterized United Fruit's operations.

Though no longer the major representative of monopoly capital in Guatemala, where U.S. multinationals now have sizable industrial investments, Del Monte is still a formidable economic and political power. It is the country's largest single private employer and totally monopolizes the export of bananas, one of the top five sources of foreign exchange for Guatemala. Del Monte continues to run the plantations like an independent enclave within the Guatemalan state, where government officials are barely tolerated. It is Del Monte, not Guatemalan officials,

1. North American Congress on Latin America—EDS.

that supplies official export statistics on bananas. Del Monte pays no tax on its lands, and has only 9,000 acres under cultivation. The remaining 48,000 acres are grazed by 7,000 head of company cattle—not to produce meat, but, as a company official explained, as a tactic designed both to keep squatters off the property and to prevent the government from expropriating it as idle land.

While Del Monte does not dominate the country's key transportation networks as United Fruit once did, it still benefits from special privileges. When its port facilities at Puerto Barrios on the Atlantic were destroyed by the earthquake in 1976, the company was immediately able to relocate to choice facilities at the nearby government port of Santo Tomás. The corporation also enjoys a special relationship with the government-run national railway, Ferrocarril de Guatemala (FEGUA). Del Monte is one of FEGUA's creditors and also repairs the company's rail cars at its plantation machine shop.

The first thing that strikes a visitor to the town of Bananera, where the plantation headquarters are located, is the highly stratified social system typical of plantations everywhere. On one side of the railroad tracks, behind fences and guard posts, is the company compound. Amidst country club surroundings, a few North American executives and their Guatemalan aides oversee Del Monte's vast lands and its 4,500 person workforce. The compound's manicured lawns, spacious tropical mansions, its pool and tennis courts, stand in sharp contrast to the dusty company town on the other side of the rail tracks. The evident poverty of the town, which exists mainly as an adjunct to the plantation, belies Del Monte's claim that its presence has a beneficial effect on the surrounding economy.

Most of Del Monte's workers and their families live on the plantation itself, isolated even from the small town of Bananera. The company-owned housing camps are conveniently clustered around the banana farms where the men work, along the edges of the railway line. The workers' housing is spartan and barely adequate, a far cry from the luxurious company compound. Since there are no roads going into the plantation, the only access to the outside world is the company operated rail wagon, which runs only twice daily—at the beginning and end of each work day. No one, neither workers, their families, nor company executives, is allowed to board the train without a special pass given out daily by a company office. To further assure "law and order" there is a Guatemalan army post in the middle of the plantation, staffed by armed Guatemalan soldiers. A company executive explained to NACLA interviewers that the soldiers take care of any disturbances which occur on the plantation. He also recalled the original reason for the post: in the late 1960s, guerrillas were active in the area, and a United Fruit pilot was killed. Given the social unrest in the Guatemalan countryside, Del Monte is clearly not taking any chances.

Plantation Workforce

Many of the workers at the BANDEGUA plantation were once peasant farmers from the neighboring provinces who were either forced off the land, or were unable to survive by farming. Now, with their sole source of sustenance the salary they receive, the plantation workers have become part of the Guatemalan proletariat. However, with salaries averaging about $870 a year, and with benefits such as free housing, water, electricity, and medical facilities, Del Monte's employees are better off than the bulk of the Guatemalan working class.

Although the policy of maintaining a *relatively* well-off workforce was originally pioneered by United Fruit, today it has become an integral part of the strategy of all the multinational banana companies. Like other monopolistic corporations, they recognize their own self-interest in ensuring labor peace by paying high salaries—something their hefty profit rates allow them to do. For the banana industry, however, a docile and cooperative labor force is a special imperative. Bananas are a highly perishable commodity, and time is critical in the marketing process. A plantation or port work stoppage of even a day can mean the loss of hundreds of thousands of dollars in overripe bananas. Thus, harvesting at BANDEGUA's plantation is carefully timed to coincide with the arrival of Del Monte's ships at Puerto Barrios. Within one day, the bananas are cut, washed, packed, and sent by train to the nearby port. There they are immediately loaded onto specially refrigerated ships which will transport them to the U.S. and European markets. The whole process must be regulated like clockwork, and delays avoided at any cost. In this context, it is possible to understand why Del Monte is willing to pay its dockworkers, who hold the key to the whole marketing process, up to $600 a month on a piece-rate basis.

The plantation workers, most of whom earn between $2.80 and $4.00 a day, are not nearly so well off. And in fact, their relative privilege is more than anything a commentary on the miserable living conditions of the rest of the Guatemalan people. In spite of the free benefits provided by the company, the salary of a banana worker is still not sufficient to sustain a family. To supplement their income, wives and children of the banana workers are usually forced to find jobs, often in the banana packing sheds, where salaries are the lowest on the plantation. According to a recent study in Guatemala, the workers and their families spend an average of 64 percent of their income on food, clothing and fuel; and 17 percent of the plantation families do not have an income adequate to obtain a minimum satisfactory diet.

Work conditions on the plantation are also extremely difficult. Banana production is highly labor intensive, and requires continual painstaking work of weeding, trimming, marking plants, and spraying with insecticides. Under the hot tropical sun, crews of workers roam among the banana trees under the constant supervision of the BANDEGUA foremen. When one of Del Monte's ships is in port, workers often do the grueling job of harvesting for twelve or thirteen hours at a time—one man cutting down the banana stem with his machete, and another carrying the stem (which can weigh up to 150 pounds) in a sack slung across his back. As one of the U.S. executives on the plantation told NACLA, "It's backbreaking work, and you couldn't get a single person in California to do it, especially for $2.80 a day. . . . I wouldn't do it for any money." But, as he explained, cheap labor is key to the company's profits. "If you can pay a worker 35¢ an hour, why buy an $8,000 tractor?"

[Due to space limitation footnotes have been eliminated. Some information is from interviews conducted by the authors with Del Monte officials in Guatemala and with Frank Ellis. References cited in the article are: Frederick F. Clairmonte, "Bananas: A Commodity Case History," in Cheryl Payer, ed., *Commodity Trade of the Third World* (New York: McGraw-Hill, 1975); Carlos Figueroa Ibarra, *El Proletariado Rural en el agro Guatemalteco* (Guatemala: University of San Carlos, 1976); UNCTAD, *The Marketing and Distribution System for Bananas* (Geneva: UNCTAD, 1974); *Forbes*, December 15, 1970; *Guatemala and Central America Report* [Berkeley], October 1972, July 1975, and February 1976; *The Wall Street Journal*, July 14, 1975; *The New York Times*, May 21, 1975; *The San Francisco Examiner*, May 21, 1975; *Inforpress* [Guatemala City], nos. 60, 64, 93, 101, 151, 165, and 191; *Central American Report* [Guatemala City], November 24, 1975; *La Nación* [Guatemala City] April 18, 1974; *El Gráfico* [Guatemala City], May 23, 1974; and July 14, 1975.—EDS.]

General Efraín Ríos Montt and General Horacio Maldonado Schaad (left) in post-coup press conference, March, 1982. *Photo credit: Jean-Marie Simon*

Chapter II:

WHO RULES GUATEMALA?

Editors' Introduction

IN the years following the 1954 coup, a parade of military leaders [1] have sat in the National Palace's presidential office, issuing commands and receiving instructions from the high-ranking generals who are often the real decision-makers behind the president. It has been widely acknowledged that these generals may unite to depose a president who steps outside the boundaries established by the military, as evidenced in the 1963 and 1982 coup d'etats (see Reading 21). General Ríos Montt, called into the presidency by the officers who staged the March 1982 coup, affirmed the military's power, commenting, "I am the one who has the power up to this moment. Within half an hour they can shoot me without any problem." [2]

Ríos Montt's statement implicitly highlights another aspect of military rule in Guatemala: it is maintained by the fatal elimination of parties, organizations, and individuals who are trying to gain entry into political life (see Reading 19). The assassination of opposition candidates limits the range of contenders for power, while the manipulation of election results by the military guarantees the final selection of the president.

It would be a mistake, however, to assume that the military alone dictates the operation of the government. The military has been able to maintain control in alliance with leading economic groups, a point recently made by General Arana, president from 1970–74: "There has never been a separation between the private

---

1. Although Julio César Méndez Montenegro, president from 1966–70, was technically a civilian, he was not able to move into office until he signed a pact with the army giving them control over the military.

2. Raymond Bonner, *New York Times,* May 20, 1982

sector and the army . . . particularly in these times which are so crucial to our country. In these times, private initiative is very much threatened and the only thing that can save private initiative is the army." [3]

Focused solely on protecting economic investments and fighting communism, the government remains unresponsive to the economic and social needs of the impoverished majority. Unlike the Mexican government, which despite huge social inequalities maintains its power through complex alliances with organizations of campesinos, workers, and intellectuals, in Guatemala there has been no program for the structural integration of the majority into political life. The Guatemalan government has created a system based on the violent exclusion of citizens from political participation.

How, then, can we characterize the government of Guatemala? United Nations Ambassador Jeane Kirkpatrick won the attention of the Reagan Administration with her analysis of military governments: "Authoritarian governments . . . have many faults and one significant virtue: their power is limited. . . . Authoritarian systems do not destroy all alternative power bases in a society. . . . Totalitarian regimes, to the contrary, in claiming a monopoly of power over all institutions, eliminate competitive alternative elites." [4]

The Guatemalan government, with its campaign to eliminate popular opposition to its rule, easily falls within this definition of a totalitarian regime, a conclusion hotly refuted by Kirkpatrick and her associates. On the other hand, the authoritarian/totalitarian distinction may be no more than a convenient theory that reinforces the ideology of intervention on behalf of the U.S.'s strategic allies: both terms describe a government which responds to its citizens needs from behind the barrel of a gun.

18. *The Militarization of the Guatemalan State* *

BY GABRIEL AGUILERA PERALTA

IN *the following reading Guatemalan political scientist Gabriel Aguilera Peralta analyzes the historical context in which the Guatemalan military has developed. He points out that the Guatemalan military has surpassed its role as a*

3. From an unpublished interview, February 1982.

4. Jeane Kirkpatrick, in "Human Rights and American Foreign Policy," *Commentary*, November 1981, p. 44.

* Reprinted from *Polémica* [San José, Costa Rica] Number 1, Sept.-Oct., 1981, by permission. Translated by Lisa Vives.

tool or branch of the government, and has instead become the government, as have militaries in Argentina, Chile, and Uruguay, among other Latin American countries. Aguilera Peralta characterizes the Guatemalan military as a political institution that protects capitalism and whose leaders have incorporated themselves into the nation's capitalist class.

Historic Development of the Armed Forces in Guatemala

IN 1821, GUATEMALA gained its independence from Spain and became a part of the Federal Republic of Central America, to which Honduras, El Salvador, Nicaragua, and Costa Rica also belonged. In 1826, the Federal Army and National Guard were created in each nation. In 1824, a training school for military officers was established and in 1826, the Federal Army and National Guard were created in each nation. The Federal Republic disintegrated later on . . . and each of the countries had formed its own national army by 1840.

By this time, the Guatemalan state had a low level of economic development based on the export of dyes and, during the period of rule by the conservative faction (1840–1870), little political integration. The armed forces lacked professionalization. . . . The "officers" were leaders of political factions. The soldiers, recruited for campaigns (principally wars against other countries in the region), had little training and few arms. The dominant sectors were mainly large landowners with semifeudal characteristics; the armed forces were their instrument of social control and articulators of their external policies.

In 1871 the so-called liberal revolution developed. Members of the coffee-growing sector, unable to develop within a very backward state, took control of the government. Under the direction of the landowner Justo Rufino Barrios, they accelerated the process of modernization, constructing communication networks and establishing modern educational, banking, and governing systems. Within its modernization policies, the Polytechnical School was founded in 1876 for the training of military officers, under the direction of a Spanish military mission.

The historical liberal period lasted until 1944. Over those seventy years, Guatemala was integrated into the world economy through the export of coffee. Despite the name "liberal," the process of reform did not include the development of a liberal democracy. On the contrary, these years were characterized by a succession of long and cruel dictatorships, particularly those of Manuel Estrada Cabrera (1898–1920), the "Señor Presidente" about whom author Miguel Angel Asturias wrote, and of Jorge Ubico (1930–1944). . . .

The circumstances in which the country's armed forces were born explain some of the aspects of its present ideology. There was not a period of heroic struggle for independence from Spain in which a military group was created. Rather, the army was created to collaborate with the national program of coffee growers, which implied a system of domination based on repression. . . . Generals, on a national level, and the political chiefs, on a local level, were essential elements of the system. The armed forces retained their character as an instrument of the dominant sectors, but their level of professionalization and technical preparation declined after the initial phases. Under the despotic regime of Estrada Cabrera, the soldiers dressed in rags and frequently begged for food (the government preferred the police as an instrument of control), while the corrupt generals became wealthy. . . .

From 1944, the year when dictator Jorge Ubico was overthrown, until 1954, a period called the October Revolution got underway (see Reading 10). During the armed actions of October 1944, which overthrew Ubico and his successor, Ponce Vaides, a good part of the young military officers joined in the rebellion. With the triumph of the revolution, the ranks of the army were cleansed of the "old generals" and structural changes were introduced into the armed forces which permitted a certain internal democratization.

The rank of Chief of the Armed Forces was created, elected internally within the officers' corps. The army began to call itself "of the Revolution" and an ideological vision formed, with a very strong identification between the process of change and the role of the uniformed forces. Nevertheless, the social contradictions were increasingly accentuated as the reforms went deeper and began not only to extend political and social rights but to modify economic structures which directly affected North American interests. These contradictions were directly reflected in two tendencies of the state: one, favorable to the revolution and the other, conservative. Gradually, the second tendency strengthened as the process continued to radicalize.

This explains why, when an anticommunist invasion by Carlos Castillo Armas took place in 1954 with the support of the North American CIA, the Arbenz government was unable to defend itself from the attack, a minor one in military terms. When the army did not fight back, it was too late to organize alternatives, such as arming popular militias. . . .

In its collective memory, the armed forces hold the events of October 1944 as evidence of identification between the army and civilian population. They do not refer to later events, nor to the triumph of the counterrevolution in July 1954. After 1955, the Guatemalan army was directly subjected to the influence of North American military missions, including training bases in Panama and the United States. This had two effects: one, to elevate the level of professionalism and armaments; two, to promulgate a strong anticommunist ideology and an identification with the United States. The roots of the revolutionary decade remained in force, however, and in November 1960, they led to a huge uprising of military officers, discontent with government corruption and with preparations being made at that time for an invasion of Cuba. The insurrection was defeated, but a group of officers who had taken part continued the rebellion and later incorporated into a guerrilla movement which started its activities in 1963.

The process of militarization presently taking place can be traced to the mid-1960s, especially since the military coup of 1963 through which the army, as an institution, officially assumed power, until 1966. This growth of military influence was a response to the military threat presented by a guerrilla movement in that period. As a consequence, it broadened the scope of its repressive apparatus.

After the military coup, the army became the decisive factor in the political system and widened its influence in the economic area. On an ideological level, this translated into a strengthening of its anticommunist vision and contributed to cementing internal cohesion.

The Armed Forces in the Guatemalan State Today

The last five hundred years have seen important changes in the country's productive structure. From a basically mono-export country (coffee), the development of the Central American Common Market in the 1960s has permitted a certain industrial and agroindustry (cotton and sugar) expansion in the 1970s. Foreign business interests, formerly based in the infrastructure and banana production, were diversified by the penetration of transnational monopoly capital in oil and nickel. Consequently, changes have occurred in the dominant sectors; the oligarchy of coffee barons, still influential, is no longer hegemonic. National investments are distributed in agriculture, industry, commerce, and finance. As minor partners in the exploration of oil and strategic minerals, national interests have a certain grade of organic integration with the large transnational operations. The policies of the Guatemalan state, particularly since 1970, have been directed by the interests of this sector, to such an extent that a careful analysis of the national development plans . . . reveals that their objective is the adaptation of the Guatemalan state to the expansion needs of transnational monopoly capital.

An example of this is the development plan of the Northern Transversal Strip, which runs along the north of the departments of Izabal, Alta Verapaz, Quiché, and Huehuetenango. Presented as a project to expand the agricultural frontier and to resolve the problem of basic grain production and the lack of land for peasants of the southern coast, the belt represented a huge state effort to transfer manual labor (indigenous migrants), communication networks (a cross-country highway, airports), energy (hydroelectric plants of Chixoy and Chulac), to an area where the most important discoveries of oil, copper, and nickel are located

On the political level, the predominance of the monopoly sector in the state apparatus has meant an accentuation of the characteristics which existed after 1954, in particular, the lack of legitimacy. Although the country appears to maintain political parties and periodic elections, these have no real meaning, being directly controlled by the government and manipulated to benefit political groups which represent the interests of the monopoly sector.

Equally important to note is that the model of economic growth demands the constant availability of abundant low-cost and docile labor, capable of absorbing inflationary effects without social protest. These inflationary effects include the real loss of buying power and the rising cost of consumer goods, which lead to the impoverishment of the urban proletariat and rural semiproletariat, and to the rural dislocation of poor campesinos from their land. . . .

The current process of militarization must be understood in the following elements:

Integration of high-ranking military officers into the monopoly sector.

While in the past one could speak of the army as a tool of the dominant class, now it can be observed that, particularly among the generals, this group is organically integrated into the monopoly sector, to the extent that they themselves have become cattle owners, owners of strategically important lands, of factories, medium and large size business. In this sense, their criteria and behavior are no longer simply as military officers, but as members of the dominant sector. High-ranking military chiefs, like ex-president Carlos Arana Osorio, are very important figures in the national economy.

The army as "the highest level of decision-making."

Major decisions which have to do with the country's political process are argued and decided within the ranks of the army. In spite of several political parties which legally represent in some form the interests of the monopoly sector (the Institutional Democratic Party, PID; the Authentic Nationalist Central, CAN; the Revolutionary Party, PR), the selection of the official and alternate candidates for presidential elections is discussed and decided on by the top levels of power and assemblies of military officials.

The army in nonmilitary activities.

It has been observed that the functions of the Guatemalan armed forces have expanded into areas not properly defined as military. Among these functions are the running of commercial enterprises (a military parking lot in the capital); industry (cement factory); and communications (TV station). These activities are added to traditional civic action projects carried out by the army, in culture (literacy campaigns, cultural magazines) or in services (medical, construction of roads).

The state practice of terrorism.

The resurgence and development of guerrilla war in the 1960s surprised an army which had fought its last battle fifty years earlier. This explains the advance of the insurgents, despite their lack of a solid base of popular support. It took North American advisors to improve the counterinsurgency strategies in the mid-1960s.

An important element of this was the introduction of the use of terrorism after 1966. This strategy was introduced into Latin America in this period and Guatemala was one of the first countries where it was tried out. The use of terrorism is based on principles derived from behavorial psychology that fear, when sufficiently exacerbated, will determine a person's conduct because it reaches one's primary feelings. A generalized and very deep fear will permit the control of a large social group. Confronted with the process of rebellion, fear can prevent popular support for the rebels. The aim is not just to combat the insurgents but mainly to intimidate the others . . . the possible collaborators or sympathizers, and even the indifferent, creating a collective victim.

When an appearance of institutional order is maintained, it is not the state organisms, openly, which carry out terrorism. In this case, the fiction of clandestine groups is employed. They carry out acts of terrorism with apparent autonomy from the government, but in reality are specialized units within the government.[1] Initially, terrorism is a police tactic, but if it is applied on a large scale over a sustained period of time, it becomes coordinated by specialized bodies within the armed forces. Originally seen as an emergency measure to eradicate the guerrillas and popular movement over a generation, terror has recurred in waves (1966–68; 1969–70; 1971–73), responsible for an estimated forty-two thousand deaths over that period. . . .

The militarization which exists in Guatemala is a necessary element in a model of domination based on repression. The absence of a democratic-liberal legitimacy, the absence of policies of redistribution or measures of social reform and the adaptation of state policies to the necessities of the transnational monopolies require a high level of ability, on the part of the state, to suppress and repress social protest.

The apparatus for that function grows rapidly and comes to be integrated with the monopoly sector. This function explains the broadening of its sphere of activities: the incursion of the armed forces into the realm of production and circulation of goods, widening an autonomous economic base and, in the area of higher education, forming its own professionals and technicians, who are also in the military. . . .

This is a special form of militarization, it is not the autonomous behavior of the army as a social force, nor a kind of Bonapartism, in which the armed forces place themselves on top of society. What is happening in Guatemala is that the armed forces acts as an integral part of the most modern dominant classes, to modernize and direct the development of the Guatemalan state according to the interests/needs of transnational monopoly capital, through repression and terrorism.

---

1. Amnesty International's report on the relationship between death squads and the government is found in Reading 26.—EDS.

Analytical Description of the Guatemalan Armed Forces Troop Strength

The Guatemalan armed forces, in its three branches, includes around 15,000 men, organized into brigades. Police and paramilitary forces add another 8,000. Apart from that, for purposes of mobilization, there is a permanent military reserve of about 7,000 men. To that must be added the category of military agents, or local army representatives based in any population center; usually they have already given military service and are equipped with light arms. The agents act as local authorities and carry out functions such as recruiting and intelligence gathering. Their number is very high, approximately 20,000 people—which is to say theoretically, the armed forces now includes more than 40,000 men. . . .

Recruiting, Training, and Specialization

The Guatemalan armed forces has close to 1,400 military officers in three branches. They are volunteers, recruited in their adolescence from five military high schools. On completion of their studies, the best prospects enroll in the Polytechnical School, located a short distance from the capital. After eight months of study, they graduate with the rank of second lieutenant in their chosen branch. After graduation most do rotating tours of service in various zones throughout the country and are upgraded every four years. Officers of the lowest rank have an opportunity to acquire combat experience in the confrontation zones with the guerrillas and they take courses in jungle warfare at centers specializing in such studies, such as the Kaibil "hell home" in the department of Petén. The Kaibil officers and soldiers are the elite troops of the Guatemalan army. Previously, they frequently visited military training camps in the United States and Panama Canal; presently these visits are rare and trips to Taiwan or Israel more common. The military technical training for officers is very thorough. After visiting the Center for Military Studies and passing military staff studies, officers may move up to become higher-ranking officers and generals.

The system of socialization of the officers tends to isolate them from society in favor of military relationships. Despite relatively low salaries, they enjoy a kind of social salary, represented by privileges such as tax-free car imports, use of the commissary which sells tax-free merchandise, use of military clubs and other such installations during their time off, family shopping vacations to Miami at low cost, educational facilities for their children, opportunities for university studies for the younger officers, a plot of land with its own house, or living quarters in an immense military colony built in Zone 5 of the capital called Santa Rosita, where the new military hospital has been constructed for the use of armed forces personnel.

All the needs of petty-bourgeois-type families (house, car, luxury items, trips, schooling) are thus assured. There also exist opportunities for upward social mobility within the army—to become a member of the middle class, to enrich oneself personally, and participate in the selection of official candidates for president. In effect, the generals are not static and the group is constantly renewed as generals retire or are replaced by a new crop of officers coming from below. In this way each official who distinguishes himself by his loyalty to the institution, by his personal ability, and by other qualities of individual competence will have a chance to become a general, and while at this level will be able to participate in the race for president.

Soldiers, for the most part, are recruited through obligatory military service, which, however, is carried out only at the base level of society. In particular, young campesinos, mostly Indian boys, are frequently recruited by force. . . .

Upon completing training they are transferred to units throughout the country, with care taken not to return them to the area they are from.

Recruits serve for varying lengths of time, generally eighteen months. They receive a low salary and some benefits. Some recruits have the opportunity to learn basic literary skills and other crafts. In some cases the so-called process of ladinoization takes place; which is to say the abandonment of Indian customs, cultural forms, and world view. An effort is made to inculcate elements of military ideology and then to maintain some tie with them (the recruits) upon completion of their military service. Those that show special capability and loyalty have the opportunity to enroll in the Mobile Military Police (Policia Militar Ambulante). . . . There is a growing resistance to signing up for military service and in many communities young men have escaped being called up with the aid of older men in their community. . . . Presumably, the gradual awakening of the indigenous community and its adhesion to the revolutionary movement are reflected in its change of attitude toward the army.

Over the medium or long run, the perspectives of the army, in this sense, can be somber. If ethnic Indian groups continue to incorporate into the revolution, it will mean unsolvable military problems for the repressive forces, in particular, the necessity to tightly control the foot soldiers in order to avoid desertions. . . . The army is also stimulating voluntary enlistment of ladinos and taking steps to create local militias in the eastern (highly ladino) part of the country, drawing on small property owners who are members of the extreme right wing party, National Liberation Movement (MLN). (The army hopes to count on four thousand local anticommunist militants in the near future.) [2] These measures cannot, however, counteract the indigenous incorporation into the guerrilla movement.

Conclusion

We have tried to summarily sketch the most important characteristics of the

---

2. Under Gen. Efraín Ríos Montt, civilians throughout the indigenous communities in the western part of the country have been pressed into militia service as part of a counterinsurgency tactic on the part of the army.—EDS.

process of militarization in Guatemala. The armed forces has become the final word on policy decisions; the fundamental force behind the state policy of terror; and the most powerful arm of the state, with activities not only in the military and public security sphere, but also in the areas of economic production and public administration.

It has been pointed out that, to explain militarization, one must understand that it has its roots in the character of the mode of domination within the country, which is based on repression and the organic incorporation of high-ranking military into the monopolistic fraction of the ruling sector, whose interest is interpreted by the army. . . . It is apparent that this model, based on an enormous amount of human suffering, is outdated, cracking under the impact of liberation movements by the people whom it has attempted to subjugate.

19. *Behind the Facade of Democracy: A Liberal Politician's Last Interview* *

BY MANUEL COLOM ARGUETA

MANUEL Colom Argueta, head of a social democratic party, the United Revolutionary Front (FUR), was an outspoken critic of the Guatemalan government in the late 1970s. He exposed the electoral system as a façade behind which small elites competed with one another for power. He was murdered on March 23, 1979, several weeks after the assasination of Alberto Fuentes Mohr, head of the Social Democratic Party (PSD). The murders occurred as both parties were in the process of winning government validation as opposition parties after years of fighting for recognition. Their deaths made a mockery of their parties' official electoral legality and signified for many the assassination of the possibility of peaceful electoral change.

THE CLASS IN POWER, which it shares with the army, is not homogeneous in its interests. It can be divided into a number of influential groups, of which one of the most powerful is the import trade sector. This group, which has strong links with General Ricardo Peralta Méndez, is particularly aggressive in the way it uses its influence and provides much of the finance for the current repression. Most favored by present government policies, this sector was the author of the assassination of Alberto Fuentes Mohr.

Equally strong is the agro-exporting sector, to which belong Raul García Granados, organizer of the Mano Blanca in 1966, and Jorge García Granados, leader

* Reprinted from *Latin American Political Report* (London), April 6, 1979, by permission.

of the Partido Revolucionario and the power behind the throne of President Romeo Lucas García. Within this sector we can distinguish between the emergent millionaires from the dynamic cotton business and the old-fashioned conservative right of the coffee growers.

There is also the traditional monopoly industrial sector, of which Colonel Enrique Peralta Azurdia is the visible head. They are now in conflict with the government. . . . It is not a question of rivalry between businessmen, but of shootouts between rival mafias.

Ever since the Araña and Laugerud administrations, the banking sector has become increasingly penetrated by foreign capital. Nevertheless, the Guatemalan financial sector is extremely strong, hidden behind the apparent holders of power. Their hegemony enables them to decide on economic policy for the government, but because of their international connections, their interests are always subordinate to the interests of foreign investment.

Each new government is chosen by the military hierarchy and the oligarchy which negotiate on a presidential candidate. It is very comfortable to have a disposable President who can be traded in every four years for another "democratically elected" one. This avoids the blemish of a personal dictatorship. A distinguishing characteristic of the present government is that it no longer has the power to arbitrate in inter-oligarchic conflicts. Corruption is the rule, and the army participates in major business deals.

The current strategy of power is selective. It intends to destroy all organized popular resistance, which has grown steadily since 1963. If you look back, you'll see that every single murder is of a key person. They are not all of the same ideological orientation, they are simply the people in each sector or movement who have the capacity to organize the population round a cause.

Much of the blame for the present violence can be laid at the door of interior minister Donaldo Alvarez Ruiz, a member of the Partido Institucional Democrático (PID). Of course the police chief, Colonel Chupina Barahona, has been involved, but the power and role of General David Cancinos Barrios should be particularly noted (army chief of staff and head of the G-2 intelligence service).

There is another reason for the repression: the civil war in Nicaragua. The September bus fares conflict gave the government the excuse it needed to act. The military government of the region adopted a joint plan of action. More people are dying here than in Nicaragua, but no one knows that there's a war going on against the population. We estimate that in the last three months there have been over 2,000 murders. Many were common delinquents, victims of the police, but there are also those killed on contract as a result of the inter-oligarchic disputes, and the victims of the government strategy of selective repression.

It is interesting to note, however, that while the ruling class is fighting it out, the army does not murder within its own ranks. The Instituto de Provisión Militar (IPM) is the army's means of ensuring loyalty among the rank and file. The army is the number one political party in this country.

We can see how periodically the decision is made to ameliorate or debilitate—but never dissolve the paramilitary forces. There are periods of certain respect or tolerance of human rights. For example, one year before the elections there is always a period of smiles and promises about the future.

Mario Sandoval Alarcón (leader of the MLN) is a buffoon straight out of the middle ages. The army uses him a lot, but he also knows how to use the army. His dispute with the PID is over how power should be shared, not over ideological issues. He knows how to blackmail the army. He is willing to accept the blame for a lot of the crimes the army commits, and he demands his share of power in exchange. He has been skillful in involving army officers in business deals with him. He wants to polarize the political struggle, to make himself and his movement indispensable as "bastions against communism."

Jorge Skinner Klee is the great de-nationalizer of our natural resources. He is the lawyer who has drafted every single unpatriotic law in this country. He was a lawyer for the United Fruit Company, he finished drafting the 1956 constitution, he is the author of the laws destroying the agrarian reform, and of those handing petroleum over to foreign interests. He is also a teacher at the school of military studies. I know him well, I know him in detail, and that is why he hates me.

The government is attempting to give itself a democratic veneer, which is why they are recognizing my party (the FUR). But in exchange, they may want my head.

20. The Army Is Apolitical *

BY GENERAL ROMEO LUCAS GARCIA WITH A POSTSCRIPT BY GENERAL EFRAIN RIOS MONTT

IN the following statements, then-president General Romeo Lucas García explains to the nation that the army has always remained aloof from politics. In the first statement, broadcast over radio and television, Lucas reminds the nation that he is neutral in the upcoming elections. Several months later, in March 1982, he explains his lack of political interest to foreign journalists gathered in Guatemala City for the presidential elections. Lucas's hand-picked candidate, General Angel Aníbal Guevara, stole the elections three days later, prompting a coup that deposed Lucas and Guevara. General Efraín Ríos Montt took over the reins of government March 23, 1982.

THE CONSTITUTION SAYS that the army is apolitical. Military men cannot select their candidates. It is the political parties who elect a candidate and they

* Reprinted from the Foreign Broadcast Information Service, July 13, 1981, and March 4, 1982.

are free to select a civilian or a military man. For a military man to be able to participate in politics, he must ask to be discharged and retire. He must have nothing to do with the army. Military men, as you say, must have nothing to do with the elections (July 13, 1981).

I have done everything possible during the four years I have been in power to provide for the people's health, social welfare and education. I feel I have done my duty. . . . I do not intend to show any preference for anyone in the electoral process . . . here in Guatemala we are going to see that elections are free, clean, and pure.

When I retire I do not wish to continue participating in politics as the leader of any party. I am leaving quietly, satisfied with what I have accomplished. I do not want anyone saying that my government was biased . . . I repeat, I do not have any personal interest in any of the candidates. As I have said before, I will hand over power to whoever wins the elections. Personally, I have no interest in continuing in politics. When my term is over, I will be back in the army as a reservist. To me, my country's interests come before anything else. I want everyone to know that in Guatemala we have a democracy. Many people know that we enjoy freedom here.

If any party is not satisfied with the results of the elections and resorts to capricious and obstinate means, we will have to put them in their place. You can be sure that we are trying to hold free elections and that everything is being handled in the open, so that no one can say that elections were shady. The army will act to maintain public order. We are in no condition to condone public disorders. The nation's security comes first. There are people waiting to take advantage of any disorder and this does not benefit the country in any way. We have the security forces to take care of those that try to disturb public order (March 4, 1982).

Ríos Montt adds his point of view:

Q: How did you get into the presidency?

Ríos Montt: The army which made the coup d'etat said to me: "General, you are in command." And now, I am commanding.

Q: Within the military, is there one person whom you consider the leader?

Ríos Montt: There are several, not only one. There are four or five officials.

Q: And among them they . . .

Ríos Montt: Among others. But it is a very special thing. Look, I didn't make the coup, but a general put me here. Go ask them. (Excerpted from an interview, May 1982, Guatemala City.)

21. *A Guatemalan General's Rise to Power* *

BY RAYMOND BONNER

DESPITE President Lucas's assertion that the 1982 elections would be clean, it was obvious to all parties that they had been manipulated again. When the losing parties protested their leaders were briefly detained and their followers forcibly dispersed. Anti-Lucas fervor reached its peak as the March 23, 1982, coup began to take form. General Efraín Ríos Montt headed up the new government junta, sharing power with General Horacio Maldonado Schaad and Colonel Francisco Luis Gordillo Martínez in a shaky coalition supported by both the Christian Democrats and the ultraconservative National Liberation Movement (MLN) (see Editors' Introduction to Part Two, Chapter III).

Some members of the Lucas government, the more notoriously corrupt, were removed from public office although they were mostly replaced with officials from past governments. Ríos Montt served as Army Chief of Staff under President General Carlos Arana Osorio (1970–74), and is accused of orchestrating the massacre of more than one hundred campesinos in 1973. Running for president in 1974 as the candidate of a coalition that included the Christian Democratic Party, Ríos Montt won the election but lost the recount and the office was given to the military candidate, General Kjell Laugerud.[1] In 1978 Ríos Montt became a born-again evangelical minister in the Christian Church of the Word, and had retired from active service until the March coup.

While urban violence appeared to subside after the March coup, in the countryside security forces' attacks escalated. According to the Committee of Campesino Unity (CUC), three thousand campesinos were killed in the first six weeks of the Ríos Montt government and a scorched-earth policy was destroying food supplies. After Ríos Montt's consolidation of power in June and the implementation of a state of siege in July, public discussion of politics, particularly in the media, has been banned, replaced with discussion of Ríos Montt's vision of government and society, "communitarianism."[2]

GUATEMALA, JULY 16—Some politicians and diplomats here are offering a version of the events surrounding Gen. Efraín Ríos Montt's rise to power that is at odds with the one given by the general and his backers.

According to one Guatemalan political source, General Ríos Montt participated in the planning of the March 23 coup, contrary to widespread reports that he did not learn about it until army units had surrounded the palace.

---

* Reprinted from *The New York Times*, July 21, 1982, by permission.

1. Kjell Laugerud's record is discussed in Reading 13.—EDS.

2. Ríos Montt expounds on his vision of communitarianism in Reading 29.—EDS.

The source said the two army officers who were members of the junta established after the coup did not resign voluntarily last month, as General Ríos Montt said, but were forced out by the general and officers loyal to him.

One of the ousted junta members initially resisted, the Guatemalans said, pulling the pin on a grenade in the presence of General Ríos Montt and several officers. Although the junta member changed his mind, the sources said, he did not sign the resignation papers. Later, he and the other dismissed junta member were offered $50,000 to remain quiet, according to the sources.

A *Foe of the Strongman*

The new version of the March 23 coup and subsequent developments was provided primarily by a Guatemalan Government official close to the events and opposed to General Ríos Montt. The version was confirmed by some political leaders and a foreign diplomat.

According to official accounts, the small group of junior army and air force officers who deposed the Government of Gen. Fernando Romeo Lucas García on March 23 seized a radio station and made a public call for General Ríos Montt to join them. The general was reported to have been in church at the time. As a result of statements by church elders and by the general, it has been widely accepted that this was the first knowledge that General Ríos Montt had of the coup.

But the Guatemalan official and a political leader said that on March 13, ten days before the coup, General Ríos Montt attended a meeting with the young officers and political leaders of the right-wing National Liberation Party. The purpose of the meeting, according to the official, was "to finish organizing the logistics" of the coup.

On the day of the coup, three successive juntas were formed, with General Ríos Montt being the only person included in all of them. The final junta, of which he was president, also included Gen. Horacio Egberto Maldonado Schaad and Col. Francisco Luis Gordillo Martínez.

"From the beginning," General Maldonado and Colonel Gordillo knew that they were not going to survive as junta members, "but not the hour and day" they would fall, the Guatemalan official said.

The end came on June 9. What the Guatemalan official called a "working breakfast" had been scheduled for 7 A.M. But, he said, it was not a working breakfast at all, but a "goodbye ceremony," with armed soldiers present to enforce the will of General Ríos Montt.

The general has said the two junta members voluntarily signed resignation papers. The official said, however, that there was nothing voluntary about the resignations.

According to the official, on the evening of June 20, a military officer in the Government called on Colonel Gordillo at his home, where he was under house arrest. He offered the colonel $50,000. Two days later, a civilian minister came to ask whether the colonel wanted the payment in dollars or in local currency.

According to a diplomat, the same offer was made to General Maldonado.

The Guatemalan official said that Colonel Gordillo had not accepted the money, and that he did not know what General Maldonado had done.

There have been no indications that the United States participated in the planning or execution of the coup. But it has acted to prevent at least one powerful faction from deposing General Ríos Montt, according to a diplomat.

It is widely accepted that the general won the 1974 presidential election, but that the victory was "stolen" from him by the National Liberation Movement Party.

According to the diplomat, the American Ambassador, Frederic L. Chapin, warned the leaders of the National Liberation Movement that United States aid would be cut off if they participated in a coup to depose General Ríos Montt.

22. *Behind Guatemala's Military Power* *

BY THE INSTITUTE FOR POLICY STUDIES

AFTER the 1954 coup, and on into the 1960s and 1970s, Guatemala was a strategic ally of the United States, a base from which to monitor and control leftist movements in the Caribbean and Central America. In return for this loyalty the United States supplied the Guatemalan government with military equipment and training necessary to fight their own battle against leftist "subversives" within their borders. This article shows the provenance of this military support. It is ironic that the U.S., which supplies aid to the Guatemalan and other right-wing governments in Central America, denounces as intolerable even the idea of any comparable military aid for the rebels. Since human rights sanctions limited U.S. military aid to Guatemala in the late 1970s, U.S. allies such as Israel and Taiwan have filled the void.

AFTER HELPING to overthrow Arbenz, the United States began to provide substantial amounts of military aid for internal security. In 1959 there were 15 U.S. advisors in Guatemala with the Military Assistance Advisory Group (MAAG). By 1965 the total reached 34, a figure which proportionately repre-

* This reading is excerpted from two Institute for Policy Studies Reports: *Background Information on Guatemala*, prepared by Delia Miller and Roland Seeman with Cynthia Arnson in June 1981, and *Update #1 Background Information on Guatemala* (Washington, D.C.), prepared by Flora Montealegre and Cynthia Arnson, July 1982.

sented the largest advisory group in Latin America. Counterinsurgency efforts were a response both to the emergence of a guerrilla movement in Guatemala in the 1960s, and to U.S. concerns with "second Cubas" in the hemisphere after Fidel Castro's triumph in 1959.

Upon request of the Guatemalan government, the U.S. Office of Public Safety (OPS), under the aegis of the Agency for International Development, began a program in Guatemala in 1957. One of the program's objectives was "to strengthen the internal security of Guatemala by improving the organization of the National Police." The program was "oriented towards the provision of technical assistance to assist the [Government of Guatemala] in the development of effective police forces capable of providing stability to the country and protection for its citizens."

Between Fiscal Year 1957 and the program's termination by an act of Congress in 1974, the U.S. government spent a total of $4,425,000 to train 435 policemen and to supply them with arms, communications, office and photographic equipment, motor vehicles and riot control gear. The program was most active in the late '60s, with expenditures doubling from $1,029,000 between 1963 and 1966 to $2,402,000 between 1967 and 1970.

Between 1958 and 1974, the OPS provided training for 404 Guatemalan policemen at the International Police Academy in Washington and another 31 at the Inter-American Police Academy in the Panama Canal Zone. Others were trained in a variety of programs within Guatemala. During the course of the program, 24 American advisors worked with their Guatemalan counterparts in the National and Judicial Police on a daily basis.

Public Safety advisors helped set up a permanent police training complex at Los Cipreseles. They also organized and equipped a rural patrol division designed to introduce mobile police units into rural areas. They developed a country-wide tele-communications network which connected the 22 departmental capitals and Guatemala City. The Communications Operations and Dispatch Center "contributed to improved coordination and efficiency of the entire [National] Police organization." OPS advisors trained and equipped the Guatemalan police in riot control, bomb disposal, fingerprinting, photography, criminalistics and motor vehicle maintenance.

Program funds were used to purchase 3,327 pistols, revolvers, carbines and shotguns; 644,000 rounds of ammunition; 444 vehicles including jeeps, trucks and buses; 6,383 tear-gas grenades and projectiles; 710 gas masks; 319 radios; 1,266 helmets, batons and safety shields.

In the 1974 phase-out study of the Public Safety Program in Guatemala, the Office of Public Safety concluded that:

> Riot control training and related phases of coping with civil disturbances in a humane and effective manner became institutionalized in the National Police within the past three years. In the mid-60s, the Public Safety Program provided

essential riot control equipment as an interim measure to establish the predicate for more humane treatment of persons involved in civil disturbances.

The record, however, was somewhat different. In 1967–68, an estimated 7,000 people were killed in the campaign of terror aimed at eliminating a guerrilla force that numbered "no more than 450 men at the peak of their activity."

The counterinsurgency effort was undertaken not only by the U.S.-trained internal security forces, but to a significant extent by right-wing para-military groups. When the guerrillas were eliminated, right-wing death squads "continued to operate, abducting and assassinating opposition leaders and their sympathizers and sometimes killing at random for the purpose of general intimidation. . . . Between 1966 and 1976 some 20,000 people had died at the hands of these para-military squads," according to Amnesty International. These include trade unionists, peasants, students, journalists, university professors, priests, and virtually anyone suspected of associating with critics of the regime.

Recent U.S. Policy and U.S. Military Assistance

Since 1977 U.S. policy toward Guatemala has been constrained by the continuing reports of serious human rights violations by the Guatemalan government. This has led the U.S. Congress to reject administration requests for military assistance, even at a time when concern over the country's mounting guerrilla insurgency was increasing. In Fiscal Years 1978, 1979, 1981, and 1982, the Pentagon requested no new military aid for Guatemala. In Fiscal Year 1980, a modest request for $250,000 in military training was overturned by the House Foreign Affairs Committee.

In the Fiscal Year 1982 budget request, the Reagan Administration told Congress that "the continuing fluidity of the political situation in Nicaragua and El Salvador, the near unanimous international support for independence of adjoining Belize, which Guatemala claims, and Cuban-supported subversion in Central America contribute to the continuing perception by the [Government of Guatemala] that the country is increasingly isolated and endangered." Thus, "a limited U.S. security assistance program can provide an effective means of maintaining an overall cooperative relationship." While the use of public funds to finance arms sales to Guatemala is still banned, equipment can be purchased on a cash basis.

During the debate over military aid in Fiscal Year 1982 (a budget prepared by the Carter administration but authorized in the first year of the Reagan administration), Representatives Michael Barnes (D-Md) and Stephen Solarz (D-NY) agreed not to introduce formal legislation banning military aid to Guatemala in exchange for administration assurances that no military sales, grants, or training would be provided without prior consultation with and approval by the House Foreign Affairs Committee.

In Fiscal Year 1983, the administration asked Congress for $250,000 in International Military Education and Training (IMET) grants in a program designed "to help the Guatemalans defend themselves against the leftist guerrillas, and to control the spread of violence of all kinds." The Defense Department also indicated that Guatemala would be permitted to purchase modest amounts of equipment for cash through the Foreign Military Sales program. The request, made prior to the Ríos Montt coup of March 1982, noted that:

> Guatemala is facing a Cuban-supported Marxist insurgency that seeks to overthrow the government. If it succeeds, neither our objectives nor those of the Guatemalan people will survive. The challenge Guatemala faces is to respond effectively to the guerrilla threat, without engaging in the indiscriminate violence to which some elements of the Guatemalan security forces have resorted.[1]

As of this writing, Congress had not finally approved the Fiscal Year 1983 foreign aid bill. However, both the Senate Foreign Relations Committee and the House Foreign Affairs Committee approved the inclusion of $250,000 in IMET funds for Guatemala. The House Foreign Affairs Committee nevertheless reiterated its expectation that "its understanding with the executive branch with respect to military assistance, military training, and foreign military sales will continue in effect for the remainder of fiscal year 1982 and fiscal year 1983; that is, that no such assistance will be provided to Guatemala without the approval of the Committee on Foreign Affairs." [2]

After the Ríos Montt coup, Assistant Secretary of State for Inter-American Affairs Thomas Enders told a House Subcommittee that "a promising evolution may have begun" in Guatemala, and that "concrete measures have been taken against corruption. . . . All political forces have been called to join in national reconciliation. We hope that the new government of Guatemala will continue to make progress in these areas and that we in turn will be able to establish a closer, more collaborative relationship with this key country."

Accordingly, the administration began consulting with members of the House Foreign Affairs Committee about a sale of $3.5 million in spare parts, mostly for helicopters crucial to the counterinsurgency war, as well as a "re-programming" of $50,000 in military training funds. A delegation of congressional aides who visited Guatemala City in May 1982, however, was told by Ríos Montt that his government had not requested military aid, and discovered that the administration's proposal for spare parts had originated with the Lucas García government. Shortly after the aides returned, Deputy Assistant Secretary of State Stephen Bosworth visited Guatemala. Following meetings with government leaders, then-

1. U.S. Department of Defense, *Congressional Presentation,* p. 461.
2. U.S. Congress, House, Committee on Foreign Affairs, *International Security and Development Cooperation Act of 1982, Report* No. 97-547, 97th Cong., 1st sess., 1982, p. 13.

junta member Colonel Francisco Gordillo announced that Guatemala needed economic and military aid from the United States.

As of early July 1982, the reaction of members of the House Foreign Affairs Committee to the spare parts and reprogramming requests was that no military aid be given pending a demonstration by the Ríos Montt government that it would make good on its pledge to curb human rights abuses.

Commerce Department Sales

Since at least mid-1981, the Guatemalan government has purchased significant amounts of equipment for military use through the Department of Commerce. These items, while not appearing on the U.S. Munitions List detailing all equipment configured for military use, are nevertheless used by the armed forces for military purposes. One such sale which stirred considerable controversy involved Guatemala's purchase of 50 2½ ton trucks and 100 jeeps in June 1981. The Commerce Department removed the trucks and jeeps from the "Crime Control and Detection" list, which contains prohibitions on sales to countries which violate human rights, and placed them in a new category of "Control for Regional Stability."

Fifty-four members of the House of Representatives wrote to then–Secretary of State Alexander Haig protesting the sale, on the grounds that it would support "terrorist elements within the Guatemalan military and [appeared] to reflect a conscious effort to undermine the human rights provisions of our arms export control laws."

In 1980 and 1981 the Guatemalan government also spent about $10.5 million on three Bell 212 and six Bell 412 helicopters sold through the Commerce Department. According to early reports, at least two of the helicopters had been mounted with .30 caliber machine guns.[3] The Bell 212 is a civilian version of the Bell UH-1N; the two have basically the same configuration but different electronics and mission kits. The 212 carries a pilot and 14 passengers. The 412 is a four-blade variant of the 212, but has a more stable flight.[4] Photos appearing in the Guatemalan press also identified the Bell 212 as a "military helicopter on a patrol mission flying over the zone of San José Poaquil."[5]

Under the consultation agreement worked out between the Reagan Administration and the House Foreign Affairs Committee, Commerce Department sales do not necessarily have to be presented for review. Indeed, given the licensing procedures in the Commerce Department, members of the State Department often are not aware that a sale is being processed.

---

3. *Washington Post*, Jan. 23, 1981.
4. John W. R. Taylor, ed., *Jane's All the World's Aircraft*, 1976–1977 and 1981–1982 editions (London: Jane's Publishers, 1976 and 1981) p. 231 and p. 299.
5. *El Gráfico* (Guatemala City), 1981 (exact date unknown).

Arms Sales by Non-U.S. Suppliers

Over the past decade Israel, France, Switzerland, Taiwan, Italy, Belgium, and Yugoslavia have also supplied arms to Guatemala. Many of these sales are reported by international research organizations such as the Stockholm Peace Research Institute (SIPRI) and the International Institute for Strategic Studies (IISS). Sales of small arms, electronics, and personal equipment, however, often escape detection. Based on our own research and press accounts, we have been able to piece together the following information:[6]

Junior officers in the Guatemalan Army have claimed that since 1975 Guatemala has spent $175 million on Italian, Belgian, Israeli, and Yugoslav weapons. Senior officers reportedly declared their value to be $425 million and pocketed the difference.

Israeli machine guns and personal equipment are now standard issue to Guatemalan troops. In 1980, however, the Israeli labor federation *Histadrut* wrote Israeli Prime Minister Menachem Begin asking that all arms sales to Guatemala be stopped. The letter called human rights violations in Guatemala "an affront to all humanity and civilization."

In July 1981 the Chairman of the Taiwan Joint Chiefs of Staff Admiral Chang Chi-Soong visited Guatemala City and offered "to continue technical military aid" against leftist guerrillas. For at least a decade, numerous Central American officers have received training in Taiwan.

In August 1981 then-Defense Minister Anibal Guevara sent to the Guatemalan Congress a bill providing for the domestic manufacture of small arms and ammunition. The legislation was designed to reduce Guatemala's dependence on foreign suppliers. The status of the legislation is unclear given the dissolution of the legislature, but many observers believe that Guatemala will soon have its own arms-producing capacity.

In November 1981, Generals Romeo and Benedicto Lucas García inaugurated in Guatemala City the Army Electronics and Transmissions School *(Escuela de Transmisiones y Electrónica del Ejército)* built with Israeli assistance and technology. During the ceremonies, attended by the Israeli ambassador to Guatemala, President Lucas García stated that "thanks to the assistance and transfer of electronic technology provided by the State of Israel to Guatemala" the Guatemalan Army has enhanced its ability to stay on top of the latest technological developments.

[Due to space limitations we have eliminated the footnotes from the text. The resources used in compilation of this piece are: *Diario Las Americas,* June 3, 1982; North American Congress on Latin America (NACLA), *Guatemala* (New York:

6. *Latin America Weekly Report,* July 31, 1981; *Washington Post,* Jan. 23, 1982; *FBIS,* July 27, 1981, and Aug. 10, 1981; *El Gráfico* (Guatemala City), Nov. 4, 1981; Latin America Working Group, *Latin American and Caribbean Labor Report,* Toronto, May 1980.

NACLA, 1974); Caesar D. Sereseres, "Guatemalan Paramilitary Forces, Internal Security, and Politics," in Louis A. Zucher and Gwen Havries, eds., *Supplemental Military Forces* (Beverly Hills, Ca:SAGE Publications, 1978); U.S. Congress, House, Committee on International Relations, Subcommittee on International Organizations, *Human Rights in Nicaragua, Guatemala, and El Salvador: Implications for U.S. Policy*, Hearings, 94th Cong., 2nd sess., 1976; U.S. Office of Public Safety, *Termination Phase-Out Study of the Public Safety Project: Guatemala* (Washington, D.C.: U.S. Agency for International Development July 1974); *Washington Post*, April 22 and June 25, 1982—EDS.]

Chapter III:

How Power Is Maintained

Editors' Introduction

THE question of how a government can maintain stability and control of its citizens while permitting their participation and dissension has been an issue central to political theoreticians for centuries. James Madison, in defending the proposed U.S. Constitution in 1788, expressed the objective of early U.S. political strategists:

> You must enable the government to control the governed: and in the next place oblige it to control itself.[1]

According to standard measures of political stability, the regimes in Guatemala since Arbenz have been notoriously fragile, a series of Madisonian nightmares, neither able to control themselves, nor, ultimately, the people they ruled. In Guatemala the specter of popular power revealed during the Arévalo and Arbenz periods was so threatening to the local elite that it struck back by abandoning a legitimization based upon participation by the people. Instead, by cynically manipulating election results, by palace coups, and mainly by brutal suppression, a shifting group, hardly deserving the term coalition, has managed to hold onto power. Lacking a coherent national ideology,[2] the government seeks legitimacy only by claiming that it is fighting communist subversion. While that may win

1. *Federalist Papers,* No. 51 (formerly attributed to Alexander Hamilton).

2. For a discussion of national ideology and nation-building in Central America and Mexico, see Mary W. Helms, *Middle America* (Englewood Cliffs, N.J.: Prentice-Hall, Inc., 1975), Chapter 18.

considerable support for a succession of Guatemalan regimes in official Washington, D.C., it has proved insufficient to ensure stability in the country itself. Terror has been the substitute.

In addition to police and military campaigns against suspected leftists and their sympathizers (see Reading 24), in 1966 the first civilian paramilitary bands joined in terrorizing eastern Guatemala. The Mano Blanca and other groups operated in conjunction with then-Colonel Carlos Arana Osorio's counterinsurgency drive in 1968. Arana, after establishing himself as the "Butcher of Zacapa," won the 1970 presidency as the candidate of the National Liberation Movement (MLN), the party with the closest involvement in death squad activity. Reflecting the ultraconservative identification with terror as an ideological rallying point, MLN 1982 vice-presidential candidate Lionel Sisniega Otero explained in 1980 why the MLN is called "the party of organized violence": "Color organized is a painting. Sound organized is a melody. Violence organized is strength." [3]

A soldier, assigned to a death squad, described his adoption of this ruthless attitude:

> They [the officers] had already filled my head with their own ideology, so I felt superior to my fellow soldiers. . . . What I thought then was that I was superior to everyone because I had managed to reach this position. . . . [I could kill] anyone who turned up, if we were told to, I could have done it then, that's how I used to feel, I'd do anything the army told me to.[4]

For those targeted for elimination by the death squads, an appropriate response was often one of rebellion. As popular resistance grew, so did the machinery of terror. By 1978 and the advent of the Lucas García regime, death squads were inextricably linked to the national government, operated from within the National Palace (see Reading 24).

The government of General Efraín Ríos Montt has not dismantled the death squads and continued kidnappings bear witness to their operation. Ríos Montt has merely added to the ideology of terror a call for religious national rejuvenation.

The military is forcing thousands of civilian campesinos to join bands of vigilantes whose attacks against other civilians are then attributed to the guerrillas. Born-again Christian Ríos Montt vowed just as this book was being completed to wipe out subversion in six months.[5] If there is not a significant victory of the

3. Cited in the Canadian Broadcasting Corporation's program, "Fifth Estate: Guatemala," aired October 1, 1980. Sisniega's role in the March 1982 coup is discussed briefly in Reading 22.

4. Quoted in Amnesty International, *Guatemala: A Government Program of Political Murder* (London: Amnesty International, 1979).

5. Raymond Bonner, dispatch from Guatemala City, *New York Times*, July 15, 1982.

forces of the left, the terror will continue. Conjuring up an image of a vengeful god, a preacher from Ríos Montt's church explained. "He who resists the authorities is resisting the will of God." [6]

23. *We Do Not Violate Human Rights in Guatemala* *

By General Romeo Lucas Garcia

DURING the government of General Romeo Lucas García (1978–82), the violence perpetrated by death squads, under presidential direction, reached staggering proportions. Tortured bodies appeared daily on the roadsides; people stopped going out at night; others fled into exile. In the following speech, excerpted from a presentation to representatives of the executive, legislative, and judicial branches of the Guatemalan government, Lucas summarized the accomplishments of his regime from a startling personal perspective.

ON BECOMING PRESIDENT three years ago, I expressed the intention of my government to promote the progress of the fatherland and to guarantee a democratic regime which respects the rights of the Guatemalans. Today, I can say that the government I head has been true to its promises and has duly complied with its decision to oversee the interests of the people, especially the majority of the people, and it has also backed the government institutions by facing international subversion within the framework of the law. My government is profoundly nationalistic and does not accept foreign guidance. Its strength is based on the judicial system and its reasoning is based on the constitutional principles that have always guided us. . . .

With our resources we are carrying out civic projects and social benefit programs for the benefit of all. We have faced up to the subversion sponsored by international groups without any help from abroad. [Applause]

For this reason, we demand that everyone stay out of our problems. We are a country that has its own laws and its own way of doing things. Within this framework, we once again demand that we be allowed to solve our own problems. As I said, we have our own way of doing things and solving our problems here in Guatemala, in our own environment. We do not want to be helped with theories or examples tried out in other countries. We know our environment. . . .

---

6. Raymond Bonner, dispatch from Guatemala City, *New York Times*, July 18, 1982.

* Reprinted from the Foreign Broadcast Information Service, July 1, 1981.

I have wanted to stress at this point that we are carrving out projects in Guatemala. We are carrying out social projects and building the infrastructure for the country's development so that foreign congressmen will not come here to tell us that we should be doing something to win over the people. We are giving what we can to the people. We know that the Guatemalan people need more and deserve much more. All of the sacrifices of my government seek to improve the living conditions of the Guatemalans. We are doing this. However, we don't allow foreigners to come here and tell us we should do something, because they don't know how to make the bed in their own houses. They have someone to do it for them.

These people come speaking a language that to us is already hackneyed. They come speaking of human rights, saying that human rights are being violated in Guatemala. We know that human rights have been violated in many countries. Here in Guatemala this has been one of the principles of my government. It has been stressed to all the officials that human rights must not be violated. Why? Because we are signatories of those human rights. We are not violating human rights in Guatemala. In Guatemala there is a war between communism and the freedoms that Guatemala needs for the enrichment and the future of our dear fatherland, Guatemala. We will defend it to the end with our blood if necessary. [Applause]

You have seen that the killings, the blackmail, and other criminal actions of the subversive groups have not been able to stop my government program. When we have exterminated that social blot, those criminals, we will be able to more rapidly advance to the collective well-being. However, each and every Guatemalan must be aware that the defense of freedom is not only up to the government. Everyone has the responsibility to participate in their trench to maintain the country's sovereignty unharmed. [Applause]

The anti-Guatemalan campaign launched abroad by foreign organizations has certainly failed. They only seek to sully our national image. Such an organization is the undesirable Amnesty International, which is an agency of the red dictatorships. Therefore when I am told Amnesty International says such and such a thing, I turn a deaf ear to those people because I know where they come from.

However, we must not let down our guard. My government is willing to resort to all the extremes that the law establishes to prevent the traitors from trying to seize power.

24. Guatemala: A Government Program of Political Murder *

By Amnesty International

In the following excerpts from a 1981 report by the respected international agency, Amnesty International, the security apparatus is clinically described. The substance of Amnesty International's earlier report on Guatemala, in December 1975, was presented as testimony to the U.S. House of Representatives Subcommittee on International Relations in June 1976, under the title "Guatemala: Death Squads and Disappearances." A more recent Amnesty International report of July 1982, "Guatemala: Massive Extrajudicial Executions in the Rural Areas under the Government of General Efraín Ríos Montt," has been presented at Congressional hearings on President Ronald Reagan's proposed "Caribbean Basin Initiative." Space considerations prevent more extensive presentation in this book of the authoritative reports from Amnesty International.

The Security Machine

NEARLY 5,000 GUATEMALANS have been seized without warrant and killed since General Lucas García became President of Guatemala in 1978. The bodies of the victims have been found piled up in ravines, dumped at roadsides or buried in mass graves. Thousands bore the scars of torture, and death had come to most by strangling with a garrotte, by being suffocated in rubber hoods or by being shot in the head.

In the same three-year period several hundred other Guatemalans have been assassinated after being denounced as "subversives." At least 615 people who are reported to have been seized by the security services remain unaccounted for.

In spite of these murders and "disappearances" the Government of Guatemala has denied making a single political arrest or holding a single political prisoner. (But in February 1980 Vice-President Francisco Villagran Kramer put the position like this: "There are no political prisoners in Guatemala—only political murders." He has since resigned and gone into exile.)

The government does not deny that people it considers to be "subversives" or "criminals" are seized and murdered daily in Guatemala—but it lays the whole blame on independent, anticommunist "death squads."

According to a distinction drawn by the government under President Lucas

---

* Excerpted with permission from Amnesty International's *Guatemala: A Government Program of Political Murder* (London), February 1981.

García "criminals" are those people who have been seized and killed by what the authorities call the *Escuadrón de la Muerte* (Death Squad) and "subversives" those killed by the *Ejército Secreto Anticomunista* (ESA)—Secret Anticommunist Army. The authorities have issued regular statistics on the killings and on occasion have come out with death tolls higher than those independently recorded by Amnesty International.

What the Government of Guatemala Says

National Police spokesmen told the local press in 1979 that the *Escuadrón de la Muerte* had killed 1,224 "criminals" ("1,142 men and 82 women") from January to June 1979 and that the ESA had killed 3,252 "subversives" in the first 10 months of 1979. Although no similar statistics have been issued for 1980, government spokesmen have continued to report on the latest victims of "anti-criminal" and "anti-communist," but allegedly independent and non-governmental, "security measures."

Amnesty International believes that abuses attributed by the Government of Guatemala to independent "death squads" are perpetrated by the regular forces of the civil and military security services. No evidence has been found to support government claims that "death squads" exist that are independent of the regular security services. Where the captors or assassins of alleged "subversives" and "criminals" have been identified, as in the cases cited in this report, the perpetrators have been members of the regular security services.

The Victims

During 1980 the security forces of the Government of Guatemala were reported to have been involved in unexplained detentions and murders of people generally considered as leaders of public opinion: members of the clergy, educators and students, lawyers, doctors, trade unionists, journalists and community workers. But the vast majority of the victims of such violent action by the authorities' forces had little or no social status; they came from the urban poor and the peasantry and their personal political activities were either insignificant or wholly imagined by their captors.

The precarious balance for the poor in Guatemala between life and death at the hands of the security services is illustrated by the testimonies. . . . A former soldier describes house-to-house searches in which the discovery of certain "papers"—leaflets or circulars—was sufficient reason to wipe out an entire family. A prisoner, who was brutally tortured and escaped only the day before he was due to be executed at Huehuetenango army base, believes that a neighbor denounced him as a "subversive" because of a dispute over the village basketball court—a good enough reason, as far as officers of the Guatemalan army were concerned, for him to be tortured and put to death.

At first glance most of the victims of political repression in Guatemala appear to have been singled out indiscriminately from among the poor; but the secret detentions, "disappearances" and killings are not entirely random; they follow denunciations by neighbors, employers or local security officials, and the evidence available to Amnesty International reveals a pattern of selective and considered official action. By far the majority of victims were chosen after they had become associated—or were thought to be associated—with social, religious, community or labor organizations, or after they had been in contact with organizers of national political parties. In other words, Amnesty International's evidence is that the targets for extreme governmental violence tend to be selected from grassroots organizations outside official control.

A more elaborate pattern is followed for dealing with Guatemalans of higher social or economic status, such as business people and professionals—doctors, lawyers, educators—or with leaders of legal political parties. Where people in these groups are suspected of "subversive" activity, past or present, the discretionary powers of security service agents do not appear to be unrestricted. Such cases are thought to require consideration by high-ranking government officials before individuals can be seized or murdered; the system appears to function hierarchically, with the official level at which a decision may be taken corresponding to the status of the suspect.

In 1980 a number of occupational groups which, in recent years, had largely escaped being the particular targets of political repression were singled out for violent attacks, resulting in numerous "disappearances" and deaths; they included priests, educators and journalists.

Father Conrado de la Cruz and his assistant Herlindo Cifuentes were detained with at least 44 other people during a demonstration in Guatemala on 1 May 1980; the pair have since "disappeared"—many of the others have been found dead. Three other Roman Catholic priests are reported to have been killed by the security services in 1980: José María Gran, Walter Voordeckers and Faustino Villaneuva. Other clergy have been formally expelled from Guatemala.

After March 1980 the teachers and administrators of the national university, *Universidad de San Carlos de Guatemala* (USAC), were singled out. By mid-September 12 members of the law faculty and 15 other teachers and administrators had been killed, including four members of the USAC executive committee. The Rector, Saúl Osorio, and some 50 staff members fled into exile.

At least 71 USAC students died or "disappeared" after detention in 1980; 53 teachers have been shot dead in different parts of the country.

The President's "Special Agency"

The evidence compiled and published by Amnesty International in recent years indicates that routine assassinations, secret detentions and summary executions are part of a clearly defined program of government in Guatemala.

New information in the possession of Amnesty International bears this out. It shows that the task of coordinating civil and military security operations in the political sphere is carried out by a specialized agency under the direct supervision of President Lucas García.

This presidential agency is situated in the Presidential Guard annex to the National Palace, near the offices of the President and his principal ministers, and next to the Presidential Residence, the *Casa Presidencial*. Known until recently as the *Centro Regional de Telecomunicaciones* (Regional Telecommunications Center), the agency is situated under two rooftop telecommunications masts on the block-long building.

The telecommunications center in the palace annex is a key installation in Guatemala's security network. For years informed sources in the country referred to the organization working from there as the *Policía Regional* (Regional Police)—although the authorities repeatedly denied the existence of such a body. In 1978 a former Mayor of Guatemala City, Manuel Colom Argueta, denounced the *Policía Regional* as a "death squad." On 23 March 1979 he was assassinated in the city center as a police helicopter hovered overhead.

The center was previously called the *Agencia de Inteligencia de la Presidencia* (Presidential Intelligence Agency); in a speech in 1966 Colonel Enrique Peralta Azurdia, head of state from 1963 to 1966, described its founding in the National Palace complex in 1964.

During 1980 sources in Guatemala City reported that the name had been changed again, to the *Servicios Especiales de Comunicaciones de la Presidencia* (Presidential Special Services for Communications); an alternative title was said to be the *Servicios de Apoyo de la Presidencia* (Presidential Support Services).

It is this presidential agency, situated in the palace complex and known by various names, which Amnesty International believes to be coordinating the Government of Guatemala's extensive secret and extra-legal security operations.

In 1974 a document from the records of a United States assistance program described the *Centro Regional de Telecomunicaciones* as Guatemala's principal presidential-level security agency, working with a "high level security/administrative network" linking "the principal officials of the National Police, Treasury Police, Detective Corps, Ministry of Government [Gobernación; alternatively translated as "Interior"], the Presidential House [Palace], and the Guatemalan Military Communications Center." (The document, which was declassified, came from the United States Agency for International Development, *Termination Phase-Out Study, Public Safety Project: Guatemala*, July 1974.)

The National Palace complex makes it possible for the security services to centralize their communications and also to have access to the central files of the army intelligence division, which are reported to be housed in the Presidential Residence itself. The files are believed to include dossiers on people who were political suspects even at the time of the overthrow of the government of Colonel Jacobo Arbenz in 1954—they include Colonel Arbenz's active supporters in the left-wing political parties of the time.

Files of political suspects were established by law in Guatemala first in the wake of the 1954 coup and more recently under the auspices of Military Intelligence in 1963, when they were incorporated into a "National Security Archive" (Decree Law 9, 1963, *Ley de Defensa de las Instituciones Democráticas*). It is believed that outdated files are still used as a basis for political persecution.

In many cases on record with Amnesty International political activities during the 1940s and 1950s appear to have been the sole motive for a detention followed by "disappearance" or by a "death squad" killing. For instance, the submachine-gun attack in September 1980 on Professor Lucila Rodas de Villagran, 60-year-old head of a girls' school, was widely attributed to her active membership in her youth of the *Partido Acción Revolucionaria* (Revolutionary Action Party), which ceased to exist more than 25 years ago.

Reliable sources in Guatemala say that the presidential intelligence agency is directed by the joint head of the Presidential General Staff *(Estado Mayor Presidencial)* and Military Intelligence. Policy decisions and the selection of who is to "disappear" and be killed are said to be made after consultations between the top officials of the Ministries of Defense and the Interior, and the Army General Staff, who command the forces responsible for the abuses.

Much of the information included in this section is general knowledge among informed Guatemalans of many political orientations. It is widely accepted that the Presidential Guard annex of the National Palace houses the headquarters for the secret operations of the security services. Entry to the center is guarded by heavily armed soldiers, with closed-circuit television cameras mounted on the corners of the building. Unmarked cars without license plates, or with foreign plates, are usually parked outside the center.

Details of the presidential coordinating agency's operations are not known—for example, Amnesty International has not been able to confirm allegations by some Guatemalans that the agency holds prisoners inside the Presidential Guard annex—but that the agency exists and that it serves as the center of the Guatemalan Government's program of "disappearance" and political murder seem, on the evidence, difficult to dispute.

The Army and the Police—the Units Accused

Most of the responsibility for the thousands of cases of human rights violations reported to Amnesty International during the presidency of General Lucas García has been attributed to either army or police units. This is how they operate:

The army—Regular uniformed units, including paratroops and *Kaibiles* (Special Forces), are those most frequently held responsible for arbitrary detentions, "disappearances" and killings in rural areas where guerrilla groups are active, notably El Quiché Province. House-to-house searches by uniformed soldiers are regularly reported throughout the country. In addition, plainclothes army squads are routinely reported in Guatemala City. Recently a number of their members have been overpowered and found to be in possession of identification cards showing them to belong to the army.

The most widely reported mass killing by regular army forces took place on May 29, 1978 in the town square of Panzós, Alta Verapaz (see Reading 33—EDS.). More than 100 Kekchí Indians, including five children, were shot dead. Soldiers positioned on rooftops and inside buildings had opened fire as the Indians gathered in the square to protest about land rights. Townspeople say that mass graves had been dug two days *before* the killings. The army issued a statement charging the Indians with attacking one of their garrisons. Two trucks filled with bodies were photographed as they were driven off to the graves.

The *Policía Militar Ambulante* (PMA)—mobile military police—is an army unit which serves in both urban and rural areas as a mobile force with powers to arrest civilians. Large landholders in the countryside and private enterprises in the cities can hire individual members of the PMA from the army as plantation or building guards—and in practice as bodyguards. The PMA is named in many reports of abuses on and around large plantations in rural areas, and of seizure and "disappearance" of trade union leaders at factories where the PMA provide security services.

The size of the PMA is a state secret in Guatemala. It is difficult to compute with accuracy: personnel are recalled from army reserves as the demand for privately contracted PMA guards rises. In 1974 there were an estimated 1,140 PMA members on active duty.

The *comisionados militares* are civilian agents of the army, serving under military discipline. Most are former non-commissioned officers. They are responsible for recruitment—forcible conscription is the norm in Guatemala—and for routine intelligence reports to regional army headquarters; *comisionados* are stationed in every hamlet in Guatemala and one of their main roles is to serve as the eyes and ears of the army. They have law enforcement functions and in some areas are heavily armed and are regularly reported to be involved in arbitrary detentions and killings.

The *Policía Nacional* (National Police)—Headed by an army colonel, the National Police is the major civil police body in Guatemala, and is particularly active in the capital, Guatemala City. The National Police works closely with regular army forces in provincial areas and in the cities it works closely with the PMA.

In 1980 the National Police was responsible for the killing of prisoners officially recognized to be in police custody—the killings took place during transfers from one prison to another, and while prisoners were receiving treatment for gunshot wounds in public hospitals. Another group of "disappearances" and killings attributed to the National Police involves people convicted of nonpolitical criminal offences, particularly recidivists, who have been found dead after being detained in Guatemala City, and of people killed immediately after their release from prison. Prisoners on El Pavón Prison Farm *(Granja Penal)*, near Guatemala City, went on strike in 1979 to protest against the systematic murder of convicts who had been released after their sentences expired. Many of the 37 bodies of victims killed by garrotte who were found in a ravine in San Juan Comalapa were identified as those of former prison inmates.

Two special units of the National Police, the *Comando Seis* (6th Commando) and the *Pelotón Modelo* (Model Platoon), have been particularly active during political demonstrations and have been identified as having detained demonstrators who subsequently "disappeared."

The *Cuerpo de Detectives de la Policía Nacional* (National Police Detectives Corps) is a semi-autonomous branch of the National Police known popularly as the *Policía Judicial* (Judicial Police) or the *Policía Secreta* (Secret Police). Detectives in this force are most frequently identified as the perpetrators of political arrests in and around the capital. The Detectives Corps was reported to have directed two mass arrests of leaders of the *Central Nacional de Trabajadores* (CNT) labor federation on 21 June at its headquarters in Guatemala City and at a Roman Catholic conference center in Escuintla on 24 August 1980. A 16-year-old girl, detained in October 1979 on the steps of the Guatemalan Supreme Court by Detectives Corps members while handing out leaflets protesting against the seizure and "disappearance" of trade unionists, was temporarily blinded as a result of being hooded, beaten and raped while in Detectives Corps custody.

The *Guardia de Hacienda* (Treasury Police) is a principal rural component of the civil police structure. Its development was described in a peasant trade union newspaper in a November 1979 report in the following terms:

> Little by little it has changed to become one of the most repressive police bodies in the countryside, especially in the highlands *(Tierra Fría)* and in the border areas. . . . Previously they were simply agents who, on the pretext of investigating the brewing of *cuxa* [a homemade alcohol] and controlling contraband, used to demand bribes with menaces from the peasants. . . . But they are now a force of control and repression . . . they enter the houses to go through our documents and to take everything they can find.

25. *A Pacification Program for Guatemala* *

BY GENERAL EFRAIN RIOS MONTT

WHILE *decrying violence, President and General Efraín Ríos Montt proposes a new path for Guatemala, a path built, as he puts it, with "fusiles y frijoles" (guns and beans). His evangelical beliefs, expressed in weekly sermons on national television, may affect some people in this deeply religious country.*

---

* Reprinted from the Foreign Broadcast Information Service (FBIS), March 24, April 12, and May 23, 1982.

He points to the lack of national ideology and talks in vague terms about "communitarianism," a system based on the authority of the traditional family and Christian morality. North American evangelical groups and the so-called Moral Majority could perhaps easily identify with Ríos Montt, a fellow conservative spokesman. In fact, the Virginia-based Christian Broadcasting Network has offered Ríos Montt funding for a model community based on his vision.

While thousands have found in Christianity revolutionary inspiration and ideology, as we show in a later section of this anthology (see Part Three, Chapter III), Ríos Montt's religion appears to be one based on fear and punishment. While he says prayer will stop violence, his government continues to wage war, toning it down a bit in the cities and increasing its pace in the countryside. A seventeen-year-old Indian woman describes an army incursion into her rural village which occurred well after born-again Christian Ríos Montt took power:

> The soldiers arrived. We went to a mountain and hid there. Some soldiers found us and they . . . killed my friends with machetes and knives. Then they asked me who the guerrillas were. I said there weren't any there. They asked me who my father was, and when I didn't tell them, they hacked me with a machete; they raped me, they cut me in the head, my whole hand and my breast. . . . They killed my father, my mother, my brothers and sisters, my little one-year-old brother. The army machine-gunned them when they arrived in the village.[1]

THERE WILL BE no more murdered people on the roadsides; anyone who acts against the law shall be executed. Let's not have any more murders. We want to respect human rights and defend them. It is the only way to learn to live democratically.

That is why I first recommend a prayer to God Our Lord to permit us to continue developing a program in peace that we shall submit to your consideration. Secondly, we ask for your cooperation, your tranquillity, and your peace. The peace of Guatemala does not depend on arms. It depends on you men, women, and children. Yes, the peace of Guatemala is in your hearts. Once there is peace in your hearts, there shall be peace in your home and our society. Please let's not have any more drinks or anything else. Let us get to work. Guatemala needs work. There are no sources of work; there is no confidence. There is no authority. . . . (March 24, 1982)

Guatemala needs peace. Peace will not be created with weapons. Peace will not be created by the police. Peace will not be created by all of the uniformed men. Peace will have to come from your heart. . . . I have been in this position of

---

1. From an interview provided by the National Network in Solidarity with the People of Guatemala [Washington, D.C., July 22, 1982].

authority for only 20 days. Neither the votes nor the bullets gave me this position of authority; neither the votes nor the bullets. God placed me here. . . .[1] Subversives, listen to me. We are able to speak politically, but we also have the ability to defend ourselves with weapons, to work with weapons, to fulfill our duty with weapons. . . . Father, Lord, I beg you to bring peace to the hearts of the Guatemalans, to bring confidence to the people and to consolidate your family. Thank you, God, in the name of Jesus Christ, Amen. (April 12, 1982) . . . Communism and fascism are two political doctrines in which authority is preserved; in one, through the dictatorship of the proletariat, and in the other one, through a good dictator. . . . Why not communitarianism? No, you may say, because that has no philosophical principle attached to it. Truly, communitarianism is a way of living much like our own. Listen, we are more than twenty nations but we lack the philosophical, legal, and conceptual framework that will allow all of the nations of Guatemala to be united and to look within that philosophical framework, based on the characteristics of each of our nations, for what we see as a nationality. That is communitarianism. . . .

Basically, we need to consolidate the family, because by consolidating the family—the father, the mother, the children—we are consolidating society. And once society is consolidated, we [achieve] human quality. At this time, materialism is destroying us. Materialism makes us leave our homes and end up in who knows what bar. This precisely is the most serious problem. We need a change, but not in the sense that I or someone else change; what we are interested in is that you change. You change! If you change, Guatemala changes! This is the only way. You are the most important thief. You are stealing from yourself. You are destroying yourself, killing yourself. Listen, change. Consider the concept of life, the human quality you can give yourself. . . .

We are going to fight violence with understanding, peace, and love, because we know of the great social inequalities, because we know that there is no peace in our hearts and because we know that there is no concept of love. We are telling you now, however, that we love you, subversives. We love you because in one way or another, you subversives have given us new insight, a new understanding that without haste, but also without pause, Guatemala deserves to find a path, a Guatemalan path.

May the Lord our God hear us. May he enlighten us. And may he allow peace and security to reign in this country, as they reign in his heart. Give him thanks. (May 24, 1982)

---

1. Ríos Montt's role in the coup preparations are discussed in Reading 21.—EDS.

Part Three:

THE POPULAR MOVEMENT

A strategic hamlet in Chajul, where the population is concentrated under army control, May, 1982. *Photo credit: NISGUA*

Editors' Introduction

TO comprehend a popular movement for radical change, such as the one contending for power with the military and the oligarchy in present-day Guatemala, at least two kinds of intellectual effort are necessary. First, a level of misery and oppression such as few readers of this book will have personally experienced must be imagined: malnutrition so severe it approaches mass starvation; inadequate sanitary water supplies so that diarrhea is a main cause of death; violence so severe that thirty to forty mutilated bodies turn up *daily*; a government so devoid of legitimacy that, aside from invocation of anticommunist faith, it hardly has any other justification of its rule, and so must practice and condone terror to retain the existing distribution of power. All of this and more is demonstrated in the previous and following sections of this book. The second important concept necessary to comprehend contemporary Guatemala, one that follows almost logically from the perception of the grim reality of that country, is that these conditions generate an opposition.

But popular opposition, even in its most innocuous stages, has faced bitter opposition from the oligarchy. Guatemalan rebels now face helicopter gunships, heavy artillery, and counterinsurgency troops in armored personnel carriers (see Part Four, Chapter I). Even earlier, the government "pacification" campaigns of the 1960s and 70s took thousands of campesino lives, driving rebel remnants into the cities where, in a systematic campaign undertaken by Colonel Carlos Arana Osorio, a whole new array of terror tactics were deployed; house-to-house searches, mass arrests, and political assassinations on an unprecedented scale.[1] In the words of two recent students of Guatemalan history, government terrorists aimed to kill "anybody tinged with liberalism. Thousands of people suddenly met

1. Gabriel Aguilera Peralta, "Terror and Violence as Weapons of Counterinsurgency in Guatemala," *Latin American Perspectives*, VII (Spring/Summer, 1980), esp. pp. 102–109.

death at the hands of unseen gunmen. . . . Few of the victims were actual guerrillas; many were middle-class professionals who had supported Arévalo and Arbenz." [2] Military aid from the United States underwrote the spread of right-wing, government terror into almost every area of Guatemalan life, even including the maiming and killing of a former Miss Guatemala beauty queen known for anti-government views.[3]

The governments that carried out these terrorist anti-insurgency campaigns were, not surprisingly, unsympathetic to any fundamental reforms in Guatemala, especially any change in the lati-minifundio system upon which the country's agro-export economy was based. One of the only economic reforms with any ostensibly positive economic content in the 1960s and 1970s was the creation of agricultural, handicraft, and consumer cooperatives, many funded with the help of U.S. government and international financial agencies. The aim was to create a prosperous rural middle class without altering the inherent disparities of the land tenure system.[4] However, in economic terms many of the cooperatives failed, as a growing dependence on expensive imports such as pesticides and fertilizers, and insufficient credit, technical and marketing advice made it difficult for them to compete with larger and wealthier private enterprises. An unintended consequence of these programs, in addition, was to stimulate the emergence of militant leadership in the countryside, which, especially during the Lucas years, became the target of government repression (see Readings 37, 44). With the failure and destruction of many of Guatemala's cooperatives in the 1970s, the ranks of the impoverished and impatient were swelled.

If human policy decisions were responsible for a large part of the desperate poverty that affected, and still affects, contemporary Central America, in the 1970s, it is also true that nature contributed as well. On February 4, 1976 Guatemala was struck by "the severest natural catastrophe in Central America during the twentieth century," a devastating earthquake that left over twenty-two thousand dead, over three times that number injured, and more than one million homeless.[5] This disaster fell mainly on the poor, least able to afford earthquake-resistant housing. Although there was a considerable influx of international as well as Guatemalan government aid programs to help reconstruct the country, the earthquake strained the already inadequate infrastructure of basic public services (drinking water, health care, roads, etc.). As the victims of the earthquake themselves began to develop programs of reconstruction, popular groups began to get a taste of how they might change their own lives. As one Guatemalan campesino leader put it:

2. Stephen Schlesinger and Stephen Kinzer, *Bitter Fruit: The Untold Story of the American Coup in Guatemala* (Garden City, N.Y.: Doubleday & Co., 1982), p. 245.

3. *Ibid.*, pp. 247–248.

4. See Roger Plant, *Guatemala: Unnatural Disaster* (London: Latin America Bureau, 1978), pp. 86–89.

5. *Ibid.*, p. 5.

> In those moments after the earthquake when thousands and thousands of people had died, all who were alive began to take their dead out from under the rubble and ruins, and in doing so they discovered a great strength. . . . The earthquake made the people discover a very important thing. What is this thing? It is their capacity, their initiative, their possibilities and their ideas of being able, as a people, to build their own lives independently of the present regime or whoever might come to power, and of the army and those . . . wealthy people.[6]

The various forms of this discovery of popular power are what this section of the book is about: how trade unionists, intellectuals, campesinos and church people learned to struggle for their own vision of a justly-governed Guatemala, and began to merge in a unified popular opposition.

---

6. This comment is drawn from a 1982 interview with Antonio Kalel of the January 31st Popular Front (FP-31), made available to the editors.

Supporters of the striking Ixtahuacán miners entering Guatemala City, November, 1977. *Photo credit: National Committee of Trade Union Unity*

Chapter I:

THE URBAN CONTEXT

Editor's Introduction

GUATEMALA'S small industrial work force[1] has built a union movement over the decades in a situation of near total adversity. In contrast to some Latin American countries, such as Mexico where the government has organizational ties to urban workers, the Guatemalan state has had few links with them and done little for them. When one of the first industrial plants, the Cantel textile mill, was established in 1876, villagers thought the factory would eat up their lands and destroy their customs, so the village elders demanded the factory leave. In response, the government stationed the national army around the factory and in the village center; in the years which followed, local police broke up labor disputes at Cantel and rounded up late and absent workers on Monday mornings.[2] In major conflicts with owners in the early twentieth century, workers always encountered government repression. For example, by sending in the army in 1924, the government ended a twenty-seven-day strike undertaken by United Fruit Company dockworkers to gain higher wages, an eight-hour day, and an end to discrimination against black workers. Several workers were killed and others deported.[3]

While in the 1930s many Latin American countries took advantage of a brief respite from North American and European economic domination, brought on

---

1. In 1974 only 3 percent of the economically active population worked in industry and mining (Carlos Sarti, "El Desarrollo Capitalista Base Objetiva de la Movilización Obrera" *Anuario de Estudios Centroamericans* (Costa Rica, 1980), p. 7.

2. Manning Nash, *Machine Age Maya* (Chicago: University of Chicago Press, 1958), pp. 17–19.

3. Mario López Larrave, *Breve Historia del Movimiento Sindical Guatemalteco* (San José, Costa Rica: Editorial Universitaria, 1979), p. 19.

by the world depression, to diversify production and industrialize under the banners of nationalism and populism, Guatemalan dictator Jorge Ubico (1931–1944) simply enforced the status quo and dissolved the country's few unions. During the time John L. Lewis was organizing the CIO in the U.S. and Latin American workers were building unions elsewhere on the continent, Guatemalan trade unionists sat in jail. The U.S. New Deal and the Latin American populism of the 1930s did not have their counterpart in Guatemala. Only later during the 1945–1954 liberal presidencies of Juan José Arévalo and Jacobo Arbenz were urban workers partially protected by the government. A 1947 Labor Code guaranteed workers a minimum wage, an eight-hour day, social security, and the right to unionize. For the first time, labor unions and federations flourished.

The 1954 coup effectively destroyed the labor movement overnight. The most important unions and federations were dissolved and their leaders killed, jailed, or deported. The few remaining unions, isolated from one another, subject to strong government controls, restricted their activities to the presentation of complaints in unfriendly labor courts. In the 1960s violent right-wing military groups countered any labor unrest. By 1974 only 27,486 workers, 1.62 percent of the economically active population, were in unions. In sharp contrast, on the eve of the 1954 coup, 100,000 workers, or 10 percent of the economically active population at that time, belonged to unions.[4]

The renaissance of union activities in the 1970s took place under siege, as Miguel Angel Albizúrez and Robert Morris describe in Readings 26 and 29. Struggles over wages and working conditions have become life and death conflicts with the state. Because workers have virtually no way to redress simple grievances within the system, progovernment and Christian Democratic currents in the labor movement have weakened and workers have become increasingly antigovernment and anticapitalist.

Another consequence of the Guatemalan state's isolation from its citizens, and the country's stifled social development, has been the radicalization of many of its urban middle-class intellectuals and students. Within Central America, Guatemalans have always played a leading intellectual role. During the colonial period Guatemala was the site of the Spanish Crown's administrative capital, and six provinces, San Salvador, Honduras, Nicaragua, Costa Rica, Chiapas, and Guatemala formed the Kingdom of Guatemala. As isolated as Central America was from the rest of the world, Guatemala was always less isolated. But from a seventeenth century peak, colonial arts plunged into marginality, and Guatemala's subsequent history has offered little structural stimulus to its intellectuals. Instead, they have been consigned to hover uneasily between a dominated rural society which could not accommodate their skills and a social structure of domination whose leaders had little use for an intelligentsia. Deprived of a stable place in the social order, intellectuals have tended to be rootless. Only during the 1944–54 period were they, like urban workers, integrated into the political structure

4. *Ibid.*, p. 76.

when Arévalo and Arbenz invited them to play a role in the work of nation-building. Intellectuals, many returning from exile, enthusiastically helped develop an educational system, publishing houses, a free press, theater groups, a national orchestra, land reform, and industrial policies. Characteristically, the only three Guatemalan movie productions in existence were all made between 1950 and 1954. After the 1954 coup, the doors shut again and Guatemala returned to being a nation without a national development plan or ideology where thinkers have little serious place or function. Thus for example, despite an official illiteracy rate of 54 percent, thirty thousand schoolteachers are currently unemployed. Furthermore, Guatemala has never had any ivory towers. The educated found it hard to respond to the situation after 1954 by isolating themselves from their country's all too apparent problems. Without status or refuge, political activism engaged them. Intensely nationalistic, often forced into exile, their lives became mortgaged to the future.

Guatemala's intellectual history is an unwritten one. Its best known figure is 1967 Nobel Prize-winner Miguel Angel Asturias, whose works such as *Men of Maize* and *El Señor Presidente*, illuminate a bitter landscape of corrupt politicians, landowners, and victimized Indians. But the past fifty years have also produced thinkers, little known in the United States, who have openly taken sides on real political issues. Their research projects have had the objective of aiding progressive social movements; their literary works have served as rallying points, giving personal expression to political involvement (see Reading 31). Books written by the older generation were banned in Guatemala before 1944 and after 1954. Books from the younger generation, often printed elsewhere, are difficult to buy in Guatemala. Today, essayist Luis Cardoza y Aragón, anthropologist Ricardo Falla, and historian Severo Martínez Peláez (see Reading 3) are in exile along with hundreds of professors, journalists, theatrical artists, and others.

Journalists, aware of the facts behind massacres and disappearances by virtue of their profession, have had a particularly difficult role to play within Guatemala. A self-censorship has been adopted by the major media in Guatemala; digression from government versions of incidents is punishable by death. At least 48 domestic journalists were killed or disappeared in the period from November 1978 to March 1982. In late 1980 two distinguished female journalists, Alaíde Foppa and Irma Fláquer were seized by "unidentified" gunmen. Before her disappearance, Ms. Fláquer, commenting on the somber limitations of her profession, pointed out, "Thinking is the worst crime one can commit." [5]

Denied a meaningful arena of activity by the state, many intellectuals and

5. Quoted in a report by the Committee to Protect Journalists (New York, March 1982) after a fact-finding mission to Central America. The report concluded: "Of the countries of Central America, none has been as inhospitable to journalists or to free press as Guatemala." A number of foreign journalists have been denied entry into the country. Others find their agendas and contacts closely controlled by the government. Since the Committee's mission, General Efraín Ríos Montt has forbidden the media to discuss politics or to print any reports other than government press releases.

industrial workers have met with rural people outside the boundaries of the system to form a worker-campesino-intellectual alliance. They joined together in 1979 in the Democratic Front Against Repression (FDCR), an organization which denounced repression to the national and international public. Three years later, members of the FDCR and other groups started the Guatemalan Committee of Patriotic Unity (CGUP) which supports revolutionary war as a "just and necessary solution"[6] to Guatemalan problems. CGUP unites generations and social groups. Among its members are individuals who played important roles in the 1944–54 reform period—Luis Cardoza y Aragón, ex-ambassador to the USSR, Chile, and Colombia; Guillermo Toriello Garrido, ex-Ambassador to the United States (see Introduction); Manuel Galich, ex-Minister of Public Education; as well as younger people such as architect Gilberto Castañeda (see Reading 30), trade unionist Miguel Angel Albizúrez (see Reading 26) and rural Indian activist Rigoberta Menchú (see Reading 32).

In this chapter we present a variety of readings by and about urban workers and intellectuals as well as part of a diary written by a miner in the countryside.

26. *The Guatemalan Trade Union Movement (1976-1977)* *

BY MIGUEL ANGEL ALBIZUREZ

BARELY a month passed between 1976 and 1978 without a sharp labor dispute breaking out in one factory or another. In these conflicts workers faced their employers, their employers' private guards, national police, military police, death squads, hostile judges, an antilabor Minister of Labor, and sometimes the army. Under these conditions the trade unions sustained their organizations with astonishing vibrancy. Unions unceasingly responded to waves of assassinations and mass firings. They built alliances, placed ads in newspapers, started petitions, went to court, held public meetings, marched, went out on strike, occupied factories and, to get international attention, on several occasions peacefully occupied foreign embassies. When, for example, bank workers' union leader Benvenuti Antonio Serrano disappeared in Guatemala City in 1979, bank workers immediately posted fliers inside the banks and throughout the city accus-

6. *Declaracion del Comité Guatemalteco de Unidad Patriótica* (Mexico City, February 1982).

* From Miguel Angel Albizúrez, "Struggles and Experiences of the Guatemalan Trade Union Movement," *Latin American Perspectives*, V. 7, Nos. 2 & 3 ([Riverside, Calif.] Spring & Summer 1980), pp. 145-158. Translated by the Guatemala News and Information Bureau.

ing the government of kidnapping him and demanding his release. When the government denied knowledge of his whereabouts, the workers started a work slowdown. The government sent soldiers into the banks; the next morning two hundred wealthy downtown shop owners found their doors soldered together and their shop windows painted with "Free Serrano" signs. It was typical of this period that as the government blocked one form of struggle, workers invented another. The leaders and labor lawyers of these conflicts became national folk heroes. Mounting repression in 1980, after the following article was written, further radicalized and unified the trade union movement and finally forced it underground.

Miguel Angel Albizúrez, author of the following article, is one of Guatemala's foremost trade unionists. Born in Guatemala City in 1945, he left school after completing the sixth grade. He has been a member of a Catholic workers' youth group, a founder of the union at the Shulton Company, a founder and secretary general of the National Confederation of Labor (CNT) and a founder of the National Committee of Trade Union Unity (CNUS). Now an activist in exile and member of the Guatemalan Committee of Patriotic Unity, he participated in many of the strikes and meetings he describes.

THE YEAR 1976 began with violent and repressive events in Guatemala. On January 6, the Policia Militar Ambulante viciously attacked peasants in Chisec, Alta Verapáz. This provoked the reaction of priests and clergymen from the area who, in one of their communiqués, stated "we cannot remain silent about blatant acts . . . since we condemn violence in all forms, in this case we are only fulfilling our obligation as Christians by denouncing such blatant violence." The communiqué, signed by forty-five priests and clergymen in the area of the Verapaces, asked also for the solidarity of popular and labor organizations. Following this and other acts of violence which bathed the Guatemalan people in blood, different labor and popular organizations decided to unite to issue joint communiqués denouncing repression aimed at workers and peasants. On February 3, 1976, an agreement was reached to begin a strong campaign against repression. Bulletins were issued one after another on February 4, by the Confederación Nacional de Trabajadores (National Confederation of Labor—CNT), the Federación Autónoma Sindical de Guatemala (Federation of Autonomous Unions of Guatemala—FASGUA), the Bank Federation, the Sindicato Central de Trabajadores Municipales (Central Union de Municipal Workers), etc. Unfortunately, the earthquake occurred the day after the agreement was reached, and all the plans to denounce repression fell apart. Instead, different labor organizations devoted themselves in whatever way possible to attending to emergencies and to confronting the bosses' attempt to take advantage of the situation to destroy the unions.

Shortly after the earthquake, the repression against the labor movement became more obvious, prompting the CNT to publish a petition directed to the President on February 13. In it the movement demanded that the massive firings stop and that employers pay workers for days they didn't work as a result of the earthquake. At the same time, it demanded that the right of free labor organization be respected.

The Appearance of the National Committee of Trade Union Unity (CNUS)

There have been, in the past, several attempts at unity between the different labor organizations in the country: the Frente Nacional Sindical (National Labor Front—FNS) in 1968, for example, and the Consejo Nacional de Consulta Sindical (National Council of Labor Consultation—CNCS) in 1973. In both processes, efforts were led by the CNT, the FASGUA and the Central of Federated Workers (CTF) with the bank workers' Federación Sindical de Empleados Bancarios (FESEB) and municipal workers joining later. These attempts failed not only because of the maneuvering of the bourgeoisie and the government but also because of the reactionary attitude of some union leaders and, even more importantly, the tendency to initiate processes from the top down with little or no rank-and-file participation.

The CNUS was the response of the Guatemalan labor movement to constant abuse, to which Guatemalan workers had been subjected, and the violation of basic civil rights and restriction of the right to organize. Its appearance testifies that the unitary aspiration of the Guatemalan working class had never died; it had only remained latent since December of 1946 when a unitary organization was formed with the same name as the current CNUS, later becoming the powerful Confederación General de Trabajadores de Guatemala (General Confederation of Guatemalan Workers—CGTG).

After a labor conflict at the AUROTEX factory, repression against the workers at the Embotelladora Guatemalteca S.A. (Coca-Cola) worsened, and on March 24, 1976, 152 workers were unfairly fired. The workers had only one real choice: they could passively accept the destruction of yet another union with the risk that this would give free reign to continued destruction of the labor movement, or they could confront their employer and defend their right to organize. The workers decided to defend their organization, taking over the plant that day at 4 P.M. The police arrived quickly and at about midnight violently threw the workers out of the plant.

In this police action, twelve workers were seriously injured and fourteen were jailed. The news spread throughout all the labor organizations, and different sectors condemned the repressive action of the National Police. The solidarity committee, Comité de Solidaridad de los Trabajadores de Coca-Cola, grew out of the conflict, issuing a bulletin signed by more than twenty labor organizations. In one section they point out that, "The present conflict doesn't only concern the Coca-Cola workers since the precedent that it would establish would put the collective bargaining process in danger, make the Labor Code even less effective, and affect all organized workers including those who would be unionized in the future. This struggle is the struggle of the entire Guatemalan working class who have to defend their interests and win their true rights." This bulletin referred to the danger facing the entire labor movement.

A national assembly of labor organizations was called on Wednesday, March 31, at 3 P.M. This meeting was called by the Federación de Trabajadores Unidos de la Industria Azucarera (Federation of United Sugar Industry Workers—FETULIA), the Federación Central de Trabajadores de Guatemala (National Confederation of Guatemalan Workers—FECETRAG), the FASGUA, the bank employees' FESEB, the labor confederacion's CNT, the paper workers' Sindicato de Trabajadores de la Papelera, the municipal employees Sindicato Central de Trabajadores Municipal, and the solidarity committee with the Coca-Cola workers. The assembly was attended by more than sixty-five labor organizations; they discussed the established points of unity, and decided that a unitary organization would be created to confront employer and government repression. A number of names for this organization were proposed at the assembly; it was Dr. Mario López Larrave who pointed out that it would be most convenient to name it the National Committee of Trade Union Unity since a committee had existed historically with that name. The proposal was unanimously approved and since then it has been the CNUS. Under the leadership elected in that same assembly, it has been in the forefront of actions resulting from the struggle of the compañeros at Coca-Cola and other struggles that have happened since then.

On April 6 of that same year, the CNUS presented the President of Guatemala with a public denunciation of the different labor conflicts: Coca-Cola; the municipal workers of Escuintla; the workers at IODESA, the *Ingenio* (sugar mill) Pantaleón, Banco de los Trabajadores, and others. In this public challenge, the CNUS pointed out that "The events that we denounce are a chronic illness that affects the Guatemalan trade-union movement," and that labor organizations cannot allow those events to continue. By agreement of the general assembly on April 5, they sought an immediate meeting with government officials to present the problems of labor and their possible solutions. They fixed a definite time period within which the government had to resolve the problems, stating that at an April 7 general assembly the date and time for a national general labor strike would be decided. In this same document they pointed out to the President that the inoperability and poor application of the minimum guarantees contained in existing legislation left only one alternative: immediate action by the highest courts or the united action of the workers' organizations. The President met with the CNUS, recognizing, in practice, its legality. On April 7, the government backed down, forcing the Coca-Cola company to resolve the conflict, reinstate the fired workers, and grant legal recognition to the union. In exchange, the CNUS suspended the general strike planned for the entire country. Although the attitude of the government apparently favored the solution of the Coca-Cola conflict, from that time on anti-union repression by various sectors of the government was more open. Likewise, the private sector, represented by the employer's association, Coordinadora de Cámaras Agrícola, Comercial, Industrial y Financiera (Chamber of Agriculture, Commerce, Industry and Finance—CACIF), tried to destroy the newly formed CNUS by every conceivable means. The offensive of the CACIF included forming a united front against union demands. That same April 7, forty workers from the Tursa bus company were fired, resisted the firings, and were reinstated twenty-seven days later. Today, three years later, their first collective pact is still at the discussion stage, and the company refuses to grant them their just demands. In general, the response of government and employers to demands is quick; they repress, jail, and assassinate union leaders.

In April, the struggle of the workers at the IODESA (a cooking-oil, margarine plant in Escuintla owned by Jorge Kong Vielman) got worse. On February 14, the CNUS had publicly announced solidarity with the workers at that plant. At the same time it began to prepare for a unified demonstration on May 1. The CNUS issued a manifesto condemning repression and maneuvering against labor organizations: the assassination, persecution, and incarceration of labor leaders, peasants and students; the de facto militarization of autonomous entities such as the city government; the utilization of worker and peasant organizations and of corrupt pseudo-labor leaders, traitors to their class, to try to divide the labor movement; the barracks-like quarters of those affected by the earthquake and the conversion of the shantytowns into concentration camps; and the presence of North American troops.

In May, labor struggles sharpened with conflicts appearing in Ingenio Pantaleón, Ingenio Palo Gordo, Ingenio Santa Ana, Parcelamiento Los Liros, GINSA, the workers' bank, TURSA buses, Reyes Transports, INCATECU, the Hospital of Jutiapa and Cordelería la Rápida, brought about by massive firings, violations of collective pacts, denial of the right to a collective contract, and land evictions. On May 13, a strike began at Ingenio Pantaleón. In this conflict, the attitude of the Ministry of Labor clearly favored the employers, demonstrated by the Ministry's prohibiting the CNUS as well as the workers' own lawyer, Dr. Mario López Larravé, from participating in the ensuing discussions. As a result of the intervention of the government's labor experts, the final agreement favored the company. The company was authorized by the Ministry of Labor to dismiss thirty workers of their choice, and logically the fired workers were the most active members of the union. A total of 100 were subsequently fired in an effort by the Herrera Ibarguen family to destroy the union, something which they have not yet succeeded in doing. The workers at Pantaleón have made history by defending their interests and their union.

Some of these conflicts were resolved favorably; others not so favorably. In the case of the IODESA workers, the organization was destroyed; in other cases the confrontation between exploited and the exploiting classes continues, one defending the right to organize and the other trying to destroy it. Examples of this type of struggle are found in the cases of the Cordelería La Rápida, Coca-Cola, Santa Ana, GINSA, etc. In response to these different conflicts, the CNUS carried out a week of solidarity, from May 21 to 28. There were assemblies, delegations, meetings, bulletins, and other forms of denunciation and protest, concluding, in an assembly celebrated May 26, that the Minister of Labor should be publicly confronted. The confrontation was not carried out as planned because anti-union repression intensified at that time. The attempt of the bourgeoisie to destroy the CNUS was first felt on June 14 when Luis Ernesto de la Rosa Barrera, leader of the teachers' Frente Nacional Magisterial and a member of the organizational commission of the CNUS, was assassinated.

Events of 1977

Like the year before, 1977 was characterized as much by government and employer repression of popular organizations, especially unions, as by the forms of organized struggle adopted by the labor movement. In this period, industry-wide demands were raised, workers improved on existing collective pacts, solidarity work-stoppages took place, workers took over a factory to defend their rights, regional workers' fronts were created, large mobilizations and mass actions took place—some with and some without official permission—and the CNUS became a universally recognized force. The development of the labor organizations showed qualitative as well as quantitative growth.

The main events within the labor movement began to take place in February when repression against workers worsened at the HelenoPlast factory, the property of foreign industrialists Nicolás Dimitrakis Pilli and Héctor Gabriel Abularach. Eight workers were fired and members of the secret police entered the factory where they captured four workers. Lawyers Pablo Emilio Valle de la Peña, Oscar Suchini y Suchini, and Mario Arriaza Ligorría represented the company in this conflict. The firings and jailings took place just a few days after a Labor Ministry-supervised union election.

Most important was the factory take-over by the HelenoPlast workers on May 8. They held the factory for sixteen days. In this case, the conflict was provoked by the illegal and unjustified firing of more than fifty workers and by all the maneuvers carried out by the company in a union election which lasted nineteen consecutive hours—a labor record. During that time an Army colonel was present as were elements of the Policía Militar Ambulante who arrived with the specific purpose of intimidating the workers. The solidarity of the labor organizations joined together in the CNUS enabled the workers to remain within the plant. The workers were forced to leave the plant on March 25 after the National Police beat and jailed twenty-six workers early that morning.

Once again the manner in which the authorities collaborated with the employers could be observed. In the case of HelenoPlast, workers from different plants stood guard day and night, held meetings and acts of protest throughout the city. They were able to make many people aware of the workers' situation especially in the working-class neighborhoods near such plants as Guajitos, Justo Rufinos Barrios, and Ciudad Real, and among unorganized workers in the area.

Workers at the Tipic, S.A., factory demonstrated their solidarity by carrying out a work stoppage and protecting the HelenoPlast workers by facing the National Police, after witnessing the March 25 police brutality. Three active members of the union at Cavisa were jailed for supporting the workers.

At the same time conflicts were developing in sectors such as bank workers, municipal workers, at the Acricasa factory, and a strike was called by high school students.

The decision of the bank workers' FESEB to present industry-wide demands was an important one. It created such a degree of pressure on the bankers that they were forced to grant 25 to 50 percent wage increases, in spite of the bargaining agreements in force at each bank. This case set a precedent for other workers uniting to demand improvements, showing them that this is the best way to obtain a favorable solution to their just demands without having to depend on the courts. Other sectors that have made collective demands are health workers and teachers. By bargaining collectively, they have almost always obtained a favorable solution to their conflicts.

In the wake of the existing strikes, the workers at Acricasa (Industrias Acrílicas de Centroamérica, a Japanese company) decided to carry out a work stoppage to demand that a collective pact be signed dealing with work conditions and putting an end to company reprisals. For fourteen days they occupied the plant, sleeping, eating, and conducting their meetings there. On the third day, riot police showed up at the request of the owners, (among them, Hideonozaky Ishiwata). The workers started the machines running and began to work when they noticed the presence of the police. The police, who thought they were going to find evidence of a strike and throw the workers out, had to leave upon seeing that things were running normally, despite the insistent orders of the owners that they remove the workers. From then on, all the owners and main supervisors refused to enter the plant, leaving it without technical or administrative management. With this, the workers decided to continue working for the next eleven days, until the raw materials were used up. Finally, the owners' tactic was to force all of the workers to take vacations. During the next ten working days production remained at a standstill.

When the workers returned to their jobs, the company began terminating contracts on the basis of the "illegal work stoppage." They presented pro-company supervisors and foremen as witnesses. Fifty-two workers succeeded in being heard in the labor court. This hearing took place from 8 A.M. until 4 A.M. of the next day (twenty hours). The workers were represented by attorney Mario López Larrave. The court's decision was unfavorable to the company. Subsequently, the discussions about collective pacts resumed and lasted for three years; in 1978 compulsory arbitration (the only case in Guatemalan labor history) fully validated a pact that the employer refused to sign. To date, Acricasa workers (90 percent of which are women) are still repressed, humiliated, and even slapped by the Japanese industrialists.

In May the repression became more intense. Labor organizations found out about a repressive anti-union plan being developed by the employers' CACIF. The CNUS issued a statement appealing to national and international public opinion on May 30 in which they pointed out that "a repressive plan exists against the entire labor movement and its leaders, which has as its objective putting an end to the workers' struggles, silencing the trade-union movement, stopping its development, or destroying it. . . . This is being done to assure that the capitalist system continues to develop without obstacles and without the unified working class being able to protest the abuses and excesses that historically go along with capitalism."

Barely a week later, the official lawyer for the CNUS, Mario López Larrave, was assassinated. In the face of this action, which was part of the repressive plan promoted by the CACIF, the CNUS issued a communiqué the same day López Larrave was murdered stating:

> [The capitalists] should know that the masses create their own organizations, their own leaders, and even their own lawyers. This is a social process and because today compañero Mario López Larrave is no longer with us, you should know that legal assistance for collective conflicts will continue: you should know that new labor and popular organizations will form and that the masses won't stop struggling for their freedom as long as they suffer from the oppression that you submit them to. We work in a collective and organized way: other compañeros will take the place of compañero López Larrave. With his death you have only continued to degrade your selves and bathe yourselves in the blood of worthy, honest, and militant men.

And this is exactly what has happened. The struggle continues, the labor movement continues to develop, and the social process hasn't stopped. On the contrary, the working class is increasingly assuming the leadership role which befits it, making historical progress toward the liberation of the Guatemalan people. López Larrave's death gave rise to a spontaneous demonstration of 15,000 people, mainly workers, protesting government and employer aggression and demanding respect for the right to organize. López Larrave's assassination dealt a hard blow to the labor movement, but it responded with greater organization and combativity, immediately facing the problem of workers at the Mil Flores company. The unions in the Amatitlán area united to carry out meetings and protest demonstrations against U.S. businessman Frank Rodríguez who had violently fired more than eighty-six workers.

In the beginning of November, labor organizations continued to struggle against the exploiters. New forms of action were put into practice after transport workers and workers from Minas de Guatemala and Ingenio Pantaleón were fired. Transport workers formed a national coordinating committee, and with the help of factory workers, refused to collect fares from passengers, flooded the city with leaflets and spray-painted slogans asking for solidarity and demanding the reinstatement of the fired workers. The painted demands for "reinstatement" and "stop firings" can still be seen on many buses.

The movement was in a critical situation in which it had to face the capitalists who at that time were trying to destroy three important organizations: Ixtahuacán mines, Ingenio Pantaleón, and the Florida busdrivers' union. Therefore, the CNUS planned a protest demonstration on November 11. Government authorities stated that it would be dealing with subversive activities and therefore permission would not be granted to hold it; if held, it would be repressed. The CNUS intensified their publicity and confirmed their determination to hold the march despite the threat by acting President Sandoval Alarcón that CNUS leaders would be prosecuted. The CNUS leaders sent Alarcón a communiqué on November 7, stating:

> The CNUS makes known: (1) that given the undeniable fact that a co-ordinated plan by the ruling sector of the country exists to destroy the trade-union organizations; (2) that in the face of indifference shown by administrative and labor court authorities to resolve existing labor disputes, on numerous occasions with the complicity of these authorities with employers; (3) that given the massive firings at Guatemala Mines, Ingenio Pantaleón, the transport sectors, and the acts of provocation at Coca-Cola, Acricasa, and other companies; we energetically agree: (1) to demand that the central government immediately solve the existing conflicts; (2) to stand firm in the face of government and employer aggression; (3) to use the total organizational and mobilizing capacity of the CNUS to confront the situation without worrying about the consequences it may incur, since we have the right to defend our union organization; (4) the time period allowed for solving the conflicts remains the same and after the eleventh of this month we will begin to take direct action.

This letter to the President demonstrates the combative and courageous attitude of the CNUS.

On November 11, information received from different sources was contradictory; some asserted that the demonstration would be repressed while others stated that wouldn't be possible; there was reliable information about orders given by the Minister of the Interior which contradicted those of President Alarcón.

At 5 P.M. workers began to gather at the municipal workers' Sindicato Central de Trabajadores Municipales. The rain didn't discourage the workers who were ready to demonstrate. The march was led by members of the executive committee and was carried out more at a run than a walk since we were all nervous. At 12th Street a patrol car stopped in front of the marchers, ordering through the loud-speaker that the march be dissolved. The demonstration advanced peacefully with marchers being encouraged by megaphone to continue. On that same street an impromptu rally was held in which the Herrera-Ibarguen family was exposed as exploiters, and demands were made that they rehire the 102 fired workers. From that time on, the patrol car stayed with the march. The executive committee of the CNUS met in the middle of the demonstration and, arriving at 9th street, decided not to pass in front of the national palace as had been planned since there could be problems and that could be the point where repression would break out. Seeing that the objectives had been achieved, it was decided to end the march with a rally in Centenario Park. The demonstration ended with mass participation, 90 percent were factory workers who were preparing to take another step: solidarity strikes. This demonstration showed the ability of the CNUS and its organization to mobilize workers as well as the courage of the workers who demonstrated in heavy rain, without official permission, and under threats, in defense of their unions.

The most outstanding mobilization of 1977 was without a doubt the historic march by the Ixtahuacán miners [see Reading 27, "A Miner's Diary"], who that same November 11 left the unsafe mines and set out for the capital. This was one of the largest mobilizations in the last thirty years of the Guatemalan labor movement. It also was a new form of struggle, since put into practice by other workers at Aguacapa, Chixoy, and Oxec Mines as well as by shantytown dwellers. As the miners passed through towns and villages, they unified peasants and factory workers, educating them about the level of exploitation suffered by workers in general. Until then, the average Guatemalan was unfamiliar with work in the mines and the unfair exploitation which the workers were subjected to. The march clarified the situation for the public and forced the Abularach family to give in to the workers' demands. The miners' case was resolved by the time the march reached Tecpán. However, out of a sense of class solidarity with the Pantaleón sugar mill and transport workers, the miners completed their 351 km. march to the capital. The march proved to be a decisive point. Both organized and unorganized workers who have traditionally been apathetic to this type of action participated in it.

At the same time, workers at the Ingenio de Pantaleón also carried out a march. On the way they mobilized workers on the southern coast and especially the Amatitlán labor organizations who accompanied them from there to the capital. Both marches united at the Trébol bridge to march to the bandshell at Centenario Park where a huge protest rally took place. It was larger than those held on May Day and on October 20 [anniversary of the 1944 revolution—translator's note] of that same year. The mobilization of people in the towns and villages of the province where the miners and ingenio workers passed was impressive, and both marches met with an enthusiastic welcome in the capital. The mobilization surpassed all calculations; more than 100,000 people took to the streets to express their solidarity with the workers involved in labor conflicts. Two radio stations provided direct coverage of the events which extended from Mixco to Central Park. The heroic marches of a handful of men struggling for freedom, through their effort and sacrifices, contributed a wealth of rich experiences to the labor movement and its leaders through their struggle against capitalist exploitation and its faithful government servants. As the march passed through Central Park, the Minister of the Interior watched helplessly from a balcony of the National Palace. The protest must have caused great indignation in the most reactionary sectors of the country who see their selfish interests in more danger every day and who are realizing that the working class in its role as a leading class will no longer give in or remain silent. This is why the repressive anti-union plan denounced by the CNUS continues.

In conclusion, among the gains of 1977 were the experiences of struggle achieved by the working class. One of these was the tactic of presenting demands by sector, as in the case of bank, transport, and public health workers. Another was the realization of solidarity strikes among different sectors like the transport workers, those of Ingenio Pantaleón and of the Ixtahuacán miners. The attitude assumed by the workers at different enterprises where no conflicts existed showed class solidarity and the awakening consciousness of the exploited class.

The growth of the CNUS also stood out with the formation of the Frente de Trabajadores del Sur-Occidente (Southwest Workers Front—FRETASO). This organization played an important role in the Ixtahuacán miners march, and under their leadership a number of demonstrations and actions on defending workers in that region have been organized. Another group is the Frente de Organizaciones Sindicales de Amatitlán (Amatitlán Labor Organization Front—FOSA), which collaborated closely with the farmworkers from Pantaleón, mobilizing its members. These fronts show how the CNUS was in a process of development and consolidation through the united action of all the workers and their organizations.

The only organizations and pseudo-labor leaders who were excluded from this unitary process were those who were associated with political parties or with the government or who were in one way or another simply puppets who did not represent the workers.

The year 1977 ended with a repressive attitude on the part of the owners of Guatemala Mines who refused to pay the wages and Christmas bonus due the workers for December. When the owners tried to throw a carrier [cargador] off of the mine, the miners began to struggle again, blocking the highway and preventing any new and dirty tactics of the mining company and its lawyers. The case of the Ixtahuacán miners ended with a collective bargaining agreement signed in April 1978. . . .

27. A Miner's Diary *

BY LUIS FEDERICO CASTILLO MAURICIO

SAN Idelfonso Ixtahuacán is a small isolated town in the Cuchumatanes Mountains; a narrow road, without bus service, connects it to the distant Pan American Highway. It is the site of the Guatemalan-owned and U.S.-financed Minas de Guatemala *where primarily Mam Indian workers mine tungsten and antimony. In 1973 the miners formed a union. They demanded what they lacked: potable water, toilets, lights, air ventilation, first aid kits, and fire extinguishers inside the mines; hard hats, gloves, boots, masks, and better tools; a medical clinic, and decent wages and death and accident compensation. Unsuccessful in their struggle for union recognition and better conditions, the miners and an organizer from the National Confederation of Labor (CNT), Mario Mujía, decided in 1977 to dramatize their conflict by marching the two hundred fifty-mile distance from their town to the capital city. Seventy miners left for Guatemala City on November 11. Marching for nine days, they were greeted, fed, and housed by villagers and townspeople along the way. As they approached Guatemala City, tensions within the capital mounted and the government forced the company to grant the workers' demands before they reached the city. The miners, however, decided to continue their march. When they arrived in the capital, workers walked off their jobs and more than one hundred thousand people in a city of one million turned out to greet them. Ladinos and Indians in the countryside and the city previously ignorant of the miners' situation, rallied to their cause. Nothing like this had ever happened in Guatemala, where the march is known as "The Glorious March of the Miners."*

Although the workers won their demands, establishing the first legally recognized union in the western mountain region, their brief victory was followed by repression. Mario Mujía was assassinated in 1978; thousands attended his funeral in the provincial town of Huehuetenango, walking behind a banner which read "Capitalism, Here is Your Victim." In 1979 and 1980 the company laid off workers and cut into the rights workers had won in their union contract. In February 1981, union leader Luis Castillo, author of this diary, disappeared and is presumed dead; in April another union leader disappeared, and in May a third was tortured to death while his wife, tied up, watched. At present, the company is attempting to close the mine temporarily and the area has become a guerrilla stronghold.

The following is an excerpt from Luis Castillo's diary. It describes the events

---

* From an unpublished diary made available by the National Confederation of Labor.

preceding the miners' decision to march, their negotiations with the company and the government, and their entrance into Guatemala City.

. . . COMPANEROS, FROM WHAT I've suffered and from what I know many other workers have been through, I ask you: what guarantees does the owner of the factory or industry give you for the well-being of yourself and your families? I'm going to give you an example. On May 18, 1977, the company owners called us in to sign a life insurance policy, and a fellow worker by the name of Julio . . . went along with us. Well, at ten A.M. he came in to sign the insurance policy for $1,000, and twenty minutes later he had an accident. The injury wasn't one that would send him to his grave, but they took him to the first-aid center of IGSS [Guatemalan Social Security Institute], where they gave him some stitches. But the anesthesia was so great that all of a sudden he fainted. When they saw that he was unconscious, they gave him two more shots, and we're sure that this is what poisoned his blood. He never spoke again.

They took him to Huehuetenango, [1] and according to what they said, he died along the way. When they took him to the hospital to carry out the legal autopsy, they informed us that he would have died anyway because he had rocks in his lungs. Well now, if he had something wrong with his lungs, why did the doctor who had just given him a check-up and extended him a medical certificate say that he was fine?

What did the company do? They just gave the wife of the deceased the minimum amount of $100 for the funeral, as if to say, "Take this; you figure out how to manage." After the funeral . . . when she went to the office to collect on the life insurance policy that the compañero had signed, they said that he hadn't signed it because he hadn't brought in the papers they'd asked for. . . . When she turned to us to see if they had asked us for any documents . . . we told her they hadn't.

It's for this reason, compañeros, and not out of pure whim, that we don't go by what a boss tells us; much less would we accept starvation wages. Like we said, considering the six years this worker had served the company, that shouldn't have been the payment given to his family. . . .

On October 31st of the same year, a notice about the November 1 holiday appeared on the bulletin board. . . . It was up ten minutes at the most. Then they took it down and put up some sheets notifying us that as of the first of November all work was suspended temporarily for a year because they had to make an exploratory study in the mine and because there was no mineral left. But the intention of the company was to break up the union and give us all our severance pay. But, broke as we were, we decided not to accept anything. . . . We prepared ourselves to convince the workers not to accept their severance pay. It took a lot of effort to make people understand the trick they were playing on us. Of the 325

1. The provincial capital where the nearest hospital is located.—EDS.

workers before the lockout, 140 didn't accept their severance pay and continued the struggle.

The same day the company put up this notice, we notified the CNT and also the labor authorities . . . indicating that this was an illegal lockout and that we were demanding prompt rehiring. Some compañeros from Huehuetenango, Quezaltenango, and from the capital were studying how we could deal with what had happened to the 140 compañeros and their families, who had been left without their daily sustenance. . . . With the advice we got, we set up union vigilance around the plant and at the entrance to the shop near the mine. We kept up this vigilance day and night for twenty days. It was during this time that we decided that . . . half of the workers would leave on a march to the capital city to demand our reinstatement from the authorities . . . because we wouldn't put up with being left out in the cold from one day to the next.

Seventy of us left San Idelfonso Ixtahuacán on November 11, 1977, at four A.M. for the capital city . . . with the hope that once the authorities knew about all of this they would tighten the screws on this company so that we would be rehired. We were leaving our families without our protection and going out ready to suffer the inclemencies of the weather.

We arrived in Huehuetenango at two P.M. The university there gave us its full collaboration as far as food and a place to sleep are concerned. The reception given us by our department capital was really good because they were aware of why we had decided to set out to tell the four winds what these unjust businessmen had done to us. . . .

[Castillo's diary continues to chronicle the warm reception the miners received in each village and town they passed as they marched toward the capital, Guatemala City. Before they reached the city, the Ministry of Labor asked the union leaders to come to Guatemala City to negotiate with the company.—EDS.]

On November 15th at 6:30 A.M. three of us union leaders and two more workers left our fellow workers because we'd been called to the capital by the Labor Minister. . . . When we arrived at the capital, we went to the CNT to figure what we were going to do at the ministry.

When the newspaper reporters found out that the miners of Ixtahuacán were at the Federation, they paid us a visit. . . . By this time we were so indignant at having been manipulated that we . . . denounced everything the company and the authorities had done to leave us out in the cold . . . and all because the company owners had the labor inspectors wrapped around their little fingers. For the first time in Guatemala it was made public that we mined antimony and tungsten in our town and that the Ministry of Mines had passed it off as lead, which has a much lower price. . . .

When we met in the afternoon, we were surprised to see the company representatives as well as the Labor Minister, who for the first time was meeting with us and learning about our problem. . . . Our lawyers explained the problem, and the

Minister asked the company officials if what our lawyers were saying was true. The company completely denied that they had closed the door and left us out in the cold, or that they had put up the notice about the temporary suspension of operations for lack of mineral. They did insist that there were no more raw materials. We replied that what they were saying was false because how could it be that from one night to the next morning the mineral would disappear and that from one moment to the next we would be left without food for our children. In addition, we pointed out that many of these company officials had never seen the extracted mineral because they never leave their desks except to collect their paychecks. It doesn't even occur to them that if it weren't for the poor miner, they'd be out of a job.

After we workers sustained a long verbal attack against the representatives of the company and against the labor inspectors, it was agreed that the mine would be opened again and that we would be reinstated and paid for the days we had been in our struggle up to the day the problem was resolved. But what they really wanted was to cancel our protest march so we wouldn't get to Guatemala City. The authorities would collaborate by giving us one of their recreation buses to use to return to our town. But we answered that before deciding whether or not to accept, we'd have to consult with our fellow workers at the site of the march. Then the Inspector General offered to intervene and go with us to where our fellow workers were waiting to find out the results of these talks.

When we got there, we found our fellow workers resting in the little place called "Los Encuentros" on the Pan American highway. Everyone paid attention to what the Inspector told them about the talks in the Ministry and the offer to return us to our town. The workers answered by saying that when they set out to do something, they were used to carrying through with it . . . and they wouldn't even consider stopping the march. They said they already knew well how these exploiters operated and they didn't believe anything they said. After they heard the Inspector, our fellow workers continued their conversation with the campesinos who had come down from Quiché to greet us, and they talked about what decision they would make in the future if the government didn't pressure the company. . . .

While our compañeros marched on, those of us on the negotiating team continued our talks with company representatives in the Technical Council of the Ministry of Labor where some inspectors and the Vice-Minister of Labor tried to resolve the conflict quickly so that the protest march wouldn't get to the capital. They were thinking about the reaction of all the workers and campesinos witnessing this example of how to struggle to stop these bosses from abusing and exploiting the poor. They were also thinking about other workers' reaction at seeing that for someone to get what he justifiably asks for, he has to go all the way to the capital to get the government to intervene. . . .

This same day [Nov. 16] in the afternoon, we met again at the Technical Council and came to an understanding that the company would reopen the mine, our source of work, but on the condition that we had to start work again at two

P.M. on Friday the 18th. But how could the company do this to us? They weren't even allowing us time to rest. The minutes taken for this meeting stated that the agreement was pending the approval of our fellow workers. . . .

The next day the march left Tecpán for Chimaltenango, and we left Guatemala City to meet them and inform them of what had been discussed, and of the decision the negotiating team was thinking of proposing: that it was preferable to lose two days' pay so that our march could make it to the capital, because we didn't want to give any enjoyment to this type of workers' enemy, and also because if we didn't finish our march, our fellow organized workers would be left wanting to know the reason for our march.

That day, the 17th of November, we met in negotiations again in the afternoon and explained what we miners had agreed upon: that we wanted to get to the capital, and we would take a two days' pay cut . . . because we also wanted to get a medical checkup from some doctors who had offered their assistance. In addition, we offered to change the sign of our march from "Protest March" to "Peaceful March." The company said they accepted this. . . .

After signing the agreement, we left for Chimaltenango because we knew that our fellow workers were resting there before leaving the next day for Mixco, which was the goal for Friday. The organizations and peasant leagues of Chimaltenango gave us a place to rest . . . so we could recuperate some of the energy we had left along the roadside. . . .

The 19th of November. The glorious day of the heroic miners, who, with their struggle, weariness, and their blistered and bleeding feet from the burning asphalt, made their entrance into the capital, showing that in order to resolve a labor conflict, it was necessary for us to walk 370 kilometers. . . . No compañeros, with this example we have given, we have seen that many organizations that exist today have taken a stand in order to gain respect and not let their dignity be trampled on for nothing.

Compañeros, we left Mixco at nine in the morning. . . . Many organizations from the capital, as well as students from several schools, met us in the outskirts of Mixco, and as we walked along, many more organizations joined our march.

Not only we, but also the people of the capital, had never seen a march like this one of the miners. You could see the emotion of so many people who knew that we had set an example. . . . Compañeros, as we went down Roosevelt Boulevard, you could hear the sounds of the crowd. Their applause and words of inspiration gave us the strength to reach our goal. The overpasses were overflowing with so many people. Good-willed people would break through the lines to give us sodas, fruit juices, and tortillas. We miners created a history that will never be erased from the minds of many compañeros nor from the minds of so many people who collaborated with us.

28. *Fight the Fare Increase* *

BY A RESIDENT OF GUATEMALA CITY

GUATEMALA'S few cities, like urban areas throughout Latin America, present sharp visual contrasts between wealth and poverty. Residential neighborhoods of elegant fenced homes, parks, fountains, and shopping centers border treeless shantytowns with names such as "El Milagro"—"The Miracle"—so-named because it survives. In Guatemala City these shantytowns are combed with deep ravines and here thousands live, without paved roads, water, garbage collection, schools, sewage, or electricity, in tin and cardboard shacks. During the 1970s, and particularly after the devastating 1976 earthquake left over a million homeless, the shantytowns developed internal cohesion as residents organized for housing, water, sewage, and other essentials of urban survival. Then, in late 1978, these organizations sparked an intense city-wide struggle against a bus fare increase. The city government raised the bus fares 100 percent, from five to ten cents on September 29; shantytown organizations immediately responded by building barricades across roads and stopping buses. The police attempted to invade the shantytowns which had already organized self-defense. The following day the trade union federations called a city-wide general strike against the fare increase and in support of workers involved in labor disputes at local factories and on neighboring plantations. For days street battles continued and the nights blazed with burning buses. Shops closed and the city's fast-food fried chicken chain, Pollo Campero, reputedly owned by Nicaraguan dictator Anastasio Somoza, was attacked to demonstrate solidarity with the then growing struggle in Nicaragua. After two weeks, and after forty people had been killed, three hundred wounded, twelve hundred arrested, and two thousand fired from their jobs, the government lowered the fare back to five cents. This was done just as the strike started to spread throughout the nation and campesinos in the distant western mountains began building barricades across the country's main artery, the Pan American highway.

This successful fight against the fare increase, cutting across factory, neighborhood, and even city lines, uniting industrial workers, street vendors, the unemployed, schoolchildren and housewives, was an important lesson in the effectiveness of alliances. The following eyewitness account by a young resident of "El Milagro" describes how people fought against the police in that neighborhood a few days after the fight against the fare increase started.

ON MONDAY I was going to work but when I got to the bus stop there were no buses because the people in Carolingia [another neighborhood] had stopped

---

* From *Noticias de Guatemala* (Guatemala City, Guatemala, October 11, 1978), pp. 9–12. Translated by Jonathan Fried and Nancy Peckenham.

them all. The residents of Carolingia had organized by themselves and in El Milagro we didn't know anything because we hadn't communicated with them. After all this we communicate more.

So, the SWAT police [riot police] arrived at seven A.M. in Carolingia but the people were well-organized to face them. The police entered easily but the people surrounded several policemen and it appears that one, who was throwing a [tear gas] bomb in a house, was attacked with a machete. Finally, the people from Carolingia were dispersed and many came to El Milagro.

Some youths here began to talk with the people, to ask for their solidarity to prevent the police from entering El Milagro, throwing [bombs and] making a mess like they had in Carolingia. So we decided to erect barricades against the SWAT police. A group of over two thousand people including youths, women, and elderly built them with stones. It wasn't just young people, all the people who were on their way to work got involved. It was impressive to see women and old men moving stones, carrying vinegar (to stop gaseous fumes) and helping. Some old men even went to get pick-axes to dig trenches in the street but it was too late. We held lightning meetings to raise peoples' spirits. We were all indignant over the brutalities committed by the SWAT police and also over what the government had done. We are poor people; there is hardly any water in our neighborhood, only a little spurt, and we have to take turns to get water. And now with this ten cent rise . . . the people can't bear it any more.

As there is only one entrance and one exit [in El Milagro] people divided into two groups to cover them. Some of the bus drivers joined us. We told one of them to help us, because after all, the bus wasn't his, but was used to exploit him. He did us the favor of blocking one side of the street with it. An old car was used for the other side, and the police could not get by. Nevertheless, a jeep and policemen on foot had already entered, but the people confronted them and they left running and firing shots. We stayed like that until three P.M. The police ran out of tear gas and began to shoot with real bullets from behind the barricades. Plainclothes police did most of the shooting, the SWAT mostly used tear gas.

At three P.M. they gained entry because they brought two thousand police and SWAT commandos. They entered through a ravine and came up behind our barricades; this was the only way they could enter. They filled up three vans with those captured. They entered in groups, as if it were an occupation, with pistols in hand. People ran to their homes, and they dispersed those who continued confronting them. The police stayed until midnight. Two men who had nothing to do with what was going on died. They were working, distributing water, because as I mentioned we don't all have water at the same time.

Wednesday they killed another man. The SWAT came after the people from the Primero de Julio neighborhood. They fled into a ravine and the police followed and killed a boy who was walking by. So we had three wakes. The people here continue like a son-of-a-bitch because of all that happened. . . .

29. *Coke Adds Life?* *

BY ROBERT MORRIS

"I earn $3.70 for an eight-hour day, which comes out to $110 a month, since we work six days a week and get paid for the seventh day. My wife takes in a little work—making blouses, sewing, things like that—which comes to another $30 a month. That makes it about $141 a month of income to support a family of six. Our rent comes to $25 a month for one room, with a little kitchen and a bathroom in the hall. Water is another $3.80 a month, and electricity is $4.20. My wife spends $22 a week on food—for which we don't eat very well—which comes to $88 per month. For fifty cents per day we eat very simply—mostly rice, beans, and tortillas, sometimes milk for the children. Occasionally we have some meat. My bus fare is another $6 a month, which brings the total to $127 a month. That leaves us $14 a month for clothes, shoes, medicine, and other expenses. One thing for sure: a 15-cent bottle of Coke is a luxury item for a Coca-Cola employee!"

—Francisco, fork-lift operator for *Embotelladora Guatemalteca, S.A.*, the U.S.-owned Coca-Cola franchise in Guatemala, December 1979 [1]

THE struggle for union recognition at the U.S.-owned Coca-Cola Bottling Company franchise in Guatemala City lasted five years and cost at least ten people their lives. Their victory in August 1980, aided by an international solidarity campaign, came at a time when the entire labor movement was being forced underground. On June 21, 1980, twenty-seven union leaders were kidnapped from the Guatemala City headquarters of the National Confederation of Labor (CNT), of which the Coca-Cola workers' union is a member. Two months later, on August 24, seventeen more CNT leaders were abducted from a Catholic retreat house in Palín, Escuintla, where they were meeting. Needless to say, none of them has ever reappeared. Currently the urban labor movement at the Coca-Cola plant and elsewhere continues organizing, in clandestinity. Lightning rallies are held, and factories are occupied.[2] Political messages, due to the danger involved, are often distributed by "pamphlet bombs," which, when they explode, shower leaflets over factories and neighborhoods. Meetings are held under the

* Published as an *ICCR Brief* by the Interfaith Center on Corporate Responsibility [New York], November 1980, by permission.

1. Scott Riklin, "Guatemala: the Revolution Approaches," 1980, unpublished.

2. A "lightning" rally or occupation is one planned in secrecy: people are told the time and location moments before they are expected to be there; they quickly rally and immediately disperse before the police or soldiers have time to arrive.

cover of soccer games and country outings, enabling a clandestine trade union organizational structure to exist.[3]

The following study of the union movement at Coca-Cola was written by Robert Morris of the Interfaith Center on Corporate Responsibility (ICCR). Morris and the ICCR played an important role in the international solidarity campaign with Guatemala's Coca-Cola workers. This is a slightly abridged version of the original article.

AS THEY CROSSED a busy street in downtown Guatemala City last April, union leader Marlon Mendizábal told a U.S. church representative, "If I am still alive in October, I would like to study abroad." After a few steps, he paused, thinking of what he had just said, and remarked, "Can you imagine that? What a thing for a 22-year-old guy to be saying." Unfortunately Mendizábal's premonition turned out to be all too real. On May 27th at 4:30 P.M. he was cut down in a hail of machine gun fire as he waited at a bus stop near his work place, the Coca-Cola franchise bottler, Embotelladora Guatemalteca.

Mendizábal was the third secretary general of the bottler's union to be assassinated in the eighteen-month period from December 1978 to May 1980. During that period, three other members of the union's executive committee were also murdered, two of those three were brutally tortured. Four additional union workers have "disappeared," and are presumed dead. Guatemalan workers clearly attribute the human rights abuses at the bottler to a systematic, coordinated union-breaking campaign orchestrated by the Coca-Cola plant's management and the Guatemalan police.

The long history of the bottler's human rights violations, the reaction by the plant's American owners and the Coca-Cola Company, and the successful intervention by a coalition of religious, labor and congressional human rights advocates makes Embotelladora Guatemalteca an interesting test case for the issue of corporate responsibility and human rights. . . .

History of the Union

Although labor rights violations and harassment of union leaders are commonplace occurrences in Guatemala, Guatemalan labor leaders have stated that the abusive union breaking campaign at the Coca-Cola franchise bottler, Embotelladora Guatemalteca, has singled the plant out as the most violent example of labor repression in Guatemala. . . .

The first union organization of Embotelladora Guatemalteca was destroyed in 1954 during the ascent of the brutal Armas regime. Within a few weeks of the Armas coup at least 200 prominent unionists were killed and the major union federations were outlawed. In 1968 there was another movement to form a union

3. Blanche Petriche, *Uno más Uno* (Mexico City) June 5, 1982.

at the bottler, but that effort was abruptly halted when a chief organizer, César Barillas, was kidnapped, tortured and murdered.

On August 11, 1975 the present union was organized with the specific purpose of enabling the workers to improve their wage rate ($2.08-$2.50 per day). Union resources cite that, at the time, some workers who had had fifteen to twenty years experience with the company were earning only $2.85 per day. Resistance from management was swift. One attempt to destroy the union occurred in March of 1976, when the bottler's management fired 154 employees and brought in non-union workers. Protesting union workers assembled outside the plant and managers called the crack riot squad of the Guatemalan police to dislodge the workers. Several workers were hospitalized from injuries related to this incident. Soon after, the Guatemalan labor courts ordered the bottler to rehire the 154 workers.

Harassment against the union members mounted steadily. On February 10, 1977 two workers, Angel Villeda and Oscar Humberto Sarti, filed a legal affidavit stating that plant manager Ricardo Mejicanos threatened them with death, if they did not quit the union. Less than three weeks later both men were machinegunned by unidentified gunmen but fortunately survived the attack. On the following day the union's legal advisors, Martha and Enrique Torres, had their car run off a highway and were seriously injured. On other occasions the two lawyers had received death threats in the form of intimidating phone calls. Enrique saw his name appear on no less than five death lists which appeared in Guatemala City and were sent to Guatemalan newspapers by the so-called Secret Anticommunist Army.

An agreement with management was reached in February of 1978 and a collective pact was signed. At that time 94 percent of the workers at the bottler had joined the union. This achievement, however, did not end the labor violence. In 1978, threats against union workers by plant managers began again. As Israel Márquez, the union's secretary general, drove up to his home on the evening of October 15, 1978, the windows of his car exploded in a burst of machinegun fire. Prior to the assassination attempt, Márquez had been death warned by plant managers on several occasions.

Soon after the attack on Márquez, union sources reported that there was a meeting between the Guatemalan Police Chief German Chupina, the bottler management and several members of a rival management-supported union, during which the police chief allegedly stated that "the union would be destroyed within six months." The well respected *Latin American Political Report* (London) has indicated that Police Chief Chupina has been directly linked to death squad activities.

On December 12, 1978 Pedro Quevedo, the union's financial secretary and former secretary general was shot and killed while making deliveries. Although the police denied complicity in the Quevedo murder, union sources reported that police involvement was evident when the unit of military police guarding the plant was reinforced with additional men, several hours before Quevedo's murder. After this, one death list of the Secret Anticommunist Army included the names of the union's entire executive committee and advisory council. Threatening notes were also sent to workers' houses. Union leaders stated the only source for the correct home addresses of these workers was the bottler's office. By this time three army lieutenants were working for the plant in the positions of personnel director, warehouse director and security director.

On January 23, 1979 the union placed an ad in the newspaper *Nuevo Diario* which detailed a chronology of violent actions that had been taken against the workers. The following day Manuel Moscoso Zaldana, a man who had rented Israel Márquez's house, was machinegunned and killed as he left the union leader's house. Guatemalan press reports indicated that Zaldana was probably confused with Márquez. Once again, several hours before the murder, the plant guard was reinforced this time to twenty men. After a third attempt on his life, Márquez was asked by the union's executive committee to go into exile. In January 1979 he sought asylum in the Venezuelan Embassy with his wife and child and a month later fled to Costa Rica.

On April 5, 1979, while on his delivery route, like Pedro Quevedo, Manuel López Balam was assassinated—beaten with an iron tube and his throat cut from ear to ear. Several months later Balam's wife told a U.S. church representative that her husband was repeatedly threatened before his assassination and that plant manager Lieutenant Rodas had verbally threatened him three times the week of his death, including once on the day he was killed. As Manuel went out to his truck, Rodas said to him, "Don't you know what happens to those who don't know how to cooperate?" Two weeks after the assassination of Balam, 22-year-old Marlon Mendizábal assumed the position as the new secretary general of the bottler's union and immediately received threats from plant managers. According to union sources he was shown a list of all his closest relatives and their respective addresses and taunted, "Don't be foolish, resign your post. Can't you see, we have the names of all your loved ones? . . . Remember, torture is extremely painful. . . ." Pressure in the form of threats and surveillance against the union continued unabated throughout the remainder of 1979.

On several occasions the CNT issued press releases describing specific death threats which various plant managers directed at union workers. Two of these press releases described threats from army Lieutenant Rodas, the plant's chief of industrial relations. On May 31, 1979 Rodas warned the union's executive committee that their movements and actions were under constant surveillance by various police agencies. On July 3, 1979 he gave death warning to the union's entire executive committee. By now the percentage of unionized workers at the plant had dropped to less than 50 percent from a high of 94 percent in early 1978. The union's leadership learned to travel in small groups and sleep in different houses.

Coke union leaders Arnulfo Gómez and Ricardo García were kidnapped on

May 1, 1980. Their torture-ridden bodies were later discovered several miles outside of Guatemala City. The sadistic details of their murders were later described to a U.S. church representative by Coke unionists—Gómez's lips were cut with razor blades, his tongue was cut off and placed in the breast pocket of his shirt, many of his teeth were broken, he had been severely beaten in the stomach and back and there was one gun shot wound at the base of his nose, from a bullet that was fired at close range. García was also tortured.

On May 14th Efraín Zamora, the leader of the management created employees association, was murdered in the midst of rumors that he wanted to resign from the association just prior to his death. On May 27, 1980 the Coke union's secretary general, Marlon Mendizábal, was gunned down. Within a month, in what seemed a bid to win popular support, the Rebel Armed Forces, a leftist guerrilla group, murdered plant manager Rodas. (Another guerrilla group had claimed responsibility for an attack on plant manager Riege during the summer of 1979.) The next day the Guatemalan police responded with yet another murder of a Coke unionist. Edgar René Aldana was assassinated by gunmen on the plant grounds in view of police guarding the plant. The same day, two more Coca-Cola union leaders were kidnapped by police along with twenty-five other Guatemalan labor leaders.

In a protest action demanding the return of the missing twenty-seven labor leaders, a strike began at the Coke plant. In response, on July 1, 1980 approximately eighty heavily armed riot police were called to the plant and began to beat the striking workers. During this attack two more Coke unionists were abducted. As a result of the violence of May and June 1980 and the simultaneous condemnation and pressure from international unions in thirty different countries, the parent Coca-Cola Company agreed to change the ownership and management of the Guatemalan bottler.

International Church and Union Pressure

What has emerged as a disturbing revelation in the violent history of the Coca-Cola bottler is not only that the human rights violations involve the most visible of American companies, but also that the franchise itself is owned and operated by American citizens. For the last twenty years John Clinton Trotter, a Houston attorney, has managed the plant on behalf of its majority stockholder Mary Hodge Fleming. Though Trotter has maintained that his role in the day to day operations of the plant is minimal, union sources have repeatedly identified him as a key element in the campaign against the union.

"Nothing moves at the plant without Trotter's permission," said union lawyer Enrique Torres. Torres indicated to religious investors of Coca-Cola that, during labor negotiations the plant's managers would rarely finalize any agreements without first consulting with Mr. Trotter. Israel Márquez stated that Trotter had personally threatened him saying, "The army is going to get you." Márquez also told Coca-Cola stockholders at the company's 1979 annual meeting that he was present at a meeting in which Trotter personally threatened Pedro Quevedo just eight days before his assassination. Concerning the union, Trotter told *Newsweek*, "They're communist . . . they're part of a ruthless worldwide communist campaign against big companies like Coca-Cola." Trotter is said to believe that any form of organized labor amounts to communism, an analysis disturbingly similar to the position of Guatemala's extreme right. . . .

By late 1978 and early 1979, religious investors of Coca-Cola began to monitor the increasing violence at the bottler on a weekly basis. On numerous occasions, the Sisters of Providence wrote to officials at Coca-Cola headquarters in Atlanta with specific details of activities at the plant, asking Coca-Cola to verify their factual information and take action with its franchise. Coke officials refused to elaborate on what, if any, action they were taking with Mr. Trotter. The religious investors felt that, apart from the moral obligation to stop the violence, Coke had the ability to revoke the franchise agreement or transfer ownership of the bottler. On more than one occasion company officials admitted that Coca-Cola's share of the Guatemalan cola market had significantly declined in recent months. Religious investors also pointed out that the company's image was being tarnished and that the two other Coke bottlers in Guatemala, though unionized, had not experienced labor violence.

The company responded that they could not intrude in the labor problems of an independent franchise. Not satisfied with the company's actions, five religious investors cosponsored a shareholder resolution at Coca-Cola's 1979 annual stockholders meeting. The resolution asked the company to require a code of minimum labor standards from its franchise bottlers. The resolution, opposed by management, was supported by only 1.6 percent of the corporation's shareholders. . . .

By early 1980 numerous organizations appealed to Atlanta to act decisively with Mr. Trotter. Amnesty International's U.S. section wrote to Trotter and requested he take immediate steps to protect the plant's workers. Copies of the Amnesty letters were sent to Coca-Cola. But by far the most significant development in the campaign to end the abuses at the bottler occurred with the intervention of the International Union of Food and Allied Workers.

The Geneva based IUF, which has 160 member unions in fifty-eight countries, began following developments at the bottler in 1977. In August 1979, IUF General Secretary Dan Gallin, was invited to participate in Amnesty International's mission to Guatemala. During that trip Gallin spoke with several of the threatened trade unionists of Embotelladora Guatemalteca. In January 1979, representatives of the IUF, affiliated U.S. unions, Israel Márquez and Enrique Torres met with Coca-Cola management in Atlanta to discuss the embattled franchise. Coke officials held firmly that they were not able to intrude into independent franchise affairs and that there was no conclusive proof of local management's complicity in the murders. On February 4, the IUF asked its international affiliates to pressure

Coca-Cola to intervene in the Guatemalan affair through union sponsored consumer boycotts, publicity campaigns and industrial actions. Affiliate unions enthusiastically responded with unique international solidarity in numerous countries including Australia, Canada, Israel, Japan, Norway, Germany, the United Kingdom, Venezuela, Denmark, France, Spain, Finland, New Zealand, Mexico and the U.S.A. These actions ranged from telegrams of support to the extensive actions taken by Sweden's IUF affiliates, which included a three-day stoppage of Coca-Cola production, four-day consumer boycott, 400 labor and general press articles and radio and TV coverage. As a result of the tremendous pressure from international unions, many of Coca-Cola's independent bottlers requested the parent company take action and Coke began to actively pursue the sale of the franchise to other owners.

In May of 1980 seven religious investors returned to the Coke annual stockholders meeting with a stockholder resolution requesting company policy requiring that subsidiaries and franchisees observe the basic human rights of their employees. Management again opposed the resolution and responded to references to the Guatemala cause by noting that "the duly constituted legal authorities in Guatemala have not brought charges against any person with respect to the acts of violence." Chairman Austin announced that a sale of the bottler was under negotiation but added that the initiative was "unrelated" to the international boycott actions.

Union Recognition

The finalized sale of the bottler was completed on August 28, 1980. In addition to the transfer of ownership, Coca-Cola agreed to other IUF demands including replacement of the plant's managers, recognition of the union, dissolution of the management-sponsored union, removal of the police force from the plant—the same actions that Coca-Cola had repeatedly told church investors since 1976 that it was incapable of performing. Beyond the IUF requests, the Coca-Cola Company even agreed to set up a fund to indemnify the families of the murdered union leaders.

Although Coca-Cola executives may well understand the differences between a subsidiary and franchise business relationship, most Guatemalans do not. Coca-Cola's reluctance to take action against its franchise until it met international boycott sanctions has certainly not enhanced the image of American business in Guatemala. As one U.S. official in Guatemala recently noted "Coca-Cola is the classic ugly American for many in Guatemala and this is damaging all U.S. investors here." One U.S. investor summed up the bottler's dismal image by stating "Coca-Cola is becoming a leading brand name of oppression here. . . . And believe me they've got heavy competition for that market."

Though undoubtedly the most notorious, the Coca-Cola Company is not the only American firm whose workers have experienced anti-union violence. Three members of the Ray-O-Vac battery factory union were tortured and killed this year. Other U.S. firms that have experienced labor problems include U.S. Steel, Del Monte, Kellogg, Bank of America, Singer and Phillip Morris. In addition several of the forty-three union leaders who "disappeared" [in the two 1980 mass kidnappings of union leaders—EDS.] work for American firms. . . .

There are two lessons that American investors can learn from the crisis at the Coca-Cola bottler. One is that abuses of human rights such as in Guatemala will not continue unscrutinized by a wide range of religious, labor, and Congressional human rights advocates. The second lesson is that increased repression directed at Guatemalan trade unionists, will only serve to strengthen their resolve. When Marlon Mendizábal was asked one month prior to his assassination if he was ever scared, or had considered abandoning the union, he replied:

> Well, the thing that gives me spirit is when I look at the children. The biggest temptation is to look at my own children and say I should leave the union for their sake. But then, one has to think of how many other Guatemalan children have lost their fathers because of the repression. When I look at them, I want to continue.

[For reasons of space, the footnote references in the original version of this article have been eliminated. Sources used by Morris include: *Nuevo Diario* (Guatemala City), Jan. 23, 1979; *New York Times,* June 6, 1976 and August 24, 1980; *Miami Herald,* Aug. 15, 1980; *Newsweek,* July 7, 1980; *Atlantic Magazine,* January 1980; *Washington Post,* Sept. 8, 1980; *Amnesty International,* "Repression of the Trade Unions in Guatemala"; and *National Public Radio,* "Guatemala: Prelude to a Struggle."—EDS.]

30. *Education Can Be a Dangerous Thing* *

BY GILBERTO CASTAÑEDA

THE University of San Carlos, Guatemala's most important institution of higher learning, has suffered the country's diverse fortunes. Founded by the Spanish Crown in 1676 as a royal school devoted to the study of theology, medicine, and languages, it was administered by Jesuits until their expulsion from Latin America in 1767. After independence from Spain in 1821, the university

* From *Frente* [Guatemala City], November 1, 1980. Translated by Jonathan Fried and Nancy Peckenham.

concentrated on training lawyers and other professionals essential to a new nation. In 1945, when liberal Juan José Arévalo assumed the presidency, the University of San Carlos was declared an autonomous one; although state funded, it became legally self-governing and immune from state control. From 1945 to 1954 the university, an intellectual center, expanded its humanities and science faculties. After the 1954 coup, despite the fact that many professors and students were forced into exile, many remained politically progressive. Although its student body is a relatively small privileged group drawn from the middle and upper classes, many students have fought to make the university's curriculum, publications, and research serve the majority of poor Guatemalans. Student groups also joined the popular movement in the late 1970s, actively supporting strikes and community struggles. Still nominally autonomous, since 1954 the university has not been immune from increasing political violence and political pressure.

In September 1980, having declared that he could not continue working in an "autonomous university that had lost its autonomy," Gilberto Castañeda, Dean of the School of Architecture at the University of San Carlos, asked for permission to leave the university temporarily "to give my decided support to the task of creating, through the struggle of our people, a revolutionary, popular and democratic government." Permission was denied and he left anyway. What follows is an excerpt from a letter by Castañeda explaining his decision.

. . . THE GOVERNMENT HAS seen in the university—autonomous, scientific, aware of its constitutional duty to participate in the solution of national problems—an element of opposition that must be eliminated. This is not done through the forceful closing of the university, or through open and brazen intervention, it is done in more subtle ways. What the government attempts, and in a way achieves, is to force university authorities to apply its policies. To close the university would be a major discredit, although prestige doesn't seem to be the government's main concern. . . . The objective, then, is to get the university authorities themselves . . . to abandon the critical and scientific function of the institution, to annul the freedom of teachers by self-censure imposed through terror. . . .

So we are faced with a national autonomous university without autonomy. Its autonomy is only preserved in the dead letter of the law, in the ritual that persists in maintaining a formal autonomy that has been violated more than once and in more than one form. And also, little by little, we are ceasing to be the national university, because it is becoming increasingly difficult to fulfill our promise to defend our national patrimony and popular causes. Without real autonomy, this role is impossible.

This objective of intervening in the university through repression, thus forcing it to abandon its scientific and progressive positions, had its clearest expression in the indiscriminate massacre of university students as they got off public buses in front of the administration building on July 14, 1980. The harassment and attacks began in 1978, when the President of the Republic refused to consider an increase in the university's budget. One of his arguments was that the university was a center of subversion. The same argument was used by the Interior Minister after the July 14 massacre, hence justifying these attacks and harassment.

On October 20, 1978, Oliverio Castañeda de León, Secretary General of the University Students' Association (AEU), was assassinated . . . one block from the National Palace right after a rally commemorating the anniversary of the 1944 revolution. On February 13, 1979, Prof. Manuel Andrade Roca, Advisor to the Secretary General of the university, was assassinated and the attacks against university installations began. Graffiti was painted on walls connecting the university to the clandestine Guatemalan Workers' Party (PGT), and a broad disinformation and defamation campaign against the institution began.

Then in 1980, immediately after the Spanish Embassy massacre . . . came the assault against the university. So far this year, over fifty university students have been assassinated, and even more have been kidnapped. Some are still missing; others have turned up dead with signs of torture. . . . Many chose the path of exile in search of security for themselves and their families.

In this process, loyal to the democratic spirit which inspires us, we tried to find a viable solution for the institution. Not only have we failed in our attempt because the objective conditions do not permit it, but as a response we have only received more repression, persecution and harassment. . . .

For all these reasons, and because I am committed to today's struggle to free our country; because I am convinced that the university has been changed by the crisis; because I am loyal to the university spirit that inspired me to assume the position as dean; because I believe it is possible to achieve a scientific and progressive university although I see today enormous obstacles to its development; because I am harassed and repressed for my way of thinking; because I am persecuted for my unshaking defense of our university, and pressured in many ways to let the regime use me for its own purposes; because I realize I am a victim of injustice and I deserve a better life; and because this bloody situation we live in at the university has shown me the true path to follow; for all these reasons, without resigning from my position as dean, I assume the commitment to temporarily leave the university to give my decided support to the task of establishing, through the force of our people, a revolutionary, popular and democratic government that sets the foundations for changing our society. This is my contribution to the definitive resolution of the crisis we are living through at the university, and only then will I exercise with propriety the position I occupy. . . .

31. *My Country, Let Us Walk Together* *

BY OTTO RENE CASTILLO

OTTO René Castillo's life highlights the situation of his generation of middle-class intellectuals. Born in the city of Quezaltenango in 1936, educated in the reform ambiance of the 1944–1954 period, enthralled by the vision of a new Guatemala, he was a youth activist in the Guatemalan Workers' Party (PGT) in high school. When Jacobo Arbenz was overthrown in 1954, Castillo, seventeen years old, sought exile in El Salvador and joined the Salvadorean Communist Party. At the same time his poems began to receive recognition in Central America. In 1957 he returned to Guatemala to study law and subsequently won a scholarship to Germany where he worked with European filmmakers interested in making documentaries about the Latin American revolution. Again, in 1964, he returned to Guatemala and continued his turbulent mix of political and cultural activity, founding a theater company, editing a student paper, and working clandestinely with the Rebel Armed Forces (FAR) guerrilla group. Deported a year later, he worked abroad politically and came back to Guatemala for the final time in 1966. He joined the FAR guerrillas in the mountains; in March 1967 he was captured by the army, tortured for four days and burned alive.[1]

His short life of continuous political activism, of repeated exile, and of commitment to imaginative art seems extraordinary, but it is not entirely atypical. Scores of intellectuals, such as poet activist Roberto Obregón, assassinated by the army in 1970,[2] *led and lead similar lives.*

Castillo was part of an "engaged generation"—writers and artists whose works, after the fall of Arbenz, reflect frustration, indignation and hope. Passionate, nationalistic, and homeless in his lifetime, Castillo is Guatemala's national poet, yet one whose works are difficult to buy in his country. Today he is a hero of urban youth, and a guerrilla brigade bears his name. Winner of several poetry awards, four volumes of his work have been published in Spanish language editions. "My country, let us walk together" is his best-known poem.

---

* "Vamonos patria a caminar," from Otto René Castillo, *Informe de una Injusticia* (San Jose, Costa Rica: Editorial Universitaria Centroamericana, 1975), pp. 208–212. Translated by Deborah Levenson.

1. Roque Dalton, "Otto René Castillo, Su ejemplo y nuestra responsibilidad," in Castillo, pp. 9–29.

2. Mario Benedetti, ed., *Poesía trunca, poesía latinoamericana revolucionaria* (Madrid. Visor, 1980), p. 259.

MY COUNTRY, LET US WALK TOGETHER

1. Our voice
2. My country, let us walk together
3. Distant from your face

1.

So that my steps do not cry for me,
so the words do not bleed through me:
        I sing.
For your face bordering the soul
born in my hands:
        I sing.
To say you have grown transparent
inside the bitterest bones of my voice:
        I sing.
So that no one can say—my land!
with all the decisiveness of nostalgia:
        I sing.
For what must not die, your people:
        I sing.

I set out walking upon my voice to tell you:
you, interrogation of fruits and forest butterflies,
you will not lose your way in the scaffolding of my shout,
because there is a Mayan potter in your heart,
who, under the sea, inside a star,
smoldering in the roots, pulsating the world,
entwines your name in my words.
I sing your name, happy as a furrowing violin,
because it comes to meet my human pain.
It searches for me from the embrace of the sea to the wind's embrace
with its command that I not tolerate nightfall in my mouth.
The sacrifice of being a man accompanies me warmly,
forever keeping me from descending to the place where evil's treason was born
tying its heart to darkness, denying you!

2.

My country, let us walk together, you and I.

I will descend into the abysses where you send me.
I will drink your bitter chalices.
I will be blind so you may have eyes.

I will be voiceless so you may sing.
I have to die so you may live,
so your face emerges flaming on the horizon
of each flower born from my bones.

It has to be this way, unquestionably.

I am already tired of carrying your tears with me.
Now I want to walk with you like lightning.
Accompany you on your journey, because I am a man
of the people, born in October [3] to face the world.
Ay, country,
The colonels who piss on your walls
we must pull them up by the roots,
hang them from a tree of sharp dew,
violent with angers of the people.
For this I ask you that we walk together. Always
with the peasants
and the union workers,
with he who has a heart to love you.

My country, let us walk together, you and I.

3.

My little country, sweet storm,
a riverbank of love lifts my pupils
and wild joy fills my throat
when I say country, worker, bird of summer.
It's simply that for one thousand years I have agonized awakening
and stretch myself out a corpse over your immense name,
afloat over liberating inspirations,
Guatemala, saying my country, little peasant.

Ay, Guatemala,
when I say your name I return to life.
I rise from weeping in search of your smile.
I climb the letters of the alphabet until A
which flows to the wind full of joy
and I come back to contemplate you as you are,
a root growing toward human light
with all the tension of the people on your back.
Damned are the traitors, mother earth, damned.
They will know the death of death until death!

---

3. The October 1944 Revolution in Guatemala—EDS.

Why are such vile sons born of a loving mother?

This is the life of the people, bitter and sweet,
but their struggle resolves everything humanly.
For that, country, dawns will be born of you,
when man luminously revises his past.
For that, country, when I say your name my shout rebels
and the wind escapes being wind.
The rivers leave their fated course
and come in demonstration to hug you.
The seas take the blue words of your wounded name
among their waves and horizons, clean,
crystalizing you into the people's precipitous cry,
where the fish swim with fins of daybreak.

The fight of man redeems you in life.

Country, small, man and land and liberty
carrying hope on the paths of dawn.
You are the ancient mother of pain and suffering
who goes with a child of corn in her arms
who invents hurricanes of love and cherry trees
and grows complete over the face of the world,
so that everyone can love a little of your name:
a brutal piece of your mountains
or the heroic hand of your guerrilla sons.
Little country, my sweet storm,
a song located in my throat
since centuries of rebel corn:
For one thousand years I have carried your name
like a tiny future heart,
whose wings begin to open to the morning.

General Benedicto Lucas García, ex-Chief of Staff, inspecting materials and handmade guns captured from guerrillas. *Photo credit: Susan Meiselas*

Chapter II:

Struggles in the Countryside

Editors' Introduction

WHY Guatemala's rural dwellers would rise up in revolt is hardly a mystery. More difficult to ascertain is why at this point in time, after almost five hundred years of exploitation and discrimination, Guatemalan campesinos have joined a nationwide rebellion of unprecedented proportions. From the campesinos of 1954, who, unprepared for Castillo Armas's counterrevolutionary onslaught, were unable to prevent the destruction of their organizations and murder of their leaders, to the almost eighty thousand campesinos who defiantly confronted security forces in the successful February-March 1980 farmworkers' strike that paralyzed the country's agro-export economy, there is, evidently, a substantial difference. The nature of this difference, and how and why it came about, will be the subject of the readings in this chapter.

The relationship between the owners of the large agro-export farms (*latifundios*), located mostly on Guatemala's Pacific, or South Coast region, and the owners and renters of subsistence plots (*minifundios*), found mainly in the central and western highlands, has its origins in patterns established during the colonial period (see Part One, Chapter I). Today, unlike the colonial and much of the post-independence period, the *minifundistas* need not be coerced into providing the labor for agro-export production; economic necessity draws them there. As each generation of *minifundistas* divides a finite amount of land among their children, the minifundio decreases in size. At the same time, many of these lands have been taken over by large landowners, or *latifundistas*, through economic pressure, legal action and brute force. Presently, only a minority of *minifundistas* cultivate plots that yield enough for them to sustain themselves year-round. Eighty-eight percent of farms in Guatemala are too small to produce enough to support the average rural Guatemalan family; and a growing number of rural Guatemalans are landless. In need of supplementing their income, over half a million *minifundistas* annually migrate to the *latifundios* on the Pacific Coast to work as wage laborers.[1] Their economic necessity serves the interests of the *latifundistas*, who because of the abundance of labor, are basically free to determine the wages they pay.

Low wages and lack of access to land have had a disastrous impact on nutrition, health, education, and the environment in rural areas. Because of economic deprivation, child labor is endemic (see Reading 32); hence, 50 percent of the children drop out of school after the first year. *Minifundio* farmers are forced to cultivate land that is rocky, steep, and poorly drained, causing soil destruction and deforestation. Ecological problems are even more serious on the *latifundios*, where, because of indiscriminate pesticide use,[2] agricultural workers have six times as much DDT in their blood as do the workers in the most exposed areas of the United States.

The 1970s saw a rapid expansion of private enterprise, accompanied by large-scale government-sponsored infrastructural projects in the countryside which succeeded in taking land from the land-starved. As Nancy Peckenham points out in Reading 33, little of this development has "trickled down" to the country's campesinos. Even land set aside for distribution to campesinos in the Petén and Northern Transversal Strip regions ended up in the hands of wealthy landowners and high military officers, and the settlers it was supposed to benefit often ended up working as laborers on the new plantations.[3]

Numerous land conflicts broke out, particularly in the latter half of the 1970s, as campesinos began to resist encroachment on their lands. When government troops and hired gunmen intervened on behalf of those usurping the land, these conflicts became violent, leading to a number of massacres, such as the one that occurred in Panzós in May 1978.

---

1. To refer to rural subsistence agriculturalists and agricultural wage workers as a whole, instead of using the word "peasant," we retain the Spanish "campesino," or "people from the fields," a broader generic term that conveys the spirit of the countryside. Peasants, according to anthropologist Eric Wolf, are "populations that are existentially involved in cultivation and make autonomous decisions regarding the process of cultivation." (Eric R. Wolf, *Peasant Wars of the Twentieth Century* [New York: Harper & Row, 1969], p. xiv.) In Guatemala, as the size of the *minigundios* decreases, dependence on wage labor increases, and the campesinos, who account for approximately two-thirds of the country's population, progressively lose their autonomous decision-making power. The majority of Guatemalan campesinos today could be said to be both peasants and workers at the same time; thus, the inappropriateness of using the term "peasant" to describe rural dwellers who work for a wage for a major part of their income.

2. Julio Quan, "Guatemalan Agriculture in 1981," *Conference on Land Tenure* (Washington Office on Latin America, March 23, 1981), pp. 16-19.

3. Nancy Peckenham, "Land Settlement in the Petén," *Latin American Perspectives* [Riverside, Ca.] VII, nos. 2 and 3 (Spring-Summer 1980); and Alan Riding, "Guatemala Opening New Lands, but Best Goes to the Rich," *New York Times*, April 5, 1979.

Since most Guatemalan campesinos, even if they have some land to farm, are dependent on a wage, the rising cost of living in the 1970s further narrowed their margin of survival. Parallel to the growing number of land conflicts, labor conflicts over wages, working and living conditions on the agro-export farms increased.

The success of the massive February–March 1980 farmworkers' strike in the midst of the violent rule of the Lucas government, demonstrated an extraordinary level of organization in the countryside (see Reading 34). The strike was organized by the Committee of Campesino Unity (CUC), formed in April 1978 from a number of smaller organizations fighting for land, higher wages, and a number of other survival issues, such as water rights and basic services. CUC rapidly developed into a national organization uniting the country's diverse campesinos, surpassing in scope, although not necessarily replacing, more traditional forms of rural organization, such as agricultural workers' unions and peasant leagues. Also, within the CUC organization and in the course of the campesinos' struggles, the traditional animosity between Indian and ladino campesinos resulting from anti-Indian discrimination—deftly used by large landowners and local power brokers—began to break down.

As popular organization and rural guerrilla activity grew, the government's reaction became increasingly violent. Beginning in 1975 in the north of the Quiché province where guerrillas reinitiated their political and military struggle against the government, the army began occupying villages, kidnapping and killing community leaders or potential leaders. By 1980, army terror spread to other parts of the countryside, particularly throughout the predominantly Indian western highlands.

In response, rural populations learned and put into practice different forms of community warning and self-defense. Repression radicalized the countryside and the city alike, motivating the uncommitted to organize and promoting a closer identification between rural and urban dwellers.

By mid-1980, the intensity of government repression forced the campesino movement, like the labor movement and other urban organizations, totally underground. Many campesinos, particularly Indians, swelled the ranks of the guerrilla movement, whose history, role as social catalyzers, and ideas will be examined later in this book (see Part Four, Chapter II); and a project for a new society began to take shape.

32. *In Guatemala We Indians Have No Childhood* *

BY RIGOBERTA MENCHÚ

MANY threads of the situation in the Guatemalan countryside are woven together here, in the story of one person. Rigoberta Menchú is an Indian and a Christian revolutionary. She worked on her family's minifundio *in a small community in the highlands that struggled to keep its land from being expropriated by a local landlord; and on the* latifundios *of the coast, as a migrant worker. She moved to the city, seeking a better life, and found dependence and disdain as a servant in a middle-class ladino household. After moving back to the countryside, where she saw members of her family murdered by the army, she became a leader of the popular movement. Today, at twenty-three years of age, she continues her political work outside of Guatemala as an opposition spokesperson, explaining to people of other countries why her country is in rebellion.*

MY NAME IS Rigoberta Menchú. I was born in the region of Quiché and I learned to speak Spanish thirteen years ago. I don't have a father or a mother, and I'm going to explain why.

In the first place, I should say that in Guatemala we Indians have no childhood. . . . Personally, I started working for a living when I was eight years old, on the plantations of the large landowners on the South Coast. I remember that I decided to start working because I could no longer bear the expression of pain on my mother's face. She was always exhausted, picking coffee or cotton while carrying her newborn baby on her back, and my other five brothers and sisters around her, hungry. Since the children who don't work are not fed by the owners, she never earned enough. My wage, when I started, was twenty cents a day.

If we migrated from the highlands to work on the plantations it was because my father only had a small piece of land that didn't produce much, only a small amount of corn and beans that lasted for four or five months. The rest of the year we were forced to go to the plantations. . . . That was what our lives were like, and that's why I say that I never had a childhood.

When I was eleven, two of my little brothers died on the plantations from malnutrition and sickness. We came from a cold region and the intense heat of the coast made us sick. One time I too almost died from fever.

When my brothers died, my mother asked for permission to bury them, because our burial ceremonies are very important to us; but permission was denied.

* From *Uno más Uno* [Mexico City], May 29, 1982. Taped by Elisabeth Burgos and translated by Javier Bajaña and Jonathan Fried.

So she took a day off, and returned to work the following day. . . . They fired us, and they didn't pay us for the fifteen days we had already worked. So we returned home, to the highlands. There my mother had to sell the few animals she had in order to feed us. A few months later, when my father returned from the plantation where he was working, he discovered that he had lost two sons.

Community Life and Tradition

We used to get up at three in the morning. Everyone had his own task. I had to feed the dogs and clean the corn for the tortillas; the other girls prepared the corn dough and lit the fire; and the men prepared their tools to go to work in the fields. For breakfast we had tortillas with salt. Sometimes, when possible, we drank "atol" [a drink made from corn—EDS.]. At four in the morning we were all ready to go to the fields. People in the village would call their neighbors in order to leave together, because we worked as a community. One of the women stayed behind in each house to do the cleaning and the cooking. In the evenings we ate tortillas with chili peppers. We women would weave sitting on the floor. Sometimes my brothers played music. By nightfall we went to sleep. The house only had one room, in which we all slept and ate together. We slept on reed mats, with our clothes on. This is why they think that we Indians are dirty. But the truth of the matter is that it gets very cold in the mountains and the houses have thatched roofs and cane walls that let the cold wind in. . . .

When I was a child I never went to town. Our customs don't permit a young girl to walk alone; there have to be at least two, because our way of life is communal. Moreover, in the village there was a community house where we had meetings and dances. Once a week we did the rituals of our ancestors, and once in a while those of Catholic Action.[1] When we were very young our parents taught us to be loyal to our ancestors, our culture, our traditions.

For example, before planting, we ask the earth for permission to make a wound in it; because for us, the earth is sacred. We only have the right to wound it for our sustenance. It is the same when we cut down a tree or limbs to build our houses. We have to hold a ceremony to ask nature's forgiveness. . . . Women, while pregnant, tell their babies everything they see while they walk through the woods; the names of plants, flowers and animals. . . . When the baby is born, he has a *nahual* or animal spirit, which varies according to the date of birth, and is always an animal. The name is not revealed to the child until he is an adult, so that the animal's character doesn't influence him.

"The Rich Made Fun of Us"

My father and mother were the leaders of our community. That is to say, they were elected and people looked for them when they had problems or someone

1. A grassroots Catholic movement; see Part Three, Chapter III, Editors' Introduction—EDS.

took ill. This is why, when I was small, I didn't see my father very often. When we returned from the plantations and were once again reunited, he was always busy defending our community from the large landowners who wanted to take our land away from us. . . . After my parents were married, they moved to the mountains and founded a small village with other people whom my father sent for. Everyone began clearing the undergrowth and planting. But naturally, the land didn't produce; we had to wait several years for the first harvest. And when the village finally had its first real harvest of corn and beans, a large landowner arrived, claiming the land was his. Then my father, who was the only one who spoke some Spanish, went to the authorities.

He began to travel, looking for support so that the large landowner would leave us alone. But no one listened to his protests; they sent him from one place to another, from Huehuetenango to Quezaltenango, to Quiché and the capital, just to sign some papers. They insisted he hire a lawyer and present witnesses. And since he only spoke a little Spanish and couldn't read or write, they often tricked him. He dedicated most of his time to the community, which meant that he didn't work enough to make a living. That is why we, his children, had to work in his place.

I remember when I was fifteen, in 1973. My father was arrested for the first time. They accused him of creating disturbances, and committing crimes against the sovereign authority of Guatemala. My mother had to leave us alone to find a lawyer who would take my father's case. She found a lawyer in Quiché who charged a lot. To pay, she took work as a maid, and all her pay went to the lawyer. Later, the sentence was announced: my father was condemned to eighteen years in prison. He was set free after a year and two months, but they threatened to jail him for life if he continued causing problems.

While my father was in jail, the rich landowners came, and since no one knew Spanish, they frightened us. They made believe they were engineers and started to measure the fields. And they told the campesinos to either leave, or stay as wage earners, because the land was theirs. Then their gunmen threatened to chase us out. They came into our homes, threw all our things out, and broke everything, because all we had was clay pots. When my father returned he decided to work even harder defending his community, and even to give his life for it. He continued making trips to the capital. At that time we still believed that only the large landowners were our enemies. We didn't realize that, in fact, it was all the rich who persecuted us campesinos.

My father got in touch with the National Institute of Agrarian Transformation, and they too made him sign some papers, and begin once again the procedures to obtain titles for our land; and they said we should continue working the land. On his way back from the city, my father was kidnapped by the landowner's gunmen, who tortured him and left him in the mountains, thinking he was dead. My mother had to leave us once more to go to the town where my father, with the help of our priests, was hospitalized. She came to see us only once every two months. One day the servants of the landowner told us that my father was going to be kidnapped once again, so some priests helped us transfer him to a private clinic. He remained there a long time, almost two years, and when he came out, he wasn't the same. He suffered a lot of pain and could not work in the fields. His way of getting even was to continue to fight the authorities.

From this point on, he never traveled alone, he would take other campesinos to the capital with him. But the rich made fun of us: they asked us for $19,000 because according to them, the land is national property, that is, it belongs to the state. We campesinos can't even save up $20. How could we, even in our wildest dreams, get $19,000?

In 1977 my father was sent to jail. This time they accused him of being a terrorist and a communist. But we knew well we were only poor. The community tried to protest to the authorities. To speak to a mayor you have to have a bondsman; to see the governor you have to have a lawyer; and to talk to congressmen or the president you have to put up with so many delays, a series of interviews where they send you to one person after another. You have to be able to wait, and we campesinos no longer have time to wait.

"For These People, an Indian is Less than a Dog"

[My father] taught me how to be an Indian and not become a ladina. He used to tell me that we Indians have to preserve our dress, or we would lose our dignity.

Many years ago I went to the city to work as a maid, thinking that everything would be different. But the rich woman I worked for asked me to take off my Indian clothing. "What will my friends say when they see you in those clothes?" she would say to me. "I'll advance you two months pay if you buy yourself clothes; if not, you'll have to leave." She knew very well that I hardly spoke Spanish and that I didn't know the city. She used to give me tortillas to eat, and gave the dog meat. Then I understood that for these people an Indian is less than a dog.

The ladinos celebrate the day of Tecún Umán, an Indian hero who fought the Spaniards. We refuse to celebrate it because we cannot accept that our struggle be relegated to the past, as if it had ended. . . . Once I heard a ladino say "I'm poor, but hear me, I'm not an Indian." And later I met ladinos who fought with us and have understood that we are like them, human beings.

The Example of the Bible and of Our Ancestors

[Soon after my brothers died on the coast] I started going to church to see the nuns and priests, and I became a catechist.[2] I worked with young people, women and children. We catechists teach the Bible. We have to memorize it in our

---

2. Lay religious and community leader—EDS.

Indian language, because we don't know how to read, write or speak Spanish. The priest came to our village only once a month. It was my father who taught me to be a Christian when I was very small, as soon as I learned how to talk. My father told us that he became a catechist when he was very young. . . .

In the community we began to reflect together on what the Bible told us. The story of Judith, for example, impressed me very much: she beheaded the king to save her people. We too understood that faced with the violence of the rich, we have to respond with another kind of violence, the violence of justice. The example of Moses also helped us a lot: Moses, who led his people across the world to save them. We started building encampments to spend nights in the mountains, in order to avoid being killed by the soldiers while we sleep. We taught the children how to guard the road during the day so that they can warn us when the soldiers come to town. This was the beginning of our self-defense. And it was because of the Bible that we organized our struggle. On the other hand, we also had the example of our ancestors, among whom there are many martyrs and heroes. To keep us pacified they wanted to make us believe that our ancestors didn't fight when the conquistadores arrived. But we know perfectly well what happened. They didn't leave any writings: that's why the Bible is useful to us. Furthermore, it is in accord with our own beliefs, because we too have only one God, the Sun, which is the heart of the sky.

That's why we got organized and the response was tremendous repression, particularly the persecution of catechists. In jail my father had met a ladino who was a political prisoner. He explained to my father that the enemy was not only the rich landowners who want to rob our small plots of land. My father also understood that our struggle could not be the same as before, and since his life was in danger, he decided to go underground and live a secret life. He was never at home anymore, and we never knew the places he traveled to, since he knew that if we were in contact with him our lives would be in danger.

It wasn't long before they found out who were the most active in the community. They learned who the leaders were through the system of cooperatives. The Committees of Campesino Unity were created in 1978; my father joined, since by this time we saw our problems from a political angle. In fact, we ourselves arrived at that understanding, something that is not surprising at all considering that the poor are the only ones who know what hunger, pain, and suffering are. After the assassination of 106 campesinos in Panzós (see Reading 33—EDS.)—men, women and children who had never tasted meat or owned a pair of shoes—we intensified our struggle. Their death gave us hope, because it would be unjust if the blood of all those people were forgotten forever. . . .

"The Most Painful Experience of my Life"

One of my brothers was a catechist. The other was secretary for a cooperative in the village; that was his only crime. They kidnapped him, and he spent sixteen days in the hands of the army, who tortured him. He was only fourteen years old. They ripped off his fingernails, cut off his tongue, they destroyed the soles of his feet and burned his skin. I saw him with my own eyes and I will never forget it! One day the army circulated a notice throughout our communities ordering everyone to come to one of the villages the following day to witness the punishment of some guerrillas. "Surely my son will be there," my mother said. And we walked all night and part of the next day to get there. My father, who had learned about my brother's disappearance, went with us. At eight A.M. a military truck arrived. They made about twenty men get off the truck; men who no longer looked human, and among them was my little brother. It was hard to identify him, so we were not absolutely sure it was him. He was so disfigured. . . . There we saw the suffering of our friends and confirmed that those they called guerrillas were people from a neighboring village or people we met on the plantations; among others, catechists and my little brother.

We had to witness that horrible thing, which was the most painful experience of my life. Up until then my greatest moment of grief came when my best friend, a catechist, died by my side, poisoned by pesticides from a fumigation plane that flew over our heads.

They lined up the prisoners, dressed up like soldiers. The captain in command gave a speech which he constantly interrupted to tell his squad to keep the prisoners on their feet. They hit them with their rifle butts to make them stand, but they would just fall down again. When he finished the speech, the captain said that all the subversives would be treated this way. And when he gave the order to undress them, they had to cut off the uniforms because the blood from the wounds made the uniforms stick to their bodies. . . . They tied them and piled them up together, then the captain ordered his soldiers to pour gasoline over them and set them on fire. I was looking at my brother. He didn't die right away, nor the others. Some screamed; others could no longer breathe so they didn't scream, but their bodies were writhing. Unfortunately there is no water in our villages so we couldn't put out the fire that was burning them. When water arrived, it was too late.

The soldiers left shouting "Long live the army!" "Long live President Lucas!" "Death to the guerrillas!" My mother was still hugging my brother's body. I was crying, we were all crying and feeling hate. We couldn't show it, by killing them like they kill us; but this reinforced our will to fight. My father didn't cry, he didn't move. He watched everything without making a gesture.

When we returned home, we were slightly crazed, as if it were a nightmare. My father left right away, saying that he had a lot to do for his people, that he had to go from town to town telling people what had happened. At that time he left the house for good. A short time later, my mother decided to travel to the regions of Chimaltenango and Huehuetenango to attest to what she had seen. She said "As a woman it is my duty to tell my story so that other mothers don't have to suffer like me, so that they don't have to witness the torture and assassination of one of their children." She took my smallest sister along. My brothers also left, and my little sister, who was nine years old, said she was going to join the guerrillas, so that she wouldn't die of hunger, nor wait to be killed by the troops.

Soon afterward my father was killed. With a group of campesinos he decided to occupy the Spanish Embassy in the capital to protest against the repression in Quiché. On that occasion twenty-one Indians from the Quiché, Ixil, Achí and Pocomchí communities, plus a worker, a shantytown dweller and four students were burned alive inside the embassy. . . . (see Reading 33—EDS.) The consequence of this blow at the embassy was the creation of the January 31st Popular Front, composed of six mass organizations, including the Vicente Menchú Revolutionary Christians, which was founded on the day following my father's death.[3] The slaughter at the embassy was one more lesson leading us to consolidate our organization.

My mother died three months later. The military chief raped her and tortured her like they did to my brother. They made her suffer a long time, to make her talk about the guerrillas. We knew they were up there, far away in the mountains. Sometimes they came down, searching for food. At first we didn't trust them, but later we understood that at least they had weapons to fight the army with, while we, when we had just begun to defend ourselves, used the same booby traps invented by our ancestors.[4] It was my mother who, while traveling from one town to another, had met the guerrillas.

When my mother was in the throes of death, the army commander ordered that they feed her intravenously and that they give her food. They revived her, and when she recovered her strength, they tortured her again. A human being can receive a lot of punishment, but resistance has its limits. My mother's agony started again. They placed her under a tree in the middle of the countryside, and her body became infested with worms, because we have a fly here that settles on wounds and immediately lays eggs. The soldiers kept guard over her body day and night to make sure that none of us tried to free her. She resisted a long time and then died under the sun and in the cold. They didn't let us recover her body. The troops stayed until the vultures and dogs ate her. That's how they hoped to terrorize us. . . .

"If I Fight, it is to be Treated like a Human Being"

We, their children, the orphans, had to find a different way to struggle. . . . My brothers and sisters chose a different form of combat. We separated. I know nothing of them and they know nothing of me. I chose the mass movement and joined the [Vicente Menchú] Revolutionary Christians. I know very well that in this kind of struggle we run the greatest risks. . . .

---

3. The formation of the January 31st Popular Front was announced one year later, in January 1981. Vicente Menchú is the name of Rigoberta Menchú's father—EDS.

4. Traps used against the Spanish are described in the *Annals of the Cakchiquels*, Reading 2—EDS.

As a woman, I have decided not to marry or have children. According to our traditions this is unacceptable; a woman should have children and we like to have them. But I could not endure it if what happened to my brother would happen to one of my children. From time to time, when I'm depressed, I wish my mother had had an abortion and never given birth to me. Before having children we have to change the situation. . . . I don't want a boyfriend because it would be one more reason to grieve. They would kill him for sure, and I don't want to cry anymore. . . . I am no longer the owner of my small existence; the world I live in is so cruel, so blood-thirsty, that it is going to annihilate me at any moment. Therefore, the only thing I can do is to struggle, to practice that violence which I learned in the Bible.

Besides, I don't believe that the Bible can be used to explain everything. As I told a Marxist colleague who was surprised that a Christian like me wants to make revolution, neither does Marxism contain all the truth. And I showed him that if I fight, it is to be treated like a human being. Only recently have I dared discuss this in this manner, especially with our male colleagues, because there is also a problem of machismo. Even now, since I have become a leader, it is difficult to criticize a male colleague and sanction him, because men don't accept it easily when it comes from a woman. . . .

This is what I can give as testimony. . . . If I have narrated my life, if I have taken this opportunity, it's because I know that my people cannot tell their story; but it's no different than mine. I am not the only orphan. . . .

33. *Fruits of Progress: The Panzós and Spanish Embassy Massacres**

By Nancy Peckenham

THE large-scale development project in Guatemala's Northern Transversal Strip is a clear example of the sort of "development" that benefits transnational corporations, large landowners, and the military rulers at the expense of those who, materially speaking, have the least to spare. The struggles of the campesinos of the Transversal region for their economic survival—resisting encroachment on their lands, and for their physical survival—denouncing the kidnappings and murders in their villages, form the backdrop of two massacres considered by many to be important watersheds in the development of Guatemala's revolution. Nancy Peckenham based this previously unpublished article on a chapter of a study done by an independent Guatemalan research group on

* An essay written for this volume.

the Panzós massacre (Centro de Investigaciones de Historia Social, Panzós: Testimonio, *Guatemala: 1979, Chapter Two: "La Masacre de Panzós"); and a detailed report by the Democratic Front Against Repression on the Spanish Embassy massacre ("The Democratic Front Against Repression of Guatemala Addresses Itself to all Peoples of the World to Inform Them of the Facts Regarding the Massacre Perpetrated Against 39 People in the Spanish Embassy in Guatemala on January 31, 1980," Guatemala: Feb. 1980).*

TWO DECADES AGO few people inhabited the humid lowlands of northern Guatemala; settlements were sparse and travel usually by foot. Over the past century many Kekchí Indians had migrated to the northern Alta Verapaz and lower Petén region, from the crowded highland towns around Coban, the local capital.

By the late 1970s this region, stretching west across the department of Quiché to Huehuetenango, was a hotbed of construction and development. A road, the Northern Transversal Strip highway, was dug out past the town of Sebol, designed to connect in the west with Huehuetenango and the Cuchumatanes mountains. Army engineers drew the plans; soldiers carried them out, paving the way for the petroleum-extracting machinery arriving en masse in Guatemala.

The international petroleum industry had been officially invited into Guatemala in 1975 when Guatemalan officials, feeling the squeeze from the 1973 oil crisis, decided to promote domestic oil production. In 1978 Basic Resources International, a consortium headed by English banker and publisher Sir James Goldsmith, began pumping oil at their Rubelsanto oil well, to the west of Sebol. Joined by other multinational oil companies (Shenandoah, Getty, Texaco-Amoco, Elf-Aquitane), Basic Resources remained in the forefront of an oil production industry that built a pipeline to the Caribbean port of Santo Tomás and exported the first barrels of crude in April 1980.[1]

As multinational attention focused on northern Guatemala, many native Guatemalans showed increased interest in the region also. Foremost among them was president Romeo Lucas García, whose family owned a one hundred thousand acre estate along the path of the pipeline, near Sebol. Other military officials and businessmen started making claims to the wilderness of the Transversal region. Some filed suits to gain ownership of now-promising land; some resorted to simple threat and intimidation.

The peacefulness that once distinguished the region disappeared as bulldozers roared through isolated villages or as private security guards and soldiers dragged campesino families from their homes and land. Many people protested the rape of the countryside and in their struggle, many of the seeds of today's larger

---

1. For a more detailed report on Guatemala's oil industry see Nancy Peckenham, "Guatemalan Peasants Lose Out in Scramble for Oil Wealth," *Multinational Monitor,* May 1981.—EDS.

revolutionary involvement took root. The most serious conflicts occurred in Panzós, Alta Verapaz, and in the Nebaj-Uspantán region of Quiché.

Panzós

Located in a tropical lowland valley touching Lake Izabal in the east, Panzós, in the late nineteenth century, was a major transit point for coffee produced in Alta Verapaz and ferried across the lake to the Caribbean port of Puerto Barrios. But by the mid-twentieth century, new transportation routes had by-passed the region and it sank into relative obscurity until large-scale copper and nickel operations came into the nearby towns of Cahaboncito and El Estor. In 1960, the Canadian-based International Nickel Company (INCO), in partnership with the U.S. Hanna Mining Company, began negotiations for mining nickel under the name of EXMIBAL. After years of negotiations, nickel extraction began in 1977, just as the first oil companies were exploring for petroleum reserves to the west. In 1979, a pipeline from the oil fields was built, passing along the old transport route to Lake Izabal.

In the 1960s, before the mining industry was in full swing, investors from Guatemala City had begun establishing cattle ranches throughout the Panzós region, incorporating the land which had been traditionally cultivated by local campesinos, mostly Kekchí Indians. Campesinos were dispossessed from their land in increasing numbers; by the late 1970s, tensions were near a breaking point.

Some of the campesinos who applied to INTA to legalize their claims to small plots of land obtained promises, others, provisional titles, and a few, permission to plant and harvest. None received permanent title to the property. By 1978, a resolution had not been reached. The large landowners continued threatening campesinos living on land claimed by both parties and the campesinos continued appealing to officials in Guatemala City for settlement.

In late May 1978, the people of Cahaboncito, near Panzós, received notice of a meeting to be held May 29, in Panzós, where some decisions would be made regarding land rights. On that morning men, women, and children set out for Panzós, carrying machetes for their afternoon work in the fields. When they arrived, tensions were high. Landowners, town officials, and government troops awaited them in the center of town. As the meeting was about to begin, according to eyewitness reports, a campesino began arguing with a soldier. The campesino, not understanding Spanish, thought he was being insulted, and attacked the soldier, who fell, wounded. Immediately all the soldiers opened fire, some climbing to the roof of the municipal building and shooting into the crowd. Plainclothed individuals, local policemen, and a local government official joined them in the shooting spree.

As the terrified campesinos fled, they met death in the parks, in the streets, in the fields, and even in the river where they had thrown themselves in panic, only to be carried off by the current. Two municipal trucks then rolled into town, picking up corpses from the roadside and carrying them to a mass grave outside town, which townspeople later reported had been dug two days *before* the massacre. Total dead: over one hundred men, women, and children.

The nation was stunned by this overwhelming act of brutality—the government's aggressive response to popular demands. In Panzós, the land problems festered unresolved. Government troops that had been called in for the "meeting" stayed on in the town. The land in question was roped off and guarded by military personnel and the survivors regrouped and reorganized, with many campesinos politicized by the massacre going on to work with other campesinos in the Committee of Campesino Unity (CUC).

The Spanish Embassy Massacre

For the campesinos living west of Panzós, in the province of Quiché, the Panzós massacre had a tremendous impact. For years representatives from various communities, among them Uspantán, Cotzal, Chajul and Nebaj, had been following similar avenues with INTA officials to resolve the question of land ownership. Frequent trips to Guatemala City proved fruitless; promises of land titles were never fulfilled and local landowners, aided by private military police, continued to harass local campesinos, burning their homes and forcefully evicting them.

In February 1979, when the military police set up their headquarters in the campesino cooperative of the town of Chajul, the kidnappings, disappearances and torture of local campesinos began. By the fall of 1979 the conflicts were reaching a climax as more and more campesinos became frustrated in their search for a solution to their problems. On November 29, 1979 the army bombed the outlying hamlets of Chajul, killing domestic and farm animals and destroying crops.

Afterward, soldiers searched village homes, breaking open boxes, tearing up documents, and smashing dishes and utensils. The military occupation of villages continued throughout December, with occasional bombings of villages and constant intimidation of the local population. Over fifty campesinos were kidnapped, and many later found dead and abandoned.

It must be remembered that the villages of Quiché province are far away from major communication centers and, were it not for the recent interest in oil and the Transversal project, far from the minds of most Guatemalan citizens. Campesinos, believing that if the country and the world knew of their suffering it might then cease, began planning ways to capture the country's attention.

In November 1979, a delegation of campesinos went to Guatemala City to try to read a declaration to the Guatemalan Congress. Once inside Congress, however, security forces chased them out, pursuing them through the streets of the city. Having failed, the campesinos returned to Quiché province where the bombings and intimidation intensified.

On January 15, 1980, a delegation of one hundred thirty campesinos again left their homes in search of a way to publicize their plight. They delivered press releases to the major media. Nothing was published. They held a press conference. It went unreported. Colleges were visited. They occupied the office of the Organization of American States (OAS) to lodge their protest. Two radio stations were taken over and their message broadcast to listeners in Guatemala City. But still no one in the government made an overture to discuss a solution to the problems in Quiché. The government broadcast messages on radio and TV, accusing the campesinos of being guerrillas, warning people not to be fooled by their appearances.

By the last week of January, the delegation was looking for new ways to gain the attention of the country and of the world. It was decided to occupy the Spanish Embassy together with representatives of worker, student, and Christian movements. An embassy of a democratic country was chosen so that, presumably, diplomatic immunity could not be violated by the security forces. The plan was to peacefully occupy the building, then make public their demands for an investigation into the repression in Quiché.

On January 31, 1980, twenty-nine people entered the embassy, explaining to the ambassador the nature of the occupation. Visiting the embassy were former Guatemalan Vice-President Cáceres Lenhoff and ex-Foreign Minister Molina Orantes. When the government was informed of the occupation, four hundred members of the security forces were dispatched to the scene and immediately surrounded the building. Elias Barahona, chief press officer at the time for the Interior Ministry,[2] was working at his office the afternoon of the massacre. Months later, outside the country, he gave this insider's view of the ensuing events:

> "... When the situation dragged on, [President] Lucas called Interior Minister Donaldo Alvarez Ruíz to ask him what was going on, why had he not settled the problem. He told him that the situation was difficult because the embassy's territory, in accordance with international law, was inviolable. Lucas told him to stop saying foolish things, that he had to solve this problem soon. He was told that former Vice President Cáceres Lenhoff and former Foreign Minister Molina Orantes were also inside. Then I remember well that Lucas told him: It does not matter. You resolve the problem. Then the minister asked him to define more precisely the order, and he told him: Take them out as you can. At that point, the police broke into the embassy throwing grenades, throwing all

2. Elias Barahona y Barahona, a journalist who worked in the press office of the Interior Minister, personally wrote the first press release of the Secret Anticommunist Army (ESA), a death squad which, according to Barahona, was created by the Interior Minister, Donaldo Alvarez Ruíz. Barahona, a member of the Guerrilla Army of the Poor (EGP), infiltrated this government office and gave first-hand reports on its operation after his departure in September, 1980.

kinds of projectiles, but the comrades who were inside the embassy went up to the last office, which was the ambassador's office, and took refuge there. The new situation was discussed and Lucas said: Set them on fire. Then the police put a metal lock on the door of the ambassador's office and launched fire bombs. The spectacle was horrible. . . . From the street, thousands of people could see how thirty-nine human beings writhed and died burning." *(Foreign Broadcast Information Service,* Feb. 5, 1982)

The Spanish ambassador, Máximo Cajal, managed to escape. Among the corpses, one body still breathed—that of Gregorio Yujá. Ambassador Cajal, whose calls to the government had been refused, and whose pleas to the security forces outside went unheard, denounced the brutality of the Guatemalan government, and left for Mexico. Mr. Yujá, the sole campesino survivor, was kidnapped from his hospital bed that night and murdered.

The news of the death and destruction within the embassy traveled around the world. Lucas's press representatives painted a picture of guerrillas who had seized the embassy and by accident set off the fire with a molotov cocktail, a story which sharply contradicted Ambassador Cajal's eyewitness testimony.

Tens of thousands of mourners poured into the streets of Guatemala City for the funeral procession of the murdered campesinos and popular leaders. The level of violence that was common in the countryside had now been seen in the city and throughout the country as well. The campesinos who had not entered the embassy returned to their towns with the understanding that the government would never cease the repression. The bombings and kidnappings continued, clearing the land for oil prospectors, cattle ranchers, and speculators. But many people disappeared underground and resurface now, armed to fight the enemy on its own terms.

34. *We Are Barefoot, But We Are Many**

A. *Campesino Cartoon. (See Appendix.)*

B. *"With the Machete We Earn Our Living, and with the Machete We Must Defend It"*

CARTOONS and drawings are often employed by Guatemala's popular movement and guerrillas as a means of communication in a country where

* From *De Sol a Sol* (Guatemala) no. 35, July 1980; and nos. 33-34, March-April 1980. Part B translated by Dina Briones and Jonathan Fried.

most people cannot read or write, and many different languages are spoken. The Appendix of this book shows a cartoon that is a regular feature of De Sol a Sol, *or "From Sunrise to Sunset," a newspaper linked to the campesino movement. Like many others of its kind, the cartoon depicts forms of organizing and self-defense, and contrasts government propaganda (in this case, radio ads and anticommunist rallies people are forced to attend) with the crude realities of daily life.*

In the Reading below are excerpts from De Sol a Sol's *issue on the February-March 1980 farmworkers' strike, the largest of its kind in post-1954 Guatemala. Written in the idiom of campesino language, the newspaper describes and analyzes the events that paralyzed agro-export production for two weeks and forced the government to raise the minimum wage for farmworkers from $1.12 to $3.20 per day. Not only was the strike carried out during a period of extreme repression of popular organizations, but for the first time it brought together a workforce traditionally divided by language and cultural differences, anti-Indian discrimination, and short-term economic interests, since the migrant workers, who are mostly Indians, were sometimes used involuntarily as strikebreakers in conflicts between the growers and the largely ladino permanent workforce.*

B. *"With The Machete We Earn Our Living, And With The Machete We Must Defend It"*

. . . WE ARE BAREFOOT, but we are many. We plant the sugar cane, weed, cut and grind it, transport and ship it. We do the same with cotton, coffee, and the products made in the factories. We produce the riches that the landowners and all the powerful count, enjoy, and waste. Therefore, when we stop working, the wealth that they enjoy stops as well. Without us, they are nothing; they don't produce anything, they have nothing to administer. That's why they trembled when we stopped working; that's why they incited the army to repress us; that's why the government had to set the minimum wage for all the cutters and farmworkers at $3.20 per day. This is a lesson we must never forget: *that we are many and we have a great force in our hands; and the landowners are few and without us they can do nothing. . . .*

On Monday, February 18, the sugar cane cutters of the Tehuantepec farm in Santa Lucía Cotzumalguapa began a work stoppage. . . . The strike began with seven hundred Indian and ladino migrant workers. . . . We demanded Q5 per ton of sugar cane. . . . The overseer of the farm made fun of us, saying that it was our same deviousness of every year, and that the following day we would be back at work.

But the following day, February 19, all of us were still on strike and we decided to go to other farms to ask for solidarity and for others to join the strike. We went to neighboring farms, and succeeded in extending the strike to the Florencia, Cristóbal, and La Guanipa farms, all belonging to the same exploiter. . . .

In the following days, the sugar plantations joined the strike, and the sugar mills also began joining. By Monday, February 25, more than sixty farms were on strike. We began to see solidarity in this struggle. Even though many migrant workers left the farms to go back to their towns, it was because the growers denied them food and they were unable to hold out until the end of the strike. But many other migrant workers stayed in the struggle, enduring hunger, but determined to stick it out until victory.

To give strength to our strike and show our determination, we used sabotage. We pierced truck tires, stopped many trucks carrying cane and made others turn back; and we also dumped sugar cane from the trucks, set fire to a truck loaded with cotton, and to the fields of a sugar cane plantation. Thus the strike reached the sugar mills, either because there was no sugar cane reaching them, or because in many places the workers decided to strike in solidarity with our struggle, and also demand better wages for themselves. On the roads we stopped buses carrying workers to the farms, who joined us in our struggle. . . .

From Santa Lucía the strike spread to Escuintla, where the women market vendors initiated their own struggle and supported ours. Soon the strike spread to the cotton and rubber plantations. . . . The roads of the coast were filled with workers in struggle, and the crowds of people were not afraid, but courageous, with machetes in hand. The women and children were also present with their machetes ready. By the end of February all the sugar cane farms and sugar mills, and fifteen thousand cotton and rubber workers were on strike. Nearly eighty thousand of us were on strike.

Confronting the Security Forces

As soon as the strike started, the repressive forces of the government and the rich arrived. The Ambulatory Military Police, the *Pelotón Modelo* [riot police], the Judicial Police, and soldiers from the Puerto San José military base filled the highways of the coast in an attempt to force us to back down. This was the order they had. While our leaders met with the Minister of Labor, the rich met with the Chief of Staff of the Army to decide how to repress us.

But the workers did not abandon our struggle and the threats and tear gas did not break our determination. All the workers who were together at kilometer 90 of Santa Lucía confronted the repressive forces with stones, sticks and machetes, and often made them pull back. The chief of the military police, the assassin Abadilla, came to the Cerritos farm and the La Papelera factory in Escuintla to threaten the workers. When he stepped out of his helicopter, he fired his machine gun. When he tried to enter La Papelera, the campesinos from the Cerritos farm joined together and surrounded him with their machetes raised high. All those machetes forced this assassin to flee. Next it was the criminal Chupina, Chief of the National Police, who came to threaten the La Papelera workers; he said that he was going to evict them with bullets. We confronted him and told him that he would die there too, because we could make the factory's boilers explode. . . . The only thing that made us leave was the threat that they were going to kill our captured leaders. In this same place four children armed with machetes prevented one of the employees of the rich from escaping from La Papelera. . . .

The landlords and the repressive forces asked us to choose our representatives, our leaders, to dialogue with them. We responded that we were all representatives and leaders. That's how we applied self-defense to protect our leaders and our struggle. All of us shouted out the response so that none of us would stand out.

In the course of the strike it became clear that only with force can we make them respect our rights. Women and children also showed combativeness in confronting the repressive forces; because self-defense is of all the masses confronting our enemies. . . .

Solidarity

Although for many years we were united by a common exploitation, individual migrant workers, migrant crews, resident farm hands and agro-industrial workers had kept ourselves divided, and many times made enemies among ourselves. The growers put this idea of divisiveness into our heads to exploit us better. Indians and poor ladinos have been put in a situation of confronting one another, and taking each other's jobs and better wages. Today we have begun to unite in the same struggle, with the same interest in ending exploitation, and the repression and discrimination that accompany it.

We have received support . . . from campesinos in the highlands, who sent us corn, and held demonstrations and carried out their own struggles on behalf of our strike. Farmworkers and sugar mill workers have also participated in a common struggle against common enemies.

We had talked many times about the worker-campesino alliance. In many demonstrations we shouted this slogan without understanding it fully. In the struggles of the coast this slogan has come to life. The clearest example of this is the Cerritos farm and the La Papelera factory, which are on the same property. The workers of La Papelera went out on strike not for their own interests, but to support the workers of the countryside. They were threatened and some have been fired for supporting our struggle. . . . In addition, workers in the capital, in Amatitlán, and bank employees began work stoppages in support of our struggles, as well as to demand higher wages. . . .

Our Victory "Was Not a Gift"

The rich wanted to increase the repression and not our wages. The government too. But the strength of the workers, united and organized . . . made them back down and give us a minimum [daily] wage of $3.20. We farmworkers are not satisfied with this minimum wage. We need more to survive. We need a minimum of $5.[1] Besides, we have to think about the unemployment that many of us suffer during a large part of the year, during which time we go into debt.

But we are glad because we took an important step. . . . It was not a gift as the government wanted it to appear. It is a victory because it benefits not only the striking sugar cane cutters and cotton pickers, but all the sugar, cotton, and cattle workers, and also the coffee workers, who make up the majority of agricultural workers and are the most exploited and discriminated against. . . .

Our struggle has not ended. . . . The government had to concede the Q3.20, causing friction with the growers. But neither the growers nor the government are complying with these promises. On the state farms and the farms of the most exploitative rich of our country, instead of granting the wage hikes, layoffs have begun and repression has increased. The growers are getting together to see how they can continue exploiting us. They have taken away water, wood, food, electricity, medicine, and other benefits from the resident farm hands and the migrant crews, fired the individual migrant workers and constantly threatened us. . . . But we are determined to take all measures necessary to conquer those rights that our ours. . . . We must prepare our defense so that our enemies cannot enter our communities. . . . *The machete must be in our hands at all times, whether we are men, women, or children. With the machete we earn our living, and with the machete we must defend it.* . . .

35. The Road to Liberty Passes through Organization *

BY J. ANTONIO BRAN

THERE is a myth associated with revolution (sometimes believed even by those who consider themselves revolutionaries) that the task of overthrowing unjust repressive societies, and creating new ones to take their place, is the job of "professionals," itinerant insurrectionaries who go through life leaving a trail of revolutions behind them. Whatever the merits and shortcomings of such

---

1. Preceding the excerpts presented here, a chart by the Committee of Campesino Unity—the organization which played a major role in organizing the strike—was displayed in the original source detailing minimum daily food and clothing expenses for a family of five in the countryside. Their estimate, which did not include expenses such as shoes, farm tools, transportation, medicine, dishes, pots and pans, utensils, pencils and paper, etc., came to $3.95—EDS.

* Excerpted from "Organizacion Popular y lucha de classes en el Campo," *Cuadernos de Marcha* [Mexico City], Segunda epoca, año II, November/December, 1980, by permission, translated by Edmond F. Robinson, Jr. and Jonathan Fried.

a notion of revolution,[1] it is not the pattern that the rebels of Guatemala have chosen. As Guatemalan sociologist J. Antonio Bran shows, the guerrilla and revolutionary movements in his country spring from the community life of the people—their religious, economic, social, and even athletic organizations. The pattern Bran reveals is a complicated one in which the breakdown of traditional rural society by the impact of capitalism (roads and highways, hydroelectric projects, petroleum exploration, tourism, etc.) renders the campesinos vulnerable to exploitation. But the very organization of campesinos that defends against this vulnerability unleashes repression, which calls forth the new forms of organization that Bran describes.

The Barrier of Terror

THE MOST WELL-KNOWN class confrontations in rural Guatemala are those involving unions and employers' organizations. . . . Here we will highlight some "minor organizations" whose political history is not well known, but very important for the evaluation of the campesinos' capacity for initiative, creativity, and enterprise.

Repression tends to become necessary for the dominant class when their domination is fragile. The "preventive" character of bourgeois power in Guatemala is nothing more than a social weakness. As such, repression accomplishes a direct function by attacking organizations and persons committed to change, and an indirect function by acting as a warning to the members of the dominated sectors concerning their potential destiny, if they try to organize to promote change. The massacres, the carved-up bodies left on the highways, the missing people, and other such phenomena, are part of this logic of violence. The so-called "barrier of terror" is formed, its objective being fundamental for the dominant class inasmuch as the popular organization it inhibits represents a prolongation of their domination. Nevertheless, the phenomenon has its limits, produced by its own dynamics. It reaches a saturation point, beyond which it tends to have a reverse effect.

In Guatemala the barrier of terror has already been passed. One could say that the Panzós massacre in 1978 and the Spanish Embassy massacre in 1980 are the two events which propelled the Guatemalan popular sectors to organize and confront their assassins with greater force. In both cases the campesinos absorbed heavy blows.

New Forms of Organization

Repression has on other occasions turned against industrial and agricultural unions, local development committees, cooperatives, peasant leagues, and what-

1. The editors do not offer any full analysis of what has been called the "foco" theory of revolution, but we do assay a preliminary exploration in Part Four, Chapter II, Editors' Introduction.

ever other forms of social organization were perceived as undesirable by the enemy. One of the usual procedures to evade control and repression has been the careful and politicized use of institutions apparently outside the arena of class struggle; in general, local institutions with a regional impact which assume a qualitatively different behavior than that for which they were created, and as such, are able to blend in with their surroundings in the presence of the enemy.

This phenomenon of organizations taking on new functions occurs frequently and with considerable success. Among other examples, we can cite the case of a county in the central-west region in which the participation of local authorities in direct repression, as well as in the accusations that led to the repression, became evident.

Before the last elections, the leaders of a traditional religious organization [in this region], the *cofradía*, discussed and decided which of its members, chosen for their honesty and their position in relation to the repression, ought to be the mayoral candidates for each one of the political parties. It was a type of "playing the winner," even against the risk of fraud. Now, regardless of the political party that nominated them, the local authorities are an objective example of the power of a *cofradía* with a new function added; and there is a sort of "sociopolitical space" in the town which has not only allowed the town to avoid brutal assaults, but as will show, also has facilitated the progress of revolutionary organization with the strong support of the town's population.

A similar phenomenon occurred in a town in the eastern part of the country, where the campesino organization was brutally repressed and controlled. There it was not the *cofradía* that modified its role, but curiously enough, the local soccer team. Young revolutionaries on the team take advantage of the weekly matches, regional championships, exhibition games, etc., to communicate with other campesino athletes, exchange information and reading materials, ask for and give assistance, and in a variety of ways support the popular movement.

More examples: In Sololá, San Marcos, and Alta Verapaz, we see a renewal of the extended family, but this time it looks like an immense protective umbrella of campesinos, with clear revolutionary content. The "mimicry" is perfect. Unions and peasant leagues are carefully watched and controlled, and many of them are in the process of becoming clandestine. Thus, at parties, or any type of family get-together, such political tasks as how to give false leads to army patrols, how to isolate spies, etc. are deliberated.

In another town in central Guatemala, a Catholic religious brotherhood, *Hermandad del Señor Sepultado* (Brotherhood of the Entombed Lord) became the political organization of popular content. Its members teach other local campesinos how to evade the landowners spying and their apparatus of terror, they give talks to men, women, young people, and children on the local and national social reality, etc. And in this case, as in other ones cited, we are speaking of organizations which have fulfilled their new functions for several years and whose political success has been shared and transmitted to other local campesino nuclei, even to the point of organizing small but effective regional networks of a popular and revolutionary nature.

One of the most effective channels of penetration that the Guatemalan bourgeoisie can count on to spread alien and conservative ideologies among the people is the radio: falsified news reports, concealment of information, soap operas, official radio stations, ideological messages, propaganda, etc.

The founding and administration of popular broadcasting stations, generally connected to parishes and with great ideological autonomy with respect to the bourgeoisie and the state, has meant a big step in raising the consciousness of the people. It has already, to some measure, broken the power of official ideology. Moreover, in western and northern Guatemala, these stations braodcast in Indian languages, thus contributing to a reevaluation of ethnicity. But this ideological counteroffensive is often obvious to the enemy. Thus, when the Guatemalan army laid siege to and occupied the town of Santiago Atitlán, one of the first things it did was to destroy the local broadcasting station and kidnap its director.

Other forms of the popular ideological counteroffensive tend to make the people conscious of their own role in the epic of resistance. For example, the march of the miners of Ixtahuacán . . . is part of the history of the popular struggles in Guatemala which, in addition, was captured in a beautiful song ("The Song of Ixtahuacán") by some anonymous composer. And today it is sung from town to town, from fair to fair.

The massacre committed on January 31, 1980 by the Lucas government in the Spanish Embassy, and which was covered worldwide by the press, also is recorded in a popular song which encourages people to get organized and fight against the dictatorship. And the song, like many others, is being recognized as their own by the campesinos. It is being sung and it is being understood.

Another example can be drawn from the experience of a village . . . in the eastern region which had a theater group presenting such religious dramas as the life of the town's patron saint, the Passion of Christ, etc. For complicated reasons, this theater group became increasingly conscious of the local and national social dynamics, and since then, they use drama, now truly popular drama, to present a great number of collective problems in a critical way, and propose some solutions. In their village of origin and in neighboring villages, the group speaks with elders and others knowledgeable of local history and by means of these interviews they uncover important events of that history (what happened during the agrarian reform of Arbenz, the fight in the village against a landowner over use of a source of water, etc.). The event is dramatized, and they tour the neighboring villages presenting it and *discussing* it. They are recovering their history and discovering common problems.

Similarly, popular theater groups, puppets, revolutionary song, poetry, etc., are also "arms" of the people. They are basic elements which, if lacking, would slow down the process of people's growing self-awareness. Abelino Chuj—campesino, poet, revolutionary—affirmed at a popular education meeting a short time ago, that "if we do not know how to sing, we will not be able to fight."

The above-cited cases are not the only ones. When the history of the Guatemalan revolution can be written, the great initiative and inventiveness of our people will be known; the way they recovered and put previous revolutionary experiences to use, and the contributions they make to other revolutions. Nevertheless, we should mention that if the *cofradía* mentioned above was not the only one who has joined the great revolutionary task, neither have all the *cofradías* taken that attitude. Many are openly reactionary and others have been broken as a local power by other organizations. The same observation can be made for our other examples: they are not the only ones of their kind, but neither have all acted with the same sociopolitical perspective.

[For reasons of space limitations we omit Bran's discussion of the Committee of Campesino Unity (CUC), a group characterized by one of its leaders as an "organization . . . of the masses not little groups. . . . We don't put faith in what the courts or tribunals tell us for the solution of our problems. . . . We have already seen that what we don't need to solve our problems is to ask for permission from the rich and the authorities. . . ." Bran concludes that CUC "has operated with courage, intelligence and fidelity. And it has demonstrated (in case it was still necessary) that the road to liberty passes through organization." Bran continues, discussing the relationship between the guerrilla movement and popular organizations, particularly the Democratic Front Against Repression (FDCR), which he calls "the *defensive* form of confronting the dictatorship, while the *offensive* form is the military front."—EDS.]

What relationships have been established between the mass front and the military front? Or more to the point of this work, what is the relationship between the organized campesinos and the left in arms? Here we have to begin by indicating that while the FDCR was originally an attempt at organized resistance to the dictatorship within the framework of the present society, and the unity of the armed left has a project for a society opposed to the present one,[2] both the FDCR as a whole and the majority of its component organizations have seen all possibilities of coexistence within the framework of a so-called "bourgeois democracy," with its mass murders, rapidly disappearing. In this light, the appearance of projects for a new society from within the FDCR should not be surprising. Such projects are the logical result of the growing awareness of its members, individually and collectively, regarding the possibilities of the immediate future.[3]

---

2. For the united political statement of the guerrilla groups, see Reading 49.—EDS.

3. In January 1981, after this essay was written, a new mass front, besides the FDCR, emerged. The January 31st Popular Front (FP-31) is made up of CUC and five other rural and urban organizations, and defines itself as a front of "revolutionary mass organizations," shedding all pretexts of working above-ground and within the system, and openly throwing its support behind the guerrilla movement.—EDS.

"We must begin to create the revolutionary, popular and democratic government," a campesino periodical editorialized about half a year ago. Similarly, it pressed for the unity of "all the forces in Guatemala that fight for justice and liberty." It also proposed a series of questions to be discussed and answered on the village, neighborhood, plantation, county, etc., level so as to have elements for the program of the new government coming from the rank-and-file. Some of the questions posed are as follows:

—What land needs do we have for farming and living?

—What crops should we cultivate and at what prices should we sell them?

—What wages should we, the workers on the farms, earn? How many hours should there be in a day's work?

—In what form should justice be done for massacres, murders and acts of repression?

—How should the defense of our communities be organized?

—What laws should there be and who should make them?

—How will we be able to see to it that Indians and ladinos have the same rights?

—What protection should the elderly and children receive?

These and other questions were posed, and the campesino readers were urged to pass them on to all the workers of the countryside. As can be seen, there is a close relationship between the questions asked by the workers of the countryside about the desired form of social organization and the proposals of the armed left. The possibility of a harmonic and even organic convergence depends upon the depth and objectivity of the answers found. The development of political consciousness is a slow, uneven process which has reached a truly high level in the popular sectors. The answer to the old question is simple and at the same time difficult to reach. But the people in Guatemala have already done it: the revolution has only one path, the armed path; but the forms are multiple and they are proposed and developed or withdrawn according to the circumstances. And in such a process the rural masses still have much to say.

[For reasons of space, most of the footnote references in the original version of this article have been eliminated. Bran's sources included *Voz* (newsletter of the Committee of Campesino Unity [CUC], Guatemala City); *De Sol a Sol* (Guatemala City); *Noticias de Guatemala* (San José, Costa Rica); *Política y Sociedad* (School of Political Science, University of San Carlos, Guatemala City); as well as personal interviews conducted by the author.—EDS.]

A church in Chajul where parishioners have dressed a statue in combat uniform, 1982. *Photo credit: Alain Keeler/ SYGMA*

Chapter III:

The Church Engaged

Editors' Introduction

THE changes that have taken place during the past several years within the Roman Catholic Church, and to a lesser extent within the Protestant churches of Latin America constitute a new and weighty variable in the volatile political equation of these profoundly Christian societies. The identification of large sectors of Catholic and Protestant clergy and religious workers with the poor and oppressed, and increasingly, with their liberation struggles, has strained the traditional alliance between the churches and the ruling elites that for centuries has been a pillar of the inequitable social order. Moreover, the involvement of Christians inspired by the Gospel in the popular movements of some Latin American countries—particularly in Nicaragua, El Salvador and Guatemala—has played an important role in these mass movements, and has contributed to their ideological plurality.

The metamorphosis of Latin America's churches cannot be divorced from the context of the unfolding social crises and struggles on the continent. The "Theology of Liberation," which provided the theoretical basis for the religious workers' and clergy's "preferential option for the poor," in fact emerged from the experiences of the churches during the 1960s and 1970s, a period of increasing social polarization.[1] These experiences were reflected in the statements of the Latin

---

1. Chilean lay theologian Pablo Richard gives an excellent analysis of the historical and social context of the development of liberation theology and the "popular church" in Latin America in "The Latin American Church: 1959-1978," *Cross Currents* [West Nyack, N.Y.], XXVIII, no. 1 (Spring 1978). Also see Penny Lernoux, *Cry of the People* (Garden City: Doubleday & Company, Inc., 1980), esp. pp. 19-31; and Gustavo Gutiérrez, *A Theology of Liberation* (New York: Orbis Books, 1977).

American Catholic bishops at Medellín (1968) and Puebla (1979), which recognized the legitimacy of the Church's newfound loyalties and many of its new activities, and reinforced them.[2]

In Guatemala, as in other Latin American countries, the social concerns of the Catholic Church during the 1960s grew, at least in part, in response to the 1959 Cuban revolution and the subsequent emergence of guerrilla struggle. Following the premise, popularized by the Alliance for Progress, that at least some minimal improvement in the political, economic, and cultural standing of Latin America's poor urban and rural masses was needed to combat communism on the continent[3]—or simply following their own conscience—many churchpeople became deeply involved in local development and educational projects, through such vehicles as the Catholic Action movement.[4] Guatemala's fledgling Christian Democratic Party and Christian Democratic-related institutions, which championed a "third way" between capitalism and communism and enjoyed close relations with the conservative Catholic hierarchy, also became involved in organizing unions, peasant leagues, and cooperatives. The party built for itself a considerable base among the rural population. The Church and the Christian Democrats also provided the institutional protection for community organization that, given the prevailing repression, would not have otherwise been possible.

Nevertheless, the extreme rigidity of the post-1954 governments toward any type of popular mobilization soon brought the work of the Church under question, and often in open conflict with the government. The intensified polarization of Guatemalan society in the 1970s—marked by the rise of the military as the country's dominant force, the independent growth of the popular movement and its repression by the government—eliminated the middle ground, and increasingly forced churchpeople to take sides. Lay leaders, and later Catholic and Protestant clergy, religious workers and Christian Democratic politicians, began to be killed. As in other Latin American countries, Guatemala's churches are today divided and reflect a wide diversity of positions. Some church pastors, missionaries, and

---

2. For the final documents of the Second General Conference of Latin American [Catholic] Bishops at Medellín, see *The Church in the Present-Day Transformation of Latin America in the Light of the Council* (Washington: U.S. Catholic Conference, Division for Latin America, 1973), v.2. The final document of the third conference of Latin American Catholic bishops at Puebla, as well as a variety of background and analysis, can be found in John Eagleson and Philip Scharper, eds., *Puebla and Beyond* (Maryknoll, N.Y.: Orbis Books, 1979). For more on the significance and background of Medellín and Puebla, see Lernoux, *Cry of the People*, pp. 37-47, and pp. 409-448; Gary MacEoin and Nivita Riley, *Puebla: A Church Being Born* (New York: Paulist Press, 1980); and *Cross Currents* [West Nyack, N.Y.], XXVIII, no. 1 (Spring 1978).

3. For a brief discussion of the Alliance for Progress see Part Two, Editors' Introduction, and Reading 14.

4. Catholic Action is a nontraditionalist Catholic movement that played an important role in local organizing throughout Latin America. First introduced into Guatemala in the 1930s, Catholic Action grew rapidly in the 1960s and 1970s. For a history of the Catholic Action movement in one rural Indian town in Guatemala (San Antonio Ilotenango, Quiché), see Ricardo Falla, *Quiché Rebelde* (Guatemala City: Editorial Universitaria, 1980).

officials continue to use religion as a means of legitimizing state authority and dampening class conflict (see Reading 36). Indeed, fundamentalist religion seems to be the main ideological trapping of General Efraín Ríos Montt, Guatemala's born-again Christian president, brought to power in Spring 1982 (see Reading 21). On the other end of the spectrum are those churchpeople who have found an increasing convergence of goals and ideals with guerrilla insurgents and identify with the emerging project of the workers and campesinos to build a new society (see Readings 37 and 38). Radicalized Christian leaders formed the Justice and Peace Committee in 1977. It grew to play an important role in the opposition movement through its denunciations, nationally and internationally, of government violations of human rights and its educational activities and organizing within the Church.

Catholic churchpeople may have in some instances served as a link between the campesinos and the popular and guerrilla organizations, and at least one priest is known to have joined Guatemala's guerrillas. But the transformation of the churches in Guatemala cannot be reduced to the radicalization of elements of the clergy and hierarchy, to the teaching of new theological doctrine, or to the pastors leading their sheep astray. Christian campesinos and workers were the first, and in most cases, those most directly affected by government intransigence and repression. Consciousness-raising within the Christian communities has been a two-way process, in which the parishioners are often responsible for the "conversion" of their pastors;[5] a conversion encompassing a renewal of Christian faith and a political commitment to the struggles of campesinos and workers, grounded in Christian beliefs.

Drawing both on Indian communal traditions and a reinterpretation of the Gospel in light of people's experiences and sufferings, a qualitatively new "popular church" has emerged. It has taken on a dynamic of its own, operating with a great degree of autonomy from official church structures and cutting across denominational lines. Particularly since religious personnel have been forced to leave some regions of the country, the "catechists" and "Delegates of the Word," female and male lay leaders who emerged from local church organizing activities, have become the communities' principal religious and political leaders. The base communities of this popular church played an important role in the formation of the Committee of Campesino Unity, and later became the foundations of support and sources of new combatants for the guerrilla movement. Of course, like so many aspects of the Guatemalan revolution, born and bred in partial or total secrecy, the full story of the popular church will not be known until conditions permit its telling.

---

5. Thomas and Marjorie Melville's *Whose Heaven, Whose Earth?* (New York: Alfred A. Knopf, 1971) is a personal account of a Roman Catholic priest and nun whose experiences in Guatemala eventually led them from an anticommunist point of view to active commitment to a revolutionary movement for change.

36. *Blessing The Powerful: An Interview with Archbishop Casariego* *

IN contrast to such outspoken Latin American church leaders as the late Archbishop Oscar Romero of El Salvador,[1] *Mario Cardinal Casariego, Archbishop of Guatemala, fits the traditional mold of the church hierarchy: close ally of the military and defender of the established order. These are excerpts from a May 1982 interview.*

Q. YOUR EMINENCE, what should the work of the Church in Guatemala be?

Cardinal Casariego: The work of the Church should follow the norms given by the Holy Church, which are the most proper ones; and in the social question, follow the same norms given by the Holy See.

Q. Could you be a bit more specific?

A. Well, for example, to work for the people, but prepare them beforehand so they understand what the social question is; and to teach them how they should live: in a Christian manner. And if they are poor, the Church should also help them put their life in order, get them a house. Pope Paul VI gave me, the Archbishop's See, the Cardinal you are speaking to, a gift to build some houses and give them to ten, fifteen, twenty families. But I thought it would be better to build a colony dedicated to the Pope who gave me this money when he appointed me Cardinal. So, the Paul VI Colony was built. And for the Indians above Antigua, in Santa María de Jesús, San Juan del Obispo, another five hundred were built in each town. And we retained a group of Colombian nuns . . . to teach our indigenous how to keep a house, how to wash their children, how to take a bath without going to the river, as is their custom.

But the work of the Church must be silent, and not something like politics, because the Church's politics are to do good, according to the Gospel, and what the right hand does, the left does not know. Now then, the Church has never done anything for propaganda's sake, nor will it, because that's not its mission.

Q. Many people are talking about the Theology of Liberation. What do you think about it?

A. I am of the same opinion as the Church. His Holiness Paul VI said that we have to liberate ourselves first, from our sins . . . our egotism, from the idea that if I have something, I don't share it with the poor. I must change. It is a change. Liberation from the devil of the world and of the flesh.

---

* From an anonymous Roman Catholic source. Translated by Jonathan Fried.

1. See Plácido Erdozain, *Archbishop Romero: Martyr of El Salvador* (New York: Orbis Books, 1981).

Now then, liberation also [means] being able to help the poor. . . . And to get governments to help the have-nots socially and to make the rich, who are more or less the same everywhere, understand that if God gave them more than others, they should share with those humans who have nothing. With love, not as charity, because if you give bread to a poor person, you don't throw it at him, you give it to him with love. And giving alms to the poor is also an obligation. But the social aspect as well is an obligation; so says the Church.

Q. There are many who have given this Theology of Liberation more of a political meaning. What do you think about this?

A. I don't accept it, and neither does the Church, because once we are dealing with politics, the Church should remove itself.

Q. What is the relationship between the Church and the State?

A. Very good [relations], as long as the Church is independent from the government. The Church respects the government. The Gospel says so: that even if the authority were bad, it must be respected. Thank God in Guatemala, despite the problems in some dioceses, in the Archdiocese we have had no problems of importance with any government. Because my goal and my idea is to follow the Pope. The Pope, the Holy See, maintains relations with everyone, with the good and the bad. And we have to get along with everyone, as long as we preserve the roles of the Church and the State.

Q. Then what is the relationship between the Church and the army here, considering the important role of the army in the government?

A. I will tell you. For over twenty-five years the army has had a chaplain in every military post, especially in the Archdiocese. And I know that other dioceses have followed the example I set since 1964. . . .

The previous governments did not allow the military school to have a chaplain, since it was a Liberal school,[2] a school that did not want relations with the Church. But thank God, in 1959, these relations were initiated. First, when I was the auxiliary bishop, I began as a professor of ethics in the school. And two months from then, I was named chaplain of the Polytechnic [military] school by the very Defense Ministry. . . .

Q. Recently you said that if you had not been a priest, you would have been a military man.

A. . . . I love military life. And I love it when it is based upon discipline, such as I believe is the case in our army, the American army, the Italian. For example, when I go to Rome, I visit the military districts, because the chaplain of the Italian military schools takes me there. . . . Here is the largest military training school, where armies from almost the whole world are trained, like you, who give scholarships to the Central American army.

---

2. Here he is referring to the anticlerical tradition dating from the 1870s, when Liberal governments expropriated Church lands to make way for the expansion of coffee plantations.—EDS.

So when the [Roman Catholic] Bishops' Conference was coming out of a meeting with the junta—we had to meet with them about the liberty of the Church, to see if it would still be respected . . . when we were leaving the office of the president, my gentlemen reporters—by "my" I mean they are Guatemalans—asked me, "What have you come for, Cardinal?" Well, we have come to speak with the junta and greet them. Nothing more. Well you know because I have said it many times: if I had not been a priest, I would have been a military man, because I like a disciplined life. The army, perhaps, is very openly disciplined. We are trained in religious houses, in seminaries, and we have a developed, conscious discipline; thus, my sympathies for the army, just as long as it carries out its duty. Up until this day, I have seen that they have done what they can for the fatherland.

Q. How is your relationship with the new government?

A. I lived thirty-eight, or thirty-six years in El Salvador as a priest, and I've never had any problems with any government. And since the Pope named me First Auxiliary Bishop, then Archbishop, many governments have come and gone, and I have gotten along with all of them. Each one in his place. I don't ask more than I should. . . .

Q. According to reports, large parts of Guatemala, like Huehuetenango and Quiché, presently have no Catholic priests or nuns. Why is this so?

A. Well, I'll tell you. Each diocese has its bishop. So the Archdiocese gives orders, the Archbishop rules in the name of the Pope. But I cannot give orders in another diocese. Therefore, I am not able to speak with clarity because I know little. . . . The bishop from there [Quiché], I don't know his motive for leaving or why he said it was better to avoid the possibility of more priests being killed.[3] If this was judicious, or less judicious, only his conscience and his superiors [can judge]. I am not his superior, I am his brother. And therefore, the great need that our army—thank God the young officers who graduated from the school since 1958 are now more religious. And they have more contact with the Church. I have no great problems in the Archdiocese because I knew them when they were cadets. Now they are government ministers. One of them, the chief of the current junta, was captain of the company of cadets way back in 1958. And today he is chief of state.[4]

Q. But doesn't it worry you that there are few nuns and priests in some areas?

---

3. The Quiché diocese was abandoned by clergy and religious personnel in July 1980 due to the repression (see Reading 37). Soon afterward, Bishop of Quiché Juan Gerardí, a Guatemalan national, visited the Pope to speak of the situation in his diocese. Upon return to Guatemala, he was refused entry into the country, thus being forced into exile—EDS.

4. Here he is referring to General Efraín Ríos Montt. Although a member of the fundamentalist Christian Church of the Word (see Reading 25), General Ríos Montt claims to have never dropped his Roman Catholic affiliation. His brother is the Roman Catholic bishop of the Diocese of Escuintla.—EDS.

A. Yes. In some dioceses, in the ones you have mentioned, there is certainly a lack of priests. In the Archdiocese I don't have a single vacant parish. Two or three priests have left me, gone to Mexico, and I don't know what contacts they have with the guerrillas. Nor have I asked them. But they haven't arrived at their destination.

In the other dioceses many have gone out of fear. But I don't believe there has been a real persecution in Guatemala. Maybe they have been very vehement in explaining the social question. And so, naturally, some have understood one thing, others have understood another. . . .

Q. Why have so many priests been killed in Guatemala?

A. What do you want me to explain to you? What I don't know I can't say. Neither can I say what I don't see nor hear with my eyes.

Q. The government told us that many priests and nuns have been involved with the subversives in rural areas. Is this true?

A. Well listen, I believe that some of what they have told you is true, because whoever doesn't get involved in anything, they leave alone. Now it could be that the subversives have catechized as well. And the priests they have indoctrinated have been caught. . . .

Q. If it is true that some of them are involved in subversive activities, what can you do to purify the ranks of the Church?

A. Well, I believe that each bishop knows his priests. So it is very easy. . . . When one asks for priests [one should] see where they come from, what ideas they bring, because, you understand that good and bad ideologies exist all over the world. We cannot say that the United States is free either. Thank God, the guerrillas haven't made their appearance [there yet], but that there are people [there] who are a little left-wing, hah, you'll see! They're probably hiding, or whatever. Let's hope that President Reagan, who is very capable, knows, et cetera, et cetera, et cetera. . . .

37. A *Priest among the People:* An *Interview with Father Celso* *

FATHER Bill Woods, a Maryknoll missioner from Texas, was the first priest to die in Guatemala in recent times under mysterious circumstances. An active priest who helped found agricultural cooperatives in the dense jungle region of Ixcán in northern Quiché, his Cessna airplane crashed into the mountains

* From an independent Roman Catholic source.

one cloudless November morning in 1976, killing him and his four passengers instantly. Many friends and observers believe his plane was sabotaged by government elements who didn't look kindly on his work with Indian campesinos.[1] *However, it wasn't until 1980, well after local lay leaders began to be hunted down and killed by the dozens, that the wrath of the Guatemalan government fell with full force on the clergy and religious personnel of the Roman Catholic and some of the Protestant churches. During 1980 and 1981, twenty Catholic priests and nuns were killed or kidnapped, including Father Stanley Rother, a U.S. priest shot to death on July 28, 1981.*[2] *Five Protestant ministers were also killed. As of September 1981, ninety-one priests and seventy-eight nuns had been forced to leave the country due to threats on their lives. Religious training centers, schools, and Church-sponsored radio stations have been closed or threatened, and parish houses and convents sprayed with machine-gun fire or destroyed. Seventy Catholic parishes no longer have priests.*

The Catholic Church has come under particularly heavy attack in the Quiché province. In July 1980, after two Catholic priests were killed and two attempts on the bishop of Quiché's life, the clergy decided to abandon the diocese. Some of the priests from the Quiché diocese left the country and founded the Guatemalan Church in Exile (IGE). In this February 1982 interview with Father Celso, a member of the IGE, he talks about his work in Quiché and the circumstances that led him and other churchpeople to take sides with their parishioners against the government.

Q. LET US BEGIN by asking you to briefly say something about yourself, your name, your history.

Father Celso: My name is Celso. I can't say more because of the situation of repression which forced me to leave Guatemala. Now I am part of the Guatemalan Church in Exile, and our work is to denounce the repression in Guatemala and to help the people in their struggle, a struggle for liberation which is taking shape.

I was born in Spain and I was trained as a missionary. When the situation changed in Guatemala in 1955, [Castillo] Armas opened the doors of Guatemala to missionaries. During this time, a large number of missionaries, especially from Europe, came. I was in a group of missionaries which arrived to work in Guatemala. All of my priestly life has been in Guatemala. I came to Guatemala with the difficult task of integrating myself into the life of the Guatemalan people and to develop a mission with them. It was difficult, but I had to do it, right? I

---

1. See Ron Chernow, "The Strange Death of Bill Woods," *Mother Jones* (May 1979).

2. See Daniel Southerland, "Does U.S. Cleric's Death Cast Doubt on Aid to Guatemala?," *Christian Science Monitor* [Boston] June 30, 1981; Patty Edmonds, "Oklahoma Priest Murdered in Guatemala," *National Catholic Reporter* [Kansas City] August 14, 1981; and "Cry from Guatemala," *New York Times* August 15, 1981, excerpts from a letter written by Rother in January 1981.

realized it would always be a temptation to want to be with these people and then to leave them. I came to understand that if one wants to identify with a people, then one has to always live with these people. For this reason, in the beginning of my work here, I decided to become a Guatemalan citizen.

Q. What work were you involved in, and in what areas did you work as a missionary?

A. From the beginning my work has been in the countryside. And it is important to understand that the majority of the campesinos are Indians, Native Americans. Hence, my life has been primarily with the indigenous people, although there were always groups of ladinos, not in towns, but in the countryside. These ladinos have a standard of living very similar to the poverty and the exploitation of the indigenous. Hence, I know these two areas very well—Indians and ladinos. . . .

For example, in 1956 my work was in the northern zone with the Kekchís, Quichés, and Ixils. I can tell you that we were some of the first persons to work in this heavily forested area when, in 1960, we began to see the possibilities of this zone as part of a solution for the poverty of our people, people who didn't have land, who didn't have homes. So we worked there primarily to help these people to organize themselves. We organized cooperatives, neighborhood committees which would help advance local agricultural projects. . . . As a missionary, I went to these areas to say mass, to offer classes in religious instruction, to offer classes designed to raise the consciousness of the people. . . . The thing that was most important about this work was the training of people through courses, through intensive workshops and classes at the neighborhood or community level.

Q. Why has the government or the army targeted so many priests, nuns, missionaries, catechists for such repression?

A. Listen, I'm going to tell you a fact. For example, one of the most difficult jobs we had was the construction of schools. I suppose I helped build hundreds of schools in this zone. . . . We would then use the schools as a means for training people, to teach them how to read, how to speak, how to defend themselves. And we gave religious instruction, there were literacy campaigns, etc. . . .

Each school was built by the Indians or the ladinos, by the poor people of a given area themselves. But the government looked at this with its feathers ruffled. Our interest was to build schools. For us, it was not important that they be constructed with the same glory and inaugural ceremonies as other schools. When our schools were opened, the people themselves had been prepared to speak, to give the opening addresses. These poor persons themselves would speak in front of the authorities. This represented a tremendous advancement. People were beginning to express themselves and were beginning to define their problems.

One day the Minister of Education arrived with the local governor to the opening ceremony of one of our new schools. We had opened eight schools in this zone in one year and in each opening ceremony the Indian leaders would speak. And the governor asked his people, "Who taught these wretches how to speak?

What can these shriveled up oranges possibly think?" That is to say, that for the governor and his people, the Indians are wretches. They are perceived as nothing more than subjects to be manipulated and suppressed. They are to be used for elections, they are to be quaint objects of interest for the tourists as though they were part of a museum. But when they saw this change among the Indians who were now beginning to speak of some of their needs, the officials were taken aback. The people began to call on others to keep struggling, struggling for running water, struggling for better roads, struggling for an improved school. . . . This is the anger they have against the Church. . . .

We wanted the day to come when the Indians would have a dignified life. That was the mission we had, to teach people how to live as persons. They told us many times, "Father, you are teaching us how to be human." And the expression "to be human" means moving from being seen as animals, as beasts of burden, to being seen as human beings. It was precisely here that our problems as missionaries began. We were committed to teaching, baptizing, offering the sacraments, and calling people to conversion. We began to speak of a liberating Gospel, of a Jesus who came to be with the poor, of a Jesus who said in his Gospel "Blessed are the poor, blessed are those who suffer." How am I going to convince them that Jesus, the Jesus we were called to proclaim, is the Good News when these people start to express to me their sufferings? They explained the weight of the oligarchy, of the rich. They talked of their oppression by those in power, even by the Church itself.

Let me be more concrete. I remember an Indian who was kidnapped, the first one I know. It took us four days to get his release. A man of a higher class, according to what he told me, had taken him. When he was in the hospital, he told me how [in earlier times] he had to carry people. Because when we first arrived in Guatemala there weren't many roads, the Pan American highway didn't exist. There were only paths for walking. For example, even the mail arrived this way. This Indian told me that he had to carry people to the capital. He was forced to carry the wife of the governor, the wife of the mayor, or his children. He was ashamed to tell me that he even carried people from the Church.

Yes, even the Church was identified with those in power during this time. It was a church of social power, of economic power. It had its social position. And then came this terrible slap in the face: a liberating Gospel. And in the light of this liberating Gospel, the people began to interpret their reality. And here our trauma began. What happened? What is reality? We began to think from this perspective, to study and to see how we could identify with these suffering people.

I have the advantage that I was born a peasant; and then soon I had the good fortune of beginning to understand the language of these people, their silences, their looks, their expressions, which were the dialogues of these people. And these dialogues revealed much about their situation. I worked alongside them as a peasant, as a worker. I have plowed the soil using oxen. I have used the machete.

From experience, I have learned all about the suffering of the campesinos. . . . From this perspective of knowing and understanding their life, our uneasiness began to increase as we searched for a road to change the situation.

Now they accuse us of being communists. Since I was born into a profoundly anticommunist family, a family which fought in the Spanish Civil War against the communists, there is no truth to the accusation that we are communists. The only thing we are guilty of is . . . having incarnated ourselves with these people. We accept this reality and we live with the people and we suffer with them. What is our sin? Why are they persecuting the Church? Because it has helped these people, it has raised their consciousness and has promoted their interests. We have moved them to think, to analyze, to become aware and to organize themselves. We have encouraged them to look for a road for change, a peaceful road. For years and years we have looked for a peaceful road—peasant leagues, cooperatives, agricultural committees, production committees, committees to study fertilizers, schools, training programs, human promotion projects. All of these efforts, always with the same results: a thick wall. We always came to the same end, an end which would enable us to go no farther. . . . After twenty-five years of work, we began to come to the conclusion that the misery of our people was not diminishing, in spite of our efforts. The misery of our people was actually increasing, because their exploitation was increasing. . . . And this led us to take another step and to be present with these people in their own dynamic and their struggle.

Q. How did the repression against the Church in Guatemala manifest itself?

A. The repression against the Church began with the repression of the leaders, not clergy or nuns, but lay leaders from the countryside, catechists, etc. Those who were first repressed were the leaders of the cooperatives, the leaders of the committees, the leaders of whatever program had been initiated. . . .

The catechists were the most motivated . . . and had the most skills in directing work at the community level. One of the governors of Quiché said of these "bastards" that it was necessary to beat their heads in, in order to stop them. The first four catechists were kidnapped back in 1964. Here is where the repression began. We can't distinguish here between repression of those in the Church and those out of it, because the religious leaders were leaders of the people. Those who had been trained in the Church were the best prepared. They had learned how to write, for example. I saw many catechists who learned how to read and write through Bible study, through study of the Catechism. . . .

But these leaders became the leaders of the community, because it is necessary to remember that when we are speaking about catechists, we are not talking about the Western style of religious leaders. We have present here many influences from the Mayan culture, which had its own religious values. This is a fundamental point. We are speaking of a people who are fundamentally religious. There are no divisions between politics, society, economy, and religion. Rather, for example, they believe that religious ideas are those which have respect for the land, for the family, respect for creation, respect for children, respect for that which has been made. We are a part of this creation, according to their religious beliefs. It is here in this creation where politics and society mix within the community. . . . Hence a catechist is not only a preacher or a teacher of a catechism. He is a person who by definition is involved in the problems of a given community. . . .

Already in 1976 rumors began to spread that all catechists' names were on [death] lists because they were suspected as potential community leaders. We didn't believe it. But in 1977 we began to see some of the fruits of this reality. Some began to disappear. Others were tortured. There were massacres and still others were killed outright. Some were taken in the middle of the night and never seen again. During this year we might say there was a selective repression against those clearly identifiable as leaders, as catechists. But beginning in 1978, this situation began to change as it became clear that the people could no longer be so easily dominated. The people were rising up. This marked the beginning of indiscriminate massacres against small villages, against rural communities. I remember that already in 1977 villages were bombed, whole zones destroyed, crops and seeds destroyed. And they began to massacre the campesinos in all areas.

We were aware that it would be difficult for them to attack the Church directly, the priests, pastoral work, etc. But the moment arrived in 1980 when we realized that this equilibrium was also breaking down. They began to attack the Church, priests and nuns. And this began because they realized that as they killed off more and more catechists, they had accomplished nothing. They realized that with the repression of the small communities, they had accomplished nothing. Then they began to think that those really responsible or guilty were the priests. But imagine—and I knew them personally, William Woods, Jose María Gran, Juan Alonso, Hermógenes López, Conrado de la Cruz—the first ones that they killed were involved in absolutely nothing. I know this because where they worked there were no organizations yet at the time they were killed, organizations such as the CUC or the FP-31 [January 31st Popular Front], these organizations that we now say are necessary for the people to have in order to defend themselves against repression. The only thing these priests did was to promote the improvement of the communities in which they worked.

And they began to attack the Church indiscriminately. They didn't just kill Guatemalans; but churchpeople from the Philippines, Spain, Belgium, Canada, the United States, as well as from Guatemala, were killed. Whoever was in this area working with the people, sharing their suffering and animating people to work, was considered dangerous. . . .

38. *Religion and Revolution: A Protestant Voice* *

ALTHOUGH they have different ideological beliefs, Christians and Marxists in Latin America have, in recent years, found common interests and goals. While to a large degree a consequence of the radicalization of Christian clergy and laymen, this process of convergence could not have occurred without accommodation on the part of those who approach society's problems from a Marxist point of view. "As far as we are concerned, we haven't tried to convert Christians," said one top Guatemalan guerrilla leader, Rolando Morán of the Guerrilla Army of the Poor (EGP), "that is, encourage them to stop being Christians in order to become ideological militants of the EGP. Rather, we have tried to create the conditions so that they, as Christians, also find their function and their role within this revolutionary groundswell that has been created in Guatemala, involving all sectors, all classes, all religions and conceptions." [1]

Most Christians who have joined the revolutionary movement in Guatemala are Catholics. The Protestant churches in Guatemala are mainly of the fundamentalist evangelical type. Having the allegiance of ten to fifteen percent of the population by the end of the 1970s, the fundamentalists, in the words of one knowledgeable observer, "tend to an 'other worldly' theology that leads members to see 'salvation' as the only important goal." [2] *Since Ríos Montt came to power some of the evangelical sects—including the general's own California-based Christian Church of the Word—have been actively involved in the political and ideological aspects of the government's counterinsurgency campaigns. In conjunction with the government they preach obedience to authorities, distribute food, and build "model villages" in war-torn areas. In some areas, Catholics are indiscriminately persecuted, motivating many Indians, according to one priest, to join fundamentalist churches in order to save their lives.*[3]

Evangelical Protestant churches in Guatemala play an increasingly active role in national politics, as journalist Marlise Simons reports: "In contrast to reform-minded, mainline Protestants working in Latin America, and activist Catholic

---

* From *Cuaderno: Guatemala* (Mexico City: Christus, 1982). Testimony compiled by Margarita García and translated by Jonathan Fried.

1. Mario Menéndez Rodríguez, "Guerra Popular Revolucionaria," *Por Esto!* (Mexico City), no. 10, Sept. 3, 1981, p. 57.

2. Philip Berryman, unpublished text, provided courtesy of the author.

3. John Dinges, "The Role of Religion in Guatemala's Fighting," *The Sun* [Baltimore], Aug. 8, 1982.

priests who are challenging the continent's authoritarian regimes, the fundamentalists claim to be apolitical—yet they tell parishioners to pray for the authorities while they themselves staunchly defend Washington's policies. Already, many signs point to a Protestant revolution that may have far-reaching consequences for the United States, the Roman Catholic Church and Protestantism itself." [4]

However, not all Protestants and fundamentalists have joined forces with the government. This reading gives the perspective of a Protestant minister who has drawn closer to the popular movement and Catholics who currently form a part of that movement at a time when social conflict has increasingly taken on the proportions of a full-blown war.

THE EXPERIENCE OF what is happening in the Guatemalan countryside and of how the Holy Spirit is moving his people down unforeseen but certain paths constitutes not only personal experiences, but what we as servants of God called upon to exercise an Evangelist Christian ministry are observing.

What God is doing amidst his people really escapes our theological comprehension, including our Christian framework; especially among the base of the Christian community, where conditioning and other types of prejudice are not an obstacle.

I would like to begin by saying that this eagerness for liberty, this enthusiasm for building a new society, this revolution, is evangelizing the Church. This may seem like heresy, but today it is the truth: never before have we seen how Evangelical Christians and Catholics can meet together in a village of the highlands to celebrate their faith, because there are no longer ministers nor priests in this zone.

This struggle has knocked down the barriers that for many years had been raised. As a Protestant minister I can testify that for years we were sectarian, jealous of having the truth; but our particular truths have crumbled [not only] with the people's suffering, but also with the people's hope.

We have had the experience of entire churches participating in the struggle, sad experiences of ministers who have been kidnapped, another assassinated with his wife and child for working for justice.

In view of these acts of blood, the enlivening of the Spirit has become palpable among the most humble; the majority of the middle classes, it must be noted, remain indifferent.

What has provoked this self-evangelizing of the church, this return to its sources?

The first thing is the tangible suffering. No member of the church in the highlands can close his eyes to what he is seeing: the kidnappings, the tortures, the bombings, the constant massacres of campesinos to wipe out the guerrillas. All

---

4. Marlise Simons, "Latin America's New Gospel," *The New York Times Magazine*, November 7, 1982, p. 47.

these sufferings cannot pass unnoticed by those who have the light of the Gospel. All these experiences form part of the daily life of the people in our country in these days.

But the church is not being evangelized only from the perspective of the pain of our brothers, but also by hope. For us it is surprising to see how the indigenous people have risen up, and not as individuals, but in large numbers which even exceed the limits and technical and educational capacities of the groups which are struggling.

There is a hope so great that for the first time we can feel it profoundly. This people which we Guatemalans had seen silent and bent over—stoic, we said—has overcome this situation to rise up proudly amidst the pain, with hope.

And there is hope in the construction of a new society, a new nation where there are no denominational barriers; and even when there are particular customs to respect, in these moments the basis for a true ecumenism is being built.

For those of us who have worked in the service of the Lord as Protestants, this is a miracle, a miracle of God that is being conceived amidst the pain, a pain that is difficult to express because it is so immense, so great. Nevertheless, a new Church is growing, the old structures are cracking, it is a true earthquake; the 1976 earthquake in Guatemala wasn't anything compared to what is happening now. All social, cultural, and religious strata are being reinterpreted or reconstructed from a faith which grows from daily life.

Another crucial fact for us Christians is to see how the compañeros who approach their struggle from another ideology respect us and accept us as colleagues. This is very important for us, since our struggle is from another calling and from our profound commitment which God has given us to be pastors amidst our people.

The sacrifices are many, the pain increases daily; compañeros, brothers, friends are physically disappearing, but at the same time there is the hope of many rising up. In some remote populations we have the testimony of seeing people who before were apathetic, but upon seeing the injustices of the government and the indiscriminate assassinations, have decided to participate in the struggle.

Nevertheless, the struggle has not ended; the enemy, who are deceivers par excellence, are expanding the channels by which they can introduce false hope. We are certain that our work is not over, that we have to continue in anonymity, in the silence of service, on the lookout for the blows of the enemy. Our churches are being manipulated from their own structures, from the structures of military power, and also by North American interests. We have the experience of how the government has been using Pentecostal preachers to approve government repression or bless its promoters. There is an open door for this type of work, while those who ask for the liberation of the people are persecuted and assassinated.

Finally, I want to give another personal testimony of how God has allowed us to work together with some priests, and I say some, because those who have been made martyrs and those who continue working in the country aren't all the priests; there remains a structure which submits to, and plays along with authority.

Nevertheless, we have found a true brotherhood with those priests who have understood the message of the Lord as participation with the people who suffer and struggle. And this is a very rich experience. Now we can share so much, side by side, without distinctions, without heated discussions, because we don't have time to discuss or theorize; rather, in these moments we contribute as best we can to those who are giving their lives so profoundly: the poor, the humble and simple people who struggle and are converting us.

Part Four:

THE WAR IN THE 1980s

Members of the Guerrilla Army of the Poor (EGP) in training exercises. *Photo credit: NISGUA*

EDITORS' INTRODUCTION

AS the mid-1980s near, Central America is aflame. The situation in El Salvador is becoming increasingly polarized, as elections in the spring of 1982, intended by the U.S. to strengthen a "third force" neither pro-rebel nor associated with the oligarchy's terror campaign against the left and the civilian population, instead confirmed the domination of the army and right-wing groups determined to crush all popular opposition. Unwilling to participate in elections that would expose its candidates to virtual certainty of assassination, the left in El Salvador evidently believes it has a good chance of winning the politico-military struggle in the country. Honduras, bordering on El Salvador, Nicaragua, and Guatemala, was the staging area for the coup against Guatemala in 1954 (see Part One, Chapter II), and today its government lends Honduran territory as a base for attacks on Nicaragua. Despite 1982 elections generally interpreted as a popular repudiation of the military, Honduras remains under the military's control. Nicaragua, where a revolution in 1979 swept the Somoza tyranny from power, is a standing threat to oligarchies in the region who fear the contagion of the Nicaraguan example. As these words are being written, Honduran troops have crossed the border into El Salvador, and the war in Central America is widening, possibly to include some kind of collective assault by right-wing governments, backed by the U.S., against the revolutionary regime in Nicaragua.[1]

Where does Guatemala fit into this pattern of increasing conflict? With what is considered to be one of the strongest armies in the region, Guatemala was once thought of as the logical candidate to intervene on the side of the government in El Salvador's civil war. This no longer appears likely on any major scale, since the war inside Guatemala "already has taken on proportions comparable to the Salvadoran conflict."[2] Guatemala's military, with its unenviable record of being the

---

1. See George Black and Judy Butler, "Target Nicaragua," *NACLA Report on the Americas,* XVI, no.1 (Jan.-Feb. 1982).
2. *Washington Post,* Jan. 22, 1982.

most violent in the region (a record amply supported by the material in this volume) has pulled out all stops in its efforts to stem the tide of revolution.

The current wave of counterinsurgency began in 1981 under the Lucas government. When a palace coup placed General Efraín Ríos Montt in power in Spring 1982, some Guatemalans and international observers felt a brief moment of hope that the cycle of death and repression would be broken. Apparently there was some effort at the time to reduce the number of assassinations carried out by death squads *in the cities.*[3] But in the countryside, the military campaigns aimed at uprooting the guerrillas' popular base of support were actually stepped up. According to the Guatemalan Association of Democratic Journalists, an organization of journalists in exile, the army committed twenty-nine massacres and killed over four thousand people in the first sixty-three days of Ríos Montt's rule, mostly in Indian villages.[4] With the July 1, 1982 declaration of a state of siege, all pretenses of a democratic opening vanished.

The types of counterinsurgency tactics now being used by the Guatemalan military—the "scorched earth" policies of burning crops and forests, the bombings, massacres, and destruction of villages, the formation of "strategic hamlets" (called "phantom villages" by a priest in Reading 39B) and "civic action" programs designed to win the hearts and minds of surviving villagers—in fact, seem to bear an ominous resemblance to U.S. actions in Vietnam. Under Ríos Montt the army, in addition, has continued the previous government's program to create civilian paramilitary squads on the order of El Salvador's feared ORDEN.[5] According to the Committee of Campesino Unity (CUC),

> These so-called civilian patrols are no more than paramilitary gangs that are led by soldiers, military agents and spies in each locality. The army in many areas has forced campesinos to participate in these gangs, saying that if we don't, they will kill us all for being subversives and burn everything. . . . They want to make us serve as cannon fodder and to massacre our brothers of class and of blood.[6]

Today's pacification campaigns, the effects of which are described in Chapter I of this section, clearly surpass in geographical scope and brutality anything previously experienced in the country. The counterinsurgency has grown for a reason:

---

3. *New York Times,* May 8, 1982.
4. *Guardian* [New York], July 14, 1982.
5. On ORDEN and other right-wing paramilitary groups in El Salvador, see Cynthia Arnson, "The *Frente's* Opposition: The Security Forces of El Salvador," in Gettleman et al., *El Salvador: Central America in the New Cold War,* Reading 15; Robert Armstrong and Janet Shenk, *El Salvador: The Face of Revolution.* (Boston, South End Press, 1982), pp. 77, 110.
6. Committee of Campesino Unity, "La voz de los pueblos sin voz," *Noticias de Guatemala* [San José, Costa Rica], Año 4, No. 80 (May 15, 1982). Also see a priest's remarks on the pressing of civilians into paramilitary service in Reading 39B.

The guerrilla opposition, strengthened by the support and participation of large numbers of Guatemalans, particularly the country's Indian campesinos, is for the first time mounting a serious threat to the regime. In Chapter II, we include the voices of men and women in arms: the stories of their lives, their literary expressions (see Reading 43) and ideas. The section ends with excerpts from a document of historic importance: the February 1982 unity statement of the merged revolutionary organizations, who if successful, will be the core around which the country's political and cultural future will take shape.

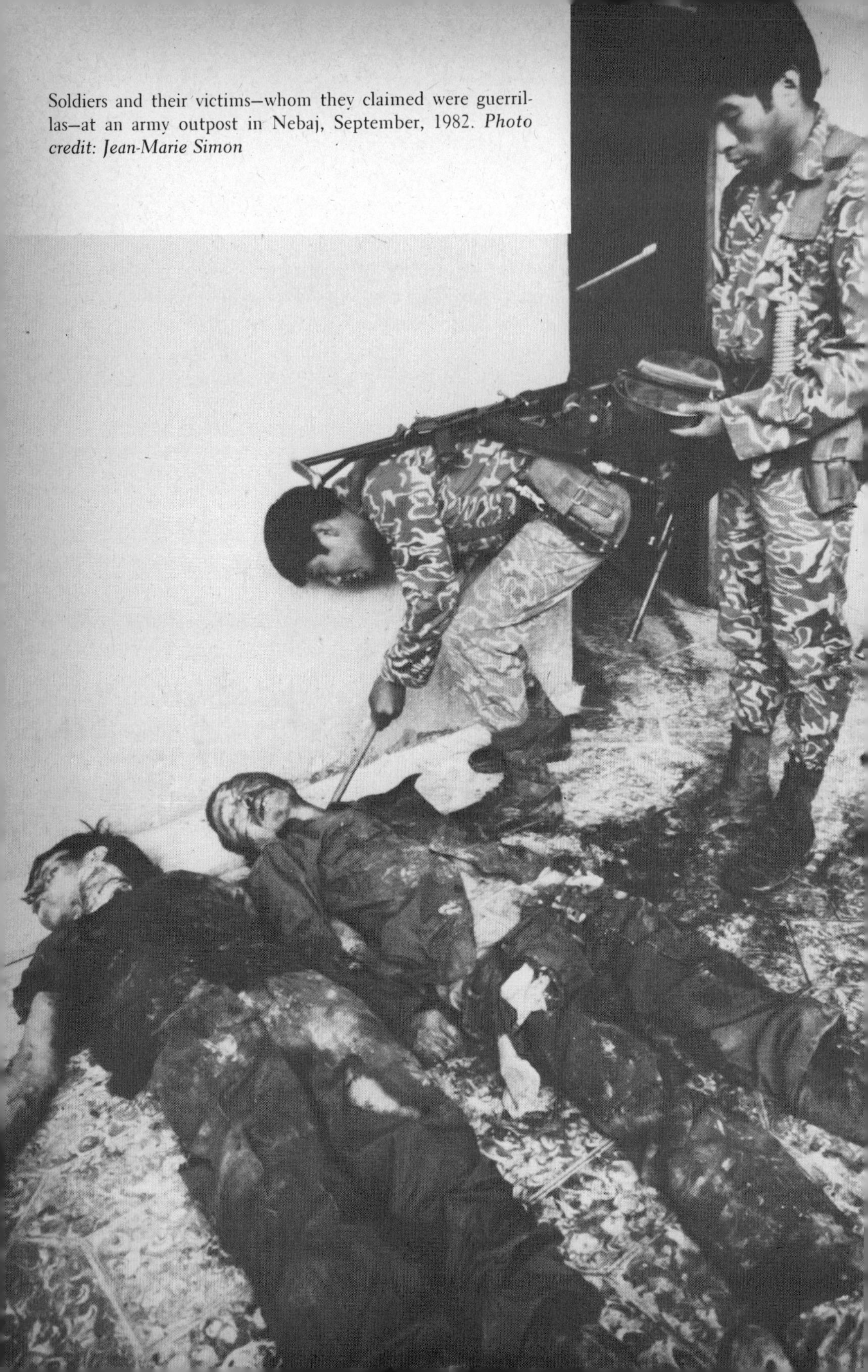

Soldiers and their victims—whom they claimed were guerrillas—at an army outpost in Nebaj, September, 1982. *Photo credit: Jean-Marie Simon*

Chapter I:

TERROR AND COUNTERINSURGENCY

Editors' Introduction

IN the heady intellectual atmosphere of President John F. Kennedy's "New Frontier" applied intelligence-gathering and counterinsurgency were seen as the solution to the problems of the United States and the world. Clearly, one of these problems was revolutionary war, and the solution was to distill the principles of this form of struggle from the very writings of its main practitioners—Mao Zedong in China, Ernesto Che Guevara in Cuba, Vo Nguyen Giap in Vietnam—and turn them against the rebels. This was to be accomplished by training American and native "special forces" to imitate the tactics of the guerrillas, to win the "hearts and minds" of villagers who otherwise would go over to the side of the revolutionaries. As one insightful student of recent U.S. policy put it, President Kennedy

> . . . put all his influence into the development of a dedicated, high-quality elite corps of specialists, capable of training local troops in guerrilla warfare, equipped to perform a wide range of civilian as well as military tasks, able to live in the jungle behind enemy lines. J.F.K.[ennedy] personally supervised the selection of new equipment. He gave the Green Berets lighter field radios and more helicopters. When all was ready he sent them out to save the world.[1]

The particular corner of the world deemed most in need of saving during the sixties was of course Vietnam, and it was in Vietnam that the theory and practice

---

1. Stephen E. Ambrose, *Rise to Globalism: American Foreign Policy, 1938-1980* (Baltimore: Penguin Books, Rev. ed., 1980), p. 273.

of counterinsurgency met its greatest defeat. There was at the outset something inherently absurd about this idea of beating the guerrillas at their own game, as if U.S. special forces, even after rigorous physical training and seminars in guerrilla warfare at Fort Bragg, North Carolina, could be parachuted into the Vietnamese jungles to win over the hearts and minds of Asian peasants. In practice, the U.S. military role in Indochina soon evolved, or degenerated, into conventional as distinguished from guerrilla warfare.[2] But native troops could be assigned to counterinsurgency, or so it was thought.

But it was the technical side of guerrilla warfare from which U.S. counterinsurgency experts tried to learn, not its political and human side. "Because guerrilla warfare basically derives from the masses and is supported by them," Mao Zedong stated, "it can neither exist or flourish if it separates itself from their sympathies and cooperation." [3] If counterinsurgency is enlisted in support of a local regime of oppression that is incapable of, or refuses to, initiate reforms that would satisfy popular aspirations, it is doomed. That doom is the story of Vietnam, and the ominous pattern seems to be repeating itself in Central America.

If the mandarins and militarists of Vietnam were unwilling to make the necessary social reforms and concessions to win the hearts and minds of the people, the same challenge in a country like Guatemala has even less of a chance. There, the local militarists and oligarchs barely pay even the most perfunctory lip-service to the "need" for reform. Instead, they rely on armed force to head off insurrection and to frighten the populace into quiescence. The readings in this chapter document this campaign of terror and counterinsurgency currently being waged in Guatemala. We give the bulk of the space to eyewitness accounts from the victims of this campaign—villagers, refugees, local priests, and guerrillas themselves. The government contention is that in conducting sweep-and-destroy missions, it is merely relieving the countryside of the depredations of subversive elements, directed from outside.

Right-wing groups and entrenched governments often claim that their opponents are outside agitators. El Salvador's rebels are now being charged with being puppets of some Cuban-Nicaraguan conspiracy, and in Vietnam in the 1960s the insurgents were seen by U.S. officials as proxies of China and/or the Soviet Union. But it is clear to all but the most biased observers that in Guatemala, the resistance is rooted in the indigenous villages, particularly as the Indian majority is increasingly mobilized in self-defense. In this context, therefore, counterinsurgency efforts mounted by the Guatemalan armed forces and their allies (paramilitary squads) amount to a kind of "ethnocide," the effort to destroy village-based culture. The brutality described in the readings therefore is not regrettable excess, but is inherent in the very process of rooting out popular resistance. Nor are the

2. A recent account of this is Larry Berman, *Planning a Tragedy: The Americanization of the War in Vietnam* (New York: Norton, 1982).

3. Mao Zedong, quoted in Eqbal Ahmad, "Revolutionary Warfare: How to Tell When the Rebels Have Won," *The Nation*, August 30, 1965.

events chronicled in this chapter a mere continuation of the traditional violence of the ruling groups in Guatemala subsequent to the 1954 coup, or a replay of the terror practiced in the early dictatorships of Jorge Ubico (1931–1944) or Manuel Cabrera (1898–1920), or by the Spanish conquistadores. Not even the U.S.-supported counterinsurgency campaigns of the 1960s could match the present ferocity.[4] It is a new and terrible phase, as the readings below show and many Guatemalans are now saying: *basta ya*, enough! And they are also asking North Americans and concerned people everywhere to help end the terror (see, for instance, Guillermo Toriello Garrido's Introduction to this book).

39. *Search and Destroy in Chupol: Daily Life in Occupied Guatemala* *

A. Indian woman
B. Catholic priest

THE view of official Washington—that insurgency in Central America is part of an outside plot to disrupt countries which unmolested would be well on the way to establishing justice for their citizens—has been amply documented in this book, and elsewhere. It is identical with the views publicly presented by the military chieftains of the region, including General Benedicto Lucas García, Chief of Staff of the Guatemalan army until President Romeo Lucas García, his brother, was ousted in Spring 1982.

Taking several journalists on a tour of western provinces late in 1981 to show that "subversive groups . . . cause great destruction to the numerous indigenous communities that reside in mountainous zones," General Lucas lamented that the rebels do "the most grave destruction and moral harm to the campesino, burning his house, killing farm animals and often kidnapping the head of the family to enroll him in the subversion under the threat of annihilating his family if he resists. . . ." The general went on to demonstrate the connection between the view of guerrillas as terrorists, and the belief that the insurgency is therefore

---

4. At least one U.S. Army counterinsurgency expert has been training Guatemalan troops since 1981, despite a Congressional ban. See Allan Nairn, "Despite Ban, U.S. Captain Trains Guatemalan Military," *Washington Post* October 21, 1982.

* This reading is made up of two sections, each of which came to the editors independently. The first consists of excerpts from a tape-recorded interview with a Guatemalan Indian woman, transcribed and translated by Christine Piotter, a German journalist. The second is part of an interview with a local Catholic priest, February 1982, supplied to the editors by another source.

externally directed.[1] *He described booby traps set up by the guerrillas to catch soldiers, and stated that they confirm once more that "the subversive elements are using what the Vietnamese did against the North American army."*[2]

> Concerning all this, we should ask ourselves something many Guatemalans are ignorant of: Are not these tricks clearly the advice of foreign experts who have come to our country? Well, we have reliable information that foreigners trained in Vietnam, Cuba and other countries of the Marxist orbit have infiltrated these groups.[3]

Lucas was speaking from the village of Chupol in the province of Quiché. In this reading we present the eyewitness accounts of residents of Chupol and nearby villages, whose experiences differ dramatically from the account given by General Lucas.[4]

A.

I CAN TELL you a little about what I lived through in a village of Chichicastenango, in the region of Quiché.

Starting on the 18th of November, we heard rumors that the Army was going around to nearby villages, massacring the people and burning houses and everything that was planted. We also heard that in several villages near the road they burned many small farms, especially in Chumanzana and in Chupol. . . . So all these people ended up in the streets, you might say, with only the clothes on their backs, without food, many of them with little children, and they couldn't even feed their children.

The days were passing and we could hear bombs falling on villages in the surrounding area. And we could hear them shooting at the people, from helicopters that had machine guns.

---

1. In an insightful study of the theory and practice of guerrilla warfare, Pakistani scholar Eqbal Ahmad ("Revolutionary Warfare: How to Tell When the Rebels Have Won," *The Nation*, August 30, 1965) concludes that while guerrilla movements are certainly not pacifist, and rebels do use armed force to attain their aims, "guerrilla warfare requires a highly committed but covert civilian support which cannot be obtained at gun point." For further discussion of this topic, see Part Four, Chapter II of this book.

2. According to Indian activist Rigoberta Menchú, these booby traps were "invented by our ancestors" (see Reading 32). A description of traps used against the Spanish may be found in the *Annals of the Cakchiquels*, Reading 2.

3. *Prensa Libre* [Guatemala City], Nov. 18, 1981. (This newspaper usually reflects the viewpoint of the Guatemalan government.)

4. The editors could easily fill a volume several times this size with material documenting antipopular terror in Guatemala. We have chosen this Chupol operation as typical of what is a daily pattern in that violent land.

One of these helicopters was blue and white and there was another one that was red. But we could see that they shot from high up in the air. They were afraid to fly low and shoot because there was a group of young people who belonged to the guerrilla; they [the guerrillas] started to shoot up into the air, at the helicopters, to defend the villagers.

All of a sudden, for a second they saw that one helicopter was shot down. Later we heard that it was destroyed and couldn't fly.

Some people also told us that in one village they saw that when the helicopter flew a little lower so it could shoot, the guerrilla groups in that village were able to shoot and kill the soldier who was shooting from the helicopter; they killed him with one of the weapons that they had. Some said that they saw him while he was falling through the air.

The people were hoping that it would be those young people who would help them, because they were without weapons, the people of the village.

The only things they had were the fireworks that they used in fiestas. They put them along the road and set them off. This frightened the army and slowed them down a little, the army that was trying to go into the villages along the road.

After all that, the people went to the villages which seemed a little safer than those that were near the road.

Again the days passed by and the army was furious because they couldn't go into the villages on foot; the people, although unarmed, had laid some traps around their fields and their houses to defend themselves. A few groups of soldiers tried to go into these villages. The only thing that happened was that they fell into the traps and died. So the army didn't dare enter the villages during the day, and were even more afraid to at night.

So the days passed and our nervousness was getting worse because around midnight every night we sensed that the helicopters were coming to bomb us; because it was always between 12 and 12:30 when they came.

The 18th of November we also heard that all the roads that lead into or out of this region in the south of Quiché were full of soldiers approaching our area. And they didn't want anybody coming into or leaving the area. On the 25th of November we began to hear big explosions and we were afraid.

People who were coming from Chupol told us that in the marketplace in Chupol there were cannons and they were shooting from there. . . . We also learned from them that the soldiers had the roads closed off. Nobody could come or go. All the roads that went to the highway—to get a bus to go to the capital or anyplace else—were completely closed off, and full of soldiers.

Whoever had the courage to try to come or go was shot. Some people who had no choice came to the village but they told us that they had to run or crawl on their hands and knees because the soldiers were shooting at them. They treated them like guerrillas, but they were just people who wanted to come to the village. They had left to do errands, had to risk their lives to come back. Some of them left to do very important things. For example, they had sick people that they had to take care of in their houses or promises they had to keep, and all of them had to take the same risk. Many of them had to stay inside the village, suffering a lot, because it wasn't possible to leave.

Every day we heard the planes and helicopters passing above us. Over our heads they were firing grenades; they were shooting at us with machine guns. And then we couldn't do anything else but flee to wherever we could, even under trees, to escape the bullets. We started to make great efforts to protect ourselves, to get ourselves into safe places. Every time a helicopter passed by, we had to run and jump into these holes. It was the only place where we felt like the grenades weren't falling right on top of us.

The days were passing. Around the 28th of November we already felt like everything was closing in on us. The people passing by told us that the number of soldiers on the highways was getting larger. And we also started to hear that the people in the area of Chimaltenango were starving to death, especially the children, because they had already been surrounded by the army for 15 days and nobody could come or go.

They said that the little children didn't have anything to eat anymore because the army burned down all the nearby stores. So they had nothing to eat. They didn't have anything except ears of corn that weren't ripe yet. They couldn't build fires because that would have given away the people's hideouts in the hills and the forest. So they could only roast them part way and this nearly raw food gave almost everyone diarrhea, nausea, and intestinal infections. Others had to hunt for leaves and roots and eat them or the little bit of food they found. All of this made their situation worse. The worst thing was that then it started to rain a lot; and it was the season when it gets very cold in that area.

The people were hiding in their places, wet; the children were crying from the cold, and there wasn't dry clothing to change into because the soldiers had burned all the clothing with the houses. So the ones that didn't die of intestinal infections died of pneumonia, especially the children and old people. There were also wounded people. . . .

On the 29th of November, we started to hear shots in the air very close by. We were alarmed because in the village that we were in there were a great number of refugees from Chupol, Pajuliboy, and other villages that have been burned to the ground. Even though there were still some farms intact around a few villages, they were completely abandoned. The people were living in the woods, as I say, without food, without warm clothes, in the rain, wet, and many people were wounded. So we had to let them stay a while and sleep for a few days, and share the same hunger and suffering together with us. In the village where I was, there were about three hundred refugees, children, women, and old people. We started to prepare ourselves for what had to come.

On the 30th of November, at dawn, we were told that the army was near some houses that were near our village. And that night they came to tell us; they were wounded people who had been in those houses. They came at night to tell us. Many of them had their open wounds. We didn't have anything to give them to ease their pain, nothing to help them. Only aspirin, which could only help a little.

We really only had a little bit of medicine. So we were alarmed because we heard that a great number of trucks, full of soldiers, were coming to the villages at night, the lights turned off, slowly, without making much noise.

The people who were hiding in the woods moved farther and farther into the woods until they came to our village. Then we were very crowded. So we had to take care of the wounded first, then the children, and then the old people. We suffered a lot, since we didn't have enough food.

That's how the first of December came. At dawn we heard shots and cannonballs from far away, shooting at us. We also heard that there was a large number of small trucks all around us. When we heard that the army had entered the village and had killed some people who were guarding the entrance, we couldn't do anything else but leave—everybody—in any way possible. At 10:00 in the morning all the women and children left and they started to cry.

A group of young people who belonged to the guerrilla helped us to organize the departure and calmed us down and told us to trust them, that they would help us. We immediately followed their instructions: first women and children left, carrying the wounded when it was possible. . . .

So our trek began, quite calmly, abut 10:00 in the morning. At about 11, when we thought we were already safe inside the woods, we heard the helicopters coming closer; they surrounded us. The children—like children are—were very restless. That's how they found out that we were there. So they started—in less than five minutes—to bomb us, to shoot us. And—I don't know how—suddenly there were small planes that flew very low. They dropped tons of bombs on us. So we started running deeper into the woods. The children started to scream and run. The women called their children, because they were getting lost. They couldn't find them. And it was a race! We were running, running, running, throwing ourselves down on the ground—a cloud of dust, of dirt, all wounded in the woods; we were going to be smashed any minute. We told the women, "Don't stand up! A bullet might hit you. Throw yourselves on the ground." But they didn't listen; many of them didn't understand "Castilla" [Spanish—EDS.]. And there were some of us who couldn't make ourselves understood in their tongue. That's how we saw many of the women fall, hit by the bullets.

Other women ran back when they saw that their little ones weren't with them. The mothers called their children; the children screamed back, calling their mothers. Only the children they carried on their backs were safe. The worst off were the ones who were four, five, or six years old and could already run by themselves. They were the ones that fell behind. That's why many women desperately ran back to get them.

But with horror we saw that all the soldiers were coming. . . . The infantry had managed to enter the village and was now coming after us, throwing grenades and shooting with machine guns. So many of the women who ran back fell, hit by these bullets. We couldn't go back to see if they were dead or only wounded, because it was impossible; those hundreds and hundreds of people of the village ran and ran, desperately.

We ran for about six hours. We were seeing people with their heads totally smashed open, their hands ripped off, their arms and legs dangling, many of them broken.

The children: sometimes we couldn't see them, their little faces, because they were full of blood. And they cried and cried and cried. All these women with their faces of anguish!

In the end I saw a woman who had given birth fifteen days earlier. She was carrying her little one on her back and another one in her arms. In one of the races she fell; the poor woman totally smashed her little one, fifteen days old. When she pulled him to her front and saw him bleeding from his ears, mouth, and nose, the woman started screaming, uncontrollably.

[She continues with a broken voice]. Our situation is very hard. Now you can imagine what all these people suffer. We rested a little, washed the wounds in the rivers that were quite dirty because it was raining a lot in those days. And we could see that some of the wounds weren't that bad, but others were. All we could do was to comfort each other.

About seven at night—we still hadn't arrived—we met people who were leaving a village where we thought we could find shelter for the night. They were carrying their clothes, with faces of anguish, and they told us: "Don't go up to our village. The army is near the school and they've already burnt the houses that are near. They're already coming after us, they will find us, let's flee together." So we had to join with this fleeing group too. We were worried about the children who wouldn't stop crying, because they hadn't eaten anything all day, absolutely nothing. They didn't understand: why all that terror? Why suffer so much hunger?

We continued walking with all the people; it was already very dark and it was raining heavily. Some of us stayed in huts that we found empty. Others who came later had to spend the night in the woods, cold, hungry, and out in the rain. At midnight one could hear the cries of the children—even screams. The people were desperate.

At dawn we continued walking, looking for a place to stay in safety. We arrived the next night in a village where the owners of the houses let us in, helped us, and comforted us. They told us with a lot of anger that they'd also heard the bombings, and that it was unfair what they were doing to us. A few months back, these villagers had lived through the same thing, but the soldiers didn't burn their houses or their crops. They just kidnapped people. So we spent some time there, resting, eating. Then we did everything possible to leave the area, because with too many people there the same would happen to all of us in this village.

After we talked more calmly about everything, we realized that the planes which had bombed us were "Pilatus" [plane for fumigation—EDS.] which they had fixed up with cannons. They had built in many things to bomb us. And the army bombed us with them.

At night we could see—and you could see it clearly from where we were—a big fire. All the villages we fled from were on fire. The houses that still stood in some places were all in flames. Then they spilled gasoline on the crops, on the corn that was ready for harvest; it was already dry. And because corn and beans are planted at the same time, they burned them both together.

After that the soldiers came to tell us, "Go back to your houses." We asked them, "What houses?" They told us, "We will protect you; don't let yourselves get fooled by the guerrillas." Well, we saw that it was the army who was destroying us. The people who were helping us to save our lives were the guerrillas.

We wanted to hear all the news on the radio, if they were going to say what happened to us. But they didn't say anything. All they said was that the soldiers had fought the guerrilla, and that they had killed many. But it wasn't the guerrillas who had died; it was the people of the village.

The next day many women returned to their villages to look for the children that were lost. They couldn't sleep or eat—nothing—they only cried and thought about their little ones. A lot of them said, "Who knows what happened to them? Who knows where they are crying, or if they're hurt? Maybe they got thrown into the river or they are in the woods and nobody can hold their hands." So we lost many women; I don't know what happened to them afterwards.

I joined up with a group that was leaving. I tried to see how to get out of all this. That's how I got out of all those places and could rest, be quiet, and start thinking about how to help all these many people without anything, without shelter.

B.

[A Priest]: Now I would like to say this. The people had to look for all means to help them defend themselves against the repression; when the army arrives it comes to destroy these rural communities. It burns and destroys villages, houses, crops . . . everything. It is here that you can really see the force and strength of the popular organizations. This zone is very well-organized by the CUC, which is a part of the January 31st Popular Front (FP-31).

The tactic of the army has two parts . . . that is three points. First the army panics. They set up a post of three hundred to five hundred soldiers, and they call together all the people and they form a road block around the post so that the people themselves are the army's defense against the guerrillas. That is to say, when the guerrillas attack, the first ones to fall then are the people themselves who have been set up by the army to be their defense. This is what they call a "phantom village," that is not a true village but only a village that has been created by the army to exist around its post.

This is what happened in Chupol. There in Chupol there is a chapel and a plaza which we built, a church, a school, chapel, market, everything, right? There in this square they placed the tanks, cannons, etc. Because from this site they could control Sololá, up until Quiché. From this site they could control Chimaltenango. And around the square, when the bombing began, all the poor people were gathered to defend the army—women, civilians, children. What was the reaction of the people? They said what the army told them to say: the guerrillas came and attacked and kidnapped thousands of campesinos. How can this be? How would they have been able to kidnap hundreds and hundreds of campesinos?

What happened is the following. These people are organized. The people knew what the army wanted to do with them. So they organized themselves and escaped, that is they escaped from the army. Faced with this, seeing the negative response of the people as they organized themselves, the army entered, seeking to infiltrate all the villages being organized. But the people had prepared themselves. They had prepared tricks, such as preparing large firecrackers, the types used at large fiestas, and used these to stall the army. While these were going off and the soldiers were seeking cover, thinking they were being attacked, the women left quickly through some hidden ravines and came towards the Motagua River. And they escaped.

When the army realized that they had been tricked and that the soldiers had not entered because of their own panic, they called in the air force. Armed helicopters with machine guns, for example the type used by the brother of Lucas himself, Benedicto Lucas García, and who himself was present and seen by the campesinos, were used. . . . These helicopters came firing, and some airplanes were sent. They also sent some smaller planes. They all came shooting. They are all firing and bombing, right? And even from the plaza of Chupol square they are shooting mortars and cannons. You can imagine the enormous holes which were left in the earth. This will give you an idea of the types of bullets and ammunition used. They continued shooting and shooting, followed by the army who burned everything in sight—crops, houses, everything. Those who lagged on behind, like the children, were lost in this insanity. Or they escaped by throwing themselves into ravines or by throwing themselves into rivers. Then some of the mothers went back to look for their children. And when they returned, these were the ones killed by the army, massacred. There are not exact numbers yet. But it is estimated that more than one thousand persons were killed in the operations in this zone. . . .

But now there is yet another point, a point that is even more terrible; I have the testimony of a person who experienced an attack on a bus by an Indian group. He got out of the bus, and the people were surprised and baffled. What is going on that the Indians are killing people?

Now we have the exact account from some Protestant ministers. In this zone there are about six hundred campesinos, both Indians and ladinos, who were armed by the army but in civilian clothes. This was done so that they would give the impression that it was fighting between the Indians and ladinos themselves. These six hundred were sent in three groups and ordered to shoot whatever moved in front of them: people, animals, children, women.

Gathered near the military post was a group who had come to play a game of soccer. They took them to the post and asked them their age. The lieutenant said: "All of those forty or over, or under sixteen, no." He was trying to calculate the ages of these persons, looking at them, saying "Take off your shirt. Take off your pants. Put on this. Take off those shoes, put on these boots," boots made of rubber, which are the kind used by the Indians and the clothes of the Indians too. He gave them arms and asked them "Have you ever killed?" What could they do? It was either kill or be killed. The army sent them off, following them, ordering them to shoot at whatever moved. And the objective? To give the impression to the outside that the people were fighting amongst themselves.

40. *Guatemalan Indians Crowd into Mexico To Escape the Widening War* *

By Marlise Simons

A report issued in April 1982, by the Guatemalan [Roman Catholic] Bishops' Conference stated that political violence in the country had driven at least two hundred thousand campesinos into neighboring countries, and had uprooted as many as a million within Guatemala.[1] *The plight of these refugees, described here by a journalist who visited the Guatemalan-Mexican border, was recently compared to the situation of refugees in Jesus's time, driven from their homes "by the terrorist reprisals of Herod," and to the persecuted Hebrews of Old Testament days seeking "liberation from Egyptian slavery."*[2] *These scriptural references remind us of the uses of religion as a form of resistance to slavery and oppression in the United States before (and after) the Civil War.*

CIUDAD CUAUHTEMOC, MEXICO—The insistent whir of a Guatemalan Army helicopter broke the silence of the hot afternoon. The helicopter circled just short of the Mexican border, then swooped down and fired into the trees below.

"Guatemalan families came running out of nowhere, screaming," recalled Carlos Gomez, a Mexican farmhand who witnessed the scene. "There was terrible panic. When they got to our side, some of the people gave away their children to the Mexicans."

No one was hurt that afternoon of Jan. 14, but by the time the chopper rumbled off, nearly 300 men, women and children had sought refuge in Mexico.

* From *Washington Post*, February 19, 1982, by permission.

1. Associated Press dispatch in *New York Times*, April 18, 1982.

2. The references are from the Iglesia Guatemalteca en el Exilio, Boletín No. 11 [Granada, Nicaragua], Febrero-Marzo, 1982.

They said they had traveled on foot much of the night, fleeing from an Army raid that they claimed had left 18 dead in the village of Santa Cataria and 16 dead in the village of El Limonar. The chopper's crew had spotted their group as they approached the border and, apparently under the impression that they were guerrillas or sympathizers, had opened fire.

The group was another trickle in the flood of about 2,000 refugees each week that is pouring into Mexico as the Guatemalan Army wages the fiercest antiguerrilla campaign in its history. Over the past six months, the Army has stepped up its hunt for a tough, often invisible guerrilla force, and the refugees say it has inflicted a brutal, scorched-earth policy on Guatemala's western highlands. As a result, entire villages and hamlets have fled, often into Mexico.

In this rugged, unpatrolled land, there are few documented statistics. The State Department in its latest annual report on international human rights estimated that nearly 100 peasants a month were killed in Guatemala's escalating guerrilla war. It estimated that an additional 250 to 300 persons were murdered each month for what appeared to be political reasons.

"Increasingly, noncombatants are the principal victims of the violence from both sides," the report said.

A Western diplomat in Guatemala recently put last year's death toll at 5,000, most of them civilians, while the newly formed Guatemalan Unity Committee, an opposition group, put the figure at 13,500.

In interviews last month with Washington Post correspondent Christopher Dickey, Guatemalan military officers in the field readily conceded that civilians caught between them and the guerrillas were considered expendable.

"These people [the guerrillas] are difficult to distinguish from most of the rest of the local population," Gen. Benedicto Lucas García, chief of staff of Guatemala's armed forces, told Dickey. ". . . Because of that, well, the population suffers."

The guerrillas have stated publicly that they at times also have killed civilians suspected of being government informants.

Guatemala's ambassador to Mexico, Jorge Palmieri, conceded in a recent interview that "there are military actions and people who have nothing to do with it are afraid to be caught up in it, [so] they travel." He contended there is evidence that the guerrillas "have manipulated people and led them to Mexico to cause upheavals."

Whatever the reason, there is no dispute that the refugees are coming here in record numbers. The Mexican Interior Ministry estimates there are 120,000 Guatemalan refugees in this country now, more than double the figure of a year ago.

The winding, 565-mile-long dividing line between North and Central America has always been porous. Marked only by an occasional border post, like here at Ciudad Cuauhtemoc, it climbs across the peaks of the Sierra Madre, becomes the Usumacinta River, then loses itself in the dense tropical jungle further north.

For as long as anyone remembers, merchants and migrant workers have freely crossed the border. But never has the flow been so large. Thousands of terrified, impoverished and often illiterate Indians have come to see the distance between their old homes and the Mexican border—often only a few hundred yards—as the difference between life and death.

Although it is quiet on the Mexican side of the mountains, the war has deeply strained the modest resources of the string of border towns where refugees have arrived. It has also unsettled officials of the Mexican government, who disclosed earlier this week that Mexico has authorized the training of a 4,000-man quick-reaction military force in part to cope with any possible spillover of the conflict.

Mexico has refused to allow the formation of refugee camps near the frontier for fear the camps would quickly turn into armed guerrilla bases and worsen the country's already poor relations with Guatemala. Instead, the refugees are scattered all over southern Mexico, working in cities or on farms or relying on the good will of religious charity groups.

Pressure has been building on the government from conservatives who argue Mexico already has enough social problems of its own and should put a stop to the new flood of penniless foreigners.

But when the government ordered the deportation of 1,800 Guatemalans last summer, it drew sharp criticism from the left as well as from Guy Prim, then the representative of the United Nations High Commissioner for Refugees, who said there was strong evidence that some deportees were being murdered on their return to Guatemala.

Most of the refugees, like much of Guatemala's highland Indian peasantry, seem conservative, devout and xenophobic. The stories they tell in broken Spanish of half-empty or deserted villages, burned homes and dismembered bodies present a picture far removed from the tight social order that for centuries has ruled one of the oldest cultures in the Americas.

Their accounts offer glimpses of a bitter, often bloody conflict that has gone largely unreported to the outside world. Few outsiders travel to the remote villages in the provinces of Huehuetenango, Quiché and San Marcos where most of the fighting has occurred, and suspicious locals seldom confide in those who do.

The Guatemalan government insists that the guerrillas bear much of the responsibility for any atrocities that have occurred. Earlier this week, the Army blamed guerrillas for the massacre of 53 Quiché Indians in the village of Chumac.

But in a week of interviews, more than two dozen refugees offered repeated accounts of brutality by the Army and none by the guerrillas.

Near Motozintla, a village tucked against a barren mountainside, Jacinto Pascual, 60, explained why he, his wife, their children and grandchildren had abandoned their home in the Guatemalan village of Tacaná last December. He said the "pintos," a Guatemalan pejorative for soldiers, had killed 40 villagers in Tacaná, including "whole families."

Pascual, whose possessions were reduced to what he could carry across the border in a plastic shopping bag, apologized for crying "right here in front of my wife. I'm not afraid of death. I've lived my time. But I'm afraid of the way the pintos kill. They first cut off the ears, then the nose, with a machete. They cut out the eyes and the tongue. I heard them say they don't want to waste their bullets."

On the flight to Mexico, he said, his family had found four bodies in a forest. "Two had their hands and feet cut off," he recalled. "Two had no more tongue."

Women express the same fears: being raped by the soldiers and being burned alive in their huts. Religious workers said that many frontier families tend their land and animals in Guatemala in the daytime and sleep in Mexico at night.

One widow who lives in Guatemala, but sleeps in Mexico, said she could no longer sleep when at home: "I've seen the fires at night. The soldiers bar the doors [of the huts], throw gasoline and burn everyone inside."

Candido, a wounded Catholic lay preacher from Nentón, said he had been dumped from an Army truck a few days earlier after faking death. Soldiers had tied his brother behind the truck, "pulling him at great speed until he died," he said. Efraín Moreno, a former government employee just arrived from Nentón, said the village had been completely abandoned.

A Mexican nurse, who said she has extracted "many a bullet" from the refugees, angrily recalled an incident two months ago when a woman from Nentón brought her badly burned 9-month-old granddaughter for treatment.

Government soldiers had come to the woman's house seeking her son. When she told them she did not know his whereabouts, she said, they held the baby's feet over burning coals in the fireplace.

"Its feet were burned to the bone," said the nurse. "I saw it with my own eyes." The nurse, who asked not to be identified because she feared that Mexican authorities disapproved of her work with the refugees, said the baby survived and subsequently was taken to a hospital for a series of skin grafts.

Sometimes the impact on Mexicans of the Guatemalan conflict is a subtle one. In the Mexican village of Niquivil, built in a high pass often covered in clouds, the villagers do not go out at night. The mountains are haunted, they say, by the souls of the scattered, unburied dead across the border.

For the past six months, peasants have pulled bodies out of the Cuilco and Selegua rivers that run from Guatemala into Mexico. "The people here have been very shocked," said a local Catholic priest. "Many of them will not eat fish from the rivers any more."

41. A Guerrilla is Captured, Confesses, Then Escapes *

BY EMETERIO TOJ MEDRANO

ON October 22, 1981, Guatemalan TV stations featured a public confession by a leader of the popular movement, Emeterio Toj Medrano, a founder of the Committee of Campesino Unity (CUC) and member of the Guerrilla Army of the Poor (EGP). Earlier he had met with a U.S. Congressional delegation visiting Guatemala, but a special assistant to Representative Thomas Harkin had doubts about the authenticity of the confession. "He seemed to be trying to signal us, 'Don't take everything I say seriously,'" recalled the aide.[1] In late November, Toj escaped; this reading is his own account. The editors present a literal translation, with no attempt to improve style or syntax. With its detail on capturing prisoners, torture, psychological warfare, and threats to family members, this reading reminds us that real war is now being waged in Guatemala.

INTERVIEWER: CAN YOU tell us the story of your capture?
Toj: Yes, look before saying anything it would be a good idea to tell you that I am an indigenous campesino who has suffered repression, discrimination and oppression at my parents' side since my childhood. My commitment to the people is a commitment from years ago, because we have gone along suffering, in our own flesh, that suffering of our people and in that sense I have been with my people in all the diverse struggles that they have been developing.

I was involved in these activities on the 4th of July of 1981, in the city of Quezaltenango. The government kidnapped me in broad daylight, publicly at about 4:30 in the afternoon. I was with my little children and another woman friend—people in the U.S. should know that in Guatemala people are assassinated in the middle of the street, in front of children, that is to say there is a total disrespect for life—and this happened to me. In front of my children, then, they grabbed me, they struck me right away, and they put me inside a car, a red one; they transferred me to the department police station in Quezaltenango where they kept me until the next day. Later they took me to the Lisandro Barillas military base in the city of Quezaltenango. There they interrogated me almost the whole night—that was Sunday the 5th of July—and of course this interrogation was accompanied by the most incredible tortures—like from what they call

* Selections from an interview with Emeterio Toj Medrano, February 1982, from an independent source.

1. Dispatch from Mexico City by Alan Riding, *New York Times*, December 18, 1981.

the "capucha," or hood, electric shock, to burning your hands—I even have various scars on my hands, all over my body; they burned my back during those two days. In Quezaltenango it was now the G-2 that interrogated me—I repeat—until the early morning so that I met the dawn on Monday with them asking me questions about my activities in Quezaltenango. Absolutely nothing came out of this because one of the commitments that I made from the beginning when they captured me, they kidnapped me, was not to reveal the work, let's say the details of our struggle because to do that would be to destroy the hope of a whole people. So I had proposed to myself that I not say absolutely anything about the work that was being carried out in those places. This cost me a lot of pain.

As much from the physical tortures as from the psychological tortures that they began that very day by saying to me that if I didn't give information that that same day they would begin to kill, one by one, my children and my family. But I resisted. I said to myself that if they are going to kill us they will kill us. It wouldn't be the first family that they had killed. You . . . know that in Guatemala they have massacred entire families. Well, I said, I'm going to be one more of those whose families are going to disappear. But it is for our people, right? And so I resisted the torture during those first forty-eight hours.

On Monday the 5th—excuse me, the 6th—they moved me to the military base in Huehuetenango where they also tortured me, in the most brutal way. They kept me for thirteen days without drinking one drop of water, without eating—they would bring me the food but they wouldn't let me eat it. That is to say; if you speak, if you talk, then we'll give it to you and if you don't then we'll take it away. They did this every little while during the thirteen days. Besides this, let's say, torture; wanting to kill me of hunger and thirst, they also hit me. For example the electric shocks. They put wires here, wires here, wires in my ears and on my feet and at the same time they plugged in the wires so that, that is to say, so that they would give electric shocks at the same time. During one of these I was going to die, I, I felt that I was going. And the torturer, who is, let's say, the guy who was directing the torture, is a major in the army—the G-2—and eight more government men, who were besides mocking me, kicking me, they spit in my face, they grabbed me and hit me with their fists, and this went on for various days. It wasn't just on one occasion, and besides that I was interred inside a bread oven. They kept me with my hands and feet tied, putting them together in a way so that my body was arched toward the back. I was under those conditions for thirteen savage days.

There were moments when I lost all awareness. During this whole time they also didn't let me sleep. That is to say they wanted to drive me crazy, to see if in delirium they could get something out of me. Besides this they put—they injected me with drugs so that I would lose all sense. They didn't let me eat, drink, or sleep during this whole time. They would tie a rope to me and pull me along every five minutes and push me with a stick inside the oven again, as a, as . . . it was a permanent torture, permanent. They did this every five minutes, and they would put sounds inside the oven, noises with some pictures, that is to say, with the end of tormenting you not only physically, but mentally as well, and to tell you the truth, in those last few days I lost all sense.

I lost all sense of time, I didn't know if it was daytime, I didn't know if it was nighttime. While I was there they came to tell me that they had my children and my family, there in the barracks at Huehuetenango, and that they were going to begin to rape my little daughters in front of me and kill them one by one. Like I told you before, if that is the price that one has to pay then, well you have to pay it, you had to pay it. What they wanted were the names of compañeros and really I don't . . . well first of all I don't know, you see, and well I'm not capable because many brothers have died already for that, this struggle. . . .[2] I couldn't be the, someone who, because, because for wanting to save my life—that I might have given information—no no I preferred death; but it didn't come, right? You resisted. Everything, all that physical and moral pain until they told me now, after ten days, that I was a member of CUC because they were putting out propaganda on the radio that I was part of CUC. I hadn't said that before; but it came out. And it was a public question, public besides that they had seen me already working with the CUC, right? So yes, I told them that I belonged to the CUC. But they didn't know anything more than about the public activities that in fact the enemy already knew. That is to say that it would be too long a story to tell you point by point about all the pain. But besides these tortures, forty-five days of physical tortures followed where they didn't let me eat one or two days—besides the time that I spent in Huehuetenango—because on the 22nd of July they transferred me to the capital of the republic to continue interrogating me—and during that time I did eat two or three days.

Interviewer: Yes, so how did you come to the point of doing the press conference publicly on television?

Toj: OK, well two reasons came into play there. They weren't killing me. They weren't killing me. I mean the moment for wanting to kill me—they had already passed you could say. They would have to kill me after getting more things out of me. I mean through the torture. . . .

[On television] you know they gave me a script and to the reporters, the pseudo-reporters because they weren't all reporters those that were there, to them they gave anticipated questions, because they gave the answers to me. And I'll tell you, it was Mr. Major Isaac Rodríguez—who is a college graduate and with the rank of major in the army for psychological operations at the National Palace, who wrote the text and passed me the questions. Well I had to come to accept this, this proposal, this prostituting proposal. But I repeat that it gave me hope . . . because this was giving them more faith in me thinking that I had passed to their side. . . . And I realized that there was no other out . . . because I was always locked up—even at the time of the escape I was in the Justo Rufino Barrios

2. At this point in the interview Toj cried.—EDS.

general barracks—so that that, let's say process of gaining faith . . . I saw that it was an alternative. Of course it wasn't the only one. Also in these actions I thought abut my compañeros, in a possible rescue . . . because in the transfer from one place to another, they could find out about it possibly, and rescue me.
Interviewer: And then, and how did you escape?
Toj: Yes, ah, well since the enemy couldn't get anything more useful out of me through torture, well they didn't kill me. They preferred to use me that way. At the same time that it was repugnant to me—because it's prostituting a person—I saw some hope for me. . . . OK, ah I prefer not to give any details for logical reasons, right? Do you understand me? . . . There are lives of other compañeros in play here and so it would be like giving information to the enemy. But yes, my organization participated in this escape . . . although there were many many contributing factors.[3] The fact, for example, that during those days the army was involved in their big genocidal offensive [4] and so inside the general barracks there weren't very many people . . . and besides, in that moment they were reckless . . . because it's true that the enemy—the army . . . and it's clear to me because I was there—the army is turned upside-down. It is not the army it was, very powerful, invincible . . . no. It is really a cowardly army. It is only brave with the civilian population, with the children that they massacre. It is, rather, an assassin, cowardly army. It is not an army that is prepared really for combat, but for massacring defenseless people. Anyway, the [televised press] conference helped to, let's say, gain a little bit of their trust by making them believe that I was with them. Also the fact that there was very little staff at the time of the escape . . . because the truth is that the army is an incapable army. It is not a professional army. I repeat: it is an army of assassins.

3. *New York Times* correspondent Alan Riding suspects that Toj was aided in his escape by allies within the armed forces. (*Times*, December 18, 1981).

4. Apparently Toj was referring to the assault on Chupol and other towns in western Guatemala, discussed in Reading 39.—EDS.

Chapter II:

People's Revolutionary War and the Guerrilla Movement

Editors' Introduction

ALTHOUGH the term "guerrilla warfare" came into use at the time of Napoleon's invasion of Spain in the early nineteenth century, the concept and practice of irregular, partisan warfare is much older. It was used by Native Americans against the colonialists, and was one of the forms of warfare carried on by the American armed forces against the British attempt to subjugate the colonies after and even before they had declared independence. After the 1775 exchange of gunfire between Redcoats and rebels at Concord in April, British troops made their way back to Boston. Along the sixteen miles of that fateful rout "Hundreds of angry and embittered Americans . . . poured upon the British line of march."

> A mile from Concord they began to shoot at the regulars from the protection of stone walls, barns, and trees, and from both sides of the road. Soon their fire was galling; before long it was deadly; and the redcoats began to slump to the ground in numbers. . . . [M]any patriots were willing to risk almost certain death to get in a shot or two at the British. . . .[1]

This bloody route back from Concord was far from the only time in the American revolution that popular forces adopted guerrilla tactics against their enemies. British Loyalists of all kinds suffered from the violence unleashed by the revolutionary patriots who are now folk heroes in the United States (some of their

---

1. John Richard Alden, *The American Revolution, 1775-1783* (New York: Harper Torchbooks, 1954), pp. 23-24.

tactics conveniently forgotten). Popular violence did not end with the American Revolution. It arose, for example, in the battle to end slavery, and in nineteenth and twentieth century struggles for labor unions and civil rights. Possibly the most important thing about this extensive record of violence is what one perceptive historian called the North Americans' "extraordinary ability, in the face of that record, to persuade themselves that they are among the best-behaved and best-regulated of peoples." [2]

Although revolutionary war may be distant in our historical memory, it is a reality of our times. In this century people in the countryside and cities of Mexico, Russia, China, Algeria, Vietnam, Nicaragua, and El Salvador, to mention the better known examples, have organized wars against their own governments. Because the U.S. government has a history, despite its own origins in revolution, of intervening repeatedly against popular revolutions, it is imperative we understand them. The State Department offers us its view, interpreting revolutionary war as a conspiracy inspired, directed, and financed from outside the country in which it takes place; a war mandated by a distant communist government as a maneuver in an international power game. A corollary of the State Department's position is that civilian populations do not really support guerrillas, their necessary cooperation is forced through violence.

The Reagan Administration voices this interpretation when it labels guerrillas in El Salvador and Guatemala "terrorists," and then vows to help stop this terrorism. Yet the weight of evidence shows that in Guatemala, as in El Salvador, most violence, and violence in its most barbaric forms, is committed by the Guatemalan government, and in El Salvador by the Salvadoran government, both of which the State Department supports.

At the same time, tens of thousands of Guatemalans are organizing a revolutionary and necessarily violent war to take power from the current repressive government and replace it with one based on different premises (see Reading 49). As we have seen in earlier sections of this anthology, throughout the 1970s each struggle, no matter how small, almost inevitably pitted people against not only, for example, the local landlord violating traditional land rights, or the factory management denying the right to organize, but against the state itself, its military, police and paramilitary forces. By mid-1980, repression was so extreme it became obvious that any form of open or legal struggle would be suicidal. This led the Committee of Campesino Unity and other groups to form a new coalition, the January 31st Popular Front, which united popular organizations to work with guerrilla groups under the banner of revolution.

Guerrilla movements have a long history in Guatemala. In 1960 discontent among young military officers led to an uprising; the uprising failed, but its lead-

2. Richard Hofstadter, "Reflections on Violence in the United States," in Richard Hofstadter and Michael Wallace, eds., *American Violence: A Documentary History* (New York: Vintage Books, 1970), p. 6.

ers went on to join with civilian activists and the small communist Guatemalan Workers' Party (PGT) to create the Rebel Armed Forces (FAR). Impressed by the success of the Cuban Revolution in 1959 and frustrated by the reformist strategy of slowly seeking social change through the electoral system, the FAR adopted the practice of guerrilla warfare based on the *foco* model. According to this model a small armed group would establish itself as a military force in the countryside, and through confrontation with the army, awaken the rural population by setting an example of how to struggle. This strategy did not call for a strongly organized popular base; Regis Debray, a French intellectual, and at one time a leading theoretician of *foco* strategy wrote in 1967, ". . . insurrectional activity is today the number one political activity." [3] Despite its commitment to armed struggle, the FAR lacked a clear vision of how it would relate to the majority of Indians and ladinos. *Foco* theory, although calling for heroic sacrifice by vanguard revolutionaries, reproduced some of the weaknesses of earlier Guatemalan movements for change. Reformers such as Arévalo and Arbenz in the 1944-54 period envisioned a small minority of educated ladino social reformers as the motor force of social change, not the Guatemalan masses. Just as Arbenz was unable to defend his government in 1954, the FAR, similarly without a structure capable of mobilizing mass support, suffered military defeat when the government launched a counteroffensive in the mid-1960s with U.S. assistance, including Green Berets.[4] By 1968, eight thousand people had been killed in "pacification" campaigns during which villages were napalmed and sympathizers murdered.

Foco guerrilla groups were born and defeated all over Latin America in the 1960s, in Venezuela, Colombia and other countries. When Bolivian troops, also aided by the U.S. Green Berets,[5] assassinated Latin American revolutionary and leader of the Cuban revolution, Ernesto Che Guevara, as he tried to build a guerrilla force in the Bolivian mountains in late 1967, many U.S. political analysts thought revolution was finished in Latin America. But massive popular movements arose throughout Central America in the 1970s; guerrilla groups persisted and, more sophisticated politically, integrated themselves into these mass movements. In Nicaragua this process culminated in the successful overthrow of Anastasio Somoza on July 19, 1979. In Guatemala the failure of the *foco* strategy and the later experiences of mass movements of the 1970s formed the political and military education of serious men and women. The older leaders of today's guerrilla organizations are veterans of the 1960s; the younger ones of the 1970s.

Today's guerrilla organizations no longer believe a brave elite with only the

---

3. Regis Debray, "Revolution in the Revolution?" *Monthly Review* [New York], August 1967, p. 116.

4. On the involvement of Green Berets and U.S.-sponsored counterinsurgency in Guatemala in the 1960s, see Eduardo Galeano, *Guatemala, Occupied Country* (New York: Monthly Review Press, 1969), pp. 69-82; and *Guatemala* (New York: NACLA, 1974), pp. 193-202.

5. Phillip Taubman, "The Secret World of the Green Beret," *New York Times Magazine*, July 4, 1982, p. 21.

briefest contact with the people can carry out insurrection in the name of the people. Instead they support the theory of people's revolutionary war. According to this theory, the war will be a long one based on mass organization. This means the guerrillas fight in such a way as to incorporate the population into their organizations as well as ally with existing groups. They do not initially fight battles for national power, but to gain and secure the ability to organize a base among the people, village by village, plantation by plantation, factory by factory. Not until the country is organized for popular rule will there be an attempt to take power from the Guatemalan government and institute a society based on popular rule. They believe the base for a revolutionary society must precede the revolution and not be created after it when disorganized people have enormous and often contradictory demands.

Currently, these guerrilla organizations have considerable authority in Guatemala. They can fight in any part of the country. Nearly the entire population of some areas, such as the Indian provinces of Quiché and Huehuetenango (see Reading 46) are organized. The guerrillas can carry out operations ranging from small ambushes and urban sabotage to major offensives. Mass multilingual rural meetings are held in complete secrecy. Under constant attack, without a defined liberated zone, the guerrillas feed, clothe, and house ranks increasingly swelled by refugees from bombed villages.

Are these revolutionary movements the work of alien conspiratorial terrorists, as the State Department maintains? An analysis of past revolutionary wars, in Vietnam or China, or the current one in Guatemala show that the use of indiscriminate violence is anathema to the guerrilla movements. These revolutionary wars have been fought by people with few arms and little money to buy them. Mass support and mobilization are the primary conditions of success; therefore winning and maintaining popular support remains the primary objective. Their use of violence is highly selective and it is obviously not directed against the people whom they seek to win over. It is such acknowledged "enemies of the people" as wealthy landowner Luis Arenas (see Reading 43) who are executed to win political support among peasants and rural workers. A guerrilla movement's success depends on its ability to integrate itself with the population, rather than on its alien connections, as the U.S. State Department spokesmen claim.

The alien force in revolutionary war is not the guerrillas but a government from whom the majority is estranged. The determination, patience, and sacrifice revolutionary war requires could only be given by a people who see no alternative but radical change. Peasants, for example, watch their cornfields being taken by rich landowners in order to grow cardamom to sell to Mideastern elites as a flavoring for their coffee. The destitute peasants protest the loss of their patches of earth and are shot by soldiers commanded by generals who own thousands of acres. This, and not conspiracy, creates revolutionary war. It is inherent in a situation where a government resists reforms, does nothing to alleviate escalating poverty, and instead confronts its citizens with increasing violence. Unwilling to satisfy its population's demands, the government loses its legitimacy.

In this situation the guerrillas offer a way to fight the government and, more importantly, an alternative to the existing system of inequality. As María Lupe describes in Reading 45, the guerrilla movement offers a different world of human relationships between men and women and ladinos and Indians. Little by little the guerrilla movement eliminates the control of the government from the countryside and builds new collective structures within which it must fulfill its promises to the people or fall into disrepute.

In this chapter, the character of revolutionary war, sketched in this introduction, is explored through the personal narratives of people who have joined the guerrillas as well as through formal political documents from these groups.

42. *The* Foco *Experience: The Guerrillas' First Years* *

BY PABLO MONSANTO

THE *Rebel Armed Forces (FAR) is the oldest of the existing guerrilla organizations in Guatemala, created as the armed branch of the Guatemalan Workers' Party (PGT). Formed in 1962, it was based in the predominantly ladino eastern region of the country. By the end of the decade U.S.-supported counterinsurgency campaigns had totally defeated the young guerrilla force and destroyed its tenuous popular bases of support. In this interview by Chilean journalist-in-exile Marta Harnecker, Pablo Monsanto, current Commander-in-Chief and long-time veteran of the FAR, recounts the bitter experiences of the FAR's first years, experiences which have had a great impact on the later development of the entire revolutionary movement. At that time, influenced by* foco *theory, the FAR's leadership, according to Monsanto, thought that "the guerrillas would be the center from which the general development of all revolutionary organization would emanate. And the masses would spontaneously join [the revolution], stimulated by guerrilla action." The defeat of that early guerrilla movement, concludes Monsanto, "was a political defeat, not a military one."*

. . . DURING THE FIRST nine months we spent our time exploring the terrain and seeking contacts with the population. These were very trying and difficult tasks.

The guerrillas' first attack was that of Río Hondo. Its purpose was to initiate hostilities and announce itself publicly. The action was carried out June 30, 1964

* Excerpted from Marta Harnecker, "De las Armas a las Masas para Ganar la Guerra," *Punto Final Internacional* [Mexico City], año IX, no. 199, January 1982, by permission. Translated by Jonathan Fried.

(Day of the Army). The second attack took place in Panzós, in October of the same year. . . .

After the Panzós action [1] . . . the reactionary army launched its first offensive against us. They reached our encampment, and a confrontation ensued. The guerrillas withdrew in disarray, leaving behind all the armament recovered in Panzós.

After a year of being in the mountains, only five of the original twenty-one guerrillas remained. We had engaged in two successful battles and had one defeat. We became acquainted with the mountain region and learned our way around it. We established our first contacts with the population. The presence of the guerrillas in the region was made known, but the people didn't join us. In that first year, only two people joined, one of whom deserted, and the other died. . . .

I should add that the base of support that we managed to organize in the Zacapa region was possible because of the work of the Guatemalan Workers' Party (PGT) years before. In this zone, in Zacapa and Izabal, where banana workers' unions existed, the PGT had done political work. Alone the guerrillas wouldn't have been able to form this social base of support. For this reason, the Río Hondo organization was the most developed. . . .

But there was no conception of war, there was no political work with the masses to prepare them for war. The idea existed that the guerrillas were going to defeat the army, but how, no one knew. We also had a faulty conception of guerrilla warfare. The lessons of the Cuban experience—to "bite" and to "run"—were poorly applied. I said to the compañeros that we hardly ever bit and were running almost all the time. . . . Even so, it must be recognized that politically we succeeded in awakening a feeling of uneasiness and sympathy toward the guerrilla movement in all the people of Guatemala.

Through all our political work we managed to acquire a knowledge of the terrain, particularly the plains, and to broaden the guerrillas' bases in all of the province of Zacapa, part of El Progreso, extending the regional organization to Chiquimula, Jalapa and Jutiapa. We opened a school, trained some seven hundred campesinos and were waiting for the possibility of recovering or buying arms to be able to form a much larger military force. . . .

At this time there were over thirty members of the guerrillas, most of them from the city, only five from the region; this, after three years of work there. But we were able to form irregular, nonpermanent guerrillas in some villages around Río Hondo. . . .

Both the guerrilla groups of César [2] and Camilo [3] were wiped out when we fell into the political trap that imperialism and the oligarchy set for us. They con-

1. This guerrilla action should not be confused with the 1978 Panzós massacre described in Reading 33.—EDS.

2. Guerrilla leader César Montes—EDS.

3. Guerrilla leader Camilo Sánchez—EDS.

vinced us to participate in the 1966 electoral campaign supporting Julio César Méndez Montenegro. We carried out "armed propaganda,"[4] and in the propaganda we included the slogan "Vote for Julio César Méndez Montenegro." . . .

Julio César won the elections. The government acted with great intelligence. First it called on the armed movement to lay down its arms and rejoin civil activity, in peace. They announced they would carry out a progressive program of government, including an agrarian reform, permit popular organizing, campesino and workers' organizations, etc. And a general amnesty for all political prisoners and guerrillas was declared. The condition was for us to hand in our arms. What was the position that the revolutionary leadership took at that moment? We refused to hand in our arms, arguing that these were needed because of the threat of a coup d'etat. But we committed ourselves to not attacking the army as long as they didn't attack us.

At the same time, the organization opened up . . . everyone participated openly in the mass organizations, everyone knew who the leaders were, who helped the guerrillas, who the guerrillas were. Everyone knew everyone else.

Precisely at that time the "Mano Blanca" [White Hand] appeared in Zacapa. They began in Gualán. They painted a white hand on the door of the houses of all the compañeros they had discovered during this time. This was the signal, and a few days later the compañeros would appear dead, captured and assassinated. Bodies began to appear, tortured, killed.

Our analysis followed from the thesis that if Julio César [Méndez Montenegro] applied his program there would be a coup d'etat, and that would radicalize the struggle, and allow us to regain the initiative, strengthening the revolutionary movement anew.

What happened was very different. On October 2, the same day that Turcios died,[5] at six P.M., the army launched an operation in the mountains, but of a different character than the previous ones. They knew we weren't going to be in the mountains, so they occupied towns, gathered the people, and talked to them.

This is how the people began to organize in militias to fight the guerrillas.[6] They captured compañeros and some of our guerrilla colleagues were lynched in the Río Hondo marketplace by the same people who had been organized by us and who had collaborated with us for such a long time.

After having gained a force of over sixty men, by the end of 1966 or beginning of 1967 we were once again a very small group of guerrillas in the mountains—only six. After four years we had, in fact, returned to our starting point.

At the Third Conference of the FAR in 1971 we analyzed the situation in which the revolutionary movement found itself. . . . We concluded that we

4. Armed propaganda is a term used to describe the military occupation of villages and farms by guerrilla forces to give political talks and messages to the local population.—EDS.

5. Luis Augusto Turcios Lima, top leader of the FAR, killed in an automobile accident—EDS.

6. A similar concept of counterinsurgency is being implemented by the Ríos Montt government—EDS.

couldn't reorganize ourselves nor develop if we continued to be estranged from the masses. . . . Also, we concluded that instead of creating a centralized guerrilla column, we needed to generalize clandestine political work throughout the country with the purpose of generalizing guerrilla warfare. Our thesis, from the experience we had lived through, was that guerrilla warfare as a method of fighting, as a method of military action, could be applied on any terrain, that neither mountains nor jungle were necessary to have guerrillas. What was basic and fundamental was to have an organized populace. . . .

43. *The Tiger of Ixcán* *

BY MARIO PAYERAS

LOS Días de la Selva (Days in the Jungle), *is a beautifully written and frank description of the Guerrilla Army of the Poor's (EGP) first years of existence in the northern jungle and mountains of Guatemala's Quiché province. Written by Mario Payeras, a member of the EGP, the book won Cuba's Casa de las Americas prize for narrative literature in 1980. The chapter excerpted below describes the EGP's first public act, its "opening shot of the popular war," the execution of an infamous landlord known as the "Tiger of Ixcán" in 1975. With the exception of the following chapter,* Los Días de la Selva *has not been published in English.*

IN THE SPRING of 1975, the various guerrilla groups concentrated in the jungle. By then the organization had spread throughout the mountains over an area of more than seven hundred eighty square miles. The original detachment, in the classic image of the cells of a beehive, had multiplied, transforming itself into two or three nuclei, dispersed and armed. However, these groups had no true cohesion nor battle experience. During the twenty-six months that the "implantation" phase had lasted, the first detail had only taken one shot at the enemy. Nevertheless at that time there were almost fifty men under arms. A constant stream of campesinos flowed toward our local cells, bringing with them their ancient burden of injustices. In great part the campesinos' sense of urgency was also the result of our efforts. There was strong popular pressure for action, but in our talks with people we also stressed the probability of imminent combat. Of course, the number of men willing to fight far surpassed the number of weapons,

* From Mario Payeras, *Los Días de la Selva* (Havana, Cuba: Casa de las Americas, 1980) "The Tiger of Ixcán" was translated by Lita Paniagua, Deborah Levenson, and Raimundo Mora.

including hunting equipment. But, spreading so rapidly, the organization had lost in quality. The existence of the guerrillas was a secret shared by thousands. And so much preparation and bustle had not gone unnoticed by the enemy. From one moment to the next we expected the first offensive against our guerrilla territory. However, we knew we were building on sand. It is not possible to continue constructing in an atmosphere of peace, an organization planned for war. Lack of military action weakened us at a national level. The organization of the city, despite its initial success, had not prospered, re-running over and over the same paths, unable to find the road that led to the popular masses. On the southern coast, the work of implantation had barely begun, despite many attempts to raise clandestine structures. How to emerge from that labyrinth of contradictions was the theme of discussion throughout the country during the month of March. From our own debates in the jungle came the first campaign plan for the highlands. Its central aim—which was to be duplicated by our other organizations in the rest of the country—was to engage in limited military activity in such a way that the enemy's reaction would not go beyond what the people could understand, nor overwhelm our own local capacity for defense. The wind we were to set loose should not be so strong as to leave without flower the tree of life. Our military forces were not, therefore, to act as a single unit, but to break up into three groups and start with armed propaganda actions. In this way the organization would enter a new phase of development and we would be able to measure the adversary's capacity for response. The guerrillas then split up into three columns and each was assigned a zone of operations. Those of us who left for the highlands had the task of punishing one of the most detested landowners in the country: Luis Arenas Barrera, better known as the Tiger of Ixcán.

The Ixcán jungle is famous for its spotted tigers. Animals of extraordinary beauty and great ferocity, the tigers are only occasionally seen, although the campesinos of the area frequently suffer the effects of their incursions. On all the sandbanks of the great rivers, the wild beast's footprints signals its close presence. Its strength and ability are legendary. In Ixcán one hears many tales narrating this jungle creature's feats of prowess. A pig is its favorite food, and it is said that the big spotted wild beast once carried off an adult male hog weighing two hundred pounds, jumping over the pigpen fence. A great hunter, the tiger's careful control of its movements reaches perfection. . . . It stole a number of dogs from the house of one of our companions, making several silent trips without the loss being noticed until the following day. The tiger's mating season starts in December. When the hunter sounds the mating call on a special horn, he immediately hears the male's roar on the horizon, responding to what it thinks is the cry of the female. A few moments later the sound of breaking branches indicates the tiger is near. It seems that when the male responds to the female's love call, it loses its sense of vigilance. The courageous wife of a campesino faced the animal alone one night in an enclosed space. Having heard suspicious sounds in the palm hut where the hogs are kept, she took a lamp and went toward the shack. Alerted by the noise of her movements the tiger hid in the loft seconds before the women entered. It remained couched in the dark, but the lights of its eyes denounced it. Recognizing the dangerous unmistakable brilliance of those pupils, the woman left immediately, shut the door behind her and went for the rifle of her absent husband. Rapidly retracing her steps, she entered the enclosure, and with one well aimed shot killed the wild beast. In the immobility of death, away from its natural ambiance, the tiger's body resembled the abandoned costume of some evil jungle spirit. Its jaws, dead, stunk of spoilage. For his cruelty and lack of compassion, this tiger's name was given by the Guatemalan campesinos to the landlord whom we were to punish.

Luis Arenas had a plantation he frequently visited at the mouth of the Xaclbal River in the highlands where this flowing water separates the central massif of the Cuchumatanes Mountains from the wooded ranges of northern Quiché. His fame began in the days of the North American intervention in 1954 when he acquired his lands with the help of the new government. The San Luis Ixcán plantation, his property, had been built with evil, utilizing the forced labor of Indians from the cold highlands. Entire contingents of workers, recruited with false promises and pretexts, were brought down to clear the jungle where there were yet no roads. Many of the men were transported in military helicopters and left to their fate for months in the middle of the jungle. Some tried to escape into the wild mountains, struggling to survive for weeks with neither food nor weapons in a vast expanse of virgin forest, but most perished in the attempt. On the La Perla plantation, men who were paying off hereditary debts formed the better part of the work force. Arenas gave an advance on the Indians' small coffee harvests and later collected in kind, adding usurious interest to the original loan. Coffee sacks were taken to the large towns by mule teams headed by his henchmen on horseback, who, wielding guns and whips, made way for the caravan. This feudal lord's name was linked to all kinds of land seizures and crimes. On some of his plantations he used special cages to punish rebellious Indians.

In the last week of April we set off for the landlord's domains. Our plan was to approach his land secretly in such a way that he would not be alerted and flee. The success of this operation would allow us to initiate military action in the mountains and practically throughout the country. Most of the members of our column were temporary recruits, with no military experience and poor weapons. Their intention was to gain both. Nevertheless they had no real idea of what this would cost them. The small tests along our way showed up the weaknesses of their convictions and how much political groundwork there was still left for us to do in the local cells. After only three days' march the men began to get demoralized. We were in the midst of the dry season and there was no water to be found. The day before, trying to assuage their thirst, many had eaten the raw flowers of a shrub palm and suffered from stomach cramps. Our destination was still several days' march away over arid and uninhabited mountains. On the afternoon when the first signs of insubordination occurred, we decided to go out into the villages, buy supplies, and shorten the march by advancing at night along the main roads. That was the only way of preventing a crisis without giving up our objective. It didn't take long for our hopes to fade. There was no water in the villages. The only well in the area was several hours away and it was used by pigs. That night on the main road we covered a distance that would have taken several days through the mountains. At midnight, exhausted, obsessed by thirst, we had to be satisfied with a puddle where animals drank. On removing the crust of slime we found a thick liquid which many of the men guzzled to the extent of bursting. By dawn, the veterans were carrying the weapons of the entire group. The recuits were tired to the point of giving up and refused to continue marching. Our limit of safety for walking along the highway was five A.M. when the early risers began to appear. Daylight surprised us still on the open ground, a few minutes from the mountains. We had to spend the day just a few steps from the road, crouched in the stubble and weeds, listening to the voices of the passersby. At night we moved on to the only spring in the zone, in the woods, where we set up camp for several days.

The war ended there for the group of recruits. Two or three days later each found different reasons for having to return to his village. Since none of them knew our plans, we let them go. We parted on good terms, keeping in mind the law of the jungle regarding the rhythm of war and the seasons, although at that moment their attitude left us profoundly disillusioned. Later we understood that if they had no idea of what that first battle signified, we too were very far from comprehending the war in all its complexity. For the bee to produce honey, it is necessary for it to carefully select pollen and patiently build the wax labyrinths wherein it will rest, awaiting the great moment of transformation. We were the bees, and the war, honey; but the honeycomb was the organization. Meanwhile our camp was a splendid arsenal of .22-caliber rifles and single barrel shotguns, weapons which we buried in hope of better days. Our brand new column was reduced then to eight stalwarts, somewhat undone by the malaria we had brought with us from the hot country. Because of a last minute mistake, our antimalaria medicine was in the backpack of one of the men who was no longer a member of our team. Under these circumstances the tasks of the healthy were heavily multiplied. In order to bring to our camp the only vial of quinine to be found in the area's communities, two of the best Ixil walkers covered sixty-five miles in three days. After a month of such vicissitudes, the guerrillas of the mountain were a band of skeletons, chasing during daylight hours after the few rays of sunlight that filtered through the thick foliage. Around that time the rains and thunder began.

The final days passed in explorıng the zone and gathering information for the execution. Conscious of his atrocities and knowing that there were guerrillas in the jungle, Arenas always moved with extreme precautions. He followed no set schedule or itinerary. Sometimes he flew to his plantation; at other times he arrived on horseback without previous warning and by different routes. Even his physical description varied according to the fear or the imagination of those describing him. The area of La Perla, where he lived, was a fortress. It was on a cliff and impossible to reach without being seen. It was protected on the west by the deforested slopes of the Cuchumatanes foothills. It communicated with the outside by radio. In view of all this we decided to watch for Arenas on the highway, dressed in civilian clothes and using light arms. As we had only three pistols, we sent messengers to the nearest base, two days away, to get more appropriate weapons. Several days later our couriers returned with a memorable arsenal: three rusty, broken-down artifacts, among which was one the Indians called a "harquebus," not the long weapon used by the Spanish Conquerors, but rather a kind of sword.

Never will the sketchy maps we used for our operation be equalled in the annals of war. The mapmakers had just learned to write and were still not accustomed to the pencil's art. Similar to those ancient explorers' maps, these contained in their tight complexity all the natural accidents and descriptions of sites and customs, a fat-cheeked sun in the west and a fanciful rose of the winds. Furthermore, they could be read backward or forward because they had the same perspective as children's drawings. Nevertheless, they were sufficient for tracing the routes for approach and retreat. After a failed ambush on the road, we decided to surprise our quarry in his own fortress. June 7 was payday, which facilitated our getting near the offices, given the crowd of workers waiting for their money. Standing in front of his administrator, with his look of a bird of prey and Spanish gentleman's mustache, the lord of the land piled up coins and unfolded rumpled bills. When he was told to put his hands up and surrender, he fixed his eyes for an instant on those who surrounded him as he instinctively reached for his pistol. A series of shots killed him at the very instant he pressed the trigger of the gun he held close to his belly. Without believing it, even though it had just happened, the workers, anxious, listened to the explanation immediately given them in their own Indian language by one of the guerrillas. But as he recalled a history of injustices, outrages, evictions, and crimes, assenting voices arose from the crowd and interrupted the speaker, adding reasons why this exploiter of another's labor deserved such a punishment. At the end, a deep ancestral clamor rose out of those throats, accustomed from the time of the arrival of the Spaniards to silence and moans. With great shouts they acclaimed the poor would live and the rich die. The guerrillas did not touch one cent of the money scattered on the table and the floor. From that moment it was said throughout the region that the men from the mountains were not strangers because they spoke the dialect of the region; neither were they thieves because they had not touched the money; and that surely they had come to make justice, because they had exemplarily punished the man who enriched himself with the sweat and the blood of all the needy. Two days of marimba music in the neighboring village of Ilom was the best testimony of the popular joy over the event. Later, when we visited the isolated dwellings of Indians, many of them, mostly the old people, would take our hands and look long into our eyes in a sign of gratitude and acknowledgment.

The news of the Tiger of Ixcán's death at the hands of Indian guerrillas rapidly spread by word of mouth through the mountains. The first shots of the popular war had been fired. The next day the sky thundered with the sound of helicopters and military planes. During the following months the enemy unleashed the largest antiguerrilla operation that had taken place in the country up to that time. Hundreds of soldiers were parachuted from old C-47 planes onto Ixcán's small landholdings, and columns advanced by land from different military bases, occupying key points in the jungle. They had only been waiting for the first shot to fling themselves across the mountains after us. They set up permanent posts in the main towns, and from there, troops trained for jungle warfare combed the mountains. For three months they blocked roads and searched villages, capturing all those who seemed suspicious or whose names appeared on their intelligence lists. The entire guerrilla territory was strategically circled. After the action at La Perla, our patrol retreated with no problems to a distant zone. From that time we cut off communications with the guerrillas in the lowlands. Troops covered the roads like columns of ants, and we learned what was happening in the jungle only through some radio broadcasts and the military helicopters' distant hum.

44. Eight Years of Silent Organizing *

By the Organization of the People in Arms

THE veterans of the guerrilla movement of the 1960s seem to agree that their defeat was in large degree a result of their isolation from the Guatemalan people. The organizations that emerged in the 1970s from that initial guerrilla experience, however, chose different paths to address the revolutionary movement's shortcomings. The FAR demobilized most of their guerrilla force to concentrate on union organizing, both among urban and agricultural workers, albeit not allowing their presence be known to the government. In the latter half of the 1970s, the EGP also became involved in urban unions, and played an important role in organizing the Committee of Campesino Unity (CUC). At the same time they continued their rural guerrilla activity, principally in the country's northwestern mountains. The Organization of the People in Arms (ORPA), in contrast, spent the first eight years of its existence in complete secrecy, without firing

* From the Organization of the People in Arms, "Historia de ORPA," in *Tercer Aniversario de Operaciones*, September 1982. Translated by Jonathan Fried.

a shot. Beginning in 1971, they quietly organized a political base in the west-central mountains, primarily among Indian campesinos, and an urban infrastructure, in preparation for future guerrilla activity. Not until September 18, 1979—with the occupation of the Mujuliá farm in the coffee-growing region of the Quezaltenango province to hold a political education meeting with the workers—did ORPA *publicly reveal its existence. Following are excerpts from* ORPA's *own story of its first, silent years.*

IN THE ENTIRE western zone there was a certain intuition about the need for armed struggle. The response to our work was immediate, quickly producing a large degree of identification with our ideas. Particularly well received were those ideas concerning the indigenous people joining our struggle, a people whose revolutionary potential was soon confirmed by our experiences.

> Such was the interest, that we had meetings with 50-100 people on different farms. We met in discreet places, at night. These meetings became real assemblies, large concentrations of people. This was one of the things that made us most enthusiastic: to see how well our statements about the need for war and the participation of the people in it were received. In these meetings they brought us food, drinks, all kinds of things. . . . We came down from our encampment in the mountains to go to these meetings every day. . . . They were long walks in the midst of a severe rainy season.[1]

The new organization emerged with a small group of combatants, two of whom were so sick they could hardly move. For all practical purposes we had no medicines to treat them, we were in the middle of an enemy siege and without material resources.

> In reality, our options for taking the initiative were reduced to the capacity of our legs to walk and our stomachs to bear hunger. Plainly speaking, these were the Organization's limits.[2]

With this christening, the Organization made ready to initiate the long stage of preparation. . . .

Beginning in June 1971, the first task we set out to accomplish in the Guerrilla Front was a double one: the formation of campesino organizers, and political education and organization among the population to create a campesino social base. For a long time this work had to be done verbally, given the illiteracy in the region. Courses were given on political and historical themes, and dealing with elements and criteria for organizing. A short time afterward we could also use our

1. ORPA, Internal Document.
2. *Ibid.*

first written materials, "Principles and Objectives" (May 1971) and "Organization" (December 1971).

All this was being carried out amidst the enormous problems of a new organization. The compañeros among us who were better prepared were overloaded with responsibilities. Sometimes a course of action had to be suspended so we could leave an area, and had to be reinitiated at a later date. There was a tremendous lack of all sorts of resources. . . .

From mid-1972 to mid-1975, the economic situation was a constant nightmare for the guerrillas. Our need was so extreme that literally survival was often our strategic objective:

> For long periods we had to eat wild plants to survive. We spent whole weeks eating only *cicil, quixtán, hierba mora,* boiled with a little salt. Often, after a 10 or 12 hour march, our supper was a hot chili pepper. When we obtained 3 or 4 green plantains—we didn't even hope to get ripe ones—it was reason to celebrate.
>
> When someone complained of hunger, we told him it was psychological—maybe for 3 or 4 days we hadn't eaten well. Not infrequently we fainted.
>
> Concerning our health, we ran the risk of complications from diarrhea or intestinal infections. Several of us nearly died from amoebiasis that sometimes lasted as long as 15 days. . . .
>
> We carried our misery from place to place. But at the same time we communicated our determination and enthusiasm without which it would have been impossible to work organizing among the population. Neither would the people have made all the efforts and sacrifices they did to support us.[3]

. . . At certain times some of our methods seemed to stamp our work with a quality of slowness; for example, the care taken in selecting militants, the exigencies of educating organizers, the meticulousness of our operations, the preparedness required of those who assumed given responsibilities, the need sometimes to defer promising work due to not having people capable of taking it on, the criteria of relying on our own forces. Nevertheless, experience has shown that in reality all these elements have turned into factors that have speeded up our development, that has allowed us to achieve greater development in the subsequent stages. . . .

Our idea was to develop a broad clandestine organization before initiating military operations, and avoiding enemy attacks in this phase; the laws of counterinsurgency indicate that this is the best time to wipe out a guerrilla force. During all this time, in addition, our Organization developed a lot of revolutionary activity of a formative and organizational type. The viability of forming a

---

3. *Ibid.*

campesino and indigenous guerrilla force—a point of hot discussion at that time—was also demonstrated.

Another interesting aspect was how the Organization's existence was kept secret during all this time. This, besides being a method of work, without a doubt has to do with the sympathy with which the people received the Organization's ideas. We didn't have to insist they guard the secret. In all the years we met people who were not organized, no one ever informed on us. It should be taken into account that discretion is one of the cultural characteristics of the indigenous people.

> Although it could be a bit adventurous to make such affirmations, I believe that this [Indian people's discretion] has to do with historical expectations that have been kept alive among the indigenous people through oral tradition. Our surprise began at the end of 1971, in the mountains and villages, upon finding stories and expressions that have been kept alive and even have acquired another level of meaning; stories relating to the grandfather of a grandfather having said that some day some men would come down from the mountains to liberate the people. Just as surprising, I've heard this story in one form or another in the Mam, Cakchiquel and Tzutuíl regions. I believe it should be interpreted as an element of tradition, of memory and of hope of a people that have been subjected to colonization and who create their legends and expectations to endure their situation.[4]

[Due to lack of space we omit the next section of the document about the formation of ORPA's Urban Front, work which began at the end of 1972 among students and the university community, and "soon extended to other sectors: workers, middle sectors, professionals and intellectuals . . ."—EDS.]

The development of our work was consolidated in the course of eight years. On September 18, 1979, the preparational stage ended. The public emergence of our Organization marked the initiation of the stage of operations: a new phase with obstacles to overcome and expectations to realize.

4. Commander Gaspar Ilom, ORPA, Internal Document.

45. *Up In the Mountains Everything Is Different: Perspective of a Subsistence Agriculturalist* *

By Maria Lupe

When the government of Julio Méndez Montenegro initiated a limited land reform in 1966, María Lupe, a ladina woman, was one of many ladino and Indian subsistence agriculturists who migrated to the region of Ixcán to colonize, without land title, a desolate region. María Lupe relates how her experiences searching for a way to make a living led her to join the Guerrilla Army of the Poor (EGP) in 1975, at about the same time the "Tiger of Ixcán" was assassinated (see Reading 43). She speaks of the special position of women and children in the popular war and how guerrilla struggle affects the family.

BEFORE, MY HUSBAND and I were very poor. We worked for the rich, on a plantation. I took care of the workers, cooking and cleaning from one in the morning until ten at night. There was not any electricity so everything was done by hand. My husband earned fifty cents a day, I only got food. Later we got a little shack and rented some land, but things went badly and we were always in debt.

Twelve years ago we decided to see if they would give us some land in the North, in Ixcán, but there things were harder. There was nothing there, the only store was a four days' walk away. We spent four months eating only tortillas and *atol* [a drink made from corn—EDS.]; a child there died of malnutrition. I was pregnant with my third daughter, I had malaria during the pregnancy and was undernourished. She was born at seven months, very very tiny and I almost lost her. Then the government engineers came and they gave us a little plot of land. During this time more people arrived and things got a little better. People came from all over, from the coast, from the east, from the mountains, from all over.

After two years, the first members of the Guerrilla Army of the Poor (EGP) arrived. I remember just when it was because we did not even have corn then. I was scared, because I did not know anything about them and a government official had told us the guerrillas just came to rob and rape our daughters. Even one of the young men, who is now a guerrilla, was frightened; he ran and hid our radio.

The guerrillas helped everyone build a house. This was the first time we worked collectively. Later they explained to us that they were poor people too, fighting so

---

* From *Compañero,* [Guatemala City: 1982] No. 5, pp. 27-30. Translated by Deborah Levenson.

that the poor could live a better life, and they said the poor were going to win. How are they going to win, I thought, when all the towns are so far apart? But now I see how the struggle has developed all over the country.

We were one of the first families that started to work with the guerrillas. I liked to raise pigs and chickens, and I sold them at a fair price to the compañeros—that's what we call the guerrillas—and even gave them some on the side. Later we gave them information and did shopping for them. Some people took advantage of them and sold them things at high prices, but when these people realized what the compañeros were doing, they stopped taking advantage of them and started to collaborate.

All the families collaborated, although at times we could only speak to the woman in the family, or only to the man, and then later they had to convince their spouse; sometimes they could not agree. Many times the men who were collaborating did not want their wives working with other men in the group, because they were jealous. So we arranged for women to work with women instead. We women organized food supplies; everyone brought food to my house and then we took it up into the mountains where the compañeros were training.

After a year spies appeared and then the army put a military commissioner in the town. There was a lack of secrecy, so everyone knew who worked with the guerrillas, especially the ones who had been the first. My husband and my oldest daughter of twelve went to train in the mountains, and there my daughter learned to read and write. They stayed there three months and then returned, but after a month they had to go back to the mountains for good because the army was pursuing them. This was at the time when Luis Arenas was executed, a very repressive landowner known as the "Tiger of Ixcán." This made the Organization public and that is when the repression really started.

I remained alone with my six children. I had once said that I could not work in the fields, but there I was planting everything. As I was already aware politically, I continued collaborating with the guerrillas. Information and food was obtained from people in the entire area. It was a rare individual who did not know of the compañeros. As people lived far from one another, we began to support one another, working collectively among twenty families or so, forming a network.

Those of us who were organized were given classes, the men and the women separately. A compañera spoke with us. We talked about discrimination against women, about why we had not been able to mix and work with men, about the lack of trust they had in us. We experienced discrimination within marriage in addition to the exploitation of the rich; husbands who say we can only be in the home, that we can not do certain things, and generally, women, not being conscious of anything else, of any other way of life, thought this was natural.

The first thing we tried to change was wife beating. It was a lot of work to change this. While we women were discussing this, the compañeros were explaining to the men that a woman is not a slave and should not be beaten. And we accomplished this, it no longer happens. It was also necessary to struggle so that men would allow women to do political work. Sometimes it was necessary, for example, for a woman to go out at night and her husband would not let her. The men came to understand that this was because they lacked confidence in women. My husband and I never had problems with this.

Other things were even harder to change. For example, among ladino agriculturalists like ourselves we marry at fifteen years of age and older, but it is freely arranged. Among the Indian population, it is different. Some Indians who lived nearby and were also collaborators and compañeros came and made an offer for my twelve-year-old daughter. We told them this was not our custom, and that if the girl consented, okay, but if not, no. They accused us of discriminating against them because they were Indians. We discussed this with the compañeros from the Organization, and they spoke with the Indians later, but you can not change customs easily. Finally the young man proposed to another girl, an Indian. They remained angry at us. Later the young man joined the guerrillas, and our two families worked together, but it is difficult to change these things. For the Indian woman it is very difficult because the life she has had is so hard. Sometimes when the compañeros come, at first the Indian women hide and if you can not speak their language, you can not communicate with them. . . .

I was the first woman to join the guerrillas, because the army pursued me; they came to take me away. I left the children with another woman, but she could not take good care of them. I had to come down from the mountains into the village, where the army knew me and was looking for me, and take my children away with me. We did this like a military operation, and we went back to the mountains with the children. We lived for months in the guerrilla encampment; sometimes I was alone there with the children, only the monkeys saw us.

Later, for safety, I left the encampment and went to live in a different town, but I lost contact with the Guerrilla Army of the Poor. I had little money and no one from the organization contacted me. So the children and I started to work, washing other people's clothes and selling tortillas. My oldest daughter took care of other people's children to earn something. How we survived I do not know! For five months we lived that way, with me telling everyone my husband had left us, that he was a good-for-nothing and they believed me—the first thing you learn how to do is to put on an act, isn't that the truth?

When I went back to the guerrilla encampment they were already doing everything: training, studying, going out to the villages to talk to people, shopping. If only the men went to the villages to buy supplies, people did not trust them, but if women also went, the villagers saw that women were participating too, and carried weapons as the men did. We gave talks to the people, about simple things, comparing an organization's growth to the growth of corn. We women talked to the women, and the men to the men.

We struggled against discrimination. When the men in the EGP arrived at a house, they always helped in the kitchen; it was very strange to women that men would do this, but little by little it was explained that both men and women could do everything. I helped in the fields, planting and harvesting; I explained to people that I had not done this work before, but that out of necessity I had learned, so that they could see that women too could work in the fields. Whenever we guerrillas arrived at a place, we always helped with everything.

In the encampment we had people from different places—from the mountains and from the jungle. At that time, there were few women, maybe four, but today there are many more. . . .

Up in the mountains everything is different; it is more collective. We organized care for the five children—the youngest was three, the oldest twelve—among all the compañeros. The oldest had already helped with the work and had participated in the meetings. They came to the training sessions with their rifles made of sticks, that is what they played with. They all learned to read there. . . .

Many say that it is bad to talk in front of the children. But children understand what is explained to them. We told them they could not talk loudly because of the army's proximity. From the time they are little they can learn to be disciplined. We explained to them that our struggle is for all the poor people, that other children remained behind without their parents and that after victory we would all be together. . . . And they understand; one day my six year old came to tell me that a spy, whom none of us had seen, and who had come to kill a compañera, was around.

In public, in the villages, the children get food, information, and guard the secret of the Organization. From the time they are twelve they can join the guerrillas. . . . You realize, in the countryside, among the campesinos, children work equally with adults from the time they are eight. . . . In general children did not join the EGP at first because it was not so necessary, there was not so much repression nor such a need for self-defense. When the repression set in many more joined. . . .

Now I have a grandson who is already one year old. My daughter and her husband are with the guerrillas. Her husband did not see his son until he was eight months old. I have three children in the guerrillas, one is sixteen, one twenty and one twenty-two. Another daughter is now twelve and she wants to join, she says she wants to be free and have something with which to defend herself. . . .

46. The People Become Guerrillas *

THE small guerrilla nuclei of the mid-1970s had become massive organizations with strong internal structures by late 1981. The Guerrilla Army of the Poor (EGP), for example, is divided into different regional fronts. The group

* From *Noticias de Guatemala* [Guatemala City], October 20, 1981. Translated by Jonathan Fried.

called the Commander Ernesto Guevara Guerrilla Front (FGCEG) operates in the mountain area of Huehuetenango province. Huehuetenango's majority Indian population lives scattered in villages often isolated from one another, and speaks diverse languages. This interview with a member of the FGCEG appeared in Noticias de Guatemala, *a magazine formerly published in Guatemala and now published abroad and distributed clandestinely in the country. For lack of space we omit a section of the interview which discusses the way the language problem has been confronted, by having locally recruited people organize in their home area and using Spanish as the lingua franca among Indian groups. In the excerpt below, an FGCEG leader describes the way the population has integrated itself with the guerrillas in an area nominally under government control.*

Q. WHAT IS THE RELATIONSHIP between the population and the guerrillas?

A: An elderly Indian man once said to us: "The enemy says that the guerrillas are in the mountains, so they are with us because we are the mountains. . . ."

In the FGCEG, as in our other rural fronts, the population has organized directly with us. This does not mean that all the people are guerrillas in the military sense of the term, but that they are organized to support the revolutionary armed struggle. Our base of support is organized and structured in two principal senses: military and paramilitary tasks, and production. A local military force is organized in each location. Generally it is made up of young men and women who undergo military training in their home village. Their role is self-defense of the population: guard duty to detect enemy presence, laying ambushes of harassment with "popular arms" and explosives, capturing unknown persons suspected of being enemy agents. They also act as messengers to guarantee communication between villages and with guerrilla units, and they carry supplies for the guerrillas. The hope of many is to join the guerrilla movement as permanent forces, but in many cases this has not been possible for lack of arms.

Another important task of the population is production and contribution of everything the guerrillas need to be able to dedicate themselves to combating the enemy. To feed the guerrillas they contribute a portion of their corn harvest, beans, potatoes, and the few other fruits and vegetables that are grown in the mountains. There is an increasing expansion of collective forms of production for the organization, that is, production on lands lent by their owners to plant and harvest for the guerrillas and where the work is voluntary and collective, for the revolution. Despite the fact that the population of this front is among the poorest in the country, their monetary contribution, cent by cent, is very great.

The organized population also wages its struggles as masses against local enemy power: logging enterprises which are stripping the hills bare, mining enterprises which remove the wealth of the soil without contributing to local development, and when necessary, against the army. They have also struggled within their communities to eliminate the bars and moonshine stills; already in many organized villages, liquor, which has caused such ravages among the Indian peoples, has practically disappeared.

Q: You speak of "local enemy power." Are you referring to the presence of the government and its military and security forces?

A: Yes, that is what we are referring to. But in vast regions of the front local power already is in great measure revolutionary power. It is this way because there is not direct economic power of the very rich, no large farms or plantations. The scant organization of the traditional and progovernment political parties now only exists on their membership lists. In these regions local political power was always weak, and now it is nonexistent. Concerning military power many local military commissioners have been neutralized or driven away, and there are no longer spies or informants.

In other words, in many regions the oppressive traditional structures of enemy control and domination have disappeared.

We say that in many places local power is already revolutionary power because all decisions pertaining to community life, legal land disputes, control and punishment of delinquency, marriages, deaths, and so on, are made by the local or the front's revolutionary structures. And all effort and work of the population beyond what is necessary for subsistence is developed as a function of the revolution. Nevertheless, these regions are still not liberated zones, because the enemy still makes incursions into them.

47. *The Indian People and the Guatemalan Revolution* *

BY THE GUERRILLA ARMY OF THE POOR

INSEPARABLE from the development of popular revolutionary war has been a reconsideration of the role of Indians in the revolution. Guatemalan intellectuals debated "the Indian question" in the 1960s and 70s. Traditional leftists understood the division in Guatemalan society as only a class one. They analyzed Indian culture as an impoverished culture of poverty, a consequence of the Conquest and colonialism, which, in its religiosity and localism, bound the Indians to a kind of real inferiority and narrowness.[1] *According to this view, the Indians as rural workers had revolutionary potential, but their culture was a negative force. On the other side of the spectrum, some argued that Indian culture was an ideal one with roots in a golden precolonial past. This perspective defined class divisions as secondary and ethnic ones as primary.*[2]

---

* From *Compañero* [Guatemala City], no. 5, 1982, pp. 11-20.

1. Severo Martínez Peláez, *La Patria del Criollo* (San José, Costa Rica: Editorial Universitaria Centroamericana, 1979), pp. 34-35; 594-616.

2. Antonio Pop Caal, "Replica del Indio a Una Disertación Ladina," *La Semana* (Guatemala, March 1973).

Discussion and experience have moved the debate to new and more sophisticated ground. Indians have generated and joined mass movements not only to defend their class interests but their cultural rights as well. Today's left-wing organizations do not identify the oppression of Indians as simply class exploitation or strictly ethnic discrimination and no left organization condemns Indian culture as monolithically conservative or romanticizes it as being ideal.

Barely the first words on Indians and the meaning of Indian culture have been written. It is clear, however, that for the first time in Guatemalan history several important things are taking place. In the first place, Indians are joining guerrilla groups in large numbers; in some they comprise a majority. Secondly, as a result, Indians who have never been united as a group are coming together across linguistic and cultural lines. Thirdly, they are uniting with ladinos, and fourthly they are doing this without giving up their distinctive customs or languages. In a country where antagonisms between Indians and Indians and ladinos and Indians have been axiomatic, all these relations are today in a process of redefinition. The current crisis and the people's revolutionary war seem to be creating a new conception of who the Guatemalan people are.

In the following document, the Guerrilla Army of the Poor (EGP), a guerrilla organization with a large Indian membership, presents what it describes as a "preliminary outline of our view of the national Indian question and an invitation to begin discussion."

The Complex Indian World

THE LANGUAGE, CUSTOMS, types of family, communal and social organization, values, traditions, psychology, which have survived from the Maya-Quiché culture, with the changes wrought by four and a half centuries of colonial domination, make up the specificity of the Guatemalan Indian culture. The ethnic-cultural atomization which characterizes the present-day Indians—variations in languages and dialects, different dress styles, distinct regional and local manifestations of one generic culture—stem from the peculiar kind of domination to which the conquistadores and colonizers subjected the Indian population throughout the colonial period. By breaking up their forms of community into so-called "Indian towns," the unity of the ethnic group was fragmented and the prehispanic social dynamic distorted to fit into the colonial regime. Many of the indigenous cultural expressions which survive today are the result of forms of economic organization, legal relations and political and ideological mechanisms stemming from the Spanish cultural influence, although shot through with the world vision inherited from the Maya-Quiché.

Although since the Conquest the main burden of producing social wealth has rested on the backs of the Indian producers, making the ethnic-cultural status of the Indian in Guatemala equivalent to the economic status of exploited, there has been a historic process of class differentiation among the Indians. This differentiation, in general, corresponds to the coexistence and the complementary nature of different forms of production in the Guatemalan social formation. In those parts of the countryside where precapitalist production relations predominate, the majority of Indians are still subsistence farmers, linked to the dependent agroexport capitalist system only through the local market. Where there is a tendency for capitalist relations of production to impose themselves, the Indian suffers a process of proletarianization. Due to the characteristics of the latiminifundio system, this process is not systematically completed, giving rise to an enormous mass of semiproletarians who produce as wage workers on capitalist plantations during certain times of the year and the rest of the time as peasants on small plots of land or minifundios. In those parts of the countryside most strongly integrated into the capitalist economy the stratification of the peasantry gives rise to rural middle sectors, who base their economy on the intensive cultivation of minifundios using terracing, irrigation and fertilizers, and produce for the national and Central American markets. The system's incapacity to absorb population growth by providing jobs or land means, on the other hand, that a growing mass of poor peasants (Indian and ladino) migrate to the cities in search of work, becoming servants or doing piecework at home for national and foreign industry, or joining the ranks of the unemployed and underemployed jammed into the marginal areas and ravines of the capital city.

Some groups of rich Indians, above all in the west but also in departmental capitals throughout the Indian area, are able to climb to the lower layers of the ruling classes, giving rise to an Indian bourgeoisie whose capital is based mainly in commerce. In spite of their class condition, they do not escape ethnic-cultural oppression and discrimination. . . .

Although they are the majority of the Guatemalan population, the ethnic-national Indian groups do not form a single nationality. They have been impeded from doing so by exclusion from political power since the Conquest, fragmentation both geographic and in terms of ethnic-cultural atomization, and disintegration as peasantry due to the advance of capitalist relations of production. However, the strength, the historically demonstrated capacity to resist and to survive, to reproduce their culture locally and regionally, to adapt to the changes four centuries have wrought in a colonized society transformed into a dependent capitalist one, can only be explained by a profound and hard to describe sense of ethnic-cultural identity. This can only be defined as the particular way of being and feeling of a collective body linked through the definitory and peculiar thought patterns produced in human beings by such complex and varied factors as the mother tongue, the place of childhood, life experiences, the relation to the land and to the basic foods it produces, habits, customs and traditions, in a place and time which cannot be either replaced or repeated.

The importance in Guatemalan society of this way of being, of seeing life and the world, cannot be quantified. It is all over, it crops up everywhere, it is Guatemala itself. The immense majority of non-Indians have something of it, in the physical traits, in the psychology, in the customs or in many of the indigenous words which have become part of our Spanish and without which we could not express much of what is ours. Guatemala is profoundly Indian and will continue to be so in the future. . . .

Dominant Culture and Dominated Culture

The colonialists' need to preserve the basic Indian economic and social organization in order to facilitate the exploitation of a rural labor force, is one of the key factors which explains why the Indian culture, revolving around precapitalist agriculture based on maize and the corresponding level of social organization, could survive in the new colonial society; but it also explains why this culture could not develop. The culture imposed by the Spanish colonialists (western, greco-latin, judeo-christian) dominated the Maya-Quiché culture, because it expressed a mode of production superior to that of the Mesoamerican Indians. No human culture can develop when the material base which sustains it is broken down by outside, superior relations of production which are essentially exclusive of the old, even if in some senses complementary. The Guatemalan Indians' cornfields were held and worked communally and the differentiation of social classes had only begun. Their traditional form of land ownership violated, forced to regroup into towns created to facilitate the exploitation of their labor, militarily defeated and subject to the ideological onslaught of missionaries, the Guatemalan Indians resisted and rejected the new relations of production and the culture of those who imposed them. Resistance and rejection went from religious syncretism to local armed uprisings, passing through all the forms of cultural resistance which the sense of ethnic identity leads oppressed people to create in similar circumstances. The sense of ethnic-cultural identity—the other key to understanding the survival of the Indian culture as we know it today—finds its scientific explanation in the relative independence of the superstructure with regard to the material base which gives rise to it at a given moment.

Cultural oppression—and discrimination as one of its practical manifestations—has, in historical terms, an economic origin and a given class content. The Spanish conquistadores and colonizers needed to justify their domination of the Indians in order to exploit them economically. The system they created gave rise to a corresponding superstructure, designed to oppress. All ladinos, even exploited ladinos, participate in maintaining this superstructure, which thus reproduces itself. The development of agrarian dependent capitalism perpetuates, deepens and sharpens this phenomenon, fusing the contradictions inherent to the social-economic structure with the specific contradictions arising from the multinational nature of the country. Today the culture of the Maya-Quiché is the dominated culture and the western culture historically imposed by the successive ruling classes is the dominant one.

Production Relations and Culture

As capitalism expands in the countryside, it breaks down precapitalist forms and relations of production which have historically characterized the Indians and on which their culture is based. As they lose their land, they also lose the base of their culture. In other words, when the precapitalist producer becomes a semiproletarian or a proletarian, he begins to incorporate cultural elements belonging to the new relations of production which forcibly immerse and encompass him. In the midst of a hostile culture which discriminates against him, the semiproletarian Indian is forced to take refuge within himself, to try to blend in with his surroundings, to accumulate hate and distrust of the system and of those who pay his wages but at the same time expropriate him, depersonalize him and deny that which he most treasures: his own ethnic-cultural identity. He is forced to learn Spanish on the plantation; the family economy based on a different view of time begins to be governed by the law of value; ceremonies, festivals, traditions depend on the free social time which the new production relations allow the disintegrating peasant community. The rubber boot replaces the leather caite or sandal, the synthetic blouse displaces the handwoven, the transistor radio takes the place of oral tradition. However, precapitalist forms do not completely disappear, surviving, reinforcing and complementing the capitalist relations of production in the dependent agroexport model. The Indian community and its specific culture thus have a certain margin for survival. The limited internal market characteristic of dependent capitalism has been an important factor in the conservation and reproduction of regional indigenous cultural expressions.

In this process, class consciousness and the sense of ethnic cultural identity become part of the complex dialectic known as the national-ethnic contradiction. Subsistence Indian farmers and semiproletarian Indians, for example, produce and think differently; they share a sense of ethnocultural identity, but differ ideologically as a result of their different social and economic status. Among subsistence farmers, who live and work in basically prehispanic and precapitalist ways, ethnic-national awareness and Indian cultural traits are in harmony with their socioeconomic situation.

Among semiproletarian Indians, ethnic-national consciousness is permeated with political and ideological elements which belong to the encompassing modern relations of production. These include an incipient awareness of exploitation, a beginning differentiation along class lines to visualize the existence of rich Indians, class consciousness in relation to exploitative and exploited ladinos. For the subsistence Indian farmer, the relation with ladinos is one of ethnic-cultural oppression and discrimination. For the semiproletarian, the ladino is also oppressor and discriminator, but he begins to understand that the exploiter is the rich. Thus, two systems of parallel and apparently incoherent contradictions are introduced into his awareness, since the logical conclusion of this second aspect is that there are also exploited ladinos, even if they are not culturally oppressed. The defensive discrimination against ladinos and more important, the awareness that both are linked by common interests against a common enemy—the exploiter, who reproduces and benefits from the system—can only be resolved ideologically and politically by assimilating a revolutionary scientific conception which explains exploitation and oppression as complementary parts of a social system affecting both Indians and ladinos. . . .

The Ethnic-National Contradiction

One of our basic political premises—perhaps the least orthodox within the programmatic objectives derived from the complexity of Guatemalan society and the problems posed by its revolutionary transformation—is the thesis that in Guatemala *the ethnic-national contradiction is one of the fundamental factors in all possible revolutionary change.* We base this political conviction on the fact that more than half of the Guatemalan population is Indian, and that the majority of these are wage or semiwage workers who have different contradictions with the system. *We call the ethnic-national contradiction the domination of the Indian peoples and their ethnic-cultural identity by the dependent agroexport capitalist system which the ruling class has historically created in our country, and the need to eliminate the economic-class and political base on which this domination rests.* The economic-class goal of the revolution is to change existing relations of production and put an end to the exploitation of some classes by others. This will be done by overthrowing the present proimperialist and landowner-bourgeois regime and carrying out an agrarian, antiimperialist, and anticapitalist revolution, through the phases and stages which the complex global balance of forces imposes on our revolutions in the area. The ethnic-national objective of the Revolution is to do away with the relations of ethnic-national domination and eliminate the oppression and discrimination to which the Indians are subject under the ruling classes' system. This objective will begin to be achieved by overthrowing the present regime and carrying out a revolution which, in addition to the abovementioned class content, has a liberating ethnic-national character. This is why we say that the class contradiction in our country is complemented by the ethnic-national contradiction, and that the latter cannot be resolved except in terms of the resolution of the former. Both are permanently intertwined, since both arose historically as essential parts of the same system of domination-exploitation, the form that early capitalism adopted in the development of its colonial modality in America. . . .

The double condition of the Indian as exploited and oppressed; clarification of the specific nature of the second contradiction; comprehension of the ethnic-national contradiction as the basic complement of the class contradiction; and the correct way of posing and solving both contradictions in terms of the totality of national problems, are keys to revolutionary strategy and what makes the Guatemalan revolution unique. The particularity of our revolutionary process in this sense resides in the fact that *the sum of ethnic-national minorities make up the majority of the population and that the class status of this majority is that of exploited.* Our task cannot be simply to design a policy on ethnic-national minorities or to reduce the question to one of class, but rather a whole program that encompasses both contradictions and correctly resolves them for the whole society. . . .

The national question is part of the general question of the Revolution. The ethnic-national Indian groups contain revolutionary forces that not only cannot remain outside the popular revolutionary war, but that constitute a decisive element of victory. But we should not forget that they also constitute decisive factors for building the new revolutionary society. The Indian culture, its strength, its deep roots in what is ours—without idealizations, but also not underestimating it—is an immense pool of human wealth which the new society cannot disregard without denying its very essence. The Indian sense of the collective, austerity, courage, valoration of human solidarity, industriousness, frankness, straightforwardness, among others, are contributions which will come mainly from those who throughout centuries of oppression and exploitation have made these qualities and these values essential parts of their most intimate nature. . . .

We can anticipate that after the revolutionary forces take power, in the class-based and ethnic-national based bodies of State leadership, by common agreement, freely and voluntarily, the Indian peoples and the ladino people will decide the economic, social and political configuration of the New, Multinational Guatemala.

48. *Indian Women in the Revolution Speak* *

BY JUANA AND LUCÍA

There is an Indian legend called "The Mountain." It speaks of a road of war. The Indians say for the road to be complete it must return to where it began. It never goes in one direction: where it goes one way, it must always go the other way as well. The road of war has been going in one direction. It has been a road of continuous plunder, of continuous pushing against the mountain, of taking away land and taking away expression. It is a road of more than four hundred years. Now they say it is time for the road to return, for the road to complete itself. The road of war went from the city to the mountains, so the road of the war's return is the other way, from the mountains to the capital.

—Priest in exile, March 1982

THE *following statements are from two Indian women who are members of the January 31st Popular Front (FP-31), a revolutionary organization that includes Indians and ladinos, as do all revolutionary organizations in Guatemala today. The cultural pride which Juana and Lucía express below occurs in the context of the greatest unity ever achieved between Indians and ladinos in Guatemala's history. A Quiché guerrilla in the Guerrilla Army of the Poor (EGP) recounts:*

Many years ago the Indians struggled alone against the invaders but the Indians fought alone so they did not achieve victory. Later ladinos organized but

* Interview with Juana by the editors, June 18, 1982; interview with Lucía from an anonymous source, February 1982.

they did not win either. Now the poor ladinos and the Indians like each other much more because we have come to understand the enemy divided us before. They would tell the ladino that we were no good, we were their enemies, and they told us the ladinos were our enemies. And it is true that at one time we saw the ladinos as our enemies, but now we have learned more, we have learned to struggle together with them.[1]

It is significant that this new unity with ladinos does not appear to mean a loss of cultural awareness and identity.

Juana and Lucía emphasize that their Indian culture has been one of resistance in which the silent barriers Indians have built over hundreds of years against total domination are now being turned into barricades of war against the government. Whether or not Indian culture has always been a culture of resistance, their remarks challenge the simple equation of cultural traditionalism with political conservatism.

The fact that both these revolutionaries are women reflects the high participation of women in the guerrilla movements, an aspect of the contemporary struggle which has not yet been fully studied.

Juana:

STRUGGLE IS VERY deep within the Indian community. Because we have always hidden our identity and we have secrets it is not hard for us to live in a state of war—it is hard but it would be much more difficult if all our structure of secrecy did not exist. In fact, many of the structures of the revolution have their roots in Indian culture, there are many things. . . . Many people are afraid that Guatemala will be converted into a socialist country even though they do not know what the structures of a socialist country would be; but in fact socialism exists within the people, it is evident that we already communicate and share, we are already members of a community. And now in the revolution, for example, why do children learn to be adults from the time they are small? Because it does not cost them to learn this, they already know it. Why do children assume a major responsibility in the revolution? Because, in fact they have always assumed responsibilities in our community. . . . There are many things we see in the revolution today which distinguish it from the other revolutionary processes in Central America because they are the expression of the Indian. And this has made our survival possible, that we have not been exterminated. In Guatemala there exists a very refined and intelligent apparatus of repression but it has not been able to destroy our organizations. Why? Because of who is in these organizations—a people who have already learned how to suffer. So I think we can see the revolution has taken great strides because of the entrance of the Indian. Without

1. From an interview with a Quiché guerrilla, anonymous source, March 1982.

the Indian maybe the revolution would not have been able to achieve the stage it has.

Lucía:

THE RICH AND the army think of us as stupid and incapable, that we know nothing, but this is a lie. Now we are proving that we Indian women are capable. We are demonstrating this as Indian women leaders of mass movements. We play important roles and carry out important tasks, and not only on the level of mass organizations but within the vanguard organizations as well. When the news that the guerrillas have occupied a village arrives, it always relates how women served as commanders among the ranks of the guerrillas. So we are playing the same role the colonels in the army play. If those colonels are capable, so are we.

They used to use us in elections. They would haul us over in trucks to vote, as if we were some kind of animals. So that we would vote they would promise us things and then after voting they would forget all that we asked for. In contrast, now we are clear and convinced that this is not the road that will take us to victory. Now we realize these elections are a lie. So now the government does not haul us around in trucks, not because they do not want to, but because we do not let them. . . .

Our culture has survived because it was not made in one month or one year. Rather, it comes from our ancestors. When more than four hundred fifty years ago the Spaniards came to conquer and invade Guatemala, they wanted to destroy our customs, our entire culture, but this was not possible because it is something within our very hearts, it is very deep within us. It is inscribed within us. Our culture and our customs are so deeply rooted within us that they go wherever we go. And now we are struggling for this entire culture. We are fighting for all those things which the rich and the colonels want by stepping on us with all their might. But it is not possible for them to win because we Indians are the majority in the country and when we are united and increase our strength they will not be able to finish us off. . . . In reality we are defending our culture, our language, our customs, our religiosity which we understand differently from the way they understand it. What they want is that we go on losing our customs, but we have carried our customs for many years, for hundreds of years, for four hundred fifty years. Ever since the Spaniards arrived in Guatemala they have been trying to destroy our customs but they have not been able to. And they will not be able to because we will keep on respecting all of that which is really ours.

Even our Indian dress has come under attack in Guatemala because we are obliged to take it off. Why? Because the rich and the army say that all of us Indian people are communists, and subversive. So for our own safety, so that they will not take us, so that they will not kidnap and torture us, we have stopped wearing our Indian dress. This is a painful thing because for us this way of dressing is also our culture. . . .

The government uses us or has used us in the past, when they thought it was in their interest. They exhibited us in our native dress as if we were in a zoological park where people would come and pay them money to see us. But now they have us as their worst enemy. They have exhibitions in their Clubs where they drink, dance, and bring their foreign friends. They exhibit our clothes and with all this, without any effort of their own, they rake in money—by showing things we make, our pots in which we cook our beans, the ceramics and earthenware which we use, our *huipiles* [2] which we weave. And to enter this exhibit costs a lot of money. So in this way the government has used us, but now we are no longer lending ourselves to these games. Now, we have realized that instead of weaving another *huipil,* we are better off picking up a weapon, picking up a bomb and throwing it in front of them.

I do not think of myself as a terrorist or a subversive because what I am doing is struggling so that our children can have a good education, housing and food, like the rich have. It's for this that we are fighting. I am not a terrorist because I will never take up a weapon and kill a person who has done nothing to me, like they do. So to the contrary, I think the government and its army—they are the terrorists because they take up their weapons, their tanks, their mortars, their airplanes and go out and massacre entire villages and all the people who stand in their way. They come to bomb. This is terrorism. By contrast I am fighting for peace, for justice, and for the liberation of my people.

49. The Revolution Will End Our People's Repression *

BY THE GUATEMALAN NATIONAL REVOLUTIONARY UNITY

IN January 1982, Guatemala's four guerrilla organizations, the Guerrilla Army of the Poor (EGP), the Rebel Armed Forces (FAR), the Organization of People in Arms (ORPA) and the Guatemalan Workers Party (PGT-leadership nucleus) formed a united front, the Guatemalan National Revolutionary Unity (URNG). The URNG signals a significant new stage in the revolutionary process. It provides a structure for powerful unified military action and has developed an important consensus over the political, social, and economic aims of the Guatemalan revolution. Although the political differences between the four groups have not always been sharp, each is autonomous and historically distinct. Exiles from the 1960s started the EGP in 1972 when they entered the northern rural region of Quiché where they slowly established a base among settlers (see

---

2. Loose-fitting handwoven Indian blouses.—EDS.

* Excerpted from "The Unity Statement of the Revolutionary Organizations—EGP, FAR, ORPA, PGT—To the People of Guatemala" [Guatemala City], January 1982.

Readings 44-46). The EGP believes that poor campesinos, particularly Indians, are potentially the greatest revolutionary force. The EGP is active in the regions of Quiché, Huehuetenango, Alta Verapaz, Baja Verapaz, Chimaltenango, Suchitepéquez, Escuintla and Guatemala City. The FAR has, since its 1960s defeat (see Reading No. 42), concentrated on building a base in urban areas and among agricultural workers on the Pacific coast and in the Petén jungles. They support what they call a worker-peasant alliance and stress that workers play a vanguard role. The ORPA did not become known to the public outside of Guatemala until late 1979. Influenced by the writings of Franz Fanon, a spokesperson of the Algerian revolution,[1] ORPA perceives Indians as the country's determining force and gives special emphasis to the Indian question. It organizes in the predominantly Indian areas of San Marcos, Totonicapán, Quezaltenango and Sololá. The fourth group, the PGT, a split from the old PGT of the 1960s, has support within Guatemala City's labor movement as well as among agricultural workers on the southern coast.

TODAY THE FLAME of the People's Revolutionary War is burning strong in all parts of the country. In the West, North, South, East and center, and in the capital city, there are victorious guerrilla operations every day, and mass sabotage and propaganda support activities. The revolutionary forces maintain a constant siege in the border areas, in the plantations, the oil zones, highways, tourist centers and the slums in the capital. Nearly all of the Indian groups have joined the People's Revolutionary War, and together with the ladino population they support thousands and thousands of guerrillas. In 1981, the guerrilla organizations moved from occupying villages and plantations to the occupation of municipal and departmental capitals, and from propaganda actions to generalized military harassment operations. We are now beginning to systematize operations which directly destroy the enemy forces. In 1981, we caused approximately 3,200 enemy casualties, including soldiers, police agents and members of the local repressive power in the countryside and in the city. Our guerrilla units have begun to recover enemy weapons, destroy military transport, and to down planes and helicopters. We have moved from operating with small units to using larger ones, and have managed, despite important blows, to completely defeat the offensives launched by the enemy in 1981 against the strongholds of the revolution in the city and the countryside. The People's Revolutionary War is spreading to more parts of the country; it is deepening its mass support and is increasing its offensive capacity. The exploited, oppressed and discriminated Guatemalan Indians have risen up and through their integration into the People's Revolutionary War, together with the masses of ladino workers, have already decided the outcome of the war. . . .

The Revolutionary, Patriotic, Popular and Democratic Government that we will construct in Guatemala commits itself to the Guatemalan people and to the

1. See Fanon's *Wretched of the Earth* (New York: Grove Press, 1965).

international community to fulfill the following five fundamental programmatic points:

I. *The Revolution will eliminate once and for all the repression against our people and will guarantee to all citizens, the supreme rights of life and peace.*

Life and peace are supreme human rights. The Revolution will end our people's repression and the political regime that has given itself the right to assassinate its opposition to remain in power. Since 1954, the government of the rich exploiters and repressors has killed thousands of Guatemalans for political reasons. Their blood represents for the Revolution, a commitment to freedom, peace and respect for life.

II. *The Revolution will set down the foundations for resolving the basic needs of the great majority of our people by eliminating the political domination of the repressive rich, both national and foreign, who rule Guatemala.*

The Revolution will put an end to this domination, and guarantees that those who produce with their own creative effort will benefit from the product of their labor. The properties of the very rich will be taken over by the Revolutionary government, which will see to it that this wealth is used to resolve the needs of the working people. The Revolution will guarantee a true agrarian reform, giving land to those who work in an individual, collective or cooperative fashion. The Revolution will guarantee small and medium-sized agricultural properties, and will distribute to those who work the land with their own hands those properties now held by the military hierarchy and the corrupt, greedy and repressive functionaries and businessmen. The Revolution will guarantee small and medium-sized commerce and stimulate the creation and development of a national industry which Guatemala needs to be able to develop. The Revolution will guarantee an effective price control to benefit the great majority and will at the same time, allow reasonable profits as long as they do not hurt the people.

The Revolution will wrest power from the very rich, both national and foreign, and thus create jobs and guarantee decent salaries to all workers in the countryside and the city. Once the people have power, we will have a base to begin to resolve the great problems of health, housing and illiteracy which afflict the vast majority of the population.

III. *The Revolution will guarantee equality between Indians and ladinos, and will end cultural oppression and discrimination.*

The domination by the rich is the root cause of the cultural oppression and discrimination which the Indian population suffers in Guatemala. The first step towards eliminating cultural oppression and discrimination is to enable Indians, who are an integral part of the Guatemalan people, to participate in political power. The participation of the Indian population in political power, together with the ladino population, will allow us to meet Indians' needs for land, work, salary, health, housing, and general welfare. Meeting these needs is the first condition toward achieving equality between Indians and ladinos. The second condition toward guaranteeing this equality is respect for their culture and recognition of their rights to maintain their own identity. The development of a culture which gathers and integrates our people's historic roots is one of the great objectives of the Revolution. Indians and ladinos in power will freely decide Guatemala's future contours.

IV. *The Revolution will guarantee the creation of a New Society, in which all patriotic, popular and democratic sectors will be represented in the government.*

The Revolution will respect the peoples' rights to elect their local, municipal and national representatives. All those citizens who with their work, skills or capital, are willing and able to help Guatemala overcome its poverty, backwardness and dependence will have a place in the New Society. Patriotic businessmen who are willing to contribute to the achievement of this great objective will have full rights, without conditions, except that they respect the interests of the working people. The Revolution will guarantee freedom of expression and of religious belief, as a way of facilitating the contribution of all citizens to the construction of a New Society. The Revolution will be severe in its judgment of the most repressive among the enemy, and of the clique of highranking military officers and their accomplices who have planned and directed the repression against our people. The Revolution will be flexible in its judgment of those who have refused orders to repress our people. The Revolution will eliminate forced conscription for military service, a practice which discriminates against the Indians. All patriotic officers and soldiers who have not stained their hands with the blood of our people will be able to participate in the new People's Revolutionary Army which the Guatemalan people will build to guarantee the security and defense of the country.

In the New Society, women will have the same rights as men, since they share the same obligations as men and even greater ones in their role as mothers. Children and the aged will enjoy the protection they deserve for the contribution they will make or have made to production of social wealth.

The Revolution recognizes the Christian population as one of the pillars of the New Society, since they have placed their beliefs and faith at the service of the struggle for the freedom of all Guatemalans.

V. *Based in the principle of self-determination the Revolution will guarantee a policy of nonalignment and international cooperation which poor countries need in order to develop in the modern world.*

In today's complex and interdependent world, it is necessary to maintain a position of nonalignment with the great powers and of international cooperation.

Poor countries need foreign investment and this must be agreed upon on the basis of respect for each country's national sovereignty, taking into account both the needs of poor countries and reasonable returns on foreign investments. Political stability is in this respect indispensable, as without it there can be no international cooperation. International cooperation is possible between nations which are different ideologically, and have different forms of government as long as there is respect for each country's right to self-determination.

PART FIVE:

THE NEW COLD WAR AND U.S. POLICY ALTERNATIVES

President Reagan meets with Guatemala's President Ríos Montt during Reagan's brief visit to Honduras, December 4, 1982. Booklet reads: "This government is committed to change." *Photo credit: United Press International*

Editors' Introduction

SINCE the early nineteenth century, when the Monroe Doctrine defined the limits of European expansion in the Western Hemisphere, the United States has assumed the role of protector and policeman for Caribbean and Latin American states. A convenient starting date is 1823, the year President James Monroe announced the "doctrine" associated with his name, but largely conceived by his Secretary of State, John Quincy Adams. At first simply a warning that "the American continents . . . are henceforth not to be considered as subjects for future colonization by any European power," [1] the Monroe Doctrine later in the nineteenth century began its extraordinary career of growth and amplification, becoming a quasi-legal claim for U.S. intervention in Central America and the Caribbean, a region increasingly conceptualized as the "backyard" of the U.S.A.

In the decades after the proclamation of 1823, groups of U.S. adventurers and capitalists began to explore the possibilities for profit and empire in Central America, and historians have long debated whether that was the intent of the Monroe Doctrine. One of the early entrants into the field of Yankee *filibusteros* [2] seeking cash and power was William Walker from Tennessee, a doctor-lawyer-editor-turned-pirate who in 1855 entered Nicaragua with a band of mercenaries, establishing himself as commander-in-chief of the Nicaraguan armed forces. He proclaimed himself president in 1856, only to be run out of the country a year later with the aid of Cornelius Vanderbilt whose lucrative transportation route across Nicaragua to the Pacific was jeopardized by Walker's idiosyncratic rule.

---

1. J.D. Richardson, ed., *Messages and Papers of the Presidents* (10 vols., Washington, D.C., 1907), II, pp. 218-219.

2. The word *filibuster,* later to mean interminable speechmaking in the U.S. Senate to block legislation, originally derived from a Dutch term for freebooters, or pirates. See William B. Scroogs, *Filibusters and Financiers* (New York: Macmillan Co., 1916).

Vanderbilt was one of several North American magnates to seek profits to be made ferrying U.S. immigrants to California's gold coast. A battleground between competing North American magnates in the late nineteenth century, Central America continued to be a target of U.S. economic and political penetration on into the twentieth century. During this period the United Fruit Company was establishing significant operations throughout Central America, generating U.S. concern about protecting its economic investments as well as protecting its access to a passageway to the Pacific Ocean.

In his famous 1904 "corollary" to the Monroe Doctrine, President Theodore Roosevelt affirmed the right of the U.S. to intervene in Latin American countries:

> Chronic wrongdoing . . . may in America, as elsewhere, ultimately require intervention by some civilized nation, and in the Western Hemisphere the adherence of the United States to the Monroe Doctrine may force the United States, however reluctantly . . . to the exercise of an international police power.[3]

Liberally interpreting Roosevelt's corollary to the Monroe Doctrine at a time when the United States needed to create a stable environment in the region where it planned to build the Panama Canal, President Taft sent marines into Nicaragua in 1912, where they remained until 1933. In the early 1920s the U.S. also intervened militarily in Haiti and the Dominican Republic.[4]

In 1933, President Franklin Roosevelt pledged that the United States would be a good neighbor, and no longer intervene militarily in the domestic affairs of its neighbors to the south. This policy was in part prompted by the need to concentrate on problems created by the Great Depression, and in part because of growing opposition to U.S. domination by Latin Americans themselves.[5] But F.D.R.'s "Good Neighbor Policy" was significantly qualified by Washington's insistence that local political authority be strengthened by military strongmen trained in the U.S. to insure a continually hospitable climate for foreign business investment. Thus, the initiatives of the early 1930s were not a repudiation of intervention, but an attempt to accomplish the goals of intervention at a cheaper cost. Operating as surrogates for U.S. business interests, a generation of Caribbean strongmen were the main local products of the "Good Neighbor Policy": Rafael Leonidas Trujillo in the Dominican Republic, Fulgencio Batista in Cuba, "Papa Doc" Duvalier in

---

3. Quoted in Thomas A. Bailey, *A Diplomatic History of the American People*, 6th ed. (New York: Appleton-Century-Crofts, 1958), p. 505.

4. On the expansionist interpretation of the Monroe Doctrine, see Dexter Perkins, *A History of the Monroe Doctrine* (Boston: Little, Brown, 1963), Chap. VII.

5. See Bryce Wood, *The Making of the Good Neighbor Policy* (New York: Columbia University Press, 1961).

Haiti, and Anastasio Somoza in Nicaragua.[6] About the last-named dictator, Franklin Roosevelt was supposed to have said: "He's a son-of-bitch, but at least he's *our* son-of-a-bitch."

The usefulness of a policy that supported "sons-of-bitches" like Somoza as an alternative to U.S. intervention wore thin when men and women decided to be governed by less repressive types. Anticommunist rhetoric permeated State Department analyses of the movements that threatened to replace these dictators and was used to justify U.S. intervention. That was, as we have seen, precisely what occurred in Guatemala in 1954, the year of a fateful U.S. intervention that annulled the Good Neighbor Policy.[7] What remained afterward was a new, officially undefined policy of intervention coupled with increased support to local strongmen deemed capable of repressing insurgency in their countries. The overthrow of Batista by Fidel Castro in Cuba in 1959 added urgency to this policy lest the revolutionary example prove contagious.

But genuine revolutionary movements are not imported from abroad; indigenous movements have sprung up almost everywhere in Central America. Augusto César Sandino, the Nicaraguan who, from 1928 to 1933, led a band of supporters in uprising against U.S. marines and their local mouthpiece, Anastasio Somoza, sparked a breed of revolutionary people whose needs for change have multiplied and metamorphized into today's struggle.

The vaunted strongmen were proving dangerously weak from Washington's point of view when in 1979 Nicaraguan rebels swept the Somoza dynasty from power. This toppling of the Somoza regime occurred just months after the coup which placed leftist Maurice Bishop in charge of the Caribbean island of Grenada, thereby undermining the U.S. government's traditional power bases in the region. As the decade of the 1980s opened, U.S. foreign policy in the region was in flux. During the last days of the Carter Administration, the United States began to increase its support of its right-wing allies in Central America. With the conservatives' ascendancy to power under Reagan, this support intensified as active insurrection swept El Salvador and Guatemala.

What policy options does the U.S. face? The readings in this chapter indicate some major alternatives. "Foggy Bottom," or the U.S. Department of State, still voices hope for a successful counterinsurgency (see Reading 50); other policy analysts (including many in the Reagan administration) cling to globalist doctrines which view the conflict in Guatemala as a matter of East-West confrontation, with the insurgency originating "in Cuba or other Soviet puppets" (see Reading 51). An as yet unspoken policy alternative is to regionalize the conflict in Central America by arranging some concerted movement among the military oligarchies of El Salvador, Honduras and Guatemala to attack the guerrilla move-

---

6. Wood, *The Making of the Good Neighbor Policy, passim.*

7. See Part One, Chapter II, for the events of 1954 and the reformist phase that preceded them.

ment as well as its presumed local base of support in Nicaragua. Another option is to negotiate with the rebels of Central America, as former U.S. Ambassador to El Salvador Robert White recently argued.[8] A final alternative, of course, would be to not intervene at all in the affairs of Central American nations, a path unlikely to be followed by State Department strategists, but widely supported within a U.S. population sobered by the experience of Vietnam. As Eduardo Galeano suggests in the final reading of the book, the U.S. government says it wants peace, yet searches for it with guns.

50. *Guatemala Through the Eyes of Foggy Bottom* *

BY THE U.S. DEPARTMENT OF STATE

WHEN Ronald Reagan won the U.S. presidential election in 1980, many Guatemalan business, government, and military leaders believed that the new administration, which shared their strong anticommunist ideology, would quickly restore aid to that country. In fact, many Guatemalans were counting on a Reagan victory to save them. A U.S. businessman described Guatemala City on election night: "It was like the liberation of Paris from the Germans. There were Guatemalans dancing in the streets, marimbas in front of the U.S. embassy, there were skyrockets, it was a terrific night. It was like we were liberated because we all felt that none of us could stand another four years of Mr. Carter's policy in these countries."[1]

Under questioning by members of two subcommittees of the House Committee on Foreign Affairs in July 1981, Stephen Bosworth, Deputy Assistant Secretary of State for Inter-American Affairs, defended the Reagan Administration's new approach to State Department policy towards Guatemala. This new policy is based in part on the assumption that human rights abuses in Guatemala actually increased when the U.S. stopped sending aid to Guatemala, and that by sending aid the U.S. should be able to influence the Guatemalan government to stop these abuses.

---

8. Robert E. White, "Central America: The Problem that Won't Go Away," *New York Times Magazine*, July 18, 1982.

* Excerpted from *Human Rights in Guatemala.* Hearings before the Subcommittees on Human Rights and International Organizations and on Inter-American Affairs of the Committee on Foreign Affairs, House of Representatives, Ninety-Seventh Congress, July 30, 1981.

1. From an interview made available to one of the editors.

Mr. Gilman (D-N.Y.): Could you spell out for us, Mr. Ambassador, what the basic goals or objectives of our policies are in Guatemala?

Mr. Bosworth: Our basic objective, or objectives, in Guatemala are to develop a relationship with the Government of Guatemala which both enhances its ability to control insurgency, to guarantee the stability of the country, and also, and we believe in a mutually reinforcing fashion, enhances its ability to improve, bring about the improvement of the human rights situation in that country.

Mr. Bonker (D-Wash.): Mr. Bosworth, the State Department Report on Human Rights Conditions, country by country, which was prepared by Mr. Palmer's department [2] . . . documents violations in every single category of torture, cruel, inhumane, degrading treatment, punishment, disappearances. Guatemala is very clearly in violation of 502(b)(which restricts the sale of military supplies to countries in gross and consistent violation of human rights).

Mr. Bosworth: . . . We have concluded that the limited security assistance of a non-lethal nature which we have proposed can be legally justified under section 502(b).

As we indicated in our testimony, we believe that furnishing such limited assistance may permit us to more effectively seek to influence the human rights policies of the Guatemalan Government, and thus to promote the policies underlying section 502(b).

Mr. Gilman: Mr. Bosworth, following General Walters' visit,[3] and our announced change in policy in the delivery of equipment, of the jeeps and trucks to Guatemala, has there been any marked change in the human rights situation in Guatemala over the past few months?

Mr. Bosworth: No, Mr. Gilman, I do not believe that there has been any marked improvement in the human rights

---

2. Stephen Palmer, Acting Assistant Secretary of State for Human Rights and Humanitarian Affairs—EDS.

3. Ambassador at Large Vernon Walters has frequently represented the U.S. State Department in Argentina and Guatemala, offering military advice to these countries' governments. This trip was made in May 1981.—EDS.

situation in the last few months. Clearly we had hoped that there would have been.

On the other hand, this is a process of violence, terrorism, which has been going on for a long period of time. Levels of suspicion, levels of hostility and polarization have set in, and it will clearly not be possible to reverse these immediately, but it is our conviction that over a period of time, given the sort of policy approach we have outlined, that it will be possible for us to begin to show an improvement in the human rights situation in Guatemala.

Mr. Gilman: What do you base your assumption on, Mr. Bosworth?

Mr. Bosworth: It is based, I think, on two facts, Mr. Gilman. One, that the previous approach clearly was not working, and there was a need for a new approach and, second, that it is important, if the Government is going to be able to bring terrorism and violence under control, that it have the self-confidence needed to do so, and not be operating out of a siege or bunker mentality, and it is our belief that a program, a moderate program, a measured program of establishing communication with that Government, will enhance our ability to bring about the sort of changes we believe are necessary.

Mr. Leach (D-Iowa): . . . Isn't it potentially counterproductive for the United States to identify very closely with such a government, and thus legitimize to some degree the opposition? These arms exchanges give the opposition the right to claim that their struggle is not only philosophic but also anticolonial. And why do we bother to make a very substantial policy shift with only a nominal change in the quantity of support given? Isn't this such a trivial arms exchange that it is a no-win proposition both for the Guatemalan Government and for the United States?

Mr. Bosworth: I think, Mr. Leach, the objective of this change is as I indicated earlier. We are trying to bring about a lowering of what some might call the siege mentality, which has been demonstrated by the Guatemalan Government over recent years, and in the view of the administration, one of the reasons for the development of that mentality was the progressive distancing of this Government from it, and in frequent cases, open confrontation.

We have deliberately chosen to move in a new policy line in a very careful and measured fashion through actions such as this, which you have termed as being symbolic, but which nonetheless, we believe will increase the level of confidence of the Guatemalan Government in the prospective relationship with the United States, and increase its own self-confidence and put it in a better position to try to deal with human rights violations in that country.

Mr. Leach: Let me just ask about your description of "careful and measured." That language is somewhat reminiscent of 1961 and 1962. We had some very "careful and measured" responses to a country in Southeast Asia.

Would you like to give us assurances, (a) that this administration does not want to walk down the road—even if it is an inapplicable analogy—of Vietnam; and (b) that the administration is more apt—does not intend to walk down the road and have perhaps the analogy of El Salvador.

Is there any likelihood that this administration will followup military equipment with military advisors?

Mr. Bosworth: No, that is not under consideration, Mr. Leach. We recognize, first, that this is an extremely controversial issue that we are dealing with, and it is one on which feelings are very deep and very strongly held. We believe that the previous policies that the United States employed toward this issue were not effective, and in fact, could perhaps at times be described as having been counterproductive. We believe that a new policy approach can be effective. We also realize, however, that we are not going to be able to carry out this new policy approach, unless we proceed in what I termed a careful and measured fashion, and I was not trying to relate that to any historical analysis.

Mr. Gejdenson (D-Conn.): One of the things that troubles me about American foreign policy under this administration and in many others is that we seem to take a very shortsighted view. We seem to feel that somehow we can plug up the dike and hold the situation in place. It seems clear if we take a look at the experiences in Cuba, in El Salvador, as it is developing in Nicaragua, as it has occurred, that American foreign policy is not best suited by tying ourselves to a repressive regime that represents a very small faction in the country. When you take a look at the situation it seems, that sooner or later, the public is going to rise, that those people in power are going to get thrown out, and American security is going to go down the drain as it has in Nicaragua, as it has in Cuba, and as it has in countless other places around the world. At some point, our foreign policy has got to take a look at not simply what is right and nice about a government that murders its own people, but at some point, we have got to take a longer view of what is happening in the world.

If we take the short-term views of holding up this present dictator because they happen to get along with us and don't like the Cubans, we are going to end up being very alone in this world.

51. *Strategic Guatemala: Next Red Plum in the Hemisphere?* *

BY EDWARD J. WALSH

WHAT are U.S. interests in Guatemala that impel the Reagan administration to push for renewed support of that country? The following piece, introduced into the Congressional Record *in October 1981 by Senator Jesse Helms (R-N.C.), exemplifies how U.S. right-wing strategists have revived the anticommunist rhetoric of the Cold War, endowing Guatemala with the characteristics of a country under siege by Soviet infiltrators. While the issue of strategic economic interests are important to Mr. Walsh's discussion of Guatemala's*

* Reprinted from *National Defense: The Journal of the Defense Preparedness Association*, [Arlington, Va.] October 1981, by permission.

problems, he makes no mention of the social inequities and violence which many observers believe are at the root of Guatemala's crisis today.

GUATEMALA IS A small, mountainous nation at the neck of the Central American Isthmus. Like its neighbors in Central America, it was for many years ignored by the United States government, although American agricultural companies have long been present in the country. Nonetheless, few regions of the world are currently receiving more attention from the U.S. than Central America. The signing of the Panama Canal treaties, and the fall of the Somoza regime in Nicaragua to the Marxist-led Sandinista Front for the Liberation of Nicaragua (FSLN) in July 1979, were undoubtedly the catalysts in the process of rethinking the strategic significance of the Isthmus, a process that is continuing today. Such rethinking must necessarily begin with Guatemala, which, although still underdeveloped, is yet the richest and most populous country in the region.

Much debate has already taken place on the subject of the Marxist threat to Central America, especially since the Nicaraguan revolution and the coup d'état in El Salvador of October 1979. It has already been suggested many times that terrorism in the region is the result of a combination of "local conditions" and Soviet-guided, Cuban-assisted agitation. I will not continue that discussion here. Instead, I will focus on the strategic importance of Guatemala to the United States as the cornerstone of opposition to the continuing growth of Soviet influence in Central America.

A glance at the map of the Central American-Caribbean region reveals Guatemala's position as the link between Mexico and the rest of the Isthmus. Guatemala shares with its neighbors (except El Salvador) access to both oceans. There are few good harbors in Central America, however, and the coastlines are thinly peopled. The sea has therefore been the obvious route for subversives into the Isthmus, mainly from Cuba, dating from early in Castro's tenure. In 1962, a gun battle took place in a remote forest area on Guatemala's Caribbean coast near Belize; the dead were identified as Czechs. Since then, Marxist agents and arms have been funneled into Central America. In March 1980, the Carter administration accused Cuba of moving arms from the Honduran coast into El Salvador and in February 1981, the State Department revealed documents captured from Salvadoran guerrillas that verified the weapons traffic from Soviet bloc nations into El Salvador through Cuba.

Antagonisms Over Belize

The Pacific littoral of Guatemala is similarly isolated, from the more developed south-central highlands, by rugged volcanic peaks as high as 14,000 feet above sea level. On the Caribbean side, Puerto Barrios is the sole population center. To the north of this city lies the perennial problem of Belize, the British colony long claimed by Guatemala. In late March [1981], an agreement was reached in London by the British and Guatemalan governments that provides for independence for Belize, but gives Guatemala the right to a corridor through Belize's territorial waters, and the right to build two oil pipelines through to Belize's harbors. Belize's opposition party, the United Democrats, is adamantly against the plan and has withdrawn from further discussions. Hostility towards Guatemala in Belize is deepset, in the fear that Guatemala's long-standing claim may prompt it to invade Belize. The antagonism between these two neighbors will not end soon.[1]

Guatemala's view of its own history provides the principal basis for its claim on Belize; however, a more immediate reason is the recent discovery of oil. Getty, Texaco-Amoco, Basic Resources Ltd., and Spanish, French and Brazilian firms are exploring a narrow belt that extends from the Mexican border to the Caribbean coast at the center of Guatemala and additional tracts in the extreme northwestern quadrant. In 1978, when Guatemala's President Romeo Lucas García invited foreign oil companies to bid on leases, oil production was 220,000 barrels. By 1980, total production reached 1.4 million barrels.

A 125-mile long pipeline links Rubelsanto in the west with a shipping terminal at Santo Thomas on the Caribbean. On April 13, 1980, the tanker *Nefeli* left Santo Thomas with 120,000 barrels of crude, bound for New Orleans, Guatemala's first petroleum export. Today, reserves in the Rubelsanto tract alone are conservatively estimated at 33 million barrels. Needless to say, the Belize right-of-way will increase greatly the capacity to transport and load oil.

It hardly needs to be pointed out that Guatemala's oil reserves are in the same petroleum basin as those of Mexico; the rich oil fields of Campeche, Chiapas, and Tabasco, with estimated reserves of more than 60 billion barrels of recoverable crude oil and natural gas equivalent, lie hard on the Guatemalan border.

The proximity of Guatemala's oil fields to Mexico's is a geological phenomenon that is widely, and I think mistakenly, considered the key to a grand Communist strategy that aims at Mexico in a kind of "soft underbelly" threat to the United States. This theory assumes that the Central American dominoes will fall inexorably northward. It glosses over the significant political differences between Guatemala and Mexico on one hand, and the broad cultural contrasts between Mexico and the five Central American nations on the other. Both Mexico and Guatemala are resource-rich but underdeveloped countries with semi-authoritarian governments, large Indian populations, and the same official language. But politically, they are at opposite ends of the spectrum, with a leftist, one-party government in Mexico oriented strongly to the "Third World," and a conservative, staunchly anti-Communist regime in Guatemala. Mexican presidents come from the educated elite, while in Guatemala the head of state has usually been a career military man who has risen through the ranks in the Latin American tradi-

1. The independence of Belize, which occurred in September 1981, is supported by Guatemala's guerrilla organizations.—EDS.

tion. Political relations between the two countries are distant, and friction is the rule. Relations with the United States are a good barometer of the political perspective of the two governments: Mexico is wary of "domination" by the U.S., and there is a residue of distrust of the United States that dates from the Mexican-American war. Guatemala, in contrast, recognizes and welcomes a special role for American interests.

Much conventional wisdom assumes that Mexico could simply enter the Communist camp if Guatemala and the rest of Central America fell to Marxist-Leninist "peoples' movements." But it is more likely that Mexico's long tradition of supporting popular revolution makes it less vulnerable to Communist subversion. Although Marxism is entrenched in Mexico's political and intellectual circles, the reality of closeness to the United States has conditioned Mexico's culture profoundly, and generally mutes the anti-Americanism in official contacts. Mexico's leftism is a peculiarly Mexican kind, a complacent, corrupt socialism that seems immune to change, either by capitalists or communists. It may be that Mexico's habit of echoing the slogans of revolutionaries has created among leftists in Mexico and elsewhere a sort of tolerance of the stagnant Mexican political atmosphere.

Central American Targets

Recent history indicates that targets of Communist agitation lie south of Mexico rather than north of Guatemala. The political climate of the Central American nations, after all, has been anything but stagnant. As in nearly all Latin countries, instability has been chronic. Today, generals rule in Guatemala and Honduras, and El Salvador is governed by a fragile civilian-military junta. Nicaragua, after 46 years of rule by the Somozas, is already a Marxist puppet state. Only Costa Rica has enjoyed a measure of calm in the past years, but that is now threatened by a declining economy and a growing Communist presence. Nevertheless, the Central American countries share a legacy of closeness to the United States through military and economic ties—one might even say economic domination—that Mexico has not experienced.

On this score, it is important to note that U.S. involvement in Central America has been a two-sided coin. American agribusinesses and military assistance have contributed the lion's share of progress in the region. U.S. companies provided investment that built factories, roads, hospitals, and schools, and today provides jobs for thousands of Central Americans. American military aid and training has buttressed the armed forces of Central America, the traditional source of trained administrators and bureaucrats in the Latin American government infrastructure. The reverse side of the coin has been that the U.S. presence has provided a target of opportunity for leftist organizations that have been infiltrated and co-opted by Communists.

At the same time, it is by no means true that Central American governments have been no more than puppets of the United States. It is reasonable to surmise that the Somoza regime could have survived with less American aid than it received over the years, by virtue of Anastasio Somoza's political abilities and the intense loyalty of his National Guard, which he had cultivated. Before he fell, Somoza had arranged to purchase weapons from Israel, which were never received because of pressure on the Israeli government by the Carter Administration, as U.S. Ambassador to the United Nations Jeane Kirkpatrick has pointed out. Had he obtained them, or weapons from another source, the outcome of the Sandinista revolution might well have been different—without American aid.

Guatemala today is a good example of the hypothesis that American economic aid and investment have been major factors in the nation's development and growth. U.S. military assistance and training over the years have produced a highly competent, seasoned cadre of officers well-versed in guerrilla warfare and counterinsurgency techniques. They command an army of 18,000 men. The political consciousness of the government and the business elite is enthusiastically, some would say definitely, conservative and pro-Western. Consequently, the economic and political institutions, developed on the U.S. model, are the target of Communist subversion and terrorist attack.

Today, however, Guatemala purchases weapons from Israel, since American aid was discontinued by the Carter Administration. The lack of American assistance has not weakened the Lucas government's determination to continue the fight, however, and the battle against the Marxist-led guerrillas continues. Currently, the guerrillas are limited to assassinations and kidnappings in the urban areas, and ambushes of army patrols in the countryside. Government officials and supporters are murdered, and leftist assaults on individuals and property are answered by private rightist groups which attack leftist students, intellectuals, union leaders, and clergymen who criticize the government. Consequently, Guatemala has become a "pariah" state, a member of a club of internationally disliked countries that includes two other major Latin nations, Argentina and Chile, as well as South Africa, South Korea, and Taiwan.

Strategic Guatemala

Like those countries, Guatemala is of strategic value to the United States because it is of strategic value to the Soviet proxies who threaten it. Guatemala shares with nearly all the above-mentioned nations certain characteristics which make them attractive to the Soviets: it commands a privileged geopolitical position adjacent to a vital waterway (the Caribbean straits); it is close to one or more countries controlled by an aggressive pro-Soviet regime (Cuba, Nicaragua); it possesses valuable natural resources (oil, nickel), and a robust free-market oriented economy. In addition, Guatemala is governed by an authoritarian regime that has been attacked from within by "indigenous forces" that include pro-Soviet elements. Furthermore, these countries have in common economic and political elites that are fiercely anti-communist, though not unqualifiedly pro-American, and have been the subject of repeated condemnations by international human rights organizations.

Of these states, Guatemala is unique in its proximity both to the United States and to weak non-communist countries with strong leftist factions. No other Central American or Caribbean nation has the same combination of assets and liabilities in terms of strategic importance, and no other nation in the region reflects the same embattled attitude toward Marxist subversion.

Today, despite the closeness of the United States and Mexico, no country in the region evidences noticeably strong political ties to either. A power vacuum of sorts exists in terms of regional leadership, in which two local centers of political and military power, Cuba and Guatemala, are contending through indirect, ideological warfare. Cuba has established valuable footholds in Nicaragua, Guyana, and in Grenada, where it is assisting the leftist government in building a modern airport with a runway capable of accommodating wide-bodied jets. Marxist elements also have made significant inroads in El Salvador, Costa Rica, and Panama. Until the election of Edward Seaga as prime minister of Jamaica last October, that country, with its rich bauxite reserves, had teetered in the Cuban orbit.

Conversely, Guatemala has no important friends in the region. Its isolation is in part due to criticism by human rights organizations that have often bypassed human rights abuses in Marxist states. Mexico, Costa Rica, and Venezuela have added their voices to those of the rights advocates, while steering clear of, for example, the issue of political prisoners in Cuba. The principal reason for Guatemala's beleaguered international position, though, is that in no other Central American or Caribbean country has the war against Marxist subversion been drawn so starkly. In El Salvador, the United States has most recently borne the brunt of criticism for supplying arms and advisers to the junta. In Guatemala, the shadow of the United States no longer falls over decision-making in the National Palace. Guatemalans see themselves in a battle for their nation that only they can win. Mexico and Venezuela, the two major economic powers in the region, have asserted their role by agreeing to convert the oil debts of nine small Caribbean countries into long term loans; both powers have confined themselves to speechmaking in the ideological war.

Despite claims by numerous diplomats and journalists that the United States no longer occupies the central political role in the Caribbean-Central American region, the U.S. will inevitably be a major player in the region's affairs. Our economic ties are too extensive, and our historical interest too deep to detach ourselves from political events there, especially when so many governments in Central America and the Caribbean hope for a stronger American hand. In seeking to reassert opposition to continually expanding Soviet influence, the U.S. must identify its logical allies and assist them as much as possible in fending off Communist agitation that originates in Cuba or other Soviet puppets. This task, of course, is separate and distinct from cooperating with authoritarian governments in repressing any domestic group it perceives to be in opposition to its policies. The first target of such U.S. attention is Guatemala. If we are to defend our interests in the region, the way to do it is to buttress the strong links in order to protect the weaker ones. Guatemala is the only stalwartly anti-communist country in the Central American-Caribbean theater with a relatively healthy economy, a capable army, and a key geopolitical position.

Strong U.S. Ties

For these reasons, Guatemala is enduring a bloody terrorist campaign conducted by pro-Soviet guerrilla tacticians. At the same time, Guatemala has a tradition of closeness to the United States: children of wealthy Guatemalans are educated in the U.S., and senior Guatemalan officers were trained in American military colleges. This longtime affection for the U.S. suffered when the country was put on trial for human rights violations in recent years, but it is as deep-rooted as America's interest in Central America. Guatemalans hope their admiration for the United States will be reciprocated. But if it is not, they are prepared to forge closer ties with the other "pariah" nations (and, in fact, have received weapons and military advice from Argentina).

It is important to note that closer cooperation between the United States and Guatemala should be based on mutual recognition and understanding of the strategic priorities in the Central-American-Caribbean region. It does not mean that human rights abuses should be ignored or condoned. Still, the United States has few reliable allies in this critically important region. We cannot help Guatemala build a more prosperous economy or refine its practice of democracy while the nation is fighting an internal war. The war should be won, and then the social problems given prompt attention, both with American assistance.

52. *Wrong Central American Policy* *

BY WAYNE S. SMITH

IN 1982 the United States continued to destabilize Nicaragua, from both inside and outside the country, allocating $19 million to underwrite counterrevolutionary activities by anti-Sandinista forces in Honduras. Raids by counterrevolutionary groups, based in Honduras, into northern Nicaragua are a clear attempt to undermine the Sandinista government. Honduras plays a key role in this de-

---

* Reprinted from *The New York Times*, October 12, 1982, by permission.

veloping crisis as the locus of anti-Sandinista activity supported by the United States. Military assistance to Honduras increased from $5.5 million in 1981 to $32.3 million in 1982, with $36.3 million projected for 1983. Unofficial military aid was reported by a senior Honduran army officer to have topped $100 million in 1981. The approximately ninety U.S. military advisers in Honduras, more than in El Salvador, and the war games scheduled for late 1982 off the coast of Honduras attest to U.S. efforts to make Honduras the planning and staging grounds for regional U.S. strategy.

Former chief of the United States Interests Section in Havana, Wayne S. Smith, privy to closed door discussions of U.S. policy in Central America and the Caribbean, believes that the effort to regain dominance in Central America through military force is a fatal error. Now senior associate at the Carnegie Endowment for International Peace, Smith argues in the following piece that U.S. interests could best be served through negotiations for a peaceful settlement to the conflicts in the region.

ALMOST TWO YEARS after they were adopted, the Reagan Administration's confrontational policies in Central America have produced not victories but, rather, widening conflict and dwindling options for peaceful solutions.

There have been recent reports that the United States has been quietly encouraging contacts between the new Government in El Salvador and the guerrillas, and President Reagan has at least professed interest in a Mexican-Venezuelan peace plan for Central America. Does this mean that the Administration is trimming its sails? Possibly. If so, one can only applaud. But don't count on it. A more accurate indicator of Administration strategy was probably the meeting convened by the United States last week in San José, Costa Rica, to endorse a formula outlawing arms trafficking, subversion and foreign military advisers. Only governments that tend to agree with ours were invited. Nicaragua, Cuba, even Mexico and Venezuela were excluded. The Administration seems not to understand that to be useful, negotiations must include the other side.

This approach follows a pattern. To date, the Administration had denigrated negotiations and grossly misanalyzed the situation in Central America. Initially, it insisted that conflicts there were not internal—rather, that they represented Soviet-Cuban expansionism and thus implied a major East-West test of wills. Incredibly, at one point the Administration even suggested that there was "no native insurgency" in El Salvador. With such a skewed, unrealistic approach to the problem, no wonder Washington is in serious trouble.

This all could have been avoided. As the Administration took office, it was in a strong position in Central America. The Salvadoran guerrillas, who had launched an all-out offensive on Jan. 10, 1981, had already been turned back. During the year, they came around, offering negotiations without preconditions. The Cubans and Nicaraguans, realizing they had miscalculated, also signaled willingness to address our concerns and seek a peaceful settlement in El Salvador. The Administration was in a good position to negotiate from strength. Had it done so, it might indeed have had a victory to its credit—a diplomatic victory. Unfortunately, it was not interested in negotiations. No, it was precisely for that sort of supine nonsense that it had berated the Carter Administration. The Reagan team thus put aside opportunities for effective diplomacy in order to demonstrate that tough talk could force a full political and military victory. It didn't work.

The Administration assures us that things are going its way in Central America. Serious observers, however, should consider the following facts:

1. The fighting has increased in El Salvador since the March elections, with the guerrillas dealing Government forces several sharp defeats. Clearly, the introduction of more United States-trained troops is not turning the tide. On the contrary, the guerrillas are more than holding their own, and give evidence of ability to fight on indefinitely. An old adage should be borne in mind: In guerrilla warfare, if the government isn't winning, it's losing.

2. While the voter turnout in March was inspiring, the hard facts are that the opposition did not participate and that the result was a right-wing Government that has further complicated our problems. The United States has prevented it from gutting agrarian reforms, and Maj. Roberto d'Aubuisson, the Arena Party's leader, has not napalmed the countryside as he had threatened. Even so, the Government's underlying anti-popular proclivities are clear and are likely to encourage erosion of its popular support, thus swinging time to the side of the guerrillas.

3. In the wake of the Falklands crisis, the United States is virtually isolated in El Salvador. We can no longer count on *sub rosa* Argentine support or backing from, say, Venezuela. In fact, Venezuela has swung around to opposing our approach in El Salvador, as do most other governments around the world.

4. Cuban support for the Salvadoran guerrillas may soon resume in earnest—if it has not done so already. In order to improve the atmosphere for broad negotiations early this year, Cuba sharply reduced, if not suspended, that support, a gesture that Washington simply ignored. The Administration, after all, had based its whole case on the assertion that this was a matter of external aggression. Intent on sustaining that assertion, it had no interest in examining any possible contradictions. Thus, even while privately acknowledging that it did not have concrete evidence of a continuing flow of arms, it publicly insisted that it did. This was obtuse, for our rejection of Cuban overtures obviated incentives for Cuban restraint.

Thus, the most elementary overview shows our situation in El Salvador to be deteriorating. We may well be headed for a bloody debacle.

Even if the Administration now wished to change course, at this late date that will not be easy. The new Government in El Salvador has no enthusiasm either for reforms or for measures to curb the excesses of its own security forces. At least until recently, the military had categorically ruled out any contacts with the guerrillas, threatening that anyone who sat down at the table with them would be finished in politics (if not finished off by death squads). As we could not have the military victory we wanted without the military, we accepted its veto. So much for the Administration's claim that doors were never closed to negotiations. Unless those doors are opened, the fighting stopped and the opposition engaged in the political process, El Salvador's 1984 elections will resolve nothing. Negotiations must be an integral part of the process just as elections must.

In Nicaragua, our confrontational approach was even more gratuitous than in El Salvador. The Nicaraguans had acceded to our demands and suspended support for the Salvadoran guerrillas, thus pointing up our negotiating leverage with them. This could have been pivotal, for the best hope of preserving democratic pluralism and of imposing subtle restraints on the Sandinists' radical tendencies was in bringing that leverage to bear within the context of the engagement-of-interest tactics pursued by Ambassador Lawrence A. Pezzullo, and in enhancing the democratic opposition's role.

Even rudimentary knowledge of the politics of nations should have informed us that if we wish to encourage moderation and pluralism in another country, we should not adopt a sharply confrontational posture. That leads ineluctably to the sort of demand for internal discipline and rally-round-the-flag mentality that work directly against moderation. Yet, that is precisely what the Reagan Administration did. The democratic opposition in Nicaragua told us that this would be counterproductive, that it would simply make it more difficult to play an effective role. Obviously. Our encouragement of right-wing Nicaraguan exile groups operating from Honduras further undermined the opposition.

Our policy makers may be tempted to see solutions in the overthrow of the Sandinist Government. But that is a dangerous road. Right-wing groups are the best organized to make such an attempt but are so discredited in Nicaragua that they could not possibly form a viable government even if the Sandinists collapsed—and our policy has already contributed to the decimation of the more legitimate opposition. In any event, these stabilization efforts would be shortsighted. We would be no more likely thus to solve the Nicaraguan problem than we solved the Guatemalan problem in 1954 with the overthrow of President Jacobo Arbenz. The one would remain to haunt us as the other has.

Meanwhile, we have also drawn in Honduras. But using it as a cat's paw against Nicaragua will not only internationalize the conflict but also undermine democratic processes and elements in Honduras. The remedy, then, is far worse than the ailment.

Guerrilla warfare is also escalating in Guatemala, where the Government's genocide against the Indians continues unchecked. Indeed, the Government's atrocities make the Sabra and Shatila massacres in Beirut pale by comparison. Guatemala may be the most dangerous powder keg in the region.

In short, the Administration's policies are not working. We should be seeking moderate solutions rather than clumsily provoking an extreme outcome unfavorable to our interests. It is perhaps not too late for broadly based negotiations.

Mexico and Venezuela have offered to be helpful; so have France, Panama and Costa Rica. Rather than attempting cleverly to maneuver around them, the United States should welcome such initiatives. Probably the best hope for peace would be an international effort to produce regional accords—perhaps with third parties trusted by both sides acting as guarantors. Restraint, of course, would have to be mutual—another fact the Administration has so far not wished to grasp.

All sides have more to gain from sensible compromise than from a regional conflict. Imaginative diplomacy, however structured, could still turn things around, if the Reagan Administration would only give it a serious try. If it does not, we may soon have on our hands a full-scale foreign policy disaster in Central America.

53. *Elections: Symbols Of Democracy?* *

BY NELSON SANTANA

MOST North Americans believe that elections are the touchstone of any system that calls itself democratic. But a moment's reflection will remind anyone that elections can serve undemocratic purposes as well, as illustrated by Adolph Hitler's manipulation of the electoral process in Nazi Germany.[1] *In the article that follows, journalist and photographer N. Santana examines four recent elections in Central America, including the March 1982 elections in Guatemala, and the coup that immediately followed. Her reportage is based upon eyewitness observation of these elections, and extensive travel in Central America and the Caribbean Basin, which she has been covering since 1974. Her journalistic reports have appeared in the* Los Angeles Times, Harpers, Rolling Stone *magazine,* The Nation, *and other publications.*

FROM NOVEMBER 29 to March 29 Central America experienced four national elections—in Honduras, Costa Rica, Guatemala, and El Salvador. Although Costa Rica and Guatemala were following their appointed schedule, Honduras and El Salvador rushed into their elections under intense pressure from the United States.

---

* From *NACLA Report* [North American Congress on Latin America, New York], June/July, 1982, specially revised for this volume, reprinted by permission of NACLA and Nelson Santana.

1. Franz Neumann, *Behemoth: The Structure and Practice of National Socialism*, 2d ed. (New York: Oxford University Press, 1944), pp. 32, 54-55; Alan Bullock, *Hitler: A Study in Tyranny* (New York: Harper & Row, 1952).

For the bemused observer on the Central American election trail, the four events had little in common other than flowery oratory and paper ballots. In Costa Rica the long-standing electoral tradition meant that one civilian party could peacefully transfer power to another, especially since there was a minuscule political distance between the two. In Guatemala, on the other hand, the electoral process merely fueled an internal conflict among military cliques that exploded after the election results were announced. In Honduras there was a vigorous registration process and a massive turnout. The less conservative of the two mainstream parties won, but the elections came about through a pact with the military, which was quick to reassert its preeminence once the votes were counted. In El Salvador the elections were preceded by a haphazard registration process under wartime conditions, while the country's highest officials quarreled over the eligibility of the left-through-liberal spectrum to participate. As expected, the U.S.-backed Christian Democrats won the largest number of votes, but their victory was snatched away by an alliance between the other five contending parties of the right. The Constituent Assembly, which was intended to give the Christian Democratic government Constitutional authority, instead shifted the government back into the hands of forces clearly identified with oligarchic interests.

The differences and the similarities between the four demonstrate how deceptive it can be to interpret elections in countries where the underpinnings of democracy have never been established. The 1981-82 elections in Central America saw the advent of computerized vote-counting systems in Guatemala under the control of parties determined to commit fraud, and satellite hook-ups to the United States to report the results of a Salvadoran election while large expanses of the country were under guerrilla control. Freedoms of the press, of speech, and of assembly have been suspended in El Salvador and Guatemala for many years. Honduras shares with them an illiteracy rate of sixty percent. Only Costa Rica, with a literate, informed populace and an absence of political repression, showed the classic face of a bourgeois democracy in a recognizable form.

What then did the other elections achieve? In Guatemala, very little, since their results were reversed within two weeks. But El Salvador's and Honduras's elections were sparked by Washington's need for regimes that could present an image of democratic pluralism to the world without making concession to guerrilla movements or their leftist allies. The aims of the elections were complemented by the formation of the Central American Democratic Community in January, made up of El Salvador, Costa Rica, and Honduras,[2] and by a series of measures taken against the Sandinista regime in Nicaragua. Elections were presented as the only answer to "tyrannies of the left and tyrannies of the right," and

2. Guatemala was excluded from the Democratic Community at its formation but joined under Ríos Montt.—EDS.

were a necessary pressure point for the U.S. Congress, which requested increasing reassurance to continue their approval of U.S. regional military aid programs.

Honduras

The 1982 Honduran elections were the posthumous legacy of the Carter human rights policy, looking to repeat the 1978 success in cleaning up the elections in the Dominican Republic. Honduran president Policarpo Paz García, who had taken power in a bloodless coup in August 1978, had come under steady pressure from the Carter Administration to hold elections for a constituent assembly in April 1980. Hondurans turned out in large numbers to vote, handing a resounding victory to the Liberal Party.

By the time Reagan took office in January 1981, Honduras had taken on a critical tactical importance in relation to the war in El Salvador, the tensions with Nicaragua, and the coming storm in Guatemala. Every last-minute effort Paz made to hold onto his office by postponing or sidestepping the elections was firmly vetoed by the United States.

Most Hondurans were only vaguely aware of Paz's machinations. For them it was a long-postponed contest between two traditional forces in Honduran politics, the conservative National ("blue") Party and the slightly less conservative Liberal ("red") Party. It was also a chance to vote against the army, which had roused widespread disgust at its corruption and mismanagement in running the economy and government. With more than sixty percent of the population illiterate, the political campaigns made frequent use of radio ads and stressed ties to party traditions—and colors—over allegiance to individual candidates. Suazo Córdova, a folksy small-town doctor with cattlelands on the side, faced the threat of party mutiny and competing personality cults. But the Conservatives were running Ricardo Zuñiga, an unsavory figure who had been publicly taken to task for crimes ranging from electoral fraud to running a small-time smuggling ring out of Miami. Suazo won easily.

As planned, the new constitutional government took over many tasks of public and economic administration from the military. But it has also abided by the rules of the game hammered out in pre-electoral talks: no investigations into military corruption, and military veto powers over key cabinet appointments. The military has exchanged a titular role as head of government for an expansion of real powers. New military strongman Gustavo Alvarez has taken on greater political visibility, engineered his own promotion to General, and succeeded in sending liberal competitors within the officers corps into genteel exile in foreign embassies. Alvarez and Suazo have publicly welcomed the possibility of U.S. military intervention in Honduras, but their new regime has suffered a sharp erosion of public confidence.

Costa Rica

The Costa Ricans celebrate their elections as the "fiesta cívica." For weeks before the contest cars jammed the streets blasting out the syllables of their candidates' names. In the capital ten different parties bloomed, including an all-female party whose only male inexplicably headed the ticket. But the race belonged to the National Liberation Party (PLN), the only party to retain the same name and institutional identity since 1953, and the incumbent Unity Party, a coalition formed in 1978 by outgoing President Rodrigo Carazo, encompassing the Christian Democats, the Democratic Renewal Party, and the Popular Union.

Costa Ricans claim their country is dominated by the "extreme center." Since 1948 it has been run without interruption as Latin America's most functional bourgeois democracy, achieving a ninety-five percent literacy rate, the outlines of a welfare state economy, and the complete dismantling of the country's military establishment. The February elections gave the country a chance to vote against the Unity Party's Carazo Administration, which led the country into a painful economic decline and a corresponding crisis in public confidence.

The PLN and its presidential candidate Luis Alberto Monge effectively attacked Unity Party candidate Rafael Calderón on the issue of Calderón's disastrous management of the national debt. But the country's economic problems were also doubtlessly rooted in the same rising energy costs, low commodity prices, and accelerated capital flight that have been plaguing the rest of Central America. About one million of Costa Rica's 2.2 million citizens turned out to hand Monge his victory. The President-elect faced the immediate problem of renegotiating the foreign debt under stringent conditions from the International Monetary Fund. The pressure was heightened by a Reagan Administration eager to use Costa Rica's international standing to lend credibility to El Salvador, Honduras, and Guatemala through the Central American Democratic Community, while ostracizing Nicaragua. The economic squeeze made the Monge government especially susceptible to such pressure.

Guatemala

For most participants Guatemala's March 7 elections were an exercise in futility and false hope. The military clique of incumbent President Romeo Lucas García had inexplicably arrived at the choice of General Aníbal Guevara as the official government candidate of the Popular Democratic Front, a coalition that one conservative businessman described as "not supported by a truly popular base or by the leadership of any person in particular" and "a purely economic convenience."

As the official candidate, Guevara had all government facilities (including vote-counting apparatus) at his disposal. Although it was commonly said that without the benefit of fraud, Guevara would place third (after Mario Sandoval of the National Liberation Movement and Alejandro Maldonado of the National Renovation Party and Christian Democrat coalition), Guevara won the election by a wide official margin.

Guevara's fraudulent victory prompted protests from the unlikely losers' alliance of Christian Democrats and the MLN. (A fourth party, the Authentic Nationalist Center, was backed by Sandoval's fellow veteran counterinsurgency master, Carlos Arana. It received lukewarm support from the business sector but ran a subdued, penny-pinching campaign.) Within two weeks the elections were rendered irrelevant by a military coup. The government was taken over by retired General Efráin Ríos Montt, who was the Christian Democratic coalition candidate of 1974, and a group of young officers allied to the MLN. There was little opposition: the Lucas dictatorship had lost all support among the private sector, the Reagan Administration, and the disaffected young officers corps in the Army, while the embittered rival parties were natural enemies.

Ríos Montt appointed himself President of the Republic in June, accepting the resignation of his two fellow junta members. Future elections have been suggested, but U.S. embassy sources have predicted that they could be postponed until 1984. But Ríos Montt may be attempting to build a new alliance against insurgency, uniting the interests of the Christian Democrats, the military, and the United States—not unlike the "moderate" regime of liberal Julio César Méndez. His administration, 1966-1970, coincided with a bloody counterinsurgency campaign in the east, directed by Carlos Arana Osorio with the assistance of U.S. military advisors.

El Salvador

The March 28 elections in El Salvador were intended to elect a sixty-seat constituent assembly, which would create a provisional government and lay the groundwork for national presidential elections to come. Never were elections so hotly debated nor so wildly misunderstood. The contest had been a linchpin for U.S. policy in El Salvador for more than a year, and the Reagan Administration pointed to it as proof that nonviolent "democracy" does indeed enjoy the popular support that the armed leftist opposition lacks.

But far from being a pat answer to El Salvador's crisis, the elections were themselves questionable at every turn. A study released by the Central American University in San Salvador questioned the "massive turnout," charging that the number of voters had been inflated by the Central Election Board. Former Ambassador Robert White questioned the "secret ballot," noting that voters were required to drop numbered slips into transparent urns as National Guardsmen stood nearby. Campaign practices were questioned as only one of the six registered parties, D'Aubuisson's National Republican Alliance (ARENA), dared to campaign outside the capital, moving down the highways in heavily armed caravans of armored cars.

The Christian Democrats never expected to win the fifty-one percent of the vote required to give them an assembly majority, but they did hope to push their total up through an alliance with Democratic Action, a small new party backed by businessmen of the center-right. Democratic Action went over to the five-party coalition after the elections under circumstances suggesting that such had been the plan all along. It was a moment rich with historical irony: the Christian Democrats had won the vote in 1972 and 1977 in their electoral alliance with the Social Democrats and the communist front organization. Now, in 1982, the Christian Democrats may have been capable of holding onto electoral office, but they lacked the allies and the votes to win the election. D'Aubuisson, the most charismatic caudillo in the new right-wing alliance, was quickly elected President of the Constituent Assembly. Alvaro Magana was given the Presidency as a gesture toward the Army and its traditional political organ, the National Conciliation Party (PCN). [The PCN, of course, was the party of General Carlos Romero before he took flight in the October 1979 coup.] It behooved no one to admit it, but the March 1982 elections brought the Salvadoran government full circle.

U.S. Policy

What did the four Central American elections accomplish regarding U.S. policy? The United States' newfound commitment to democratically elected office holders in Latin America is startling in light of historical record. The CIA participation in coups to overthrow constitutional presidents Arbenz of Guatemala in 1954 and Allende of Chile in 1973 are but the two most obvious examples. The 1965 intervention of more than twenty thousand U.S. marines in the Dominican Republic was directed against forces fighting to restore democratically elected President Juan Bosch, in favor of the heirs to the Trujillo dictatorship. In other cases, Washington's silence has spoken louder than words. Nicaragua's Anastasio Somoza's elections were accepted at face value, as he won, unchallenged, by "popular acclamation" for term after term.

The State Department continued this tradition in Guatemala in March, lending credence to a clean Guevara victory in its private analyses and public congratulations when Guatemalans ranging from his fellow officers to the Chamber of Commerce were denouncing the fraud and plotting his downfall.

One difference between Santo Domingo in 1965 and San Salvador in 1982 is that U.S. policy needs an electoral facade. U.S. public and congressional opinion have scrutinized Central American policy as they never did in the Dominican Republic. They will still listen to past geopolitical arguments cast in terms of an East-West conflict, but they bring a skepticism tempered by the fatal miscalculation of Vietnam.

In the careless imperialism of earlier days, it would have been easier to appoint Salvadoran Defense Minister García as Washington's president-designate and let him carry out desired counterinsurgency measures. Such leaders were perfectly responsive and responsible to U.S. interests in a way that even fraudulent elections can never be.

But if the superficial mechanics of the electoral process can be shown to be "clean"—an obsessive aim in El Salvador—then elections are more convenient to U.S. policy makers than a more thoroughgoing participatory democracy. Democracy is more than a piece of paper. Democratic institutions required centuries to develop out of feudalism in Western Europe and North America. Until Central Americans achieve effective equality under the law, unbonded labor, fundamental civil liberties, and the means to receive, understand, and promulgate information, their elections will be controlled by the same minority elites who dictate the law, bond the labor, repress opposition, and own the media. When the United States backs elections without taking human rights and democratic institutions into account, it is only aligning itself more solidly to the same entrenched interests that have proven themselves enemies to a meaningful democratic process.

54. *Did History Lie When It Promised Peace and Progress?* *

BY EDUARDO GALEANO

EDUARDO Galeano, an Uruguayan in exile, is the author of Open Veins of Latin America, *the classic study of how foreign domination has distorted the development of Latin American societies. Galeano knows Guatemala well. He traveled with guerrilla groups active in the eastern mountains of Guatemala in the 1960s and wrote a study of the period,* Guatemala: Occupied Country. *In the following essay, written fourteen years after* Occupied Country, *Mr. Galeano denounces injustice in Latin America and delves into the ties that bind those nations to the Western world.*

ONE TAKES A glance at international statistics and asks: what kind of a world is this we live in? A gigantic insane asylum? A slaughterhouse? Who has written this play that we are obliged to perform? Some crazy or euphoric executioner? Did history lie when it promised peace and progress?

Ten thousand persons die from starvation every day, but every day the world spends more than $1 billion on armies and weapons. The comparison between figures for military expenditures and the statistics for illiteracy, disease, and backwardness makes one shudder in horror if one thinks that for the cost of one tank five hundred classrooms could be equipped, that one jet fighter equals forty thousand drug stores, and with the money spent on one destroyer electricity could be provided for nine million people. Even if weapons were stored and never fired,

* Reprinted from *Proceso* [Mexico City], May 15, 1982, by permission. Translated by Marianne Dugan and Ernesto Castillo.

they would still devour the resources of the world economy. And to be sure, they are fired. But not against hunger; against the hungry.

A war economy during times of peace? What peace? Even if not a single shot were fired nor a single bomb exploded, a secret and undeclared war would still take thirty million victims each year in countries such as El Salvador or Guatemala. Thirty million people die of starvation each year. In the world? Ah, no, in the Third World, that is to say, in another world. This term has met such a sad destiny. It was created by Alfred Sauvy years ago, never suspecting it would serve as an alibi for the opulent countries. The so-called Third World is part of the capitalist world for the simple reason that underdevelopment is not a stage of development, but the historical consequence of someone else's development. Some countries are poor because other countries are rich, in the wake of a long history of plunder; a disguised and deceiving history, but painfully real.

Waste of resources, or resources to defend the waste? Could the world's unequal organization sustain itself even one day longer if the privileged countries and social classes, who are accustomed to squander, weren't armed to the teeth? The misery of the many threatens the wealth of the few. There are reasons for them living in a state of alarm, sleeping with one eye open, this fistful of countries sick from consumerism, ostentatiously stuffed with unnecessary objects and voraciously bent on razing the riches of this earth. In a recent work, Jean Ziegler points out that the contemporary world, a world of starving people, produces enough grain to feed a population three times larger than its current size. A third of this grain goes to the bowels of cows; and in the rich countries four out of ten people die not from hunger, but from gluttony, an excessive consumption of meat and fat.

At the same time, in another recent work, Jacques Choncol has demonstrated that Latin America produces more calories and protein than is needed by its population. Nevertheless, half of Latin Americans are children and half of these children are malnourished. According to the Food and Agricultural Organization of the U.N., thirty-five of every hundred Latin Americans suffer from serious malnutrition, the name that specialists give to hunger. Would it surprise anyone that the exploited countries spend the same on arms as they do on agricultural development? This fact can and should provoke indignation; but surprise, never. Do these countries, by chance, have no owners? And these owners, do they not have reason to feel harassed? The underdeveloped countries—which out of modesty or hypocrisy are called "developing countries"—have doubled their military expenditures between 1970 and 1975. In the same period, they lowered food production per person.

Without a bayonet behind every back, how would those who drowned Chile's democracy in blood be able to govern? What other way is there to sustain a situation in which millions of Chileans survive eating noodles, while the victors eat french bread flown in each day from Paris and drink whiskey from Scotland?

Within this framework, the crisis in Central America has exploded. It is within this general scheme of things that Nicaragua is bombarded with threats, that charges are leveled against Cuba—the red devil with horns and a long tail that, like God, is everywhere—and imperialist intervention in El Salvador and Guatemala once again surfaces.

The revolutionary fervor of Central America is a profound reply to the secret war that kills hungry children and the invisible violence that imprisons peoples and countries. The wars shaking up this tormented region, we could say, are wars against war; liberation wars that attack the causes of war, wars against the daily war that drains the working class, wars against the false peace of the prisons and the cemeteries, wars of the people for the only peace that deserves to be called peace, peace with dignity. The popular challenge for profound change collides with the system and unmasks its true character: the imperial power, threatened within its domain, gives extermination orders and the terrorism of the State shows all its teeth. The owners of terror, the uniformed terrorists, call their victims terrorists. But take a look at one illustrative fact from the last report of the group on disappearances of the United Nations Human Rights Commission: In El Salvador, eighty-seven children under fourteen years of age have been captured by the armed forces. These children were not accused of terrorism. These children have disappeared.

In a press conference, Jeane Kirkpatrick, President Reagan's UN representative, stated that Somoza was preferable to the Sandinistas. She could have said, even more sincerely, that William Walker was even more preferable. William Walker was a North American pirate who more than a century ago, in 1856, proclaimed himself president of Nicaragua and El Salvador and reestablished black slavery in both countries. The United States, after having spent half a century refusing to recognize the independence of Haiti, immediately recognized this filibuster's government and sent him an ambassador. The following year Walker was expelled by Central American patriots, but President Buchanan announced from Washington: "This is the destiny of our race. Our emigration will continue southward and no one will be able to halt it. Within a short time, Central America [will be ours]. . . ."[3] Ten years before, a North American military invasion had uprooted half of Mexico's territory.

The history of North American intervention in Central America, the Caribbean and the rest of Latin America—a history of incessant infamies and atrocities—accompanies step-by-step the history of the emergence and consolidation of the United States as a world power. We are not going to tell that history here. It is enough to look at the present reality of countries where the dictator or transient figurehead president behaves as if he were the Ambassador of the United States, the Ambassador of the United States acts like a viceroy and the Minister of Economy like his tax collector, at the same time the commander-in-chief of the armed forces runs around scalping the heads of the defeated Indians. And it is

---

3. James D. Richardson, ed., *A Compilation of the Messages and Papers of the Presidents* (Washington, D.C.: U.S. Government Printing Office, 1907)

enough to remember, for example, that the present tragic cycle in Guatemala began almost thirty years ago, in 1954, when the U.S. armed and accompanied an invasion that liquidated by fire and sword a democratically elected government that had the subversive idea of carrying out an agrarian reform. Years later, in the 1960s, in order to crush the struggle of the dispossessed campesinos, the U.S. converted Guatemala into a laboratory for applying the "dirty war" techniques they had begun testing in Vietnam. Guatemala was the first Latin American country where the technique of "disappearance" was developed on a large scale. Today this method continues to be applied in Guatemala, as well as in El Salvador and other countries ruled by kidnappers. In Argentina there have been no less than twenty thousand victims whom the power apparatus has devoured, hoping to erase any traces.

For many years now reality has painfully shown that North American training centers for Latin American militaries mass-produce dictatorships. In these centers the generals who exercise power have learned to chop human flesh and to rule by treason, either directly or through some civilian masquerade. This is the case in most of our countries.

Sometimes these intermediaries lose their balance before the onslaught of the people's rage. The United Nations Human Rights Commission has just reported that the armed forces and the paramilitary squads of El Salvador are responsible for almost all of the political murders committed last year, eleven thousand assassinations over and above those killed in military confrontations. Meanwhile, some expert journalists believe the true number to be much higher and point out that the Salvadoran military kills forty civilians for every guerrilla eliminated. But nevertheless, it is useless. The CIA advises President Reagan that the war will not be won without the direct and massive intervention of U.S. troops. Up until now, the growing shipment of arms and "advisors" has multiplied the deaths, but not the strength of the dictatorship.

From the point of view of most of the Western world's media, there are, in the world, deaths of a second category. They are the victims of programs for readjusting the nuts and bolts of imperialism in countries of a second category. Fifty crimes per day in El Salvador and Guatemala belong to the "natural order of things," they are "normal" and rarely deserve anything more than a macabre photograph or some article describing the bizarre quality of the horror. In the inequality of the organization of the world, there are those who deserve solidarity and those who deserve, at most, charity or pity.

What would have happened to Andrei Sakharov if he'd been born in El Salvador? Would Lech Walesa have been so famous if he were a union leader in Guatemala? Would Lech Walesa be alive if he were a union leader in Guatemala? The dictatorship of José Napoleón Duarte announced with pomp and circumstance the capture of the military men guilty of the rape and murder of four North American nuns in El Salvador. But Duarte has never announced the capture of those military men guilty of the horrendous murders of thousands and thousands of his countrymen, castrated campesinos, beheaded or burned alive.

The murder of the North American nuns was a dangerous mistake made by the regime; the massacre of Salvadorans is a necessity and a merit.

The drama of Poland—a drama of the divorce between the working class and those in power who claim to represent them—has given place, of late, to the most boisterous festival of hypocrisy. We have seen the jailers, the executioners and the interrogators of Turkey, Uruguay, and Guatemala shedding oceans of tears for the badly wounded liberty of the Polish workers, as if the shipyard workers of Gdansk were natural allies of the dictatorships of the so-called "free world."

The dialectic of mutual blackmail rules international politics. Be careful of sticking your foot into an old trap. To denounce those responsible for the butchery in Central America does not imply indifference or compliance regarding the coup d'état in Poland. To condemn the Soviet invasion of Afghanistan—which in practice negates the proclaimed right of nations to self-determination—does not imply any form of complicity with the criminal capitalist apparatus. To point out that the fear felt by the privileged is the principal cause of the insane arms build-up should not lead us to imply that the growing militarization of the socialist bloc is merely a result of the long history of blockades and threats by the imperialist powers. We know very well that the Eastern-bloc countries have used and are using their military strength for defense and international solidarity objectives, but we also know of other uses. In repeated and lamentable occasions, this military strength has been and continues to be used to prevent or punish "heterodoxy" and "deviations," imposing a determined model of socialism, according to which contradictions and doubts are signs of heresy and treason.

An immense apparatus of manipulation seeks to return us to Cold War times. The maneuver is not innocent: it is an attempt to reduce the Central American revolution to the terminology of East-West conflict, thereby attributing it to a Soviet conspiracy and concealing its deep national roots. It is an attempt, above all, to hide and absolve those guilty of so much bloodshed. Did you know that in Guatemala there is a functioning human rights office? In this country, converted into a slaughterhouse by foreign intervention, the office monitors the violation of human rights in the Soviet Union.

The alibis for incessant imperialist intervention in Latin America make one's heart indignant and offend one's intelligence.

The United States was the first country the Sandinists went to in search of economic and military aid after the defeat of Somoza. They were met with closed doors, conditional and reduced credit terms and threats. The most powerful empire in history considers Nicaragua—a small nation in ruins, devastated by a long dictatorship, an earthquake and a war—to be a danger. "Somoza is a son-of-a-bitch, but at least he's our son-of-a-bitch," [Franklin Delano] Roosevelt is quoted as saying. When Nicaragua wants to be Nicaragua, and through its revolution begins to discover itself, President Reagan draws his Colt .45. In order to develop hydroelectric and geothermal energy, Nicaragua needs $800 million. This would give them the leverage to take great steps forward. It seems like a huge figure, but it is 845 times smaller than the amount the U.S. spent to keep Vietnam from becoming Vietnam during the long war in Southeast Asia. Killing the Vietnamese, the U.S. wasted $676 billion; on explosives alone, they wasted the equivalent of two hundred Hiroshima-type bombs.

How much are they spending and will they spend to keep El Salvador from becoming El Salvador? We know the pretexts. Who can honestly believe that Soviet agents are to blame for the Salvadorans having the lowest caloric intake in Latin America? Out of every ten Salvadoran children, eight are malnourished. From this violence comes the violence. Before, democracy in El Salvador was the realm of fourteen families. Now it is the realm of 244 families, and of farcical elections held under a state of siege, elections that no one believes in. From this violence comes the violence. Two years ago the armed forces of El Salvador occupied the countryside. They distributed five percent of the land to peasant cooperatives and called this "agrarian reform." Before the end of 1980, the armed forces had assassinated two hundred leaders of these cooperatives. From this war comes The War.

20
12
XXHOMBRE
81

Cemetery with unmarked graves, Antigua, March, 1982.
Photo credit: Susan Meiselas

CHRONOLOGY

1524	Spanish conquest initiates colonial era.
Sept. 15, 1821	Independence from Spain.
1871	"Liberal Reform" begins. Church and Indian lands are expropriated for coffee production.
June 1944	Popular pressure forces dictator Jorge Ubico to resign, giving way to a military triumvirate.
Oct. 20, 1944	A coalition led by the urban middle class and dissident military officers overthrows the military junta, initiating a ten-year period of democratic reforms.
1945	Juan José Arévalo is elected president.
1951	Colonel Jacobo Arbenz takes office after winning presidential elections.
1952	The Agrarian Reform law is adopted.
1953	The Arbenz government confiscates four hundred thousand acres of uncultivated United Fruit Company land and begins land redistribution.
1954	Arbenz is overthrown and Colonel Carlos Castillo Armas installed in a CIA-planned and -financed invasion and coup. Land reform is reversed, popular organizations crushed and thousands killed.
1957	Castillo Armas is assassinated.
1958	General Miguel Ydígoras Fuentes is elected president.
1959	The Cuban Revolution; Fidel Castro takes power.
1960	Ydígoras allows the United States to train Cuban exiles in Guatemala for the Bay of Pigs invasion of Cuba.
	The Central American Common Market is formed.
Nov. 13, 1960	A major military uprising against Ydígoras, involving one-third of the army, is suppressed.

Mar.-Apr. 1962	Massive demonstrations by students and workers in Guatemala City against the Ydígoras government.
Dec. 1962	The Rebel Armed Forces (FAR) guerrilla organization is formed and begins antigovernment activity in the mountains of northeastern Guatemala.
Mar. 1963	Ydígoras is overthrown in a coup led by Colonel Enrique Peralta Azurdia.
1965	The chief of the U.S. military mission is killed and a state of siege declared.
1966	Julio César Méndez Montenegro is elected president.
1966–1969	United States increases military and economic aid to Guatemala, and army counterinsurgency campaigns and repression by right-wing paramilitary squads intensify. U.S. sends Green Berets, guerrillas are decimated and thousands are killed.
1970	Colonel Carlos Arana Osorio is elected president. A one-year state of siege is imposed in November and a new wave of government repression begins.
1974	Official presidential candidate, General Kjell Eugenio Laugerud García, is chosen over apparent election winner General Efraín Ríos Montt.
1975	The Guerrilla Army of the Poor (EGP) initiates guerrilla activity in the northern part of the Quiché province.
Feb. 4, 1976	A massive earthquake leaves over 22,000 dead, 77,000 injured and one million homeless.
Apr. 1976	The National Committee of Trade Union Unity (CNUS) is formed.
Nov. 19, 1977	A protest march of miners from Ixtahuacán, Huehuetenango is met by one hundred thousand supporters in Guatemala City.
Mar. 1978	A public workers' strike shortly before presidential elections forces the government to approve wage hikes.
	General Fernando Romeo Lucas García is elected president in an openly rigged contest.
Apr. 1978	The Committee of Campesino Unity is formed.
May 29, 1978	Over one hundred Kekchí Indians are killed by govern-

	ment troops and armed landowners in Panzós, Alta Verapaz.
July 1978	Lucas assumes power.
Oct. 1978	A general strike and large spontaneous protests in Guatemala City force the government to revoke a 100 percent city bus fare hike.
Oct. 20, 1978	Oliverio Castañeda de León, president of the Association of University Students, is gunned down two blocks from the National Palace in Guatemala City.
Jan. 25, 1979	Dr. Alberto Fuentes Mohr, former government minister and leader of the Democratic Socialist Party, is assassinated in Guatemala City.
Feb. 24, 1979	The Democratic Front Against Repression (FDCR) is formed.
Mar. 23, 1979	Manuel Colom Argueta, founder and leader of the social-democratic United Revolutionary Front party, is killed in Guatemala City.
July 19, 1979	Sandinists overthrow Somoza dynasty in Nicaragua.
Sept. 18, 1979	The Organization of the People in Arms (ORPA), a guerrilla organization, announces its existence.
Jan. 31, 1980	Part of a group of campesinos who had come to Guatemala City from Quiché to protest army repression in their villages occupies the Spanish Embassy together with supporters. Police storm and firebomb the embassy building, killing thirty-nine.
Feb.-Mar. 1980	Nearly eighty thousand Indian and ladino farmworkers go out on strike, forcing the government to raise the minimum wage for farmworkers.
May 1, 1980	Forty thousand turn out for the May Day protest march in Guatemala City, the last above-ground demonstration to take place in Guatemala. Dozens of demonstrators are kidnapped in the course of the march.
June 21, 1980	Twenty-seven trade union leaders are kidnapped from the Guatemala City headquarters of the National Confederation of Labor (CNT).
July 14, 1980	Armed men indiscriminately shoot at students stepping off public buses at the University of San Carlos, killing several.

July 20, 1980	After the murder of two priests and two attempts on the life of the bishop, the Catholic Diocese of Quiché is closed.
Aug. 1980	The army gathers residents of San Juan Cotzal, Quiché, and shoots sixty male villagers.
Aug. 24, 1980	Seventeen trade union leaders from the CNT are kidnapped from a Catholic retreat house in Palín, Escuintla.
Aug. 28, 1980	A violent five-year-long labor conflict at Guatemala's U.S.-owned Coca-Cola franchise is resolved after an international union-led boycott forces the parent company to intervene.
Sept. 6, 1980	The army attacks the town of Chajul, Quiché, bombing the convent, beating and interrogating residents and killing at least thirty-six.
Oct. 1980	ORPA joins EGP, FAR and the Leadership Nucleus of the Guatemalan Workers' Party (PGT) in a guerrilla alliance.
Jan. 1981	The guerrilla alliance initiates a coordinated campaign aimed at preventing the intervention of Guatemalan troops in El Salvador during the Salvadoran guerrillas' general offensive.
	The January 31st Popular Front (FP-31) announces its formation.
Feb.-Mar. 1981	An estimated fifteen hundred Indian campesinos are reported killed in army massacres in the Chimaltenango province.
Apr. 9, 1981	Twenty-four people are massacred by machete in the village of Chuabajito in San Martín Jilotepeque, Chimaltenango.
Apr. 15, 1981	Forty to one hundred campesinos are massacred in the village of Cocob in Nebaj, Quiché.
Apr. 31, 1981	At least thirty-six campesinos are killed in an army attack on the town of San Mateo Ixtatán, Huehuetenango.
May 1981	The army bombs and lays siege to the villages of Tres Aguadas, El Caoba, El Remate, and Paxmacán in the Petén province. Five hundred seek refuge in Mexico and within days are deported back to Guatemala.
June 1981	Nineteen rural cooperatives in the Petén province are

attacked by the army. At least fifty people are killed and 3,500 flee to Mexico.

June 10, 1981 The Reagan administration approves the sale of $3.2 million worth of military jeeps and trucks to the Lucas government.

July 1981 Most of the campesinos from the Petén cooperatives who had sought refuge in Mexico are deported back to Guatemala.

July 19, 1981 Two hundred soldiers attack the village of Coyá, Huehuetenango, as residents attempt to resist with machetes, sticks and stones. One hundred fifty to three hundred villagers are killed.

Among a series of guerrilla actions commemorating the 1979 Nicaraguan revolution, five hundred guerrillas occupy the tourist town of Chichicastenango, Quiché.

July 28, 1981 U.S. priest Stanley Rother is killed in Santiago Atitlán, Sololá.

Aug. 12, 1981 As many as one thousand campesinos are killed in army attacks on two villages in San Sebastián Lemoa, Quiché.

Sept. 1981 The army kills about seven hundred in San Miguel Chicaj and Rabinal, Baja Verapaz.

Oct.-Dec. 1981 Soldiers burn homes, crops and kill as many as one thousand in the Chupol region of Chichicastenango, Quiché.

Oct. 10, 20, 1981 Guerrillas launch a series of bombing and military attacks on police, government and economic targets in Guatemala City.

Oct. 28, 1981 Guerrillas simultaneously mount attacks on two provincial capitals, Mazatenango and Sololá, and briefly occupy the latter.

Nov. 1981 The army carries out a major counterinsurgency offensive in the Chimaltenango province.

Nov. 22, 1981 Emeterio Toj, leader of CUC and EGP member, escapes from a Guatemala City military base close to four months after he was kidnapped by government security forces.

Dec. 2, 1981 Five hundred guerrillas attack army posts in Santa Cruz del Quiché.

Jan. 1982	A major counterinsurgency offensive is launched in the Quiché, Chimaltenango, Huehuetenango and San Marcos provinces.
Jan. 19, 1982	A large guerrilla force attacks and nearly overruns the San Juan Cotzal, Quiché military base.
Feb. 7, 1982	The EGP, FAR, ORPA and the Leadership Nucleus of the PGT announce their unification under the umbrella of the Guatemalan National Revolutionary Unity (URNG).
mid-Feb. 1982	Exiled leaders of different organizations, sectors, and ideological persuasions form the Guatemalan Committee of Patriotic Unity (CGUP), endorsing the URNG and their points for a program of government.
Mar. 7, 1982	General Angel Aníbal Guevara, official presidential candidate, wins a plurality in elections amidst charges of fraud by the three right-wing opposition candidates.
Mar. 23, 1982	A bloodless palace coup overthrows the Lucas government before power is transfered to Guevara. General Efraín Ríos Montt is installed as head of a three-man military junta.
	Five hundred people are killed by soldiers in the villages of Parraxtut, El Pajarito and Pichiquil, Quiché.
Mar. 24-27, 1982	Helicopter bombing raids kill one hundred in the villages of Las Pacayas, Cisirám, El Rancho, Quixal, and Chuyuc in San Cristóbal Verapaz, Alta Verapaz.
Mar. 28-Apr. 10, 1982	Soldiers kill two hundred fifty and burn down the villages of Estancia de la Vírgen, Chicocón, Choatalún and Chipilá in San Martín Jilotepeque, Chimaltenango.
Apr. 3-5, 1982	Soldiers kill most of the residents of Chel, Juá and Amachel in Chajul, Quiché. In one of the villages the women are raped, the men beheaded, and the children tossed against the rocks of a river bed.
	Over one hundred are killed in the village of Mangal in Chajul, Quiché.
Apr. 12, 1982	The army burns down houses, fields, and forests in San Antonio Ixchiguán, San Marcos.
Apr. 15, 1982	Soldiers kill over a hundred children and seventy-three women in Río Negro, Baja Verapaz. The bodies of the

women are found hanging from the trees with their children on their backs.

Apr. 18, 1982 The villages of Agua Escondida and Xugüexá II in Chichicastenango, Quiché, are abandoned after the houses and fields are set afire.

Fifty-four persons are beheaded in Macalbaj, Quiché, and the entire village burned down.

Apr. 20, 1982 One hundred campesinos are massacred in the village of Josefinos in La Libertad, Petén.

Apr. 29, 1982 Two hundred campesinos are killed in Cuarto Pueblo, Quiché, and houses, crops and forests burned down.

June 1982 One hundred campesinos are killed in the village of Pampach in Tactic, Alta Verapaz.

One hundred sixty of the one hundred eighty families living in the town of Chisec, Alta Verapaz, are massacred.

June 9, 1982 General Ríos Montt declares himself president and sole ruler of Guatemala and the two other junta members resign.

July 1, 1982 Ríos Montt declares a state of siege.

Jan. 7, 1983 The Reagan administration lifts the five-year-old embargo on arms sales to Guatemala, approving the sale of over $6.3 million worth of helicopter spare parts and military equipment.

Jan. 25-26, 1983 Guatemalan soldiers and government civil patrols enter Mexico and kill four refugees at Santiago el Vértice and La Hamaca refugee camps in Chiapas.

Mar. 3, 1983 Six men are shot by firing squad three days before the arrival of Pope John Paul II, and despite his pleas for clemency. This was the second mass execution of persons tried in Guatemala's secret military tribunals.

[These sources were particularly helpful for compiling this chronology: Shelton H. Davis and Julie Hodson, *Witnesses to Political Violence in Guatemala*, (Oxfam America, 1982), pp. 47-52; Susanne Jonas and David Tobis, eds., *Guatemala* (Berkeley: North American Congress on Latin America, 1974), pp. 10-11; *Guardian* [New York], 1981 and 1982 issues; and *Noticias de Guatemala* [San José, Costa Rica], May 15, 1982 and July 15, 1982.]

APPENDIX

"We the Campesinos Are Awakening"

BY MEANS OF OUR SELF DEFENSE WE ARE ABLE TO DEFEND OUR COMMUNITIES, OUR LEADERS, OUR STRUGGLE, TO PREVENT THEM FROM MASSACRING US AS THEY HAVE OUR QUICHÉ BROTHERS AND SISTERS.

*Reproduced from *De Sol a Sol* [Guatemala City] July, 1980; text translated by the editors; cartoon re-inked by Todd Anton.

SELECTED BIBLIOGRAPHY

BOOKS

Adams, Richard N. *Crucifixion by Power: Essays on Guatemalan National Social Structure 1944-1966*. Austin, Texas: University of Texas Press, 1970.

Amnesty International, *Guatemala: A Government Program of Political Murder*. New York: Amnesty International, 1981.

Armstrong, Robert and Janet Shenk. *El Salvador: The Face of Revolution*. Boston, South End Press, 1982.

Arévalo, Juan José. *The Shark and the Sardines*. New York: Lyle Stuart, 1963.

Arévalo, Juan José. *Anti-Kommunism in Latin America*. New York: Lyle Stuart, 1963.

Asturias, Miguel Angel, *El Señor Presidente*. San José, Costa Rica: Editorial Universitaria Centroamerica, 1973.

Cardoza y Aragón, Luis. *Guatemala: Las Líneas de Su Mano*. Mexico City: Fondo de Cultura Económica, 1955.

Cardoza y Aragón, Luis. *La Revolución Guatemalteca*. Montevideo, Uruguay: Ediciones Pueblos Unidos, 1956.

Carmack, Robert. *The Quiché Mayas of Utatlán*. Norman, Oklahoma: University of Oklahoma Press, 1981.

Concerned Guatemala Scholars. *Guatemala: Dare to Struggle, Dare to Win*. Brooklyn, N.Y.: Concerned Guatemala Scholars, 1981.

Cook, Blanche. *The Declassified Eisenhower*. Garden City, New York: Doubleday & Co., 1981.

Davis, Shelton H. and Julie Hodson. *Witness to Political Violence in Guatemala*. Boston: Oxfam America, 1982.

Falla, Ricardo. *Quiché Rebelde*. Guatemala City: Editorial Universitaria, 1978.

Galeano, Eduardo. *Guatemala: Occupied Country*. New York: Monthly Review Press, 1969.

Galeano, Eduardo. *Open Veins of Latin America*. New York: Monthly Review Press, 1973.

Gettleman, Marvin E., Patrick Lacefield, Louis Menashe, David Mermelstein, and Ronald Radosh, eds., *El Salvador: Central America in the New Cold War*. New York: Grove Press, 1981.

Greenhalgh, Kurt and Mark Gruenke, eds. *The Church Martyred: Guatemala*. Minneapolis, Minn.: Guatemala Solidarity Committee of Minnesota, 1981.

Gutiérrez, Gustavo. *A Theology of Liberation*. New York: Orbis Books, 1977.

Helms, Mary. *Middle America: A Culture History of Heartland and Frontiers.* Englewood Cliffs, N.J.: Prentice-Hall, 1975.

Immerman, Richard H. *The CIA in Guatemala: The Foreign Policy of Intervention* Austin, Tex.: Univeristy of Texas Press, 1982.

Jonas, Susanne and David Tobis, eds. *Guatemala.* Berkeley: North American Congress on Latin America, 1974.

Jones, Chester Lloyd. *Guatemala, Past and Present.* Minneapolis, Minn.: University of Minnesota Press, 1940.

Kelsey, Vera and Lilly de Jongh Osborne. *Four Keys to Guatemala.* New York: Funk & Wagnalls, 1939.

King, Arden R. *Coban and the Verapaz, History and Cultural Process in Northern Guatemala.* New Orleans: Tulane University, 1974.

Kinzer, Stephen and Stephen Schlesinger. *Bitter Fruit.* Garden City, N.Y.: Doubleday & Co., 1981.

Klare, Michael T. and Cynthia Arnson, *Supplying Repression: U.S. Support for Authoritarian Regimes Abroad.* Washington, D.C.: Institute for Policy Studies, 1981.

La Farge, Oliver. *The Year Bearer's People.* New Orleans: Tulane Univeristy, 1938.

Larrave, Mario López. *Breve Historia del Movimiento Sindical Guatemalteco.* Guatemala City: Editorial Universitara, 1979.

MacLeod, Murdo J. *Spanish Central America: A Socio-Economic History 1520–1720.* Berkeley: University of California Press, 1973.

Martínez Peláez, Severo. *La Patria del Criollo.* San José, Costa Rica: Editorial Universitaria, 1976.

Melville, Thomas and Marjorie. *Whose Heaven, Whose Earth?* New York: Alfred A. Knopf, 1971.

Melville, Thomas and Marjorie. *Guatemala: The Politics of Land Ownership.* New York: Free Press, 1971.

Nash, Manning. *Machine Age Maya.* Chicago: University of Chicago Press, 1958.

National Lawyers Guild and La Raza Legal Alliance. *Guatemala: Repression and Resistance.* New York: National Lawyers Guild, 1980.

Pearce, Jenny. *Under the Eagle: U.S. Intervention in Central America and the Caribbean.* London: Latin America Bureau, 1981.

Petras, James and Maurice Zeitlin, eds. *Latin America: Reform or Revolution.* New York: Fawcett, 1968.

Plant, Roger. *Guatemala: Unnatural Disaster.* London: Latin America Bureau, 1978.

Rarihokwats, ed. *Guatemala!: The Horror and the Hope.* York, Pa.: Four Arrows, 1982.

Reina, Ruben E. *Chinautla: A Guatemalan Indian Community.* New Orleans: Middle American Research Institute of Tulane University, 1972.

Stavenhagen, Rodolfo. *Social Classes in Agrarian Societies.* Garden City: Anchor, 1975.

Schneider, Ronald. "Guatemala: An Aborted Communist Takeover," in Thomas Hammond, ed. *The Anatomy of Communist Takeovers.* New Haven: Yale University Press, 1975.

Stephens, John L. *Incidents of Travel in Central America, Chiapas and Yucatan.* Two vols. New York: Harper, 1841.

Tax, Sol, et al. *Heritage of Conquest.* Glencoe, N.Y.: Free Press, 1952.

Thompson, J. Eric. *Maya History and Religion.* Norman, Oklahoma: University of Oklahoma Press.

Toriello, Guillermo. *La Batalla de Guatemala.* Mexico City: Ediciones Cuadernos Americanos, 1955.

Warren, Kay. *The Symbolism of Subordination: Indian Identity in a Guatemalan Town.* Austin: University of Texas Press, 1978.

Wolf, Eric. *Sons of the Shaking Earth.* Chicago: University of Chicago Press, 1959.

Wolf, Eric. *Peasant Wars in the Twentieth Century.* New York: Harper and Row, 1969.

Woodward, Ralph Lee, Jr. *Central America: A Nation Divided.* New York: Oxford University Press, 1976.

World Bank. *Guatemala: Economic and Social Position and Prospects.* Washington: Latin American and the Caribbean Regional Office, The World Bank, 1978.

ARTICLES AND COLLECTIONS OF ARTICLES

Aguilera Peralta, Gabriel, "The Massacre at Panzós and Capitalist Development in Guatemala," *Monthly Review* (New York) XXXI (7), Dec. 1979.

Center for Information, Documentation and Analysis of the Latin American Workers' Movement (CIDAMO), "The Workers' Movement in Guatemala," *NACLA Report on the Americas* (New York) XIV (1), Jan.-Feb., 1980.

"Central America: The Strongmen are Shaking," *Latin American Perspectives* (Riverside, Calif.), Issues 25 & 26, VII (2 & 3), Spring and Summer 1980.

"Guatemala," *Cuadernos de Marcha* (Mexico City) II (10), Nov.-Dec., 1980.

NACLA Report. Special report on Guatemala, January-February and March-April 1983. North American Congress on Latin America.

Riding, Alan, "Guatemala: State of Siege," *New York Times Magazine,* August 24, 1980.

Torres-Rivas, Edelberto, "Guatemala—Crisis and Political Violence," *NACLA Report on the Americas* (New York) XIV (1), Jan.-Feb., 1980.

Wasserstrom, Robert, "Revolution in Guatemala: Peasants and Politics Under the Arbenz Government," *Comparative Studies in Society and History,* 17, 1975.

PERIODICALS

English

Between the Lines, Guatemala Information Center, P.O. Box 57027, Los Angeles, Calif. 90057.

Central America Report, Inforpress Centroamericana, 9 Calle "A" 3-56, Zona 1, Ciudad de Guatemala, Guatemala, C.A.

Foreign Broadcast Information Service, Daily Reports [Latin America] (of monitored radio broadcasts).

¡Guatemala! (bilingual, English and Spanish), Guatemala News and Information Bureau, P.O. Box 4126, Berkeley, Calif. 94704.

Latin America Regional Report: Mexico and Central America and *Latin America Weekly Report,* Latin American Newsletters Ltd., 91-93 Charterhouse Street, London, BEC1M 6LN, England.

Latin Perspective, Agencia Latinoamericana de Información (ALAI), 1224 Ste.-Catherine O. #403, Montreal, Que., Canada H3G 1P2.

News From Guatemala, P.O. Box 335, Station R, Toronto, Ont., Canada M4G 4C3.

This Week: Central America and Panama, Apartado Postal 1156, Ciudad de Guatemala, Guatemala, C.A.

Update on Guatemala, Committee of Solidarity with the People of Guatemala, P.O. Box 270, Wyckoff Heights Station, Brooklyn, N.Y. 11237.

Spanish

Coyuntura, Instituto Centroamericano de Investigaciones Sociales, Apartado 174, Sabanilla, Montes de Oca 2070, San José, Costa Rica.

Guatemala, Centro de Servicios para la Solidaridad con el Pueblo de Guatemala, Apartado Postal No. 20-108, México 20, D.F., México.

Inforpress Centroamericana, 9 Calle "A" 3-56, Zona 1, Ciudad de Guatemala, Guatemala, C.A.

Noticias de Guatemala, Apdo. Postal 463, San Juan de Tibás, San José, Costa Rica.

Polémica, Apartado Postal 7481, San José, Costa Rica.

Servicio Informativo, Servicios Especiales and *Documentos Especiales,* Agencia Latinoamericana de Información (ALAI), 1224 Ste.-Catherine O. #403, Montreal, Que., Canada H3G 1P2.

ORGANIZATIONS

National Network in Solidarity with the People of Guatemala (NISGUA), 930 F St. N.W., Suite 720, Washington, D.C. 20004.

ILLUSTRATIONS

INDEX

This is a highly selective index containing significant names and subjects that cannot be readily found through the table of contents.